Wild Flowers

The Wild Flowers of Britain and Northern Europe

Wild Flowers

*The Wild Flowers of Britain
and Northern Europe*

Marjorie Blamey

Richard Fitter

Alastair Fitter

with a foreword by

Geoffrey Grigson

COLLINS
ST JAMES'S PLACE, LONDON

William Collins Sons & Co Ltd
London · Glasgow · Sydney · Auckland
Toronto · Johannesburg

Originally published in 1974

© in this edition 1977 Marjorie Blamey,
Richard Fitter, Alastair Fitter

ISBN 0 00 219757X

Designed by B. E. Rockett

Filmset by Jolly and Barber Ltd, Rugby

Reproduction by Adroit Photo Litho Ltd,
Birmingham

Made and printed in Great Britain by
Wm Collins Sons and Co Ltd., Glasgow

Contents

Foreword

The *Wild Flowers* of Britain and Northern Europe – has it occurred to you that we make a slight difficulty for ourselves in talking about plants as 'flowers'? Often the habit gets writers into trouble. Yet it is a wise, or poetic trick, to our credit. On the whole it is by their flowers that we first distinguish one species from another. Plants, at the right time, hold up their flower-faces, white, coloured, streaked, or spotted, and 'flowers' we call them. In 'flowers' – still attached to pedicels, stalks and leaves – we find our commonest lyricism, valid and comforting.

I do not know a modern flower-book – 'flower' again, you see – as concisely pleasing and efficient as this one, especially in its new enlarged form. It harmonizes – intellectual elements apart – with flowers as carnival and treasure-hunt. In the British Isles and northern Europe – certainly in the British Isles – we do have what is called an 'impoverished' flora. But that amounts to curtailment of the number of species rather than curtailment of the spectacle of flowers. The year comes round, primroses, then foxgloves, blossom down a Cornish cliff to the shag's nest and the sea almost, and on Yorkshire drumlins (rounded hillocks of glacial drift), orchids and Bistort in the grass parade all their pink spikes. No doubt of the yearly carnival.

Then, bad as 'impoverished' or 'impoverishment' may sound, it amounts as well to an expression of rarity; or in reverse, rarity goes with our impoverishment. For one reason or another, soil, climate, exposure, geological history, landscape history, human history, some plants are rare; and rarity introduces the lyricism of the treasure-hunt, of the find.

In many lives, over many centuries, thrilling moments have included the finding of some rare plant, at last; some plant – some flower I must say – known by plate and fame, encountered at last rooted firmly and happily into its natural home.

Pleasure derives, too, from local abundance, contrasting with scarcity or absence in some more familiar locality. Grow up in Cornwall (as I did), and you grow up with the best, biggest, softest, most freshly scented primroses; but you know nothing of cowslips. Grow up in Wiltshire, and you know cowslips as well as primroses; but nothing of oxlips – that requires a shift to Essex – and nothing of birdseye primrose, the little deliciously pink primula of the northern moors.

When – after that Cornish childhood – I was in the flush of discovering the northern limestone and becoming acquainted with Birdseye Primrose, I realized one day – suddenly – the significance (which no editor had spotted or recorded) of some lines in one of the most ecstatic English poems, Christopher Smart's *Song to David*:

> The grass the polyanthus cheques,
> And polish'd porphyry reflects,
> By the descending rill.

The polyanthus was Birdseye Primrose, the polish'd porphyry was the polished limestone of a little waterfall. Christopher Smart was remembering his childhood in Teesdale, in Co. Durham.

To the flower pleasures, then, of carnival and treasure-hunt must be added such human-historical pleasures.

Since the eighteenth century, the wild flowers of these islands have been so loved, so studied by professional and amateur field-botanists, that a delightful history could be written of the relationships of flowers and men. When I see the artificial, still unexplained Silbury Hill, part of the prehistoric complex of Avebury, I often remember how, in search of plants, Silbury was climbed, some time in mid-sixteenth century, by the Flemish botanist de l'Obel (eponym of the species *Lobelia*). On the way up or the way down, Matthias de l'Obel found Squinancywort, and recorded it, the first time the species had been recognized in Britain.

In the most curious ways flowers will thread our lives, flowers will lead to new experiences and tie them inextricably with the older experiences. When I lived in Cornwall, few flowers gave me more local patriotic pleasure than the minute Cornish moneywort, scrawling over damp rock. We know that as a 'British plant' it was first discovered – in Cornwall – by the great naturalist, John Ray, on July 1st, 1662, near St Ives. Its specific name *Sibthorpia* led me to facts about John Sibthorpe, Oxford botanist of the eighteenth century, led me to his memorial in Bath Abbey, a relief by Flaxman which shows Sibthorpe in ancient Greek costume, with a bunch of flowers in his hand, stepping ashore in Elysium or Greece (he compiled a huge *Flora Graeca*), led me to the journal of Sibthorpe's flower explorations in Cyprus, which in turn led me to decide I must go to Cyprus, and see one flower he described, *Hyoscyamus aureus*, Golden Henbane, a beauty with violet, almost black throated flowers of yellow. Sibthorpe said it grew on the old walls of Kyrenia; and there it was, there it was. After which – all because of a minute, obscure plant in a Cornish ditch – I went on to the other delights of Cyprus, floral and archaeological.

Yet all floral pleasures depend on recognition, on wild flower guides, on keys, and descriptions, and on the flowers pictured. As aid to identification, colour photos are inferior to paintings. They cannot point sharply to the finer, irrefutable characteristics. One of the least of Marjorie Blamey's watercolours shows this, in a way which happens to involve just one more experience of my own. Lately, in April, in falling, then melting snow, I looked for a mill in the north of France which was described in his reminiscences by the dramatist Ionesco. He had been farmed out there as a child. I found the mill, and beside the stream, on black, wet ground, below alders, were splashes, or clumps, of the most singing, startling purple flower I had ever seen. A toothwort, yes – that was obvious; in fact Purple Toothwort (*Lathraea clandestina*). But it could be identified at once from Mrs Blamey's watercolour (93), although she had found space only for a single blossom.

There is more than help in these plates. One after another the best of them concentrate that lyricism of flowers. I admire the sombre poetry of the green and yellow plates, or green and brown plates, the Willows (2, 3) and other catkin bearers (4, 5). I admire (seldom as well done) the white umbellifers (65) and the white crucifers (34, 35). But then look at those outbursts of organized colour, the knapweeds and star thistles (107), the irises, gladiolus, crocuses (119), the poppies (28), and the cranesbills (53). There you have the Earth Carnival, all right, the gaiety of the business.

GEOFFREY GRIGSON.

Introduction

The decision to issue *The Wild Flowers of Britain and Northern Europe* (first published in 1974) in a new, large format was prompted mainly by the immediate and enthusiastic reception given to the 126 plates painted for the book by Marjorie Blamey. In this larger format, these plates can now be seen to their best advantage. Furthermore, advances in techniques of colour reproduction since the original edition of the book have meant that the plates have gained considerably in clarity and accuracy. For these reasons alone, the book would serve as an admirable complement to any identification guide. But more than that, the plates do bring out, far better than those of the earlier volume, the sheer beauty and variety of our native flora.

The intentions of this book are thus different from those of its predecessor. It is hoped that the present volume will serve less as an identification guide, and more as an introduction to, and a reminder of, the pleasure to be had from a knowledge of wild flowers: and that it will familiarise people with rare and uncommon flowers that they might not otherwise notice in the countryside around them.

Some notes on the criteria used in the compilation of this book, and on the best way in which the book itself may be used, are given below.

Area Covered The area covered by this book lies roughly between Arctic Norway in the north and the river Loire in western and central France and the river Danube in Germany in the south. Its boundary runs along the Loire from its mouth on the Atlantic coast of France eastwards to Dijon and Basle and thence along the Danube and the foothills of the Alps to Munich, so as to include the Vosges and the Black Forest, but excluding the Jura and the Alps. At Munich it turns northwards across Germany through Regensburg, Bayreuth, Erfurt and Brunswick to reach the Baltic at Lübeck, and thence up the Gulf of Finland and the eastern frontier of Finland to the Arctic Ocean. Iceland is included. These boundaries are shown on the map on p. xi.

The Plates The plates have been grouped together in the first section of the book, rather than interleaved with the caption pages. The sequence follows that of *The Wild Flowers of Britain and Northern Europe*. Thus, with the exception of the flowering trees and tall shrubs, which are placed at the beginning for convenience, the order is in agreement with established taxonomic convention.

Each plant is labelled with its English common name. These names follow in most cases the list approved by the Botanical Society of the British Isles.

On each plate, there is a reference to the text page(s) on which the descriptions of the plants illustrated will be found.

Most of the plants are shown one-and-a-half times life size, but where there is any deviation from this rule, a single flower of the plant in question is also shown at one-and-a-half times life size. Only the Iris plate (Plate 119) is painted to the smaller scale of three-quarters life size. Where two or more plants resemble each other closely, only one of them has been shown in full: the remainder are illustrated simply with their distinguishing characteristics.

The Text The text in this edition, apart from some minor revisions, has been little altered from the text of *The Wild Flowers of Britain and Northern Europe*. There are fewer abbreviations and only those plants illustrated are actually described, each with a reference to the plate on which it occurs.

The species descriptions are arranged under family and generic headings, and group descriptions of families and genera are given wherever possible, so as to avoid constant repetition of common characters – for example, the shape of a pea flower or the nature of a composite flower. They should therefore always be read carefully and in conjunction with the species descriptions. The group descriptions refer only to species mentioned in the text.

Each text description includes standardised information, giving details that are largely confined to points such as height, flowering period, habitat, and distribution, which are either difficult to illustrate or which, by their very nature, cannot be illustrated at all. The major diagnostic features distinguishing the plant from other similar plants with which it might be confused, are shown in italics. A number of assumptions are made in the descriptions: unless otherwise stated, plants are erect and herbaceous, leaves are stalked, flowers are open.

Latin scientific names in general follow *Flora Europaea* (where available), otherwise as in Polunin's *A Field Guide to the Flowers of Europe* or Dandy's *List of British Vascular Plants*.

Plants native to Britain, or commonly naturalised in the British Isles, are preceded by an asterisk.

Height is indicated as follows:

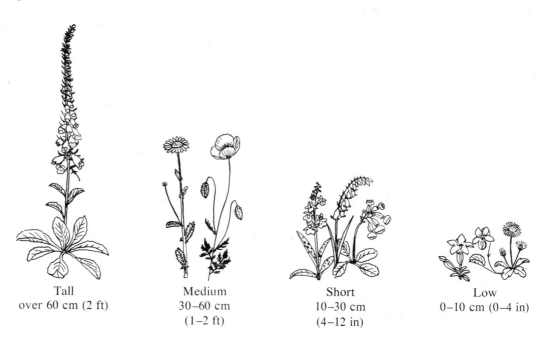

Tall	Medium	Short	Low
over 60 cm (2 ft)	30–60 cm (1–2 ft)	10–30 cm (4–12 in)	0–10 cm (0–4 in)

Plant sizes can vary greatly according to altitude, climate and soil. Plants are more likely to be found smaller than is indicated here than larger.

Annual, biennial or perennial status is given in each case. Perennials are usually stouter than annuals, and of course are much more likely to be seen above ground in winter.

Leaf shapes and flower shapes and arrangements are also described. The terms used may in some cases be unfamiliar, but all are defined in the Glossary (page xiii). Flower sizes are diameters unless otherwise stated. Flower colour refers to petals or to sepals when there are no petals. It is more variable in some species than others. Most pink, mauve, purple and blue flowers produce white forms from time to time, and many white flowers can be tinged pink. Some, such as milkworts (Plate 55), are exceptionally variable. But a normally coloured flower is usually to be found nearby.

Flowering time refers to the central part of the area, and may be earlier in the south, near the sea and in forward seasons, and later in the north, on mountains and in backward seasons.

Fruits are usually only described where important for identification.

Habitats, such as fen and bog, are used here in their strict sense, see Glossary (page xiii). Areas with lime (chalk or limestone) in the soil are shown in the map opposite.

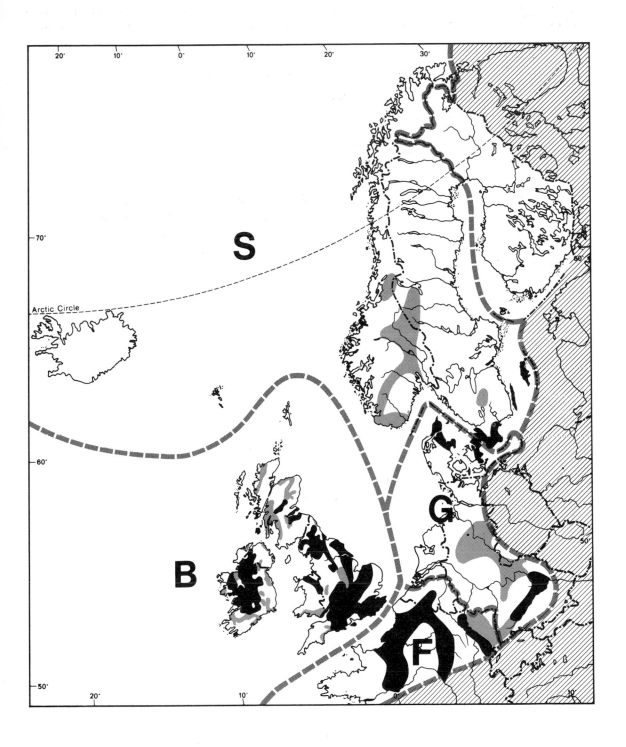

region not covered by this book

boundary between distribution areas

major outcrops of chalk and limestone

scattered outcrops of chalk and limestone

The following symbols show whether the plant occurs, either commonly or uncommonly, within each region. If it has only a very few localities, 'rare' is added, and if it is mainly found, e.g., in the south of the region, the word 'southern' is also added.

T – Throughout the area covered by the book (see above).

B – Great Britain, Ireland, Isle of Man.

F – France, Belgium, Luxembourg, Channel Islands.

G – Germany, the Netherlands, Denmark.

S – Norway, Sweden, Iceland, the Faroes.

If parentheses enclose the symbol – for example, (G) – the plant is introduced, not native. The great majority of introduced plants occur on waste or disturbed ground, roadsides, or other habitats much affected by human activity. Only rarely, as with New Zealand Willowherb (Plate 61), do they succeed in invading natural or semi-natural habitats, such as heaths, moors and calcareous grassland.

Abbreviations used in the Text

Sp.	Species (singular)
Spp.	Species (plural)
Ssp.	Subspecies
Var.	Variety
*	Native or commonly naturalised in Britain.
B, F, G, S,	Found in Britain, France, Germany, Scandinavia, and
and T.	Throughout respectively. See above.
( )	Indicates the plant is introduced, not native.

Glossary

Acid soils have very few basic minerals and are formed on rocks such as sandstone. Peaty soils are usually acid since plant humus is often so.

Alternate: neither opposite nor whorled.

Anther: the part of the flower producing the male pollen.

Annual plants live for a year or less. They are usually shallow rooted and never woody.

Appressed: flattened against the stem.

Berry: fleshy fruit.

Biennials: live for two years. Usually the first year's growth produces a leaf-rosette, the second the flowers.

Bog: a habitat on wet, acid peat.

Bracts are small, usually leaf-like organs just below the flowers, and sometimes, as in Daisies, numerous and overlapping.

Bulbs are underground storage organs, composed of fleshy leaves.

Bulbils are small bulb-like organs at the base of the leaves or in place of the flowers, breaking off to form new plants.

Calyx refers to the sepals as a whole, usually used when they are joined.

Casual: plant appearing irregularly, without fixed localities.

Catkins are hanging flower-spikes, the individual flowers of which are usually rather inconspicuous.

Cluster: loose group of flowers.

Composite: member of the Daisy Family, Compositae.

Corms are bulb-like underground storage organs, comprising a swollen stem.

Coppice: trees or shrubs cut to the ground and growing from the old stools.

Corolla refers to the petals as a whole, usually when they are joined.

Crucifer: member of Cabbage Family, Cruciferae.

Deciduous: with leaves falling in autumn.

Deflexed: bent downwards.

Dunes are areas of wind-blown, usually lime-rich shell sand near the sea, with intervening damp hollows, termed *slacks*.

Epicalyx is a ring of sepal-like organs just below the true sepals (calyx). Common in Rose Family.

Female flowers contain styles only, no stamens.

Fen: a habitat on wet, lime-rich peat, not acid as in a bog (q.v.).

Florets are small flowers, part of a compound head.

Flower: the reproductive structure of a plant.

Flower parts comprise petals, sepals, stamens, styles, and sometimes other organs.

Alternate

Anther

Appressed

Bracts

Bulbil

Calyx

Catkins

Cluster

Composite

Corolla

GLOSSARY

Fruits are composed of the seeds and structures surrounding them.

Head: used when flowers are grouped in more or less compact terminal groups.

Heath: area, often dominated by heathers or related shrubs, on acid soils.

Hips are usually brightly coloured false fruits, characteristic of roses.

Hoary: greyish with short hairs.

Honey-leaf; see **Nectary.**

Introduced plants are not native to the area, but brought in by man.

Labiate: belonging to the Labiate Family, Labiatae.

Lanceolate: spear-shaped, narrowly oval and pointed.

Lax: of a flower-head with the flowers well spaced; not dense.

Lime: strictly the product (Calcium oxide) of the burning of limestone rock (Calcium carbonate), but here used loosely to include limestone and chalk, and also soils formed on them; the opposite of acid. Lime-rich soils are those formed on limestone.

Linear: almost parallel-sided.

Lobed: of leaves deeply toothed, but not formed of separate leaflets; cf. pinnate.

Male flowers contain stamens only, no styles.

Marsh: a community on wet ground, but not on peat.

Microspecies: species produced by complex reproductive processes which result in a large number of biologically distinct units, only distinguished with difficulty, and often on microscopic characters.

Midrib: central vein of a leaf, usually thick and raised.

Moor: usually heather covered, upland areas.

Morphology: the study of the shape, form or appearance of plants.

Nectar: sugary substance attractive to insects and secreted by many flowers.

Nectary: organ in the flower producing nectar.

Net-veined: of a leaf with the veins not all parallel.

Node: point of origin of leaves on the stem.

Opposite: of leaves arising opposite each other on the stem.

Palmate: with finger-like lobes or leaflets.

Parasites: are plants, usually without green colouring, that obtain nutriment from other plants.

Peat is a soil composed of undecayed plant matter, often acid.

Perennial: plant surviving more than two years; often stouter than annuals and sometimes woody.

Petals: usually conspicuous organs above the sepals, and surrounding the reproductive parts of the flower.

Pinnate, Pinnatifid: see Figure.

Pod: fruit, usually long and cylindrical and never fleshy; as in peas.

Rhizome: horizontal underground stem, and therefore bearing leaf-scars.

Rosette: flattened, rose-like group of leaves at the base of the stem.

xiv

Deflexed

Disc florets

Epicalyx

Female flower

Lobed

Male flower

Midrib

Nectary

Net-veined

Nodes

Pinnate

Rhizome

Rosette

Runners

Runners are horizontal above-ground stems, often rooting at the nodes.

Samara

Samara: a winged key-shaped fruit.

Scale: small appendage not resembling a leaf. Normally small, brown, and papery.

Scales

Sepals form a ring immediately below the petals and are usually green or brown and less conspicuous.

Shrub: much-branched woody plant, shorter than a tree.

Shy flowerer: plant often passing whole years without flowering and for which other characters are therefore important for identification.

Species: the basic unit of classification.

Sepals

Spike: flower-head with flowers arranged up a central axis in a cylinder. Stalked spike has individual flowers stalked.

Spine: straight, sharp-tipped appendage; cf. thorn.

Spreading: standing out horizontally or at a wide angle from the stem.

Spike

Stamens: the male organs in a flower, comprising a filament and a pollen sac, the anther (see Figure). Distinguished from styles (q.v.) by lying outside the centre of the flower usually in a ring, and by the usually coloured anthers.

Stamens

Stigma: the surface receptive to pollen at the tip of the style.

Stipules are scale- or leaf-like organs at the base of the leaf-stalk.

Styles: the columns of filaments leading from the female organs to the stigma (q.v.); see Figure. Distinguished from stamens (q.v.) by lying in the centre of the flower, within the ring of stamens.

Stigma

Subspecies: the division in the classification of organisms immediately below the species. Subspecies are morphologically distinct from each other, but interbreed freely and are therefore included in the same species.

Stipules

Tendrils are twisted filaments forming part of a leaf or stem and used for climbing.

Thallus: plant body not differentiated into stems and leaves.

Thorn: sharp-tipped, woody appendage, straight or curved.

Tree: tall, woody plant, with a single woody stem at the base.

Trefoil, Trifoliate: with three leaflets.

Style

Umbel: a flowerhead with the flowers in a spike but the lower branches longer so that all are level. **Umbellifers** are members of the Umbelliferae, characterised by having flowers in umbels.

Undershrub: low, often creeping woody perennial, often quite unlike taller shrubs.

Tendrils

Variety: a distinct form of a plant, of even lower rank than a subspecies.

Waste places: areas much disturbed by man, but not cultivated.

Whorl: where several organs arise at the same point on a stem; cf. opposite

Winged: with a flange running down the stem or stalk.

Wings: see page 26.

Thorn

Whorl

Winged fruit

Winged stem

Winged flower

PLATE 1
page 1

Silver
Fir

Douglas
Fir

Norway
Spruce

Western
Hemlock

Scots
Pine

European
Larch

Maritime
Pine

Joint
Pine

Lawson's
Cypress

Yew

Juniper

PLATE 2
pages 1–2

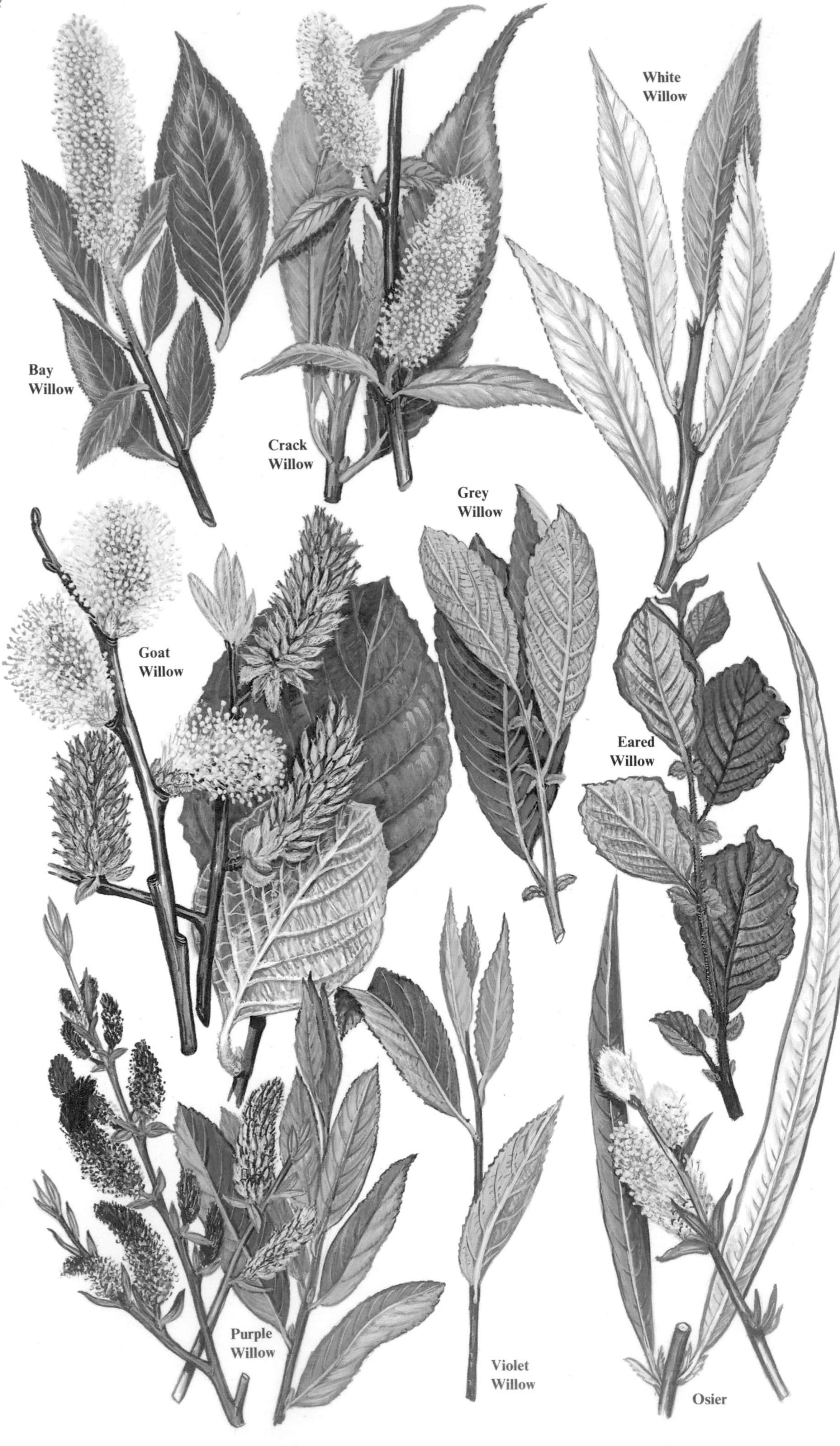

Bay
Willow

Crack
Willow

White
Willow

Goat
Willow

Grey
Willow

Eared
Willow

Purple
Willow

Violet
Willow

Osier

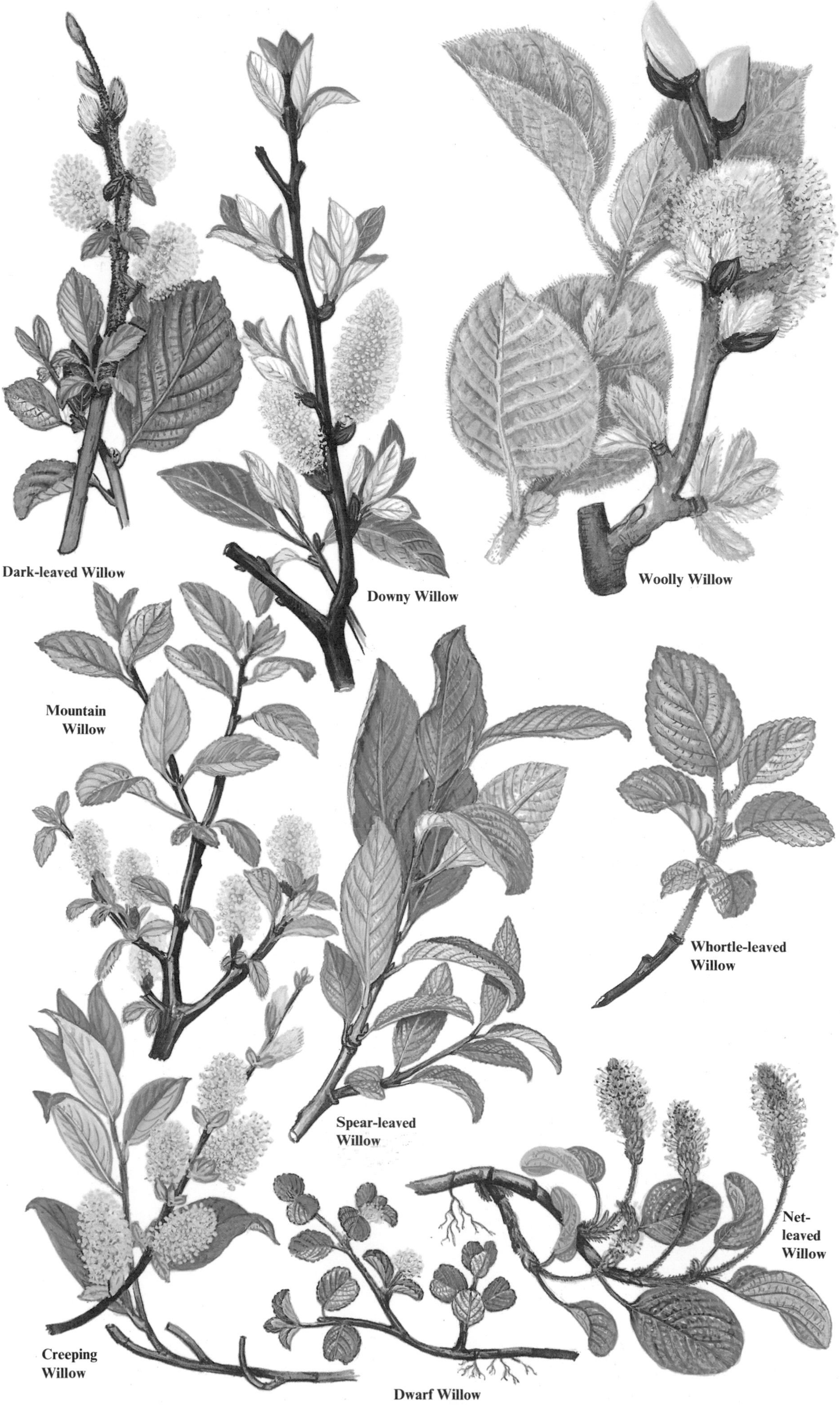

PLATE 3
page 2

Dark-leaved Willow

Downy Willow

Woolly Willow

Mountain
Willow

Whortle-leaved
Willow

Spear-leaved
Willow

Net-
leaved
Willow

Creeping
Willow

Dwarf Willow

PLATE 4
page 3

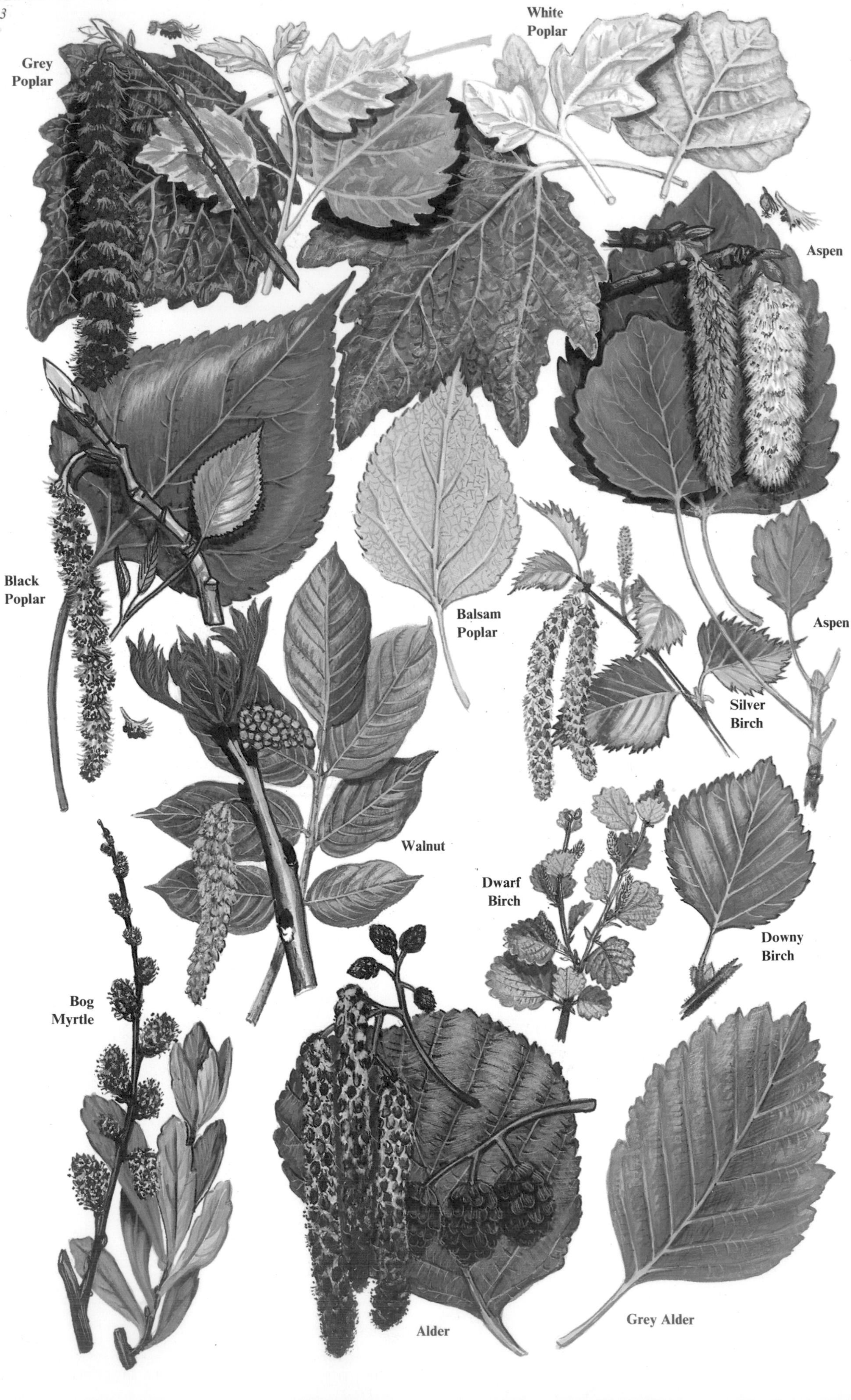

Grey
Poplar

White
Poplar

Aspen

Black
Poplar

Balsam
Poplar

Aspen

Silver
Birch

Walnut

Dwarf
Birch

Downy
Birch

Bog
Myrtle

Alder

Grey Alder

PLATE 5
pages 3–4

Hornbeam

Hazel

Beech

Sweet
Chestnut

Evergreen
Oak

Sessile
Oak

Pedunculate
Oak

Turkey
Oak

Red Oak

PLATE 6

page 4

Wych
Elm

English
Elm

Small-
leaved
Elm

Norway
Maple

London
Plane

Sycamore

Montpelier
Maple

Italian
Maple

Field Maple

PLATE 7
pages 4–5

Horse Chestnut

Holly

Small-
leaved
Lime

Large-
leaved
Lime

Ash

Tree of
Heaven

PLATE 8
pages 5–6

Asarabacca

Mistletoe

Birthwort

Bastard
Toadflax

Hop

Pellitory
of
the
Wall

Hemp

Nettle

Annual Nettle

PLATE 9
page 6

Bistort

Amphibious
Bistort

Redshank

Pale
Persicaria

Alpine
Bistort

Water-
pepper

Sea Knotgrass

Buckwheat

Knotgrass

PLATE 10
pages 6–7

Copse Bindweed

Black Bindweed

Japanese Knotweed

Himalayan Knotweed

Iceland Purslane

Hottentot Fig

Spring Beauty

Pink Purslane

Blinks

PLATE 11
page 7

Common Sorrel

Sheep's Sorrel

Sheep's Sorrel

Broad-leaved Dock

Clustered Dock

Fiddle Dock

Water Dock

Marsh Dock

Mountain Sorrel

PLATE 12
page 8

Good
King
Henry

Fat
Hen

Red
Goosefoot

Maple-
leaved
Goosefoot

Many-
seeded
Goosefoot

Grass-
leaved
Orache

Spear-
leaved
Orache

Common
Orache

Sea
Beet

Polycnemum

Frosted
Orache

PLATE 13
page 8

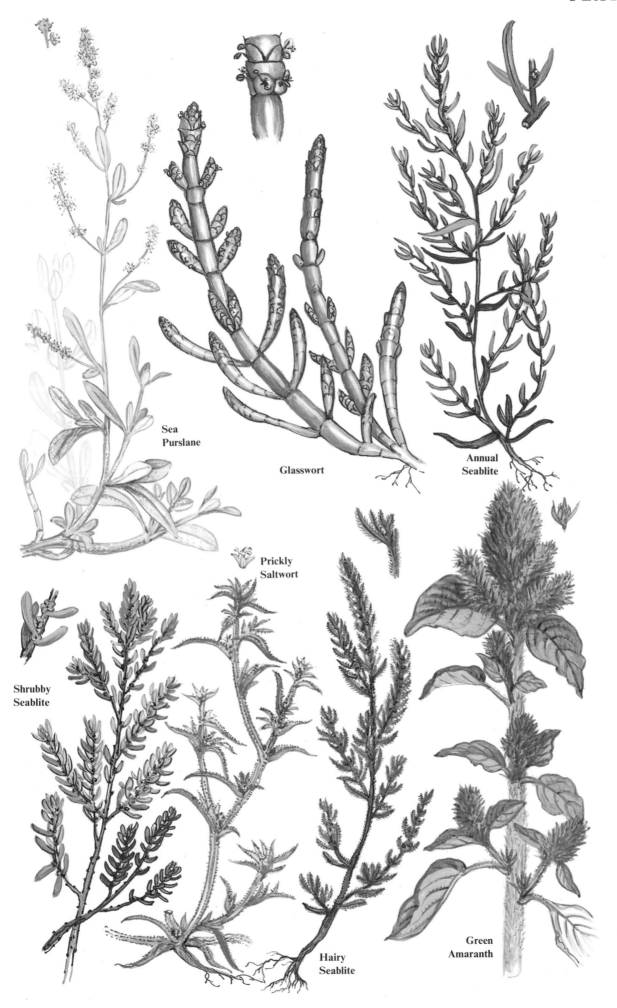

Sea
Purslane

Glasswort

Annual
Seablite

Prickly
Saltwort

Shrubby
Seablite

Hairy
Seablite

Green
Amaranth

PLATE 14
page 9

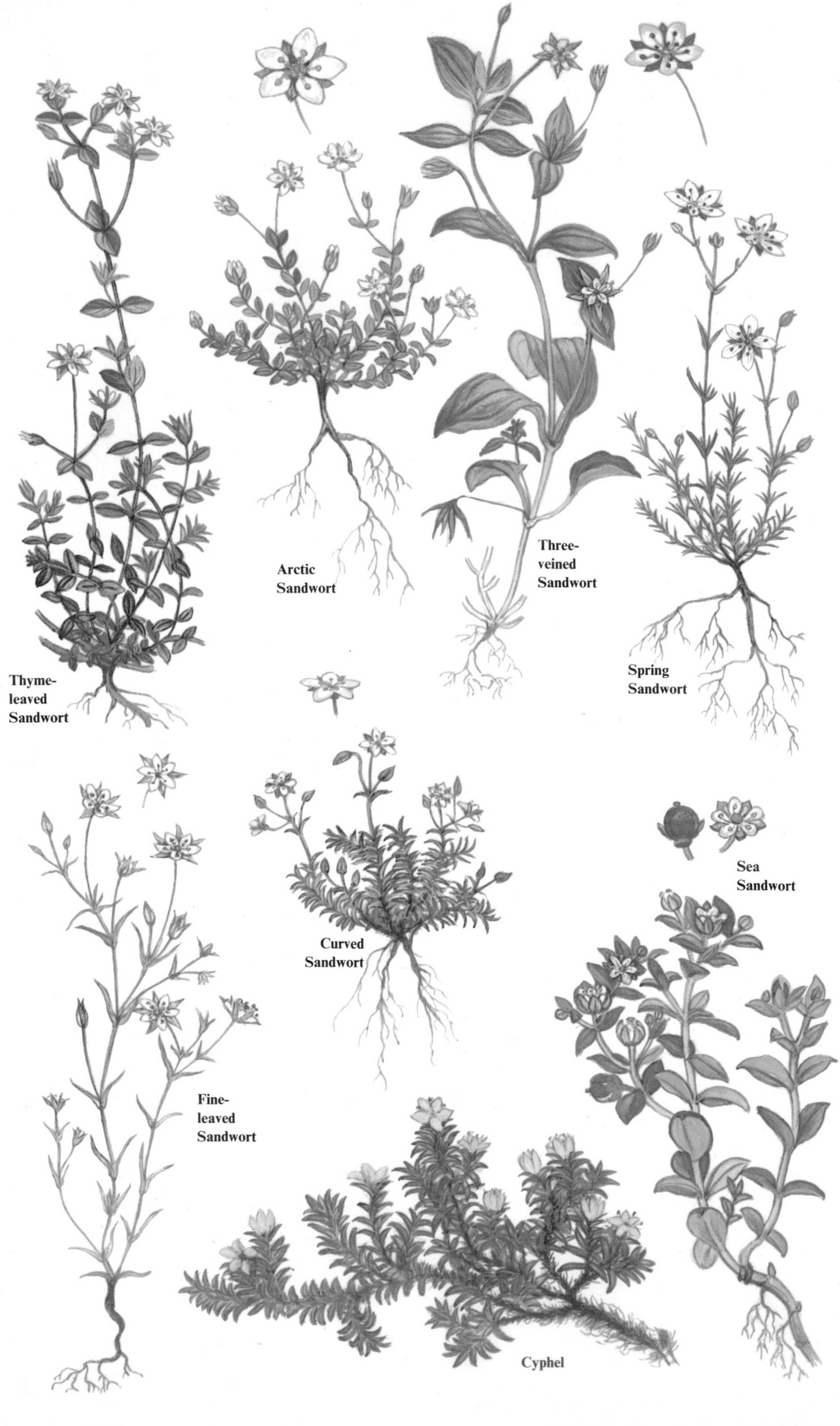

Thyme-
leaved
Sandwort

Arctic
Sandwort

Three-
veined
Sandwort

Spring
Sandwort

Fine-
leaved
Sandwort

Curved
Sandwort

Sea
Sandwort

Cyphel

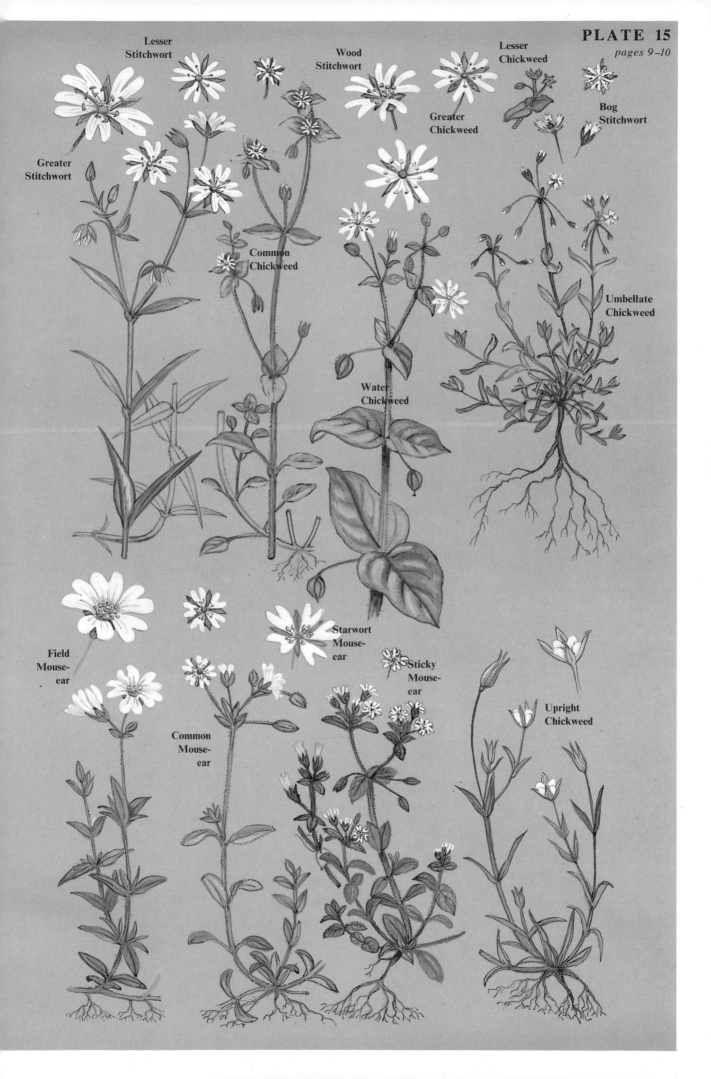

PLATE 15
pages 9–10

Lesser
Stitchwort

Wood
Stitchwort

Lesser
Chickweed

Greater
Chickweed

Bog
Stitchwort

Greater
Stitchwort

Common
Chickweed

Umbellate
Chickweed

Water
Chickweed

Field
Mouse-
ear

Starwort
Mouse-
ear

Sticky
Mouse-
ear

Upright
Chickweed

Common
Mouse-
ear

PLATE 16
page 10

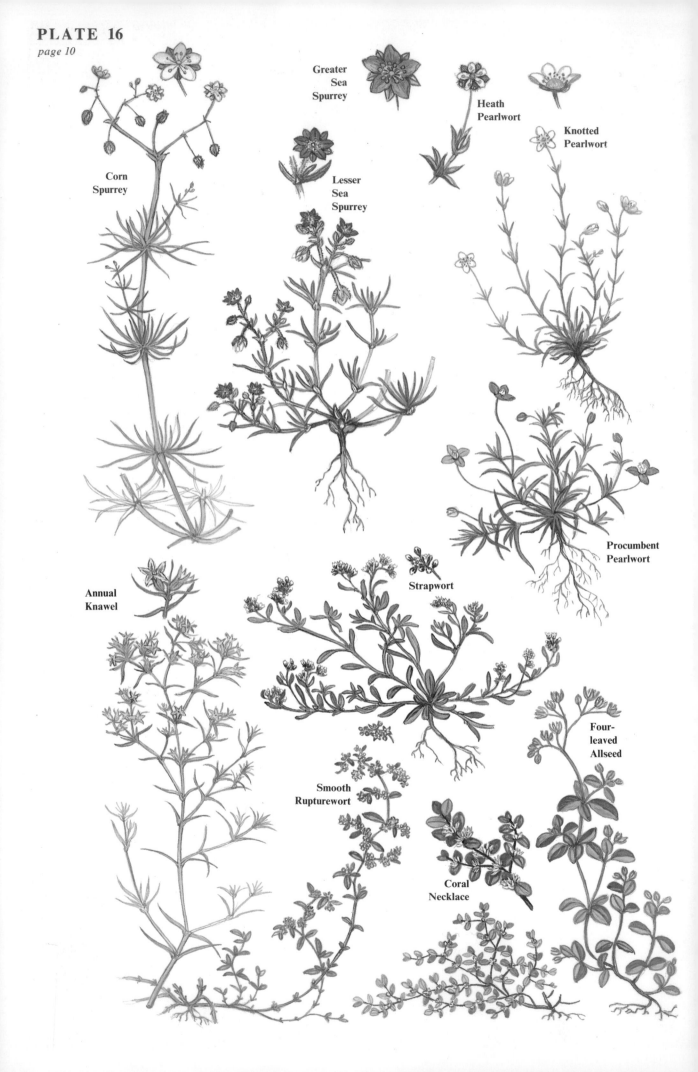

Greater
Sea
Spurrey

Heath
Pearlwort

Knotted
Pearlwort

Corn
Spurrey

Lesser
Sea
Spurrey

Procumbent
Pearlwort

Strapwort

Annual
Knawel

Four-
leaved
Allseed

Smooth
Rupturewort

Coral
Necklace

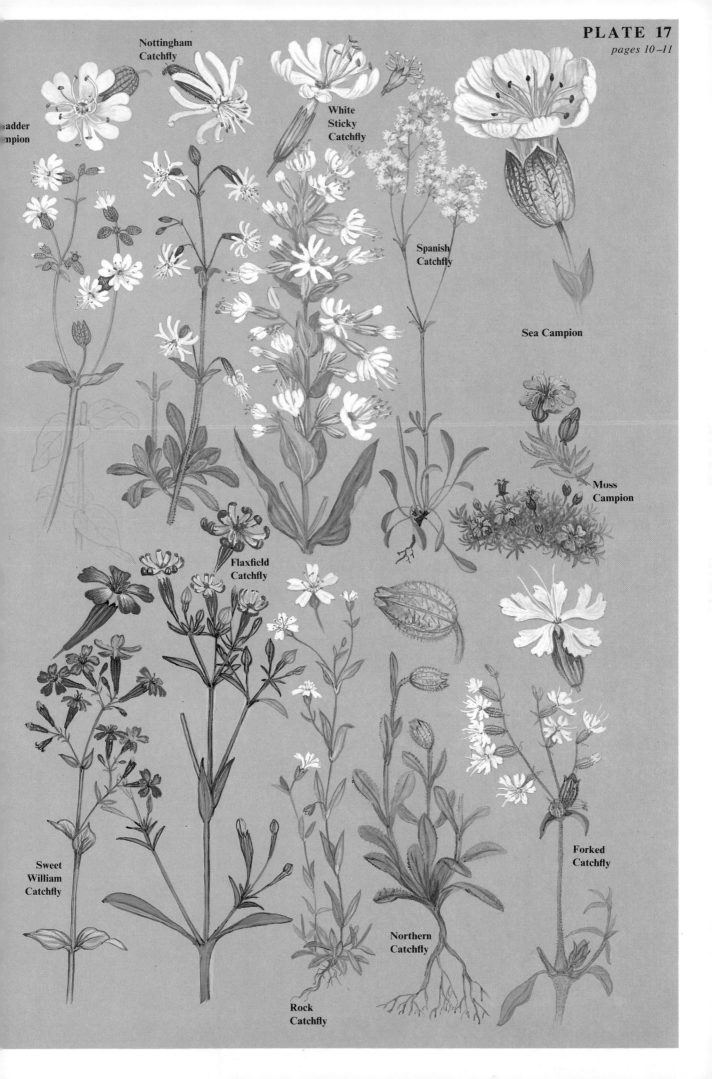

PLATE 17
pages 10–11

Nottingham
Catchfly

White
Sticky
Catchfly

Bladder
Campion

Spanish
Catchfly

Sea Campion

Moss
Campion

Flaxfield
Catchfly

Sweet
William
Catchfly

Forked
Catchfly

Rock
Catchfly

Northern
Catchfly

PLATE 18
page 11

Red
Campion

White
Campion

Night-
flowering
Catchfly

Ragged
Robin

Sticky
Catchfly

Alpine
Catchfly

Corn
Cockle

Soapwort

PLATE 19
pages 11–12

Small-flowered Catchfly

Sand Catchfly

Berry Catchfly

Fastigiate Gypsophila

Cow Basil

Tunic Flower

Proliferous Pink

Annual Gypsophila

PLATE 20
page 12

Cheddar
Pink

Clove
Pink

Wild
Pink

Jersey
Pink

Deptford
Pink

Carthusian
Pink

Large
Pink

Maiden
Pink

PLATE 21
pages 12–13

Stinking
Hellebore

Green
Hellebore

Love-in-
a-mist

Winter
Aconite

Yellow
Water-
lily

White
water-
lily

Least
Water-
lily

PLATE 22
page 13

Globe
Flower

Marsh Marigold

Meadow
Buttercup

Bulbous
Buttercu

Creeping
Buttercup

Greater
Spearwort

Lesser
Spearwort

Lesser Celandine

PLATE 23

pages 13–14

Celery-
leaved
Buttercup

Corn
Buttercup

Goldilocks
Buttercup

Small-
flowered
Buttercup

Large White
Buttercup

Glacier
Buttercup

Common
Water
Crowfoot

Ivy-
leaved
Crowfoot

PLATE 24
page 14

Common
Meadow-
rue

Greater
Meadow-
rue

Lesser
Meadow-
rue

Alpine
Meadow-rue

Baneberry

Traveller's
Joy

Alpine
Clematis

PLATE 25
pages 14–15

Columbine

Monkshood

Wolfsbane

Forking Larkspur

Varie-gated Monks-hood

Yellow Pheasant's-eye

Summer Pheasant's-eye

Large Pheasant's-eye

Mousetail

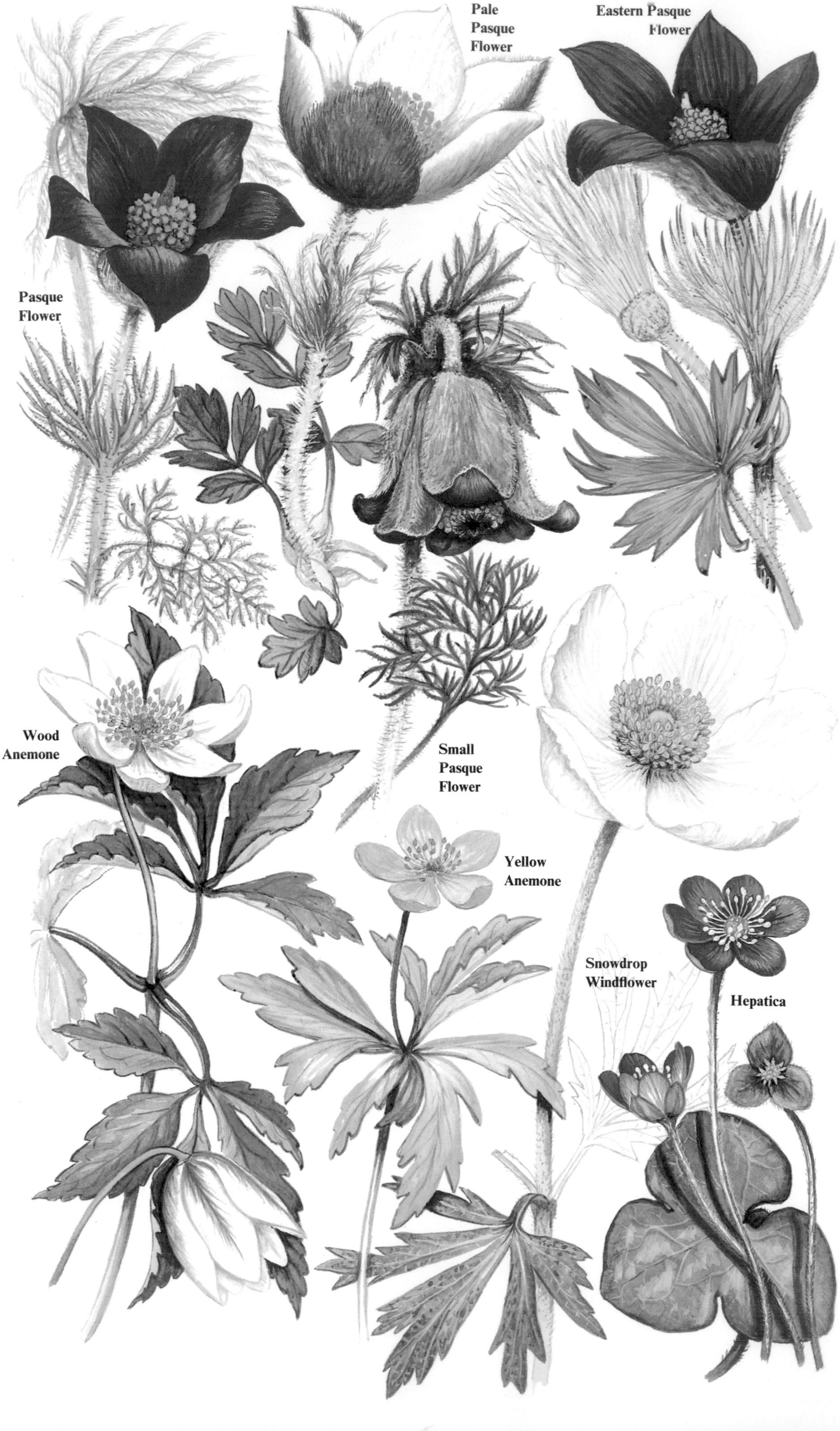

PLATE 26

page 15

Pale
Pasque
Flower

Eastern Pasque
Flower

Pasque
Flower

Wood
Anemone

Small
Pasque
Flower

Yellow
Anemone

Snowdrop
Windflower

Hepatica

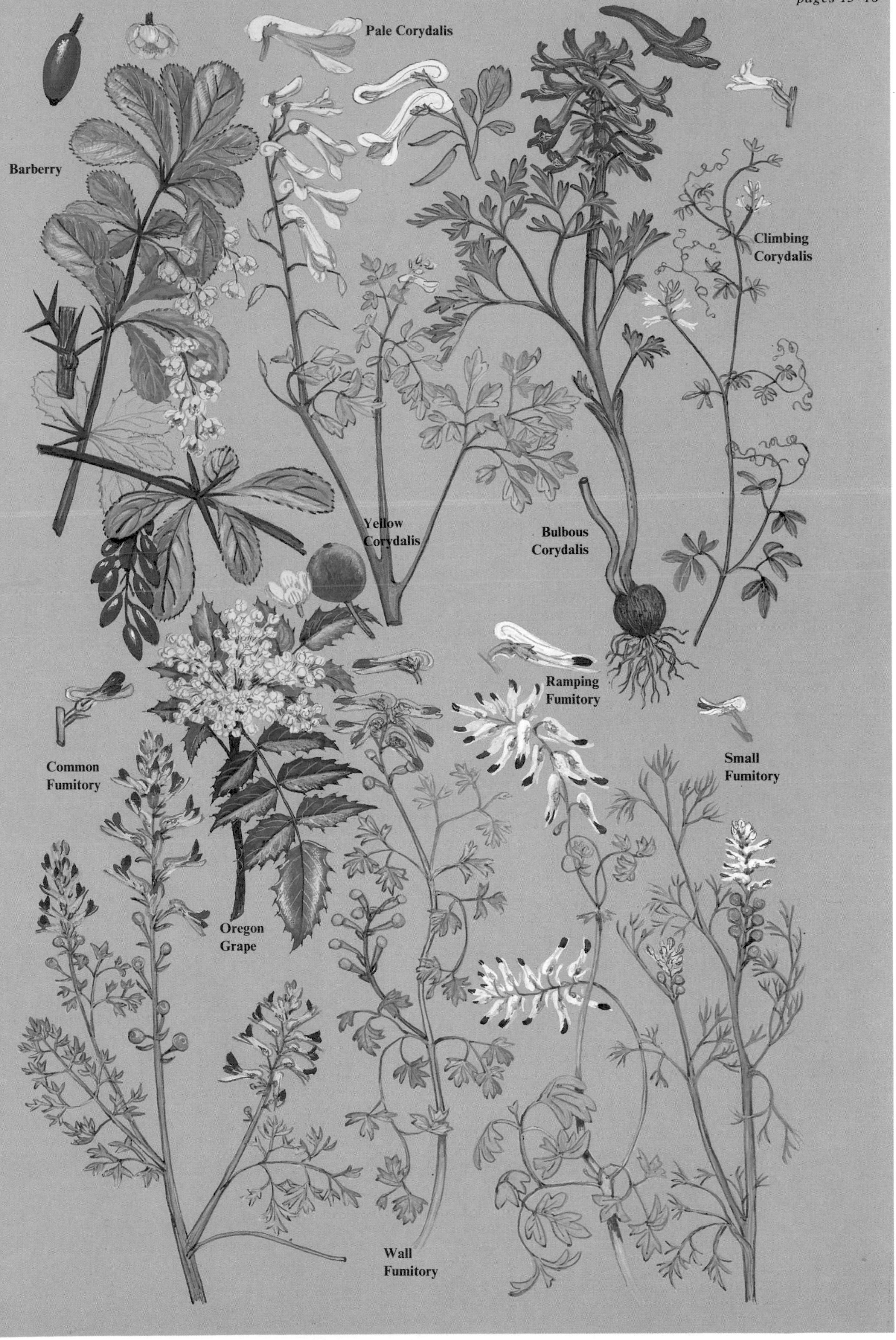

PLATE 27
pages 15–16

Pale Corydalis

Barberry

Climbing
Corydalis

Yellow
Corydalis

Bulbous
Corydalis

Ramping
Fumitory

Small
Fumitory

Common
Fumitory

Oregon
Grape

Wall
Fumitory

PLATE 28
pages 16–17

Common Poppy

Prickly Poppy

Rough Poppy

Long-headed Poppy

Opium Poppy

Arctic Poppy

Yellow-Horned-Poppy

Welsh Poppy

Greater Celandine

PLATE 29
page 17

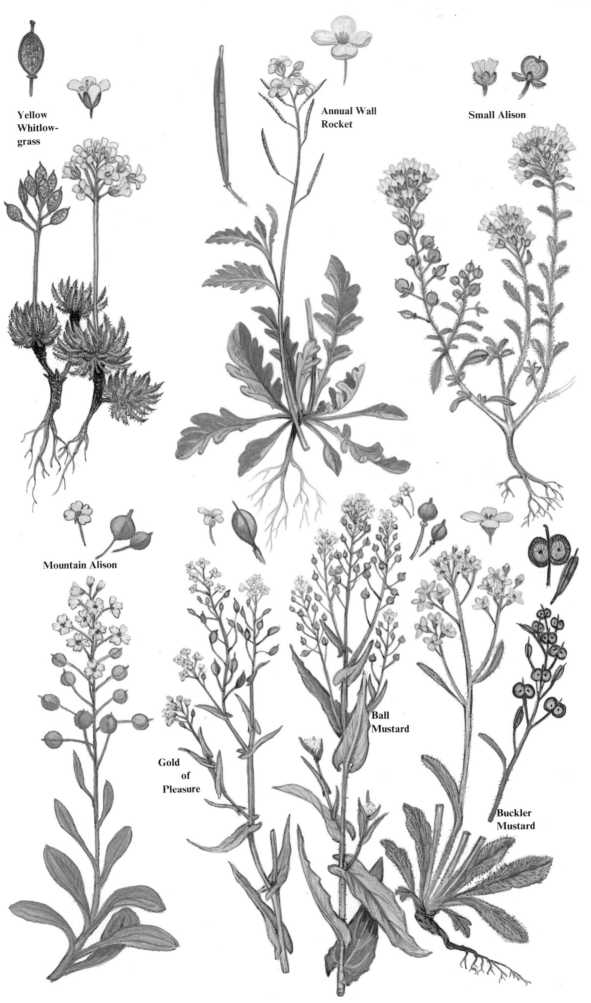

Yellow
Whitlow-
grass

Annual Wall
Rocket

Small Alison

Mountain Alison

Gold
of
Pleasure

Ball
Mustard

Buckler
Mustard

PLATE 30
pages 17–18

Wallflower

Hedge
Mustard

Tall
Rocket

Flixweed

Woad

Marsh
Yellowcress

Warty
Cabbage

Common
Wintercress

Creeping
Yellowcress

Treacle
Mustard

Great
Yellowcress

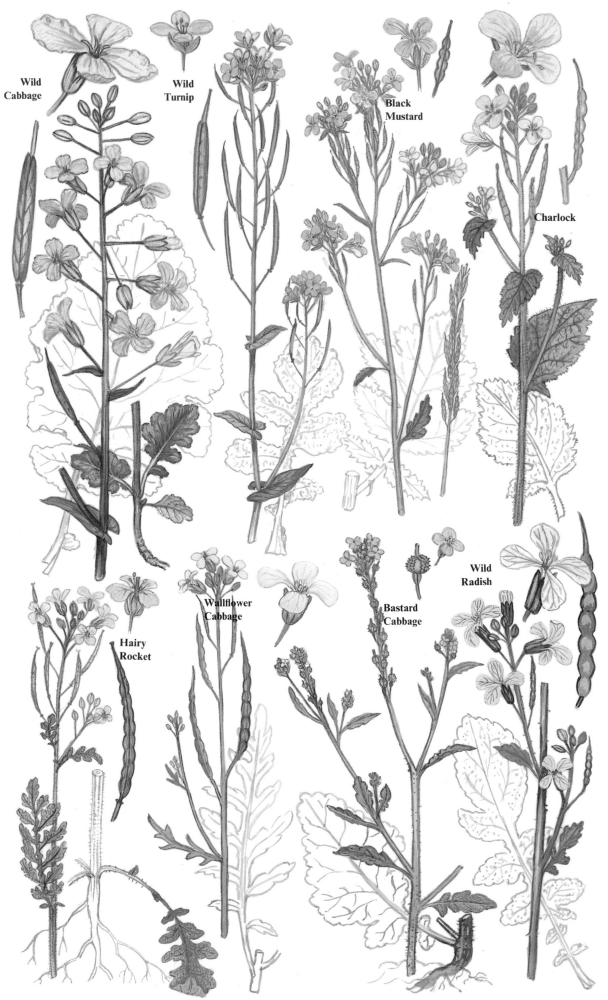

PLATE 31
page 18

Wild Cabbage

Wild Turnip

Black Mustard

Charlock

Hairy Rocket

Wallflower Cabbage

Bastard Cabbage

Wild Radish

PLATE 32
pages 18–19

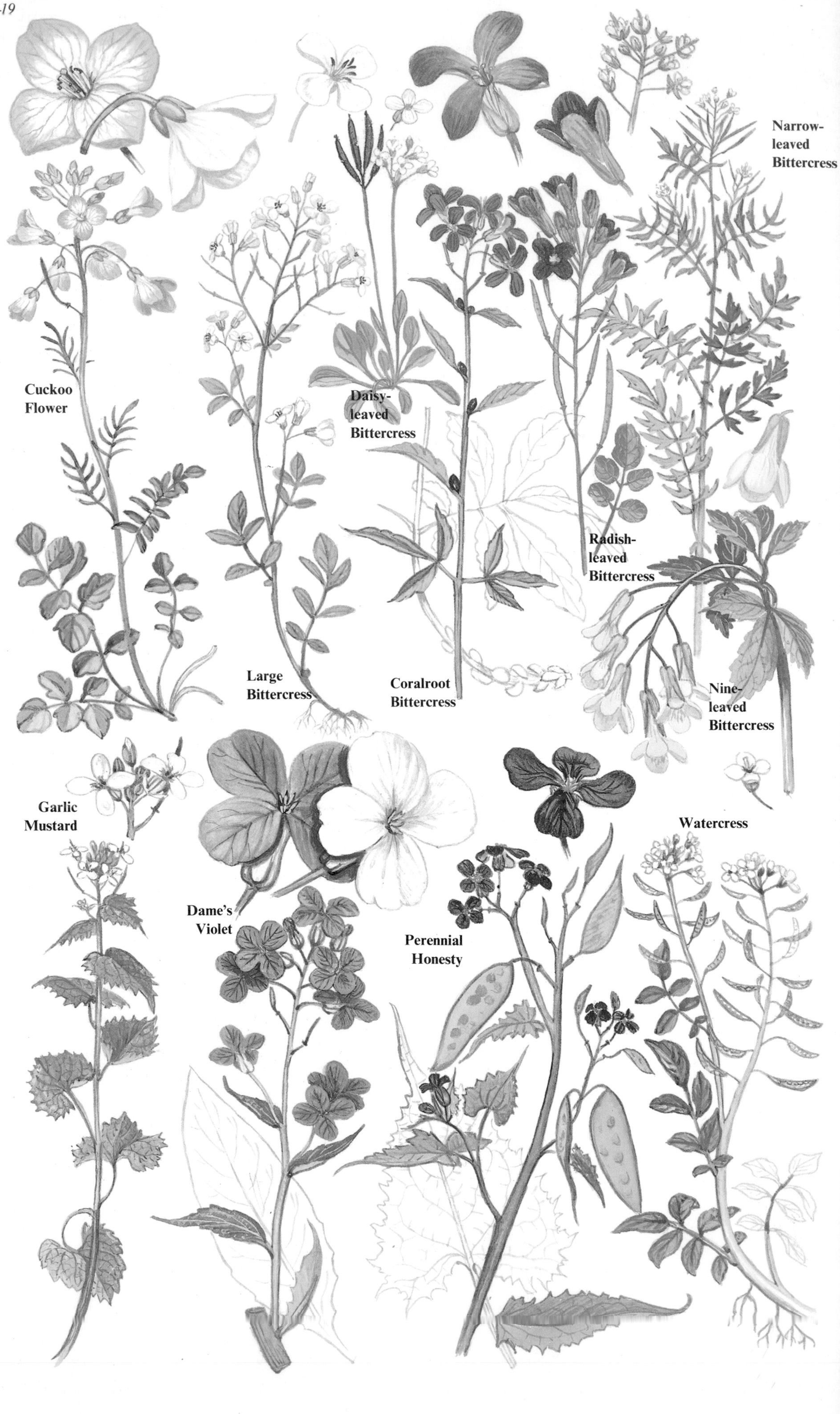

Narrow-
leaved
Bittercress

Cuckoo
Flower

Daisy-
leaved
Bittercress

Radish-
leaved
Bittercress

Large
Bittercress

Coralroot
Bittercress

Nine-
leaved
Bittercress

Garlic
Mustard

Watercress

Dame's
Violet

Perennial
Honesty

PLATE 33
page 19

Sea Kale

Sea
Rocket

Hoary
Stock

White
Ball
Mustard

Horse-
radish

Common
Scurvy-
grass

Early
Scurvy-
grass

Dittander

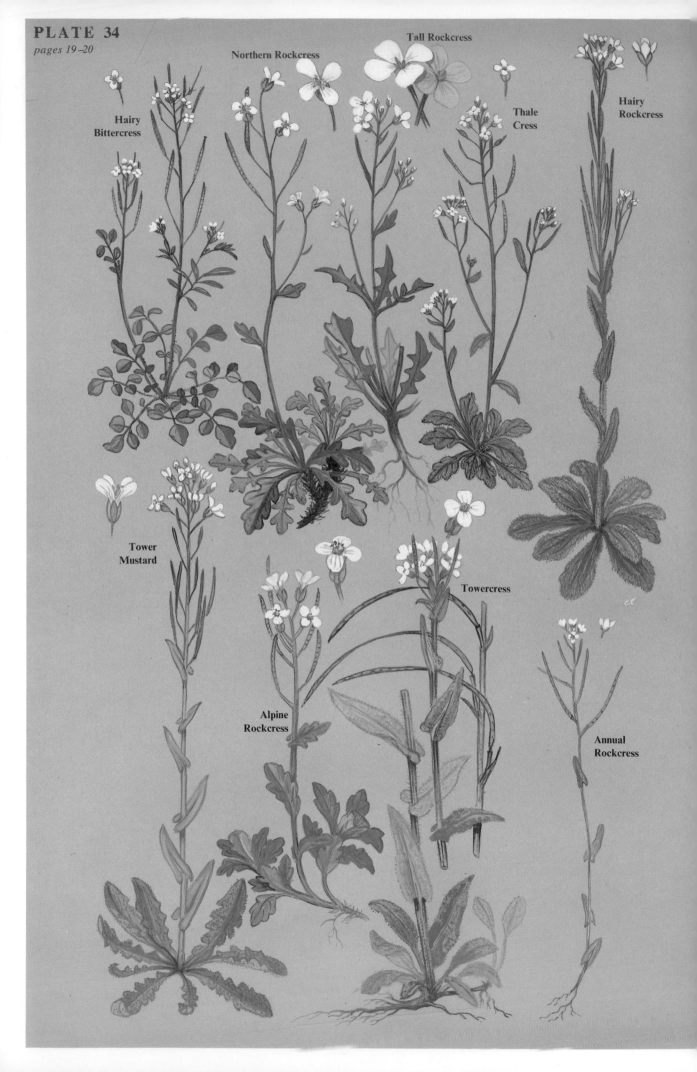

PLATE 34
pages 19–20

Northern Rockcress

Tall Rockcress

Hairy Bittercress

Thale Cress

Hairy Rockcress

Tower Mustard

Alpine Rockcress

Towercress

Annual Rockcress

PLATE 35
page 20

Wild Candytuft

Shepherd's Purse

Shepherd's Cress

Hoary Alison

Sweet Alison

Wall Whitlow-grass

Common Whitlow-grass

Hutchinsia

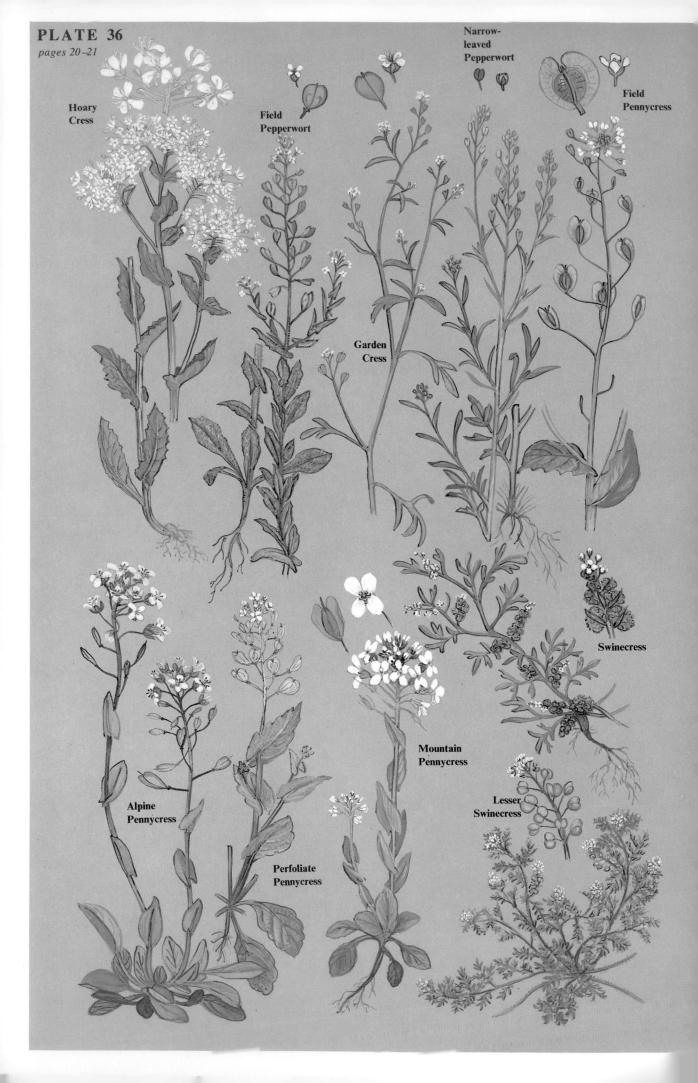

PLATE 36
pages 20–21

Hoary Cress

Field Pepperwort

Narrow-leaved Pepperwort

Field Pennycress

Garden Cress

Alpine Pennycress

Perfoliate Pennycress

Mountain Pennycress

Swinecress

Lesser Swinecress

PLATE 37
pages 21–22

Weld

Wild
Mignonette

Great
Sundew

Oblong-
leaved
Sundew

Common
Sundew

Alternate-
leaved
Golden
Saxifrage

Grass of Parnassus

Opposite-
leaved
Golden
Saxifrage

Navelwort

Roseroot

PLATE 38
page 22

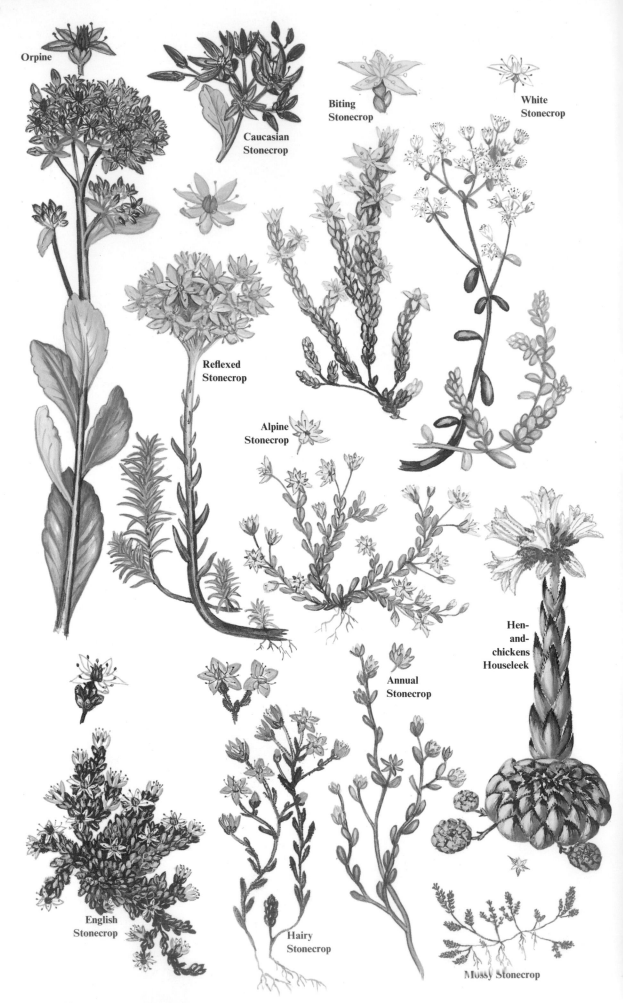

Orpine

Caucasian
Stonecrop

Biting
Stonecrop

White
Stonecrop

Reflexed
Stonecrop

Alpine
Stonecrop

Hen-
and-
chickens
Houseleek

English
Stonecrop

Annual
Stonecrop

Hairy
Stonecrop

Mossy Stonecrop

PLATE 39
pages 22–23

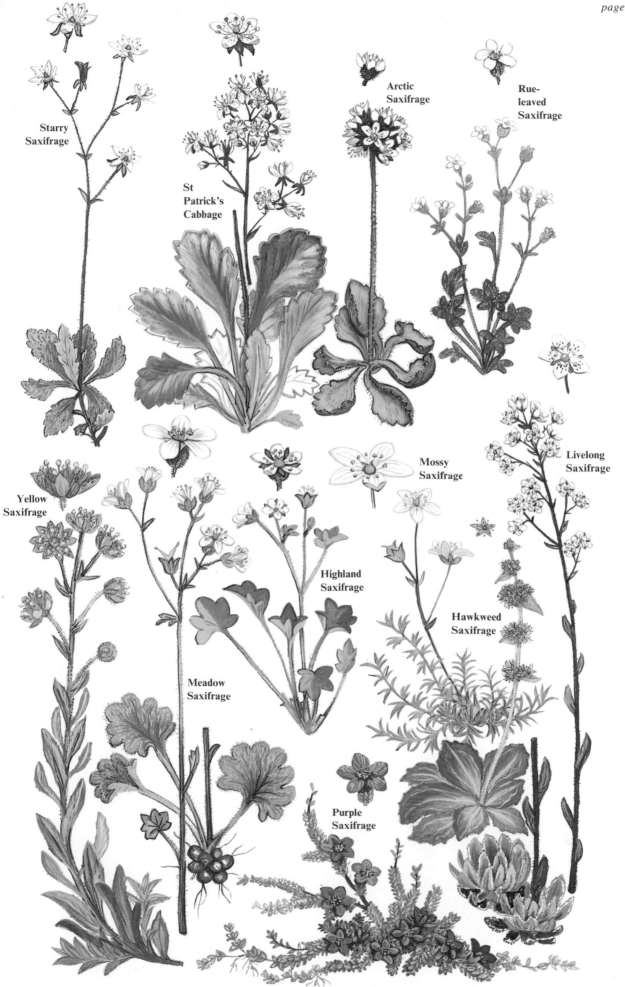

Starry
Saxifrage

St
Patrick's
Cabbage

Arctic
Saxifrage

Rue-
leaved
Saxifrage

Yellow
Saxifrage

Mossy
Saxifrage

Livelong
Saxifrage

Highland
Saxifrage

Hawkweed
Saxifrage

Meadow
Saxifrage

Purple
Saxifrage

PLATE 40
page 23

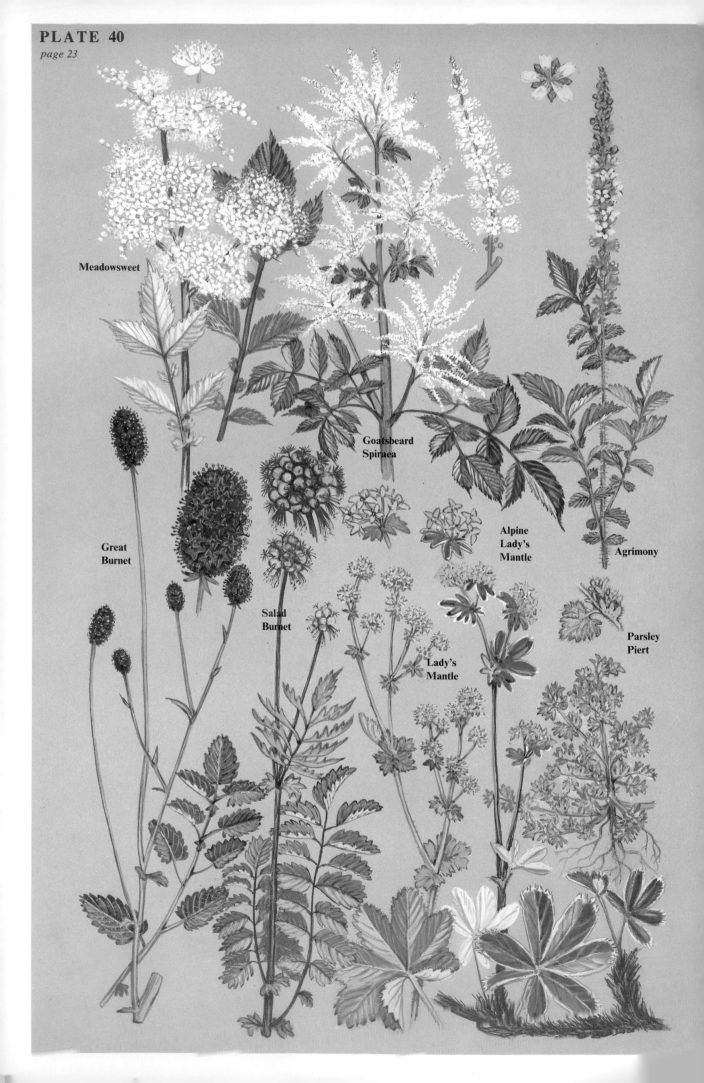

Meadowsweet

Goatsbeard
Spiraea

Great
Burnet

Salad
Burnet

Lady's
Mantle

Alpine
Lady's
Mantle

Agrimony

Parsley
Piert

PLATE 41
pages 23–24

Dog
Rose

Burnet
Rose

Field
Rose

Downy
Rose

Stone
Bramble

Bramble

Cloudberry

Arctic
Bramble

Raspberry

PLATE 42
pages 24–25

Wild
Strawberry

Hautbois
Strawberry

Rock
Cinquefoil

Marsh
Cinquefoil

Barren Strawberry

Water
Avens

Herb Bennet

Mountain
Avens

PLATE 43
page 25

Shrubby
Cinquefoil

Trailing
Tormentil

Creeping
Cinquefoil

Snow Cinquefoil

Tormentil

Hoary
Cinquefoil

Spring
Cinquefoil

Sulphur
Cinquefoil

Grey
Cinquefoil

Silverweed

Sibbaldia

PLATE 44
pages 25–26

Whitebeam

Hawthorn

Crab
Apple

Wild
Pear

Wild
Cherry

Bird
Cherry

Blackthorn

Amelanchier

Wild
Cherry

Wild
Cotoneaster

Small-
leaved
Cotoneaster

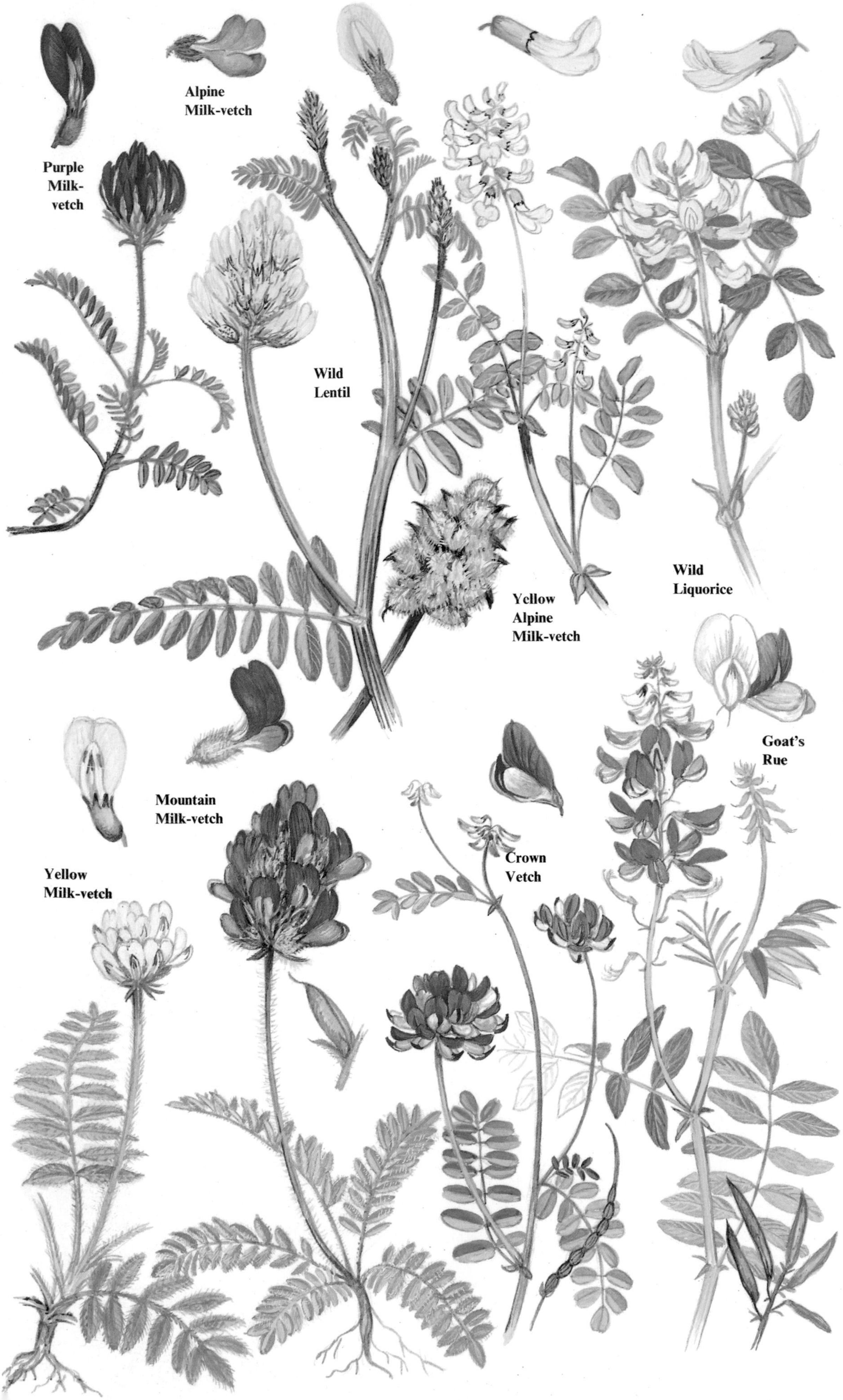

PLATE 45

page 26

Alpine
Milk-vetch

Purple
Milk-
vetch

Wild
Lentil

Yellow
Alpine
Milk-vetch

Wild
Liquorice

Goat's
Rue

Mountain
Milk-vetch

Crown
Vetch

Yellow
Milk-vetch

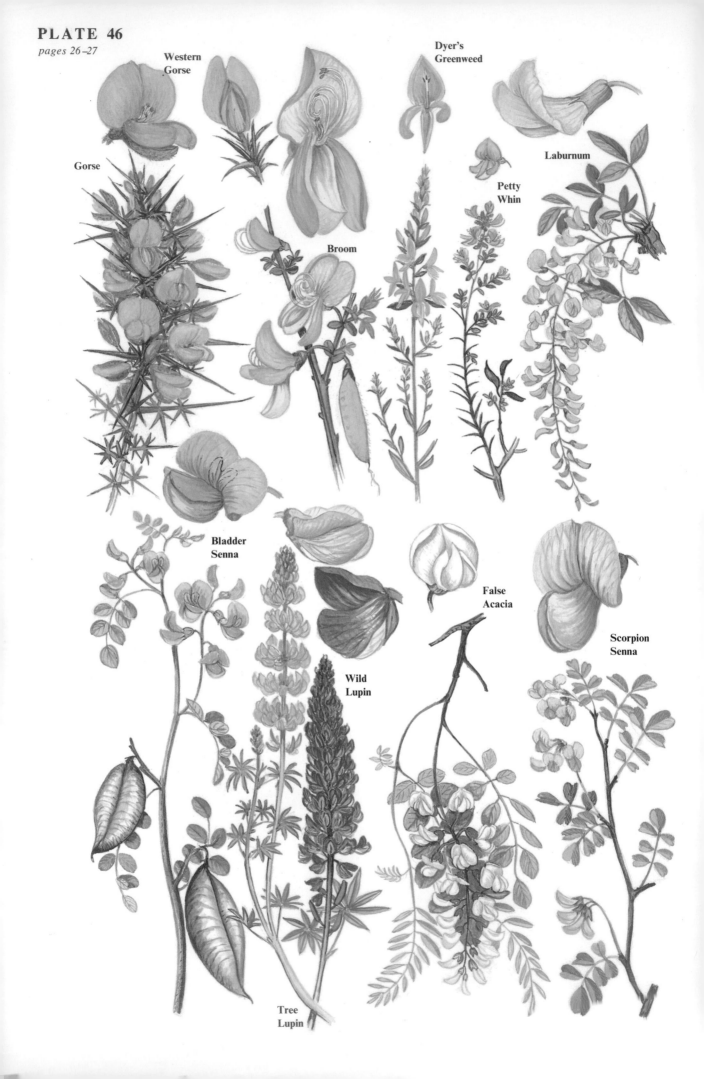

PLATE 46
pages 26–27

Western Gorse

Dyer's Greenweed

Gorse

Laburnum

Petty Whin

Broom

Bladder Senna

False Acacia

Scorpion Senna

Wild Lupin

Tree Lupin

PLATE 47
pages 27–28

Fodder Vetch

Tufted Vetch

Bush Vetch

Upright Vetch

Wood Vetch

Spring Vetch

Slender Tare

Smooth Tare

Bithynian Vetch

Common Vetch

Hairy Tare

Yellow Vetch

PLATE 48
page 28

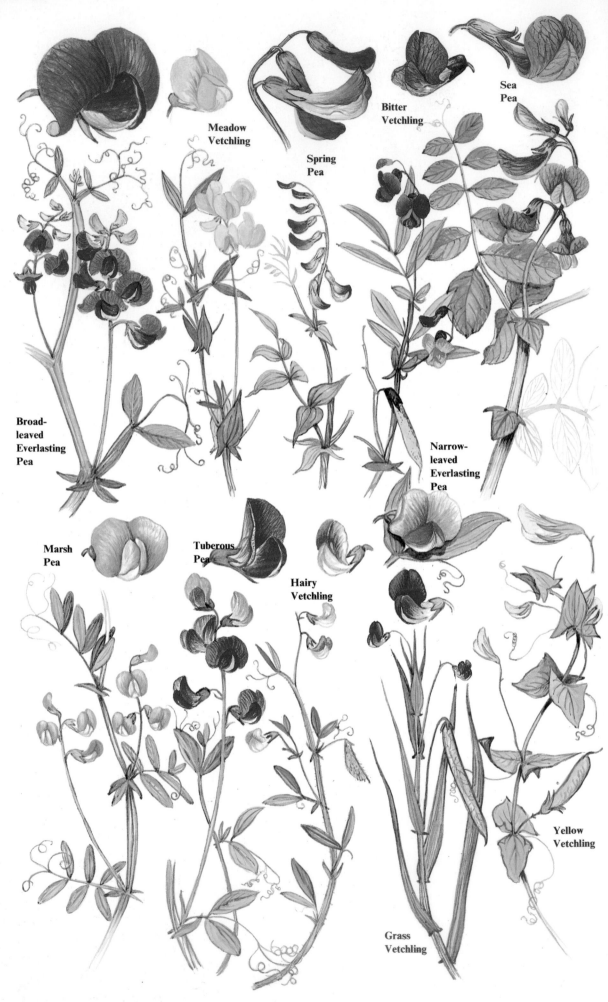

Meadow
Vetchling

Bitter
Vetchling

Sea
Pea

Spring
Pea

Broad-
leaved
Everlasting
Pea

Narrow-
leaved
Everlasting
Pea

Marsh
Pea

Tuberous
Pea

Hairy
Vetchling

Yellow
Vetchling

Grass
Vetchling

PLATE 49
pages 28–29

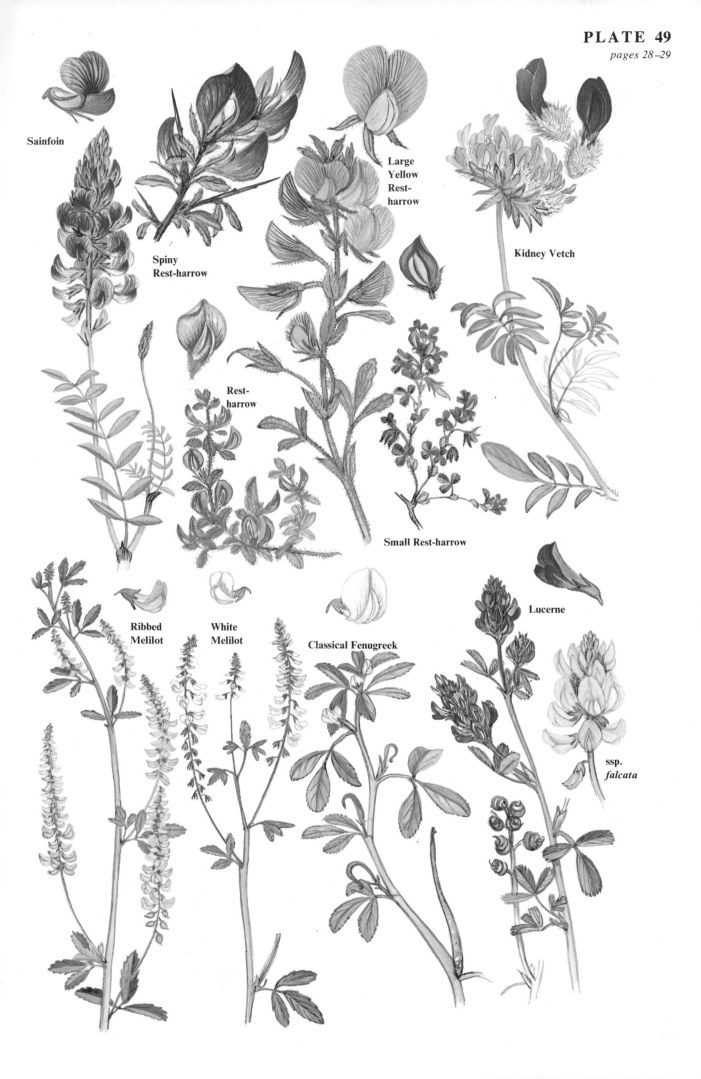

Sainfoin

Spiny
Rest-harrow

Large
Yellow
Rest-
harrow

Kidney Vetch

Rest-
harrow

Small Rest-harrow

Ribbed
Melilot

White
Melilot

Classical Fenugreek

Lucerne

ssp.
falcata

PLATE 50
page 29

Birdsfoot
Trefoil

Hairy
Birdsfoot
Trefoil

Dragon's
Teeth

Horseshoe
Vetch

Orange
Birdsfoot

Slender
Trefoil

Lesser
Trefoil

Narrow-
leaved
Birdsfoot
Trefoil

Birdsfoot

Spotted
Medick

Black
Medick

Hop
Trefoil

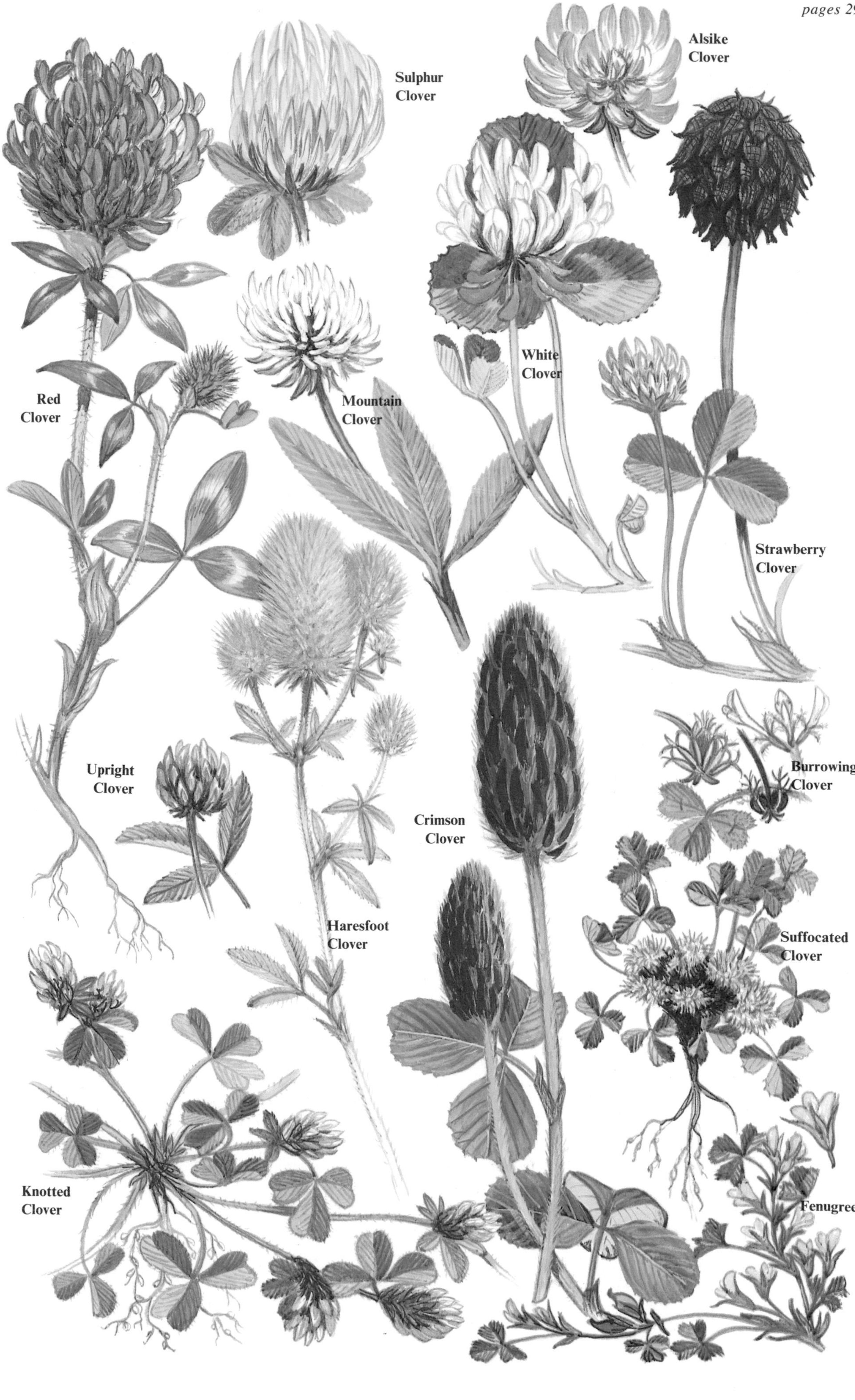

PLATE 51
pages 29–30

Sulphur
Clover

Alsike
Clover

Red
Clover

Mountain
Clover

White
Clover

Strawberry
Clover

Upright
Clover

Burrowing
Clover

Crimson
Clover

Suffocated
Clover

Haresfoot
Clover

Knotted
Clover

Fenugreek

PLATE 52
pages 30–31

Wood-sorrel

Yellow Oxalis

Pink Oxalis

Bermuda Buttercup

Common Flax

Perennial Flax

Pale Flax

Yellow Flax

Common Storksbill

Sea Storksbill

Purging Flax

Allseed

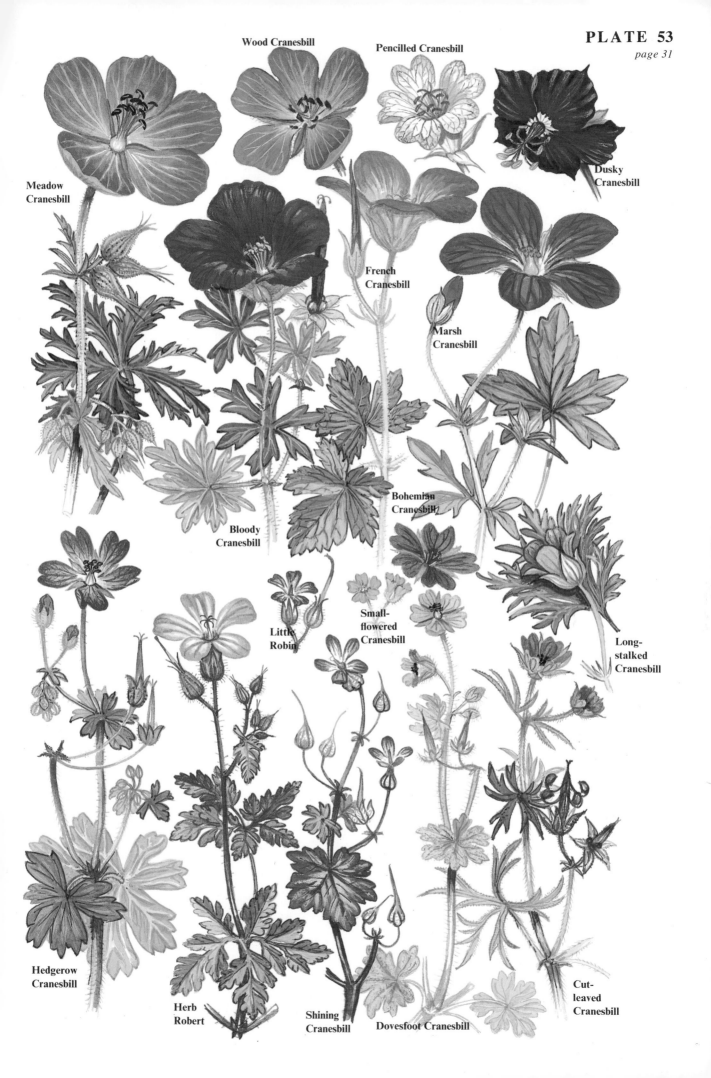

PLATE 53
page 31

Wood Cranesbill

Pencilled Cranesbill

Dusky Cranesbill

Meadow Cranesbill

French Cranesbill

Marsh Cranesbill

Bloody Cranesbill

Bohemian Cranesbill

Long-stalked Cranesbill

Little Robin

Small-flowered Cranesbill

Hedgerow Cranesbill

Herb Robert

Shining Cranesbill

Dovesfoot Cranesbill

Cut-leaved Cranesbill

PLATE 54

page 32

Cypress
Spurge

Wood
Spurge

Irish
Spurge

Sea
Spurge

Portland
Spurge

Caper
Spurge

Sun
Spurge

Dog's
Mercury

Broad-
leaved
Spurge

Petty
Spurge

Dwarf Spurge

Purple Spurge

PLATE 55
pages 32–33

Small
Balsam

Touch-
me-
not
Balsam

Orange
Balsam

Himalayan
Balsam

Burning
Bush

Spurge
Laurel

Annual
Thymelaea

Shrubby
Milkwort

Common
Milkwort

Heath Milkwort

Mezereon

PLATE 56
pages 33–34

Red
Currant

Black
Currant

Mountain
Currant

Gooseberry

Box

Buckthorn

Spindle-
tree

Bladder-
nut

Alder
Buckthorn

Sea
Buckthorn

Tamarisk

PLATE 57
page 34

Dwarf Mallow

Least
Mallow

Musk
Mallow

Common
Mallow

Smaller
Tree
Mallow

Tree
Mallow

Marsh
Mallow

Rough
Mallow

PLATE 58
ﾅﾅﾅﾅﾅﾅ ﾅﾅﾅﾅ

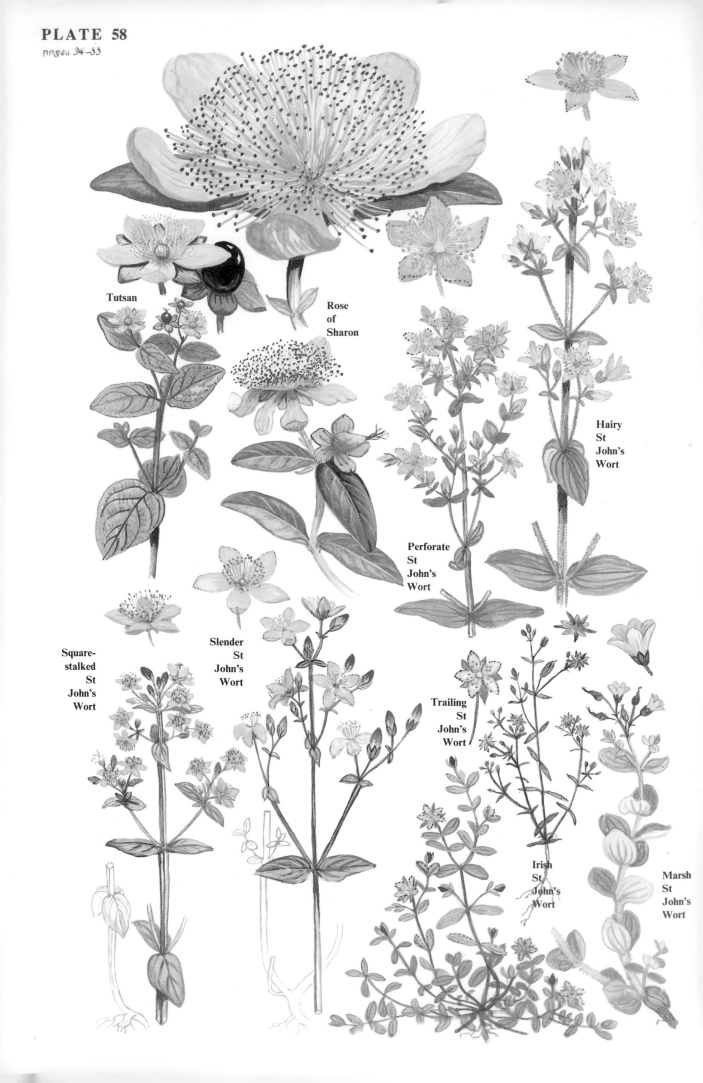

Tutsan

Rose
of
Sharon

Hairy
St
John's
Wort

Perforate
St
John's
Wort

Slender
St
John's
Wort

Square-
stalked
St
John's
Wort

Trailing
St
John's
Wort

Irish
St
John's
Wort

Marsh
St
John's
Wort

PLATE 59
pages 35 –36

Sweet Violet

Early
Dog
Violet

Pale
Dog
Violet

Meadow
Violet

Common
Dog
Violet

Northern
Violet

Heath
Dog
Violet

Marsh Violet

Mountain
Pansy

Field
Pansy

Yellow
Wood
Violet

Wild
Pansy

Dwarf
Pansy

PLATE 60
page 36

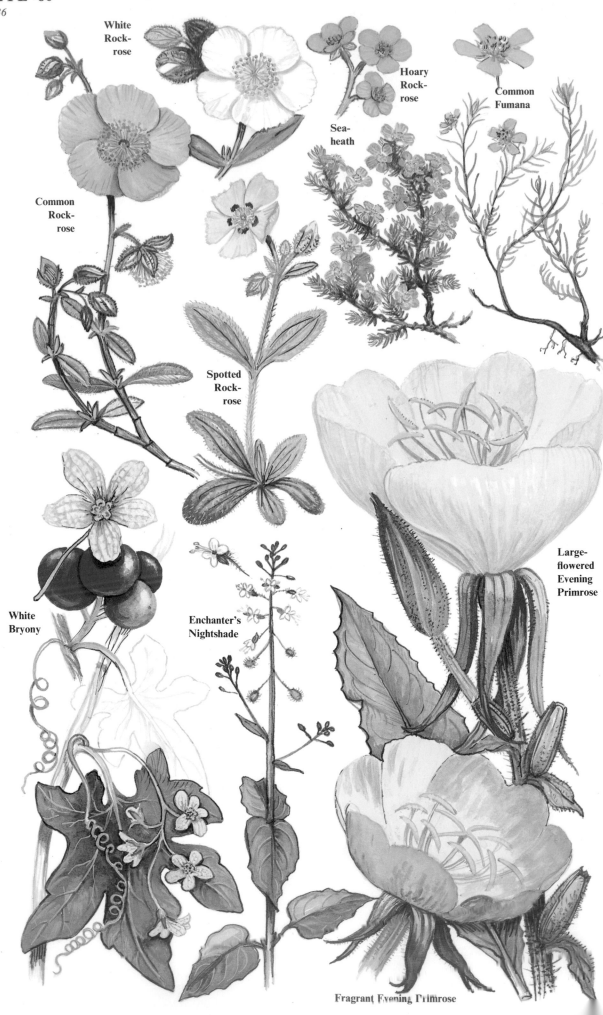

White Rock-rose

Hoary Rock-rose

Common Fumana

Sea-heath

Common Rock-rose

Spotted Rock-rose

White Bryony

Enchanter's Nightshade

Large-flowered Evening Primrose

Fragrant Evening Primrose

American
Willowherb

PLATE 61
pages 36–37

Pale
Willowherb

Hoary
Willowherb

Marsh
Willowherb

Square-
stemmed
Willowherb

Purple
Loosestrife

Broad-
leaved
Willowherb

Grass Poly

Great
Willowherb

Rosebay
Willowherb

New Zealand
Willowherb

Alpine Willowherb

PLATE 62
pages 37–38

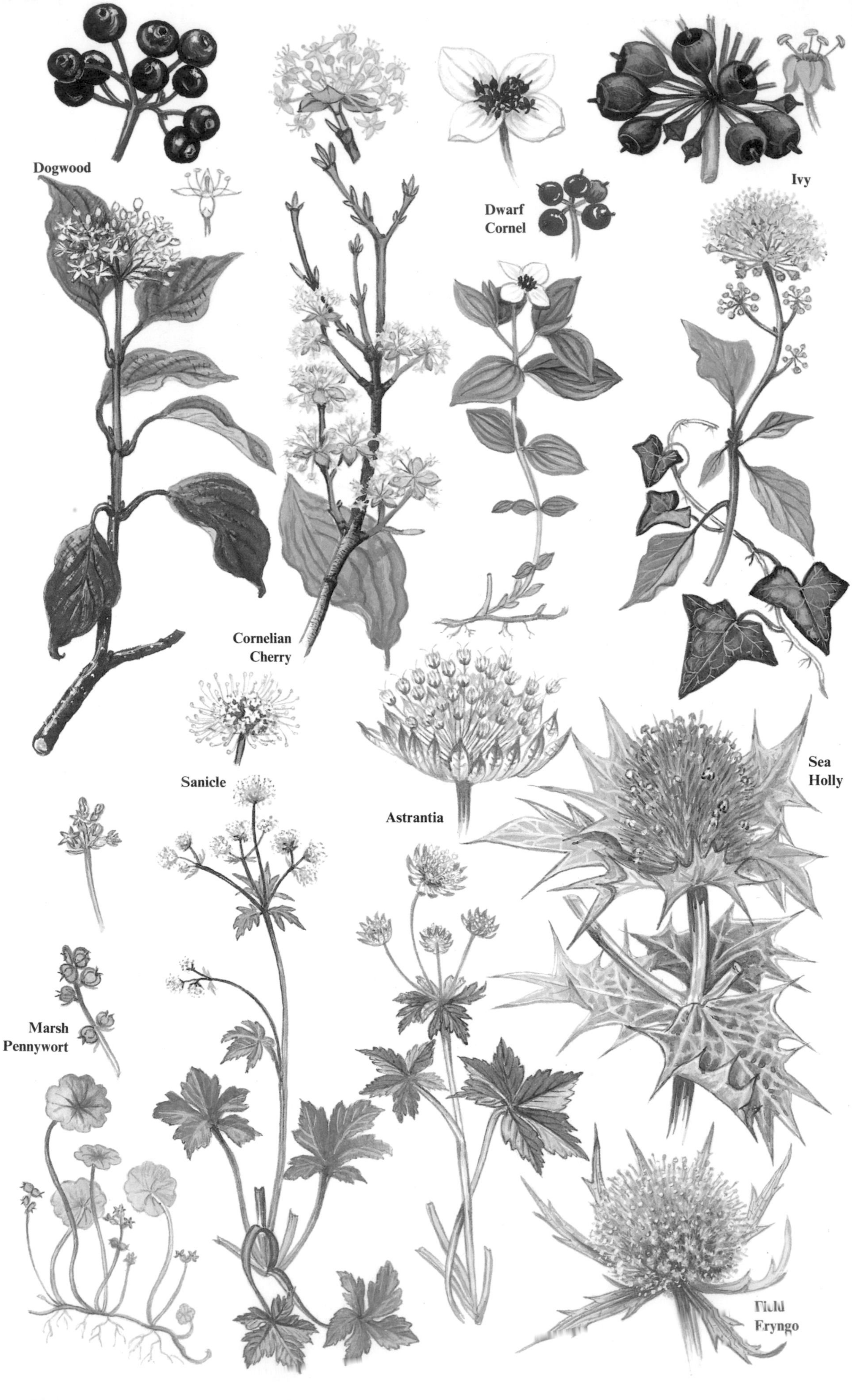

Dogwood

Ivy

Dwarf
Cornel

Cornelian
Cherry

Sanicle

Astrantia

Sea
Holly

Marsh
Pennywort

Field
Eryngo

PLATE 63

page 38

Cow Parsley

Sweet Cicely

Bur Chervil

Upright Hedge Parsley

Knotted Bur Parsley

Rough Chervil

Caraway

Coriander

Greater Bur Parsley

Whorled Caraway

Wild Carrot

PLATE 64
pages 38–39

Pignut

Burnet
Saxifrage

Shepherd's
Needle

Ground
Elder

Moon Carrot

Spignel

Bladderseed

Honewort

Fool's
Parsley

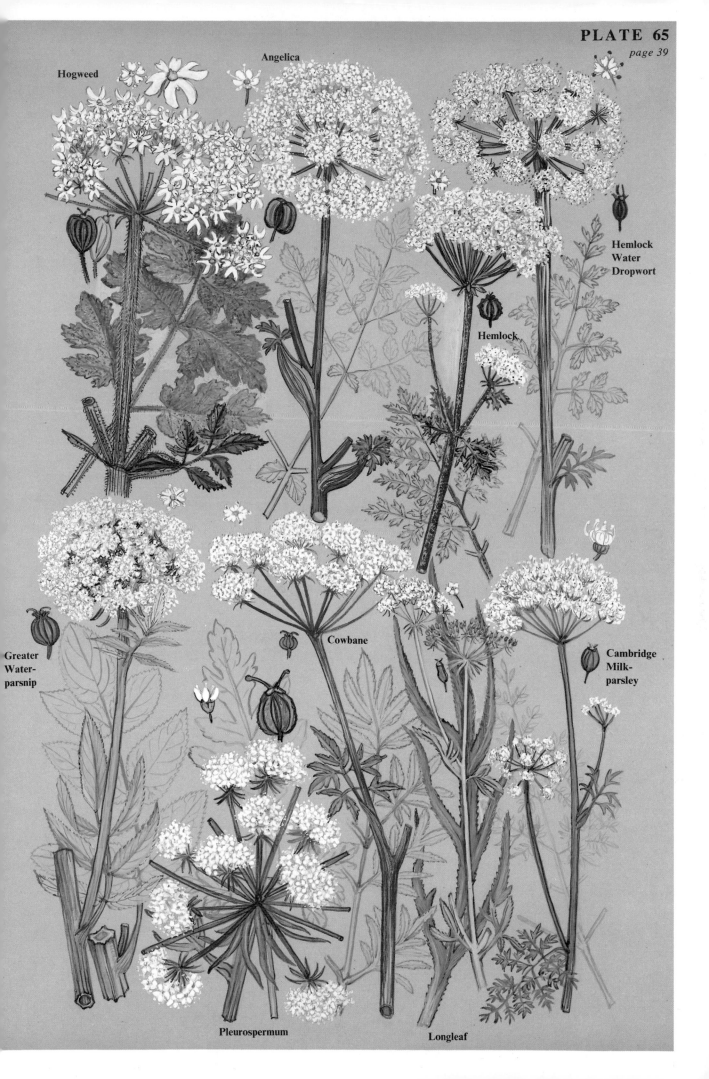

PLATE 65
page 39

Hogweed

Angelica

Hemlock Water Dropwort

Hemlock

Greater Water-parsnip

Cowbane

Cambridge Milk-parsley

Pleurospermum

Longleaf

PLATE 66

pages 39–40

Fool's
Watercress

Wild
Celery

Tubular
Water
Dropwort

Lesser
Water-
parsnip

Parsley
Water
Dropwort

Fine-
leaved
Water
Dropwort

Stone
Parsley

Corn
Parsley

PLATE 67

page 40

Hog's Fennel

Milk Parsley

Masterwort

Hartwort

Sermountain

Slender Hare's-ear

Cnidium

Scots Lovage

PLATE 68
pages 40–41

Fennel

Wild Parsnip

Alexanders

Rock Samphire

Pepper
Saxifrage

Lovage

Thorow-wax

Sickle
Hare's-
ear

Small
Hare's-
ear

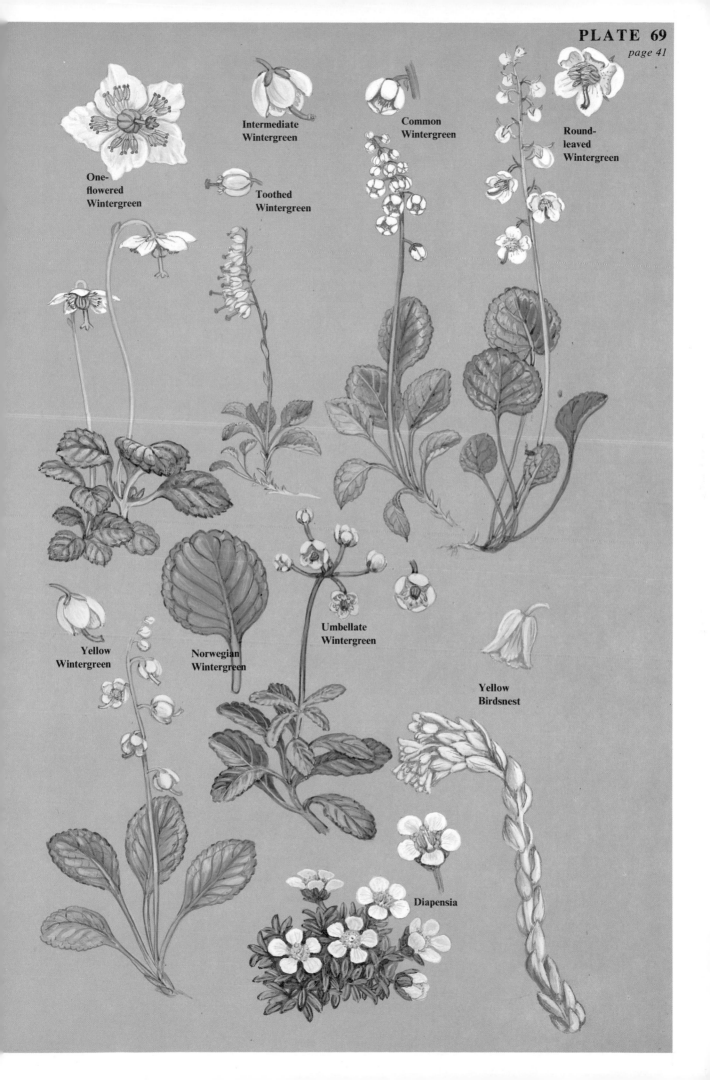

PLATE 69
page 41

One-flowered Wintergreen

Intermediate Wintergreen

Toothed Wintergreen

Common Wintergreen

Round-leaved Wintergreen

Yellow Wintergreen

Norwegian Wintergreen

Umbellate Wintergreen

Yellow Birdsnest

Diapensia

PLATE 70
pages 41–42

Heather

Bell
Heather

Dorset
Heath

Cross-
leaved
Heath

Cornish
Heath

Arctic
Rhododendron

Bog
Rosemary

Irish
Heath

Mountain
Heath

St
Dabeoc's
Heath

PLATE 71
page 42

Bilberry

Northern Bilberry

Cowberry

Labrador Tea

Alpine Bearberry

Cranberry

Leatherleaf

Cassiope

Wild Azalea

Crowberry

Strawberry Tree

PLATE 72
page 43

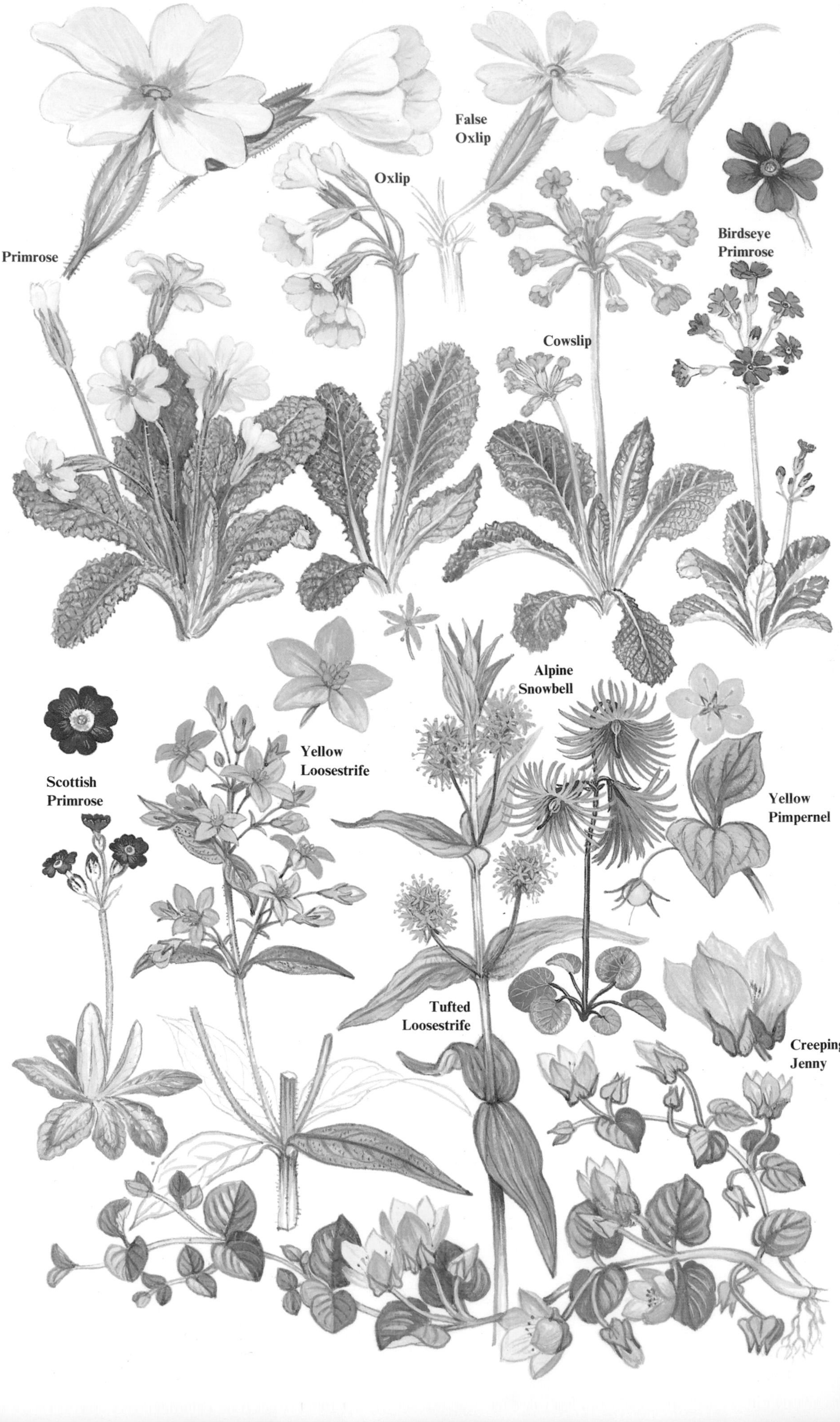

False
Oxlip

Oxlip

Primrose

Birdseye
Primrose

Cowslip

Scottish
Primrose

Yellow
Loosestrife

Alpine
Snowbell

Yellow
Pimpernel

Tufted
Loosestrife

Creeping
Jenny

PLATE 73
pages 43–44

Water Violet

Cyclamen

Chickweed
Wintergreen

Brookweed

Sowbread

Chaffweed

Scarlet
Pimpernel

Northern
Androsace

Sea
Milkwort

Blue
Pimpernel

Bog Pimpernel

PLATE 74
page 44

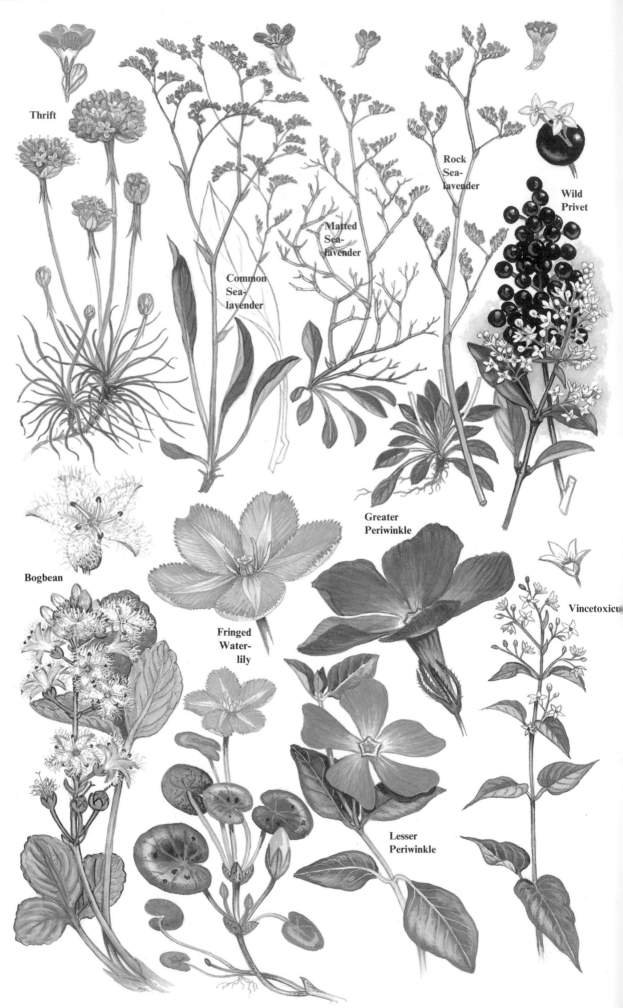

Thrift

Rock
Sea-
lavender

Wild
Privet

Matted
Sea-
lavender

Common
Sea-
lavender

Bogbean

Greater
Periwinkle

Fringed
Water-
lily

Vincetoxicu

Lesser
Periwinkle

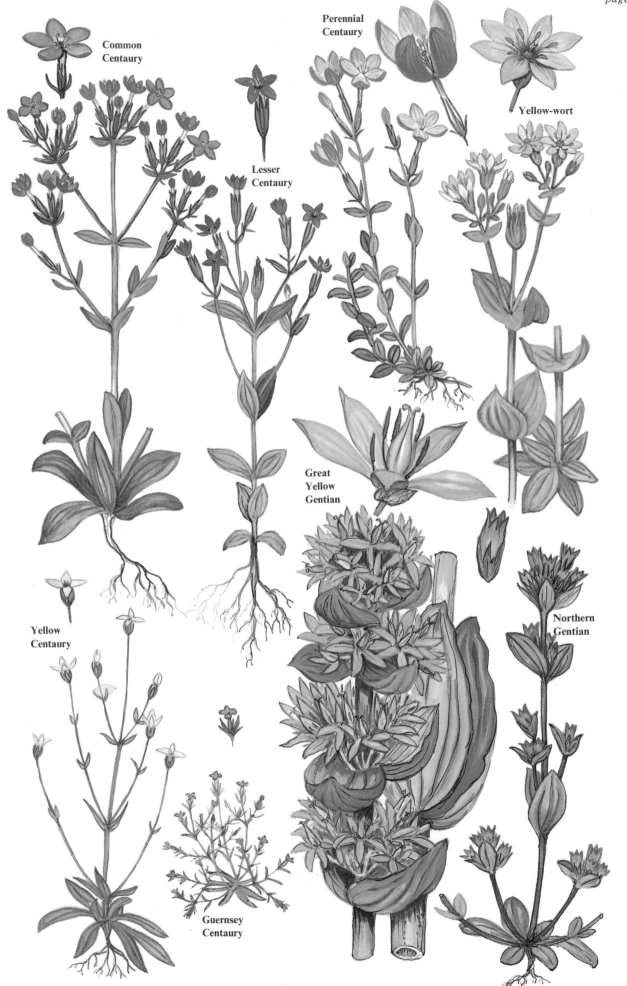

PLATE 75
page 45

Common
Centaury

Perennial
Centaury

Yellow-wort

Lesser
Centaury

Great
Yellow
Gentian

Yellow
Centaury

Northern
Gentian

Guernsey
Centaury

PLATE 76
pages 45–46

Marsh
Gentian

Purple
Gentian

Spring
Gentian

Cross
Gentian

Alpine
Gentian

Chiltern
Gentian

Autumn
Gentian

Field
Gentian

Marsh
Felwort

Slender
Gentian

Fringed
Gentian

PLATE 77
page 46

Hedge
Bindweed

Great
Bindweed

Jacob's
Ladder

Sea
Bindweed

Field
Bindweed

Field
Madder

Woodruff

Blue
Woodruff

Common
Dodder

Squinancywort

PLATE 78
pages 46–47

Hedge Bedstraw

Northern Bedstraw

Crosswort

Wild Madder

Heath Bedstraw

Marsh Bedstraw

Lady's Bedstraw

Common Cleavers

PLATE 79
page 47

Russian
Comfrey

Common
Comfrey

Amsinckia

Yellow
Alkanet

Houndstongue

Nonea

Corn
Gromwell

Common
Gromwell

Purple
Gromwell

PLATE 80
pages 47–48

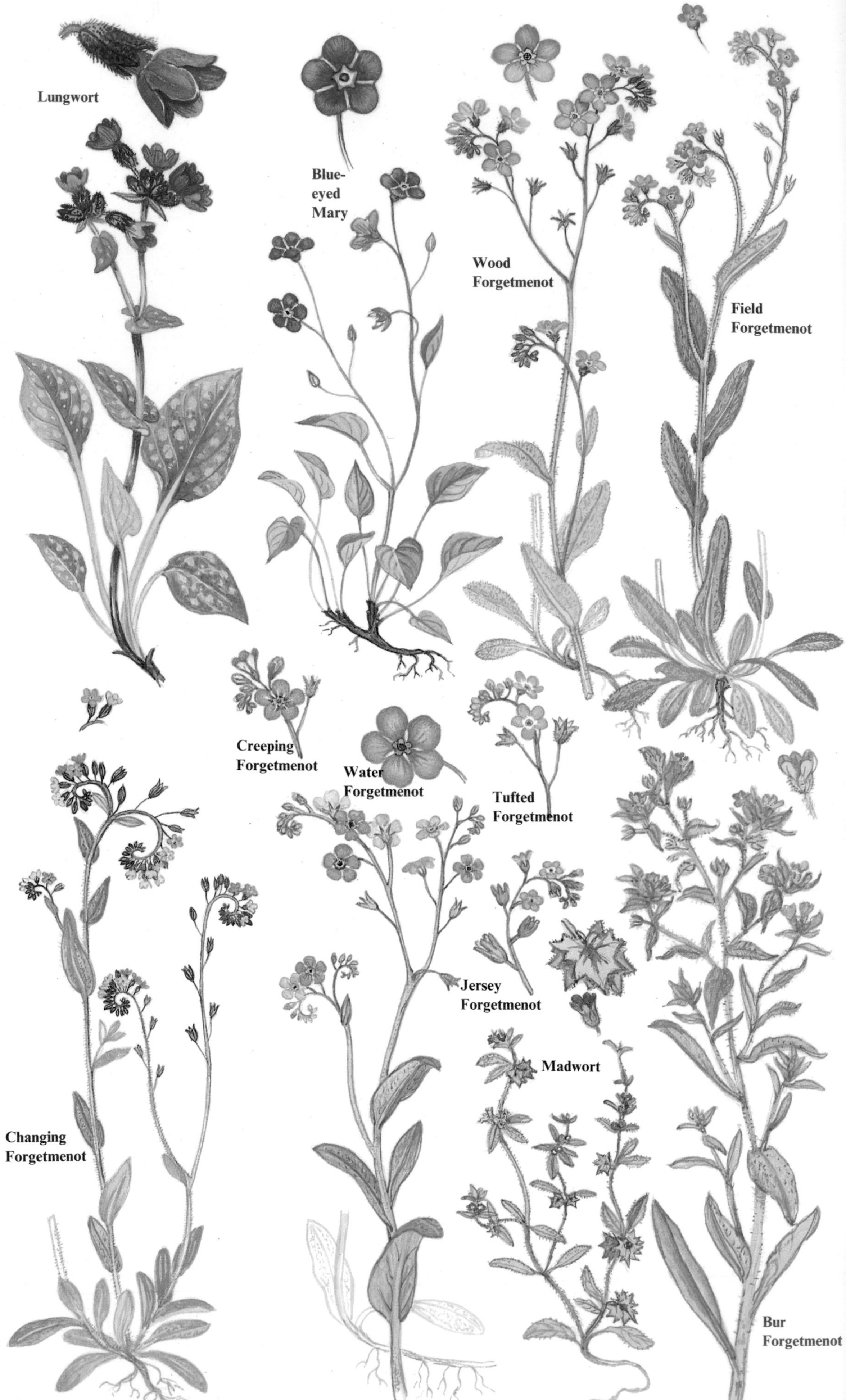

Lungwort

Blue-
eyed
Mary

Wood
Forgetmenot

Field
Forgetmenot

Creeping
Forgetmenot

Water
Forgetmenot

Tufted
Forgetmenot

Changing
Forgetmenot

Jersey
Forgetmenot

Madwort

Bur
Forgetmenot

PLATE 81
page 48

Viper's
Bugloss

Green
Alkanet

Borage

Bugloss

Alkanet

Oyster
Plant

Vervain

PLATE 82
page 49

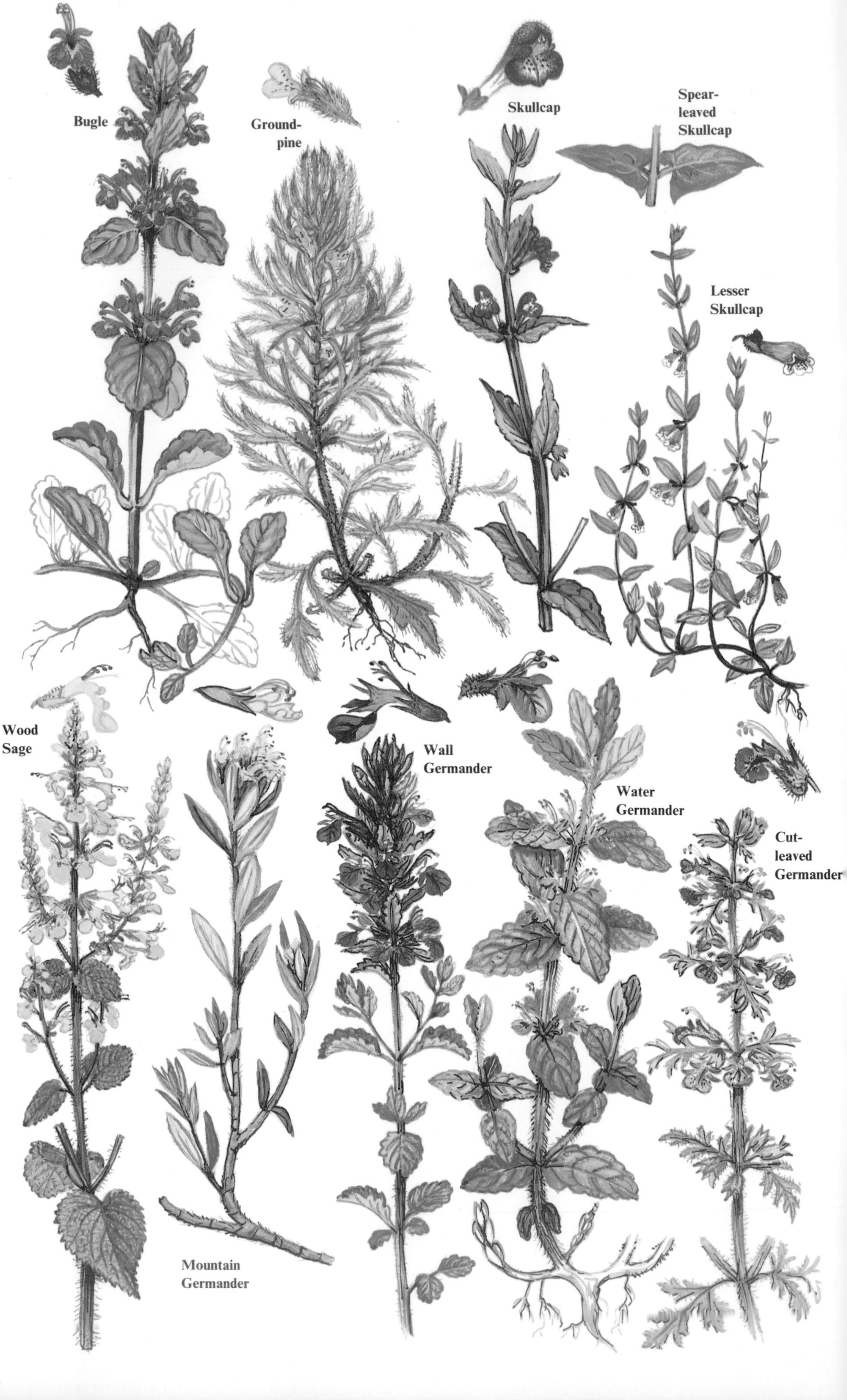

Bugle

Ground-
pine

Skullcap

Spear-
leaved
Skullcap

Lesser
Skullcap

Wood
Sage

Wall
Germander

Water
Germander

Cut-
leaved
Germander

Mountain
Germander

PLATE 83
pages 49–50

Self-heal

Large Self-heal

Ground Ivy

White Horehound

Catmint

Cut-leaved Self-heal

Hairless Catmint

Black Horehound

Hyssop

Bastard Balm

Winter Savory

PLATE 84
page 50

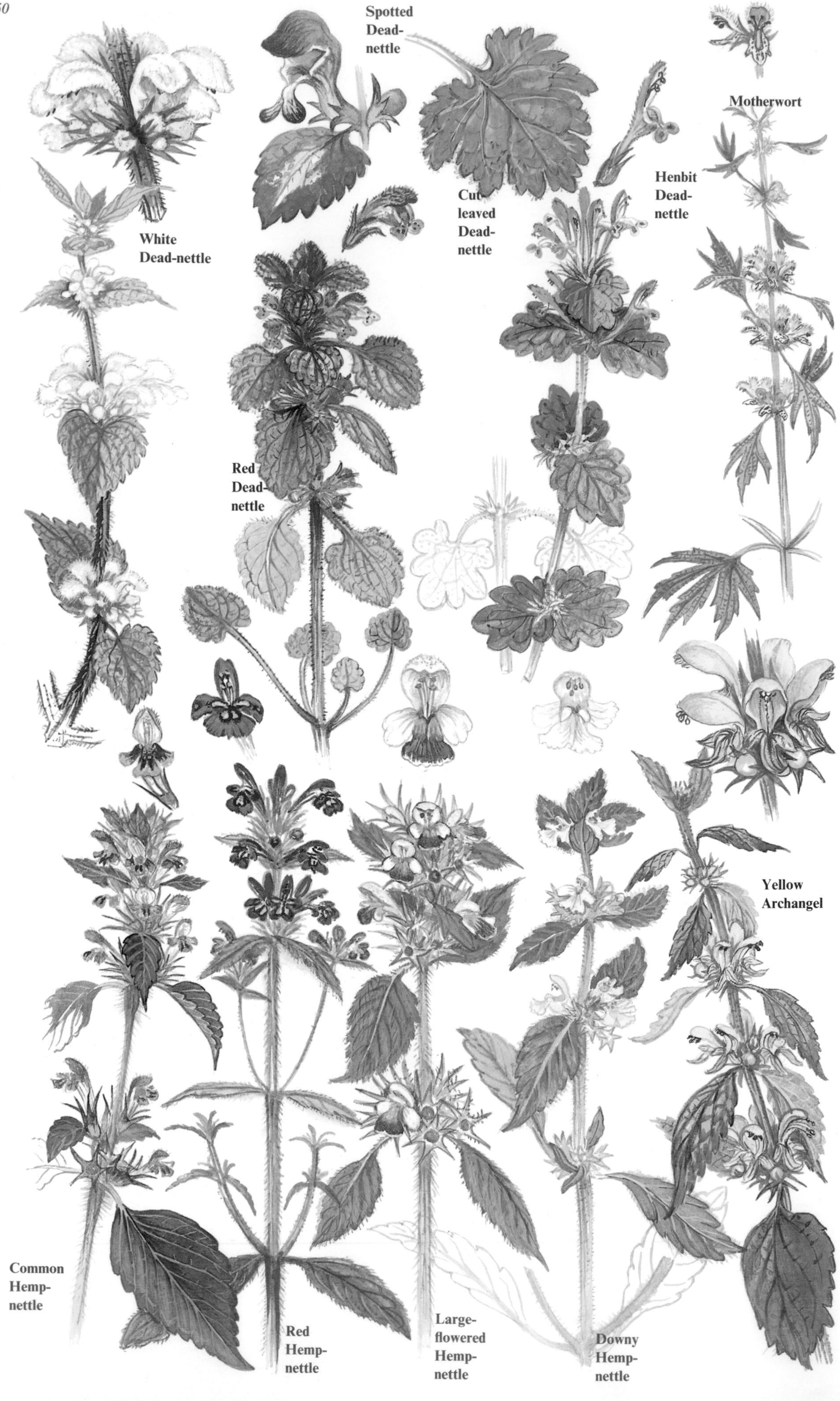

Spotted
Dead-
nettle

Motherwort

Cut-
leaved
Dead-
nettle

Henbit
Dead-
nettle

White
Dead-nettle

Red
Dead-
nettle

Yellow
Archangel

Common
Hemp-
nettle

Red
Hemp-
nettle

Large-
flowered
Hemp-
nettle

Downy
Hemp-
nettle

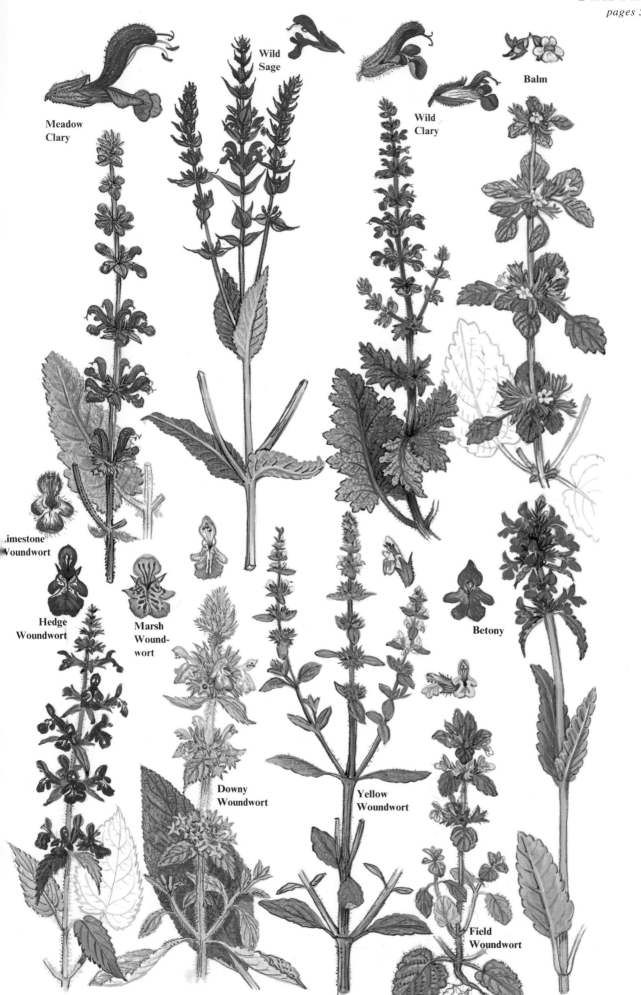

PLATE 85
pages 50-51

Wild
Sage

Balm

Meadow
Clary

Wild
Clary

imestone
Woundwort

Hedge
Woundwort

Marsh
Wound-
wort

Betony

Downy
Woundwort

Yellow
Woundwort

Field
Woundwort

PLATE 86

pages 51–52

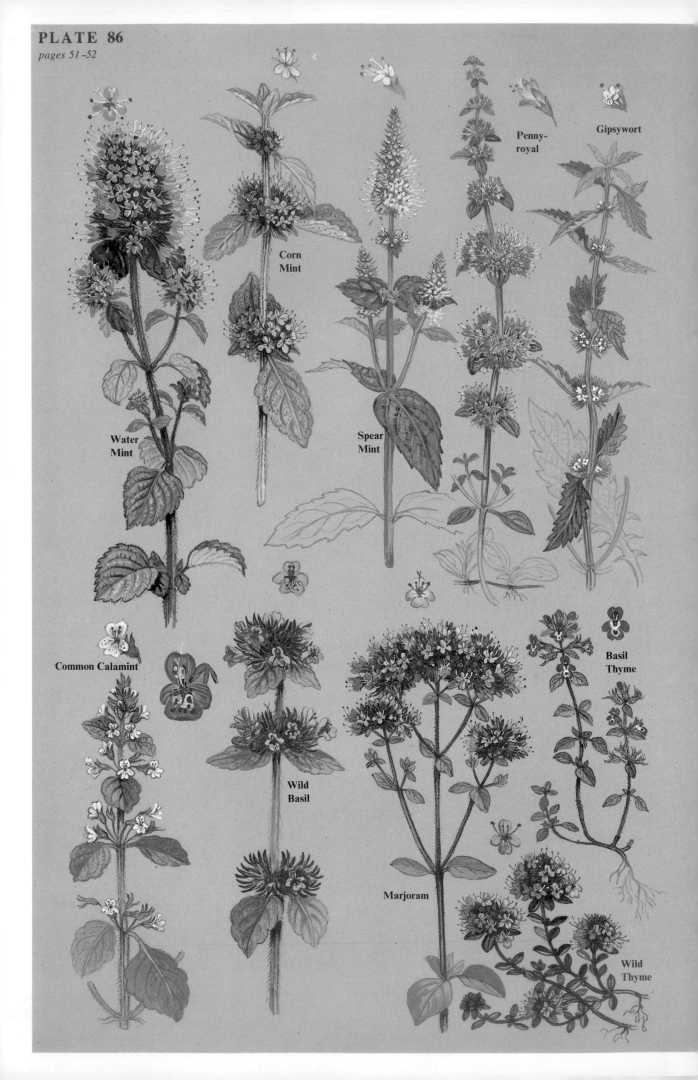

Penny-
royal

Gipsywort

Corn
Mint

Water
Mint

Spear
Mint

Common Calamint

Basil
Thyme

Wild
Basil

Marjoram

Wild
Thyme

PLATE 87
page 52

Black
Nightshade

Hairy
Nightshade

Deadly
Nightshade

Bittersweet

Small
Tobacco
Plant

Henbane

Apple
of
Peru

Thorn-
apple

PLATE 88
pages 52-53

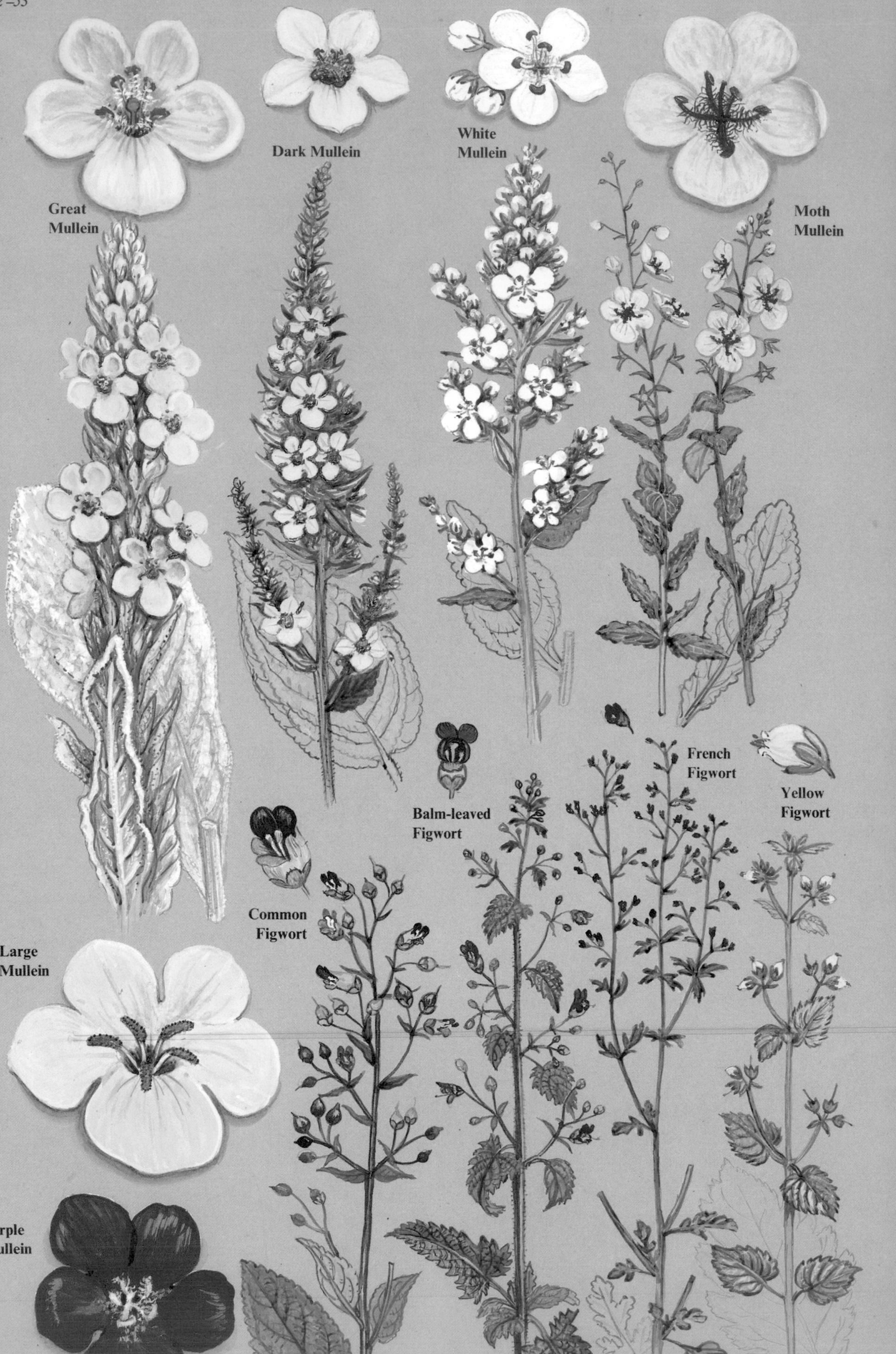

Dark Mullein

White
Mullein

Great
Mullein

Moth
Mullein

French
Figwort

Yellow
Figwort

Balm-leaved
Figwort

Large
Mullein

Common
Figwort

Purple
Mullein

PLATE 89

pages 53–54

Snapdragon

Common
Toadflax

Sand
Toadflax

Lesser
Snapdragon

Jersey
Toadflax

Alpine
Toadflax

Round-
leaved
Fluellen

Daisy-
leaved
Toadflax

Field
Toadflax

Pale
Toadflax

Purple
Toadflax

Ivy-leaved
Toadflax

Small
Toadflax

Sharp-
leaved
Fluellen

PLATE 90
page 54

Monkey Flower

Musk

Blood-drop
Emlets

Foxglove

Small
Yellow
Foxglove

Large
Yellow
Foxglove

Gratiola

Red
Bartsia

Fairy
Foxglove

Yellow
Odontites

Alpine
Bartsia

Yellow
Bartsia

PLATE 91
pages 54–55

Spiked Speedwell

Large Speedwell

Germander Speedwell

Common Field Speedwell

Ivy-leaved Speedwell

Brooklime

Water Speedwell

Heath Speedwell

Wall Speedwell

Thyme-leaved Speedwell

Wood Speedwell

Green Field Speedwell

Smooth Speedwell

Grey Field Speedwell

Slender Speedwell

Alpine Speedwell

humifusa

Rock Speedwell

Pink Water Speedwell

PLATE 92
pages 55–56

Yellow Rattle

Marsh Lousewort

Lousewort

Moor-king

Eyebright

Field Cow-wheat

Small Cow-wheat

Common Cow-wheat

Crested Cow-wheat

Leafy Lousewort

Cornish Moneywort

Wood Cow-wheat

PLATE 93
pages 56–57

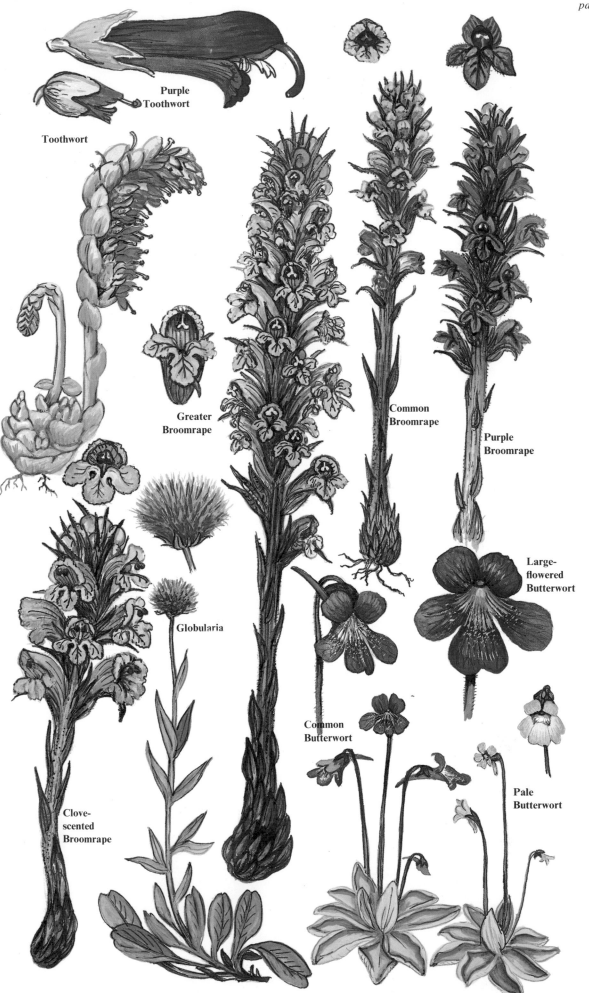

Purple
Toothwort

Toothwort

Greater
Broomrape

Common
Broomrape

Purple
Broomrape

Large-
flowered
Butterwort

Globularia

Common
Butterwort

Pale
Butterwort

Clove-
scented
Broomrape

PLATE 94
page 57

Branched
Plantain

Sea
Plantain

Hoary
Plantain

Greater
Plantain

Ribwort
Plantain

Rannoch
Rush

Marsh
Arrow-
grass

Sea
Arrow-
grass

Moschatel

Buckshorn
Plantain

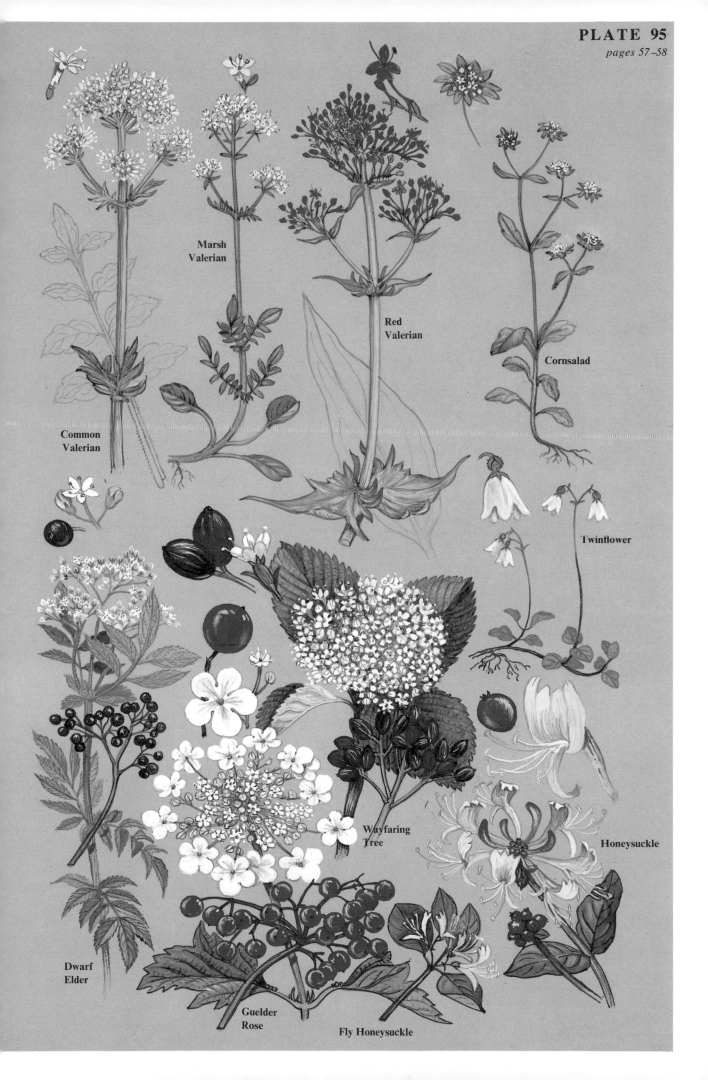

pages 57–58

Marsh
Valerian

Red
Valerian

Cornsalad

Common
Valerian

Twinflower

Dwarf
Elder

Wayfaring
Tree

Honeysuckle

Guelder
Rose

Fly Honeysuckle

PLATE 96
pages 58–59

Field
Scabious

Yellow
Scabious

Grey
Scabious

Small
Scabious

Devilsbit
Scabious

Small
Teasel

Round-
headed
Rampion

Teasel

Spiked
Rampion

Sheepsbit
Scabious

PLATE 97
page 59

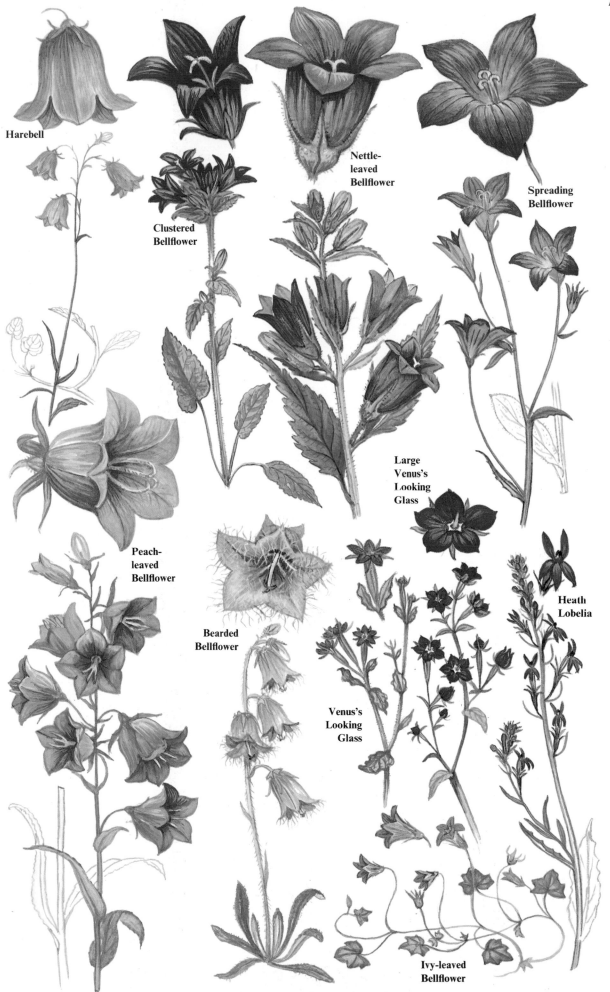

Harebell

Clustered
Bellflower

Nettle-
leaved
Bellflower

Spreading
Bellflower

Peach-
leaved
Bellflower

Bearded
Bellflower

Large
Venus's
Looking
Glass

Heath
Lobelia

Venus's
Looking
Glass

Ivy-leaved
Bellflower

PLATE 98
pages 59–60

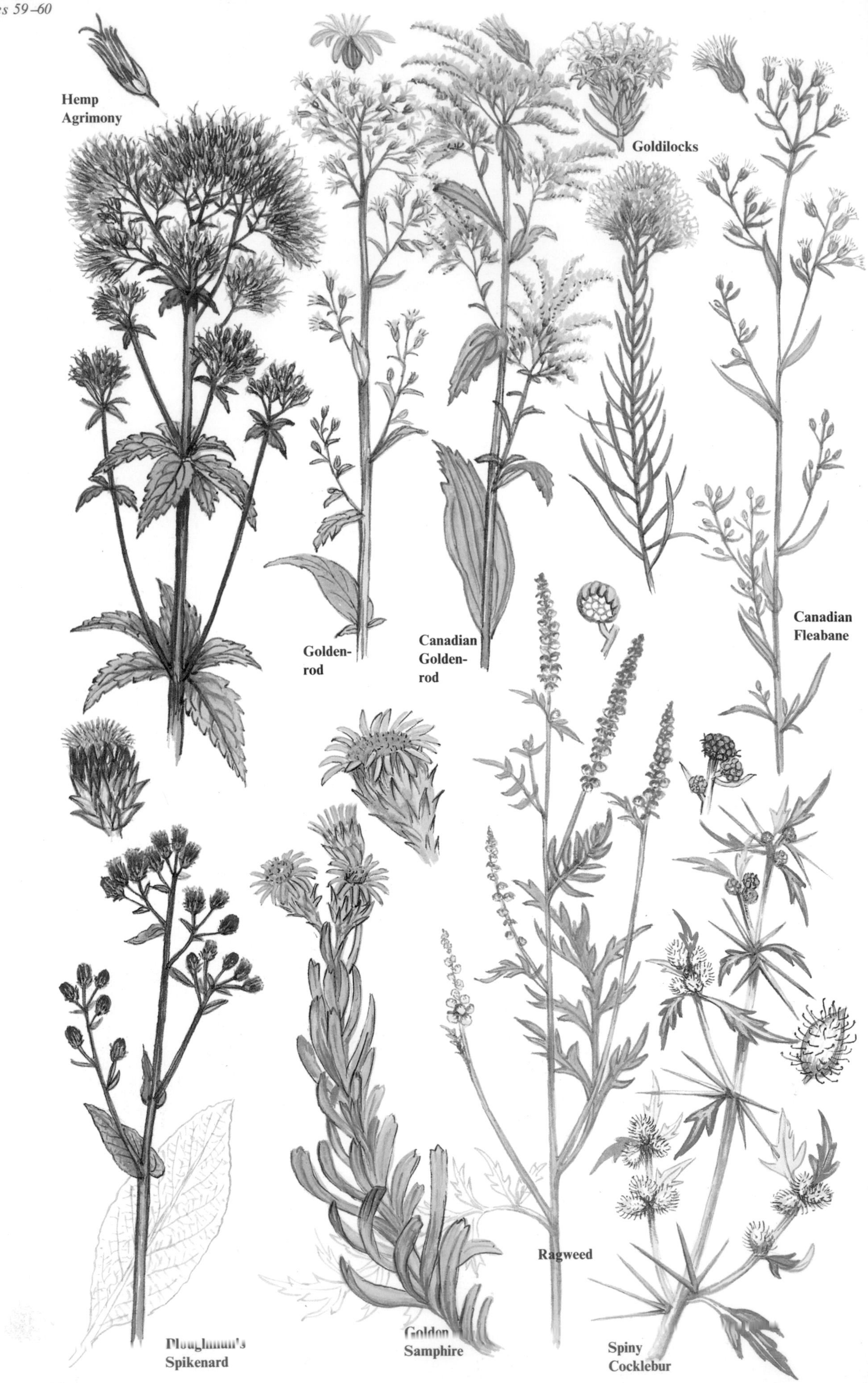

Hemp
Agrimony

Goldilocks

Golden-
rod

Canadian
Golden-
rod

Canadian
Fleabane

Ploughman's
Spikenard

Golden
Samphire

Ragweed

Spiny
Cocklebur

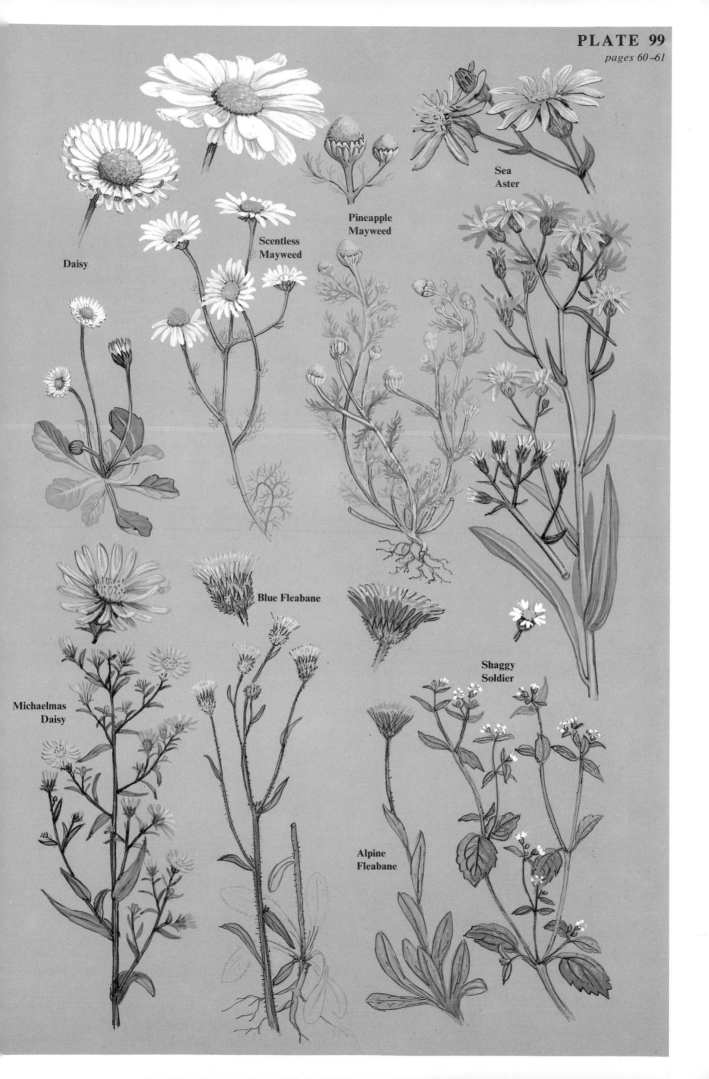

PLATE 99
pages 60–61

Sea
Aster

Pineapple
Mayweed

Scentless
Mayweed

Daisy

Blue Fleabane

Michaelmas
Daisy

Shaggy
Soldier

Alpine
Fleabane

PLATE 100
page 61

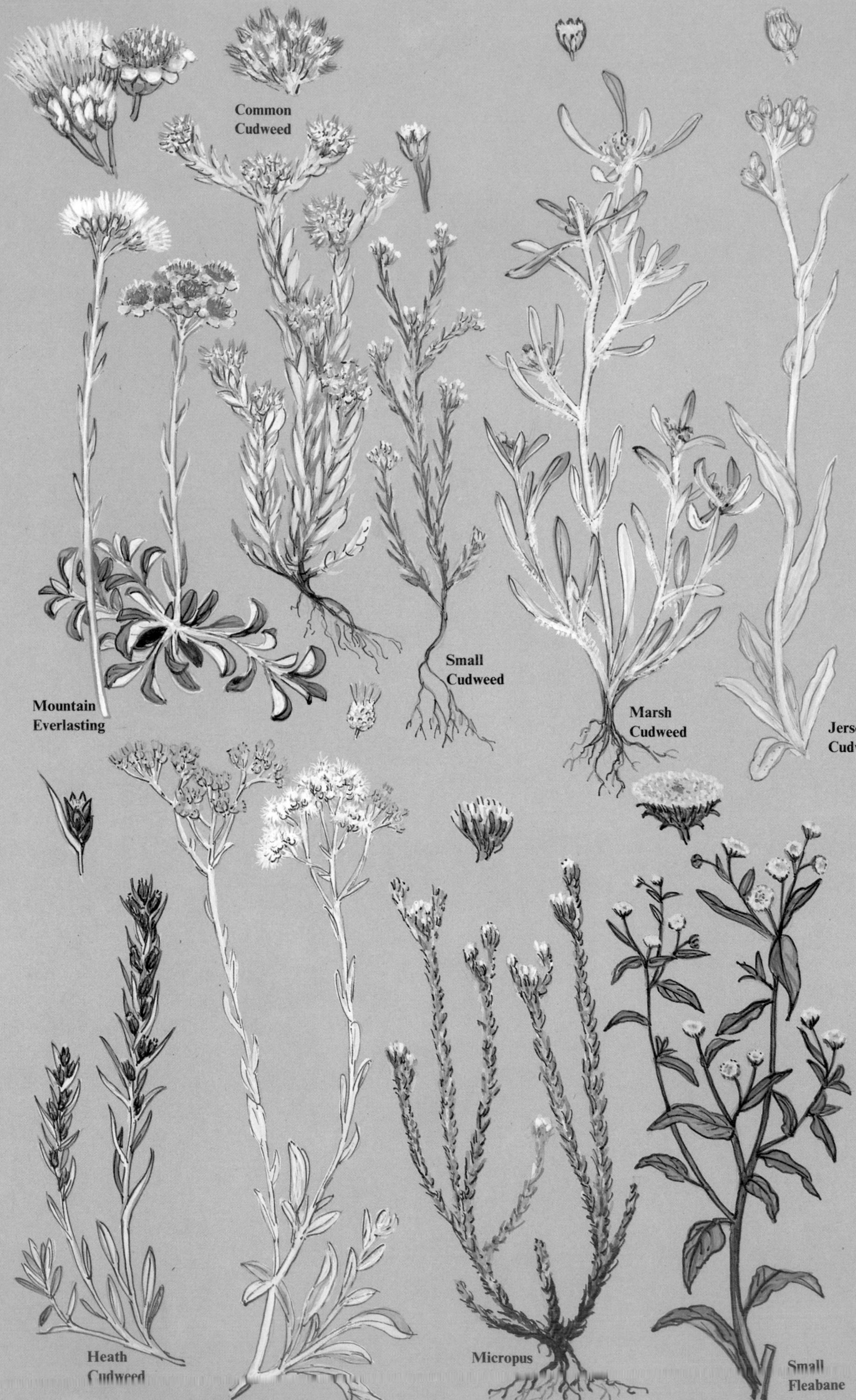

Common
Cudweed

Mountain
Everlasting

Small
Cudweed

Marsh
Cudweed

Jersey
Cudweed

Heath
Cudweed

Helichrysum

Micropus

Small
Fleabane

PLATE 101
pages 61 –62

Common
Fleabane

Irish
Fleabane

Yellow
Ox-
eye

Cone
Flower

Elecampane

Perennial
Sunflower

Arnica

Yellow Chamomile

Leopardsbane

PLATE 102
page 62

Butterbur

Winter
Heliotrope

Yarrow

Sneezewort

Mugwort

Trifid
Bur
Marigold

Buttonweed

Sea
Wormwood

Cottonweed

PLATE 103
pages 62–63

Ox-
eye
Daisy

Feverfew

Tansy

Corn
Marigold

Coltsfoot

Purple
Coltsfoot

Garden
Marigold

PLATE 104

page 63

Fen
Ragwort

Ragwort

Oxford
Ragwort

Marsh
Fleawort

Alpine
Ragwort

Silver
Ragwort

Field
Fleawort

Groundsel

PLATE 105
pages 63–64

Globe Thistle

Carline
Thistle

Lesser
Burdock

Alpine
Sawwort

Milk
Thistle

Stemless
Carline Thistle

Cabbage
Thistle

Cotton Thistle

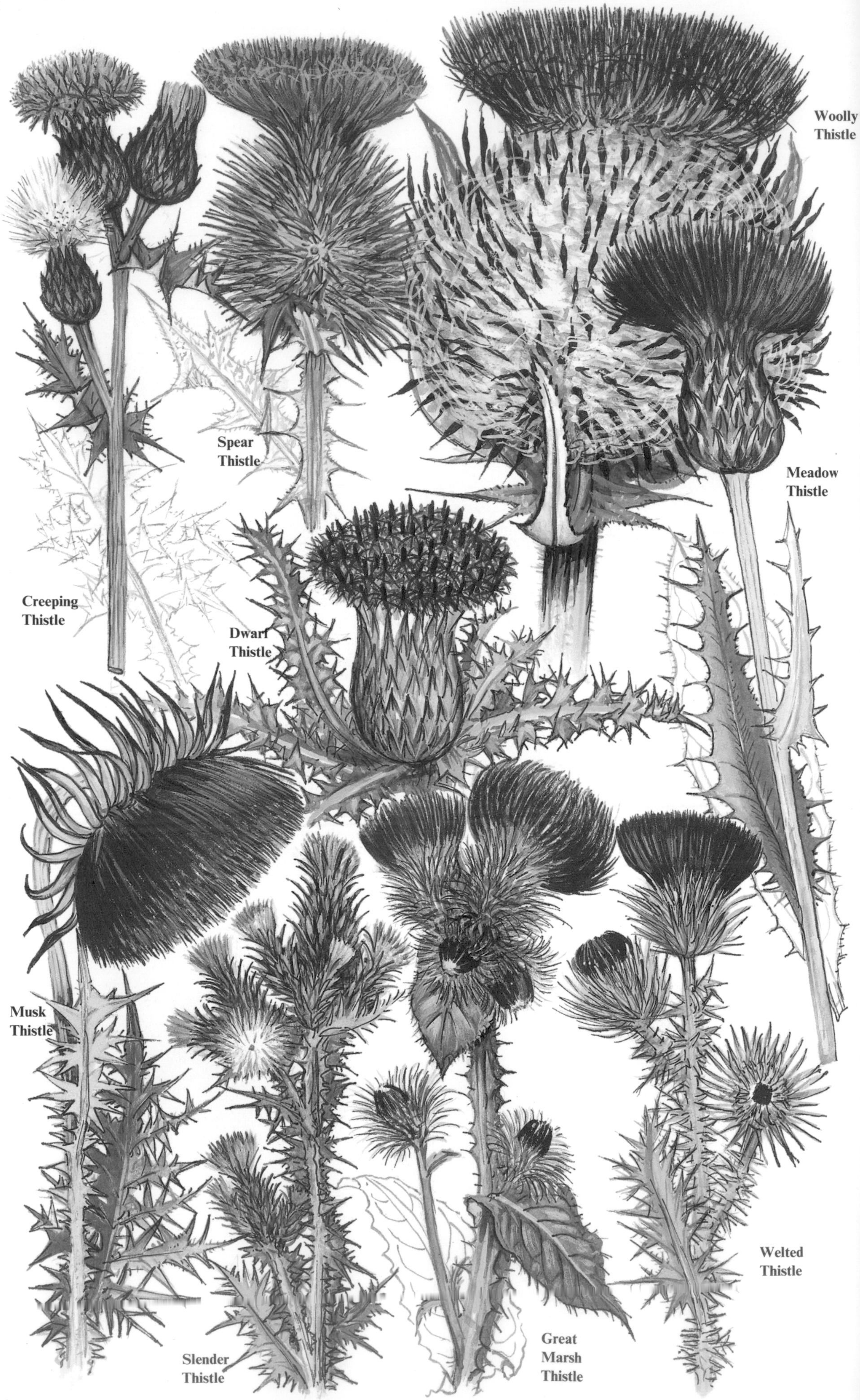

PLATE 106
page 64

Woolly
Thistle

Spear
Thistle

Meadow
Thistle

Creeping
Thistle

Dwarf
Thistle

Musk
Thistle

Slender
Thistle

Great
Marsh
Thistle

Welted
Thistle

PLATE 107
pages 64–65

Black
Knapweed

Cornflower

Greater
Knapweed

Perennial
Cornflower

Black
Knapweed

Sawwort

Yellow
Star-
thistle

Red
Star-thistle

PLATE 108
page 65

Goatsbeard

Salsify

Purple
Viper's
Grass

Viper's
Grass

Chicory

Purple
Lettuce

Alpine
Sow-
thistle

Blue
Lettuce

PLATE 109
pages 65–66

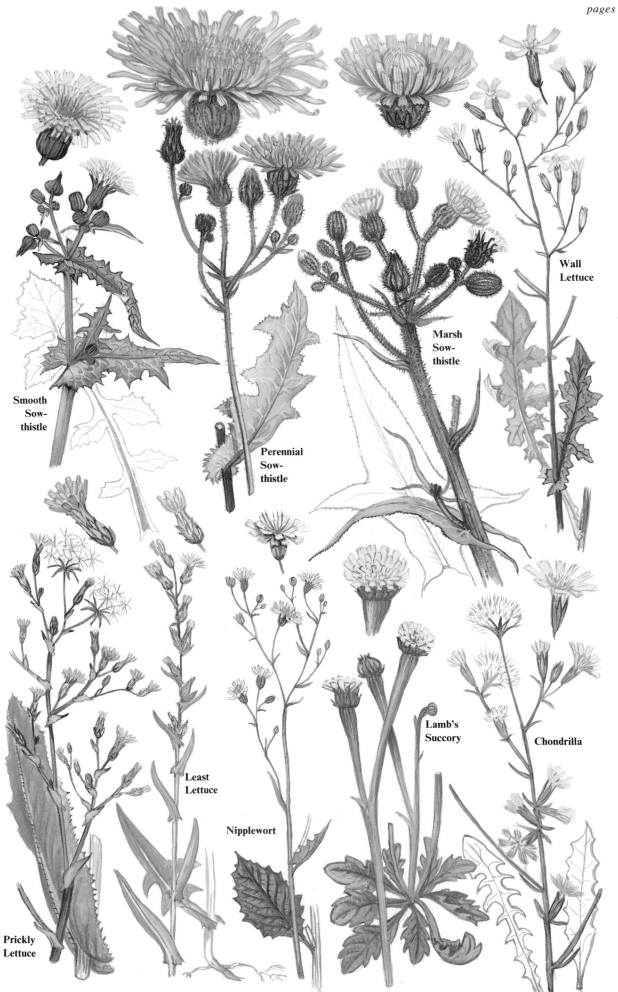

Wall
Lettuce

Marsh
Sow-
thistle

Smooth
Sow-
thistle

Perennial
Sow-
thistle

Least
Lettuce

Nipplewort

Lamb's
Succory

Chondrilla

Prickly
Lettuce

PLATE 110
page 66

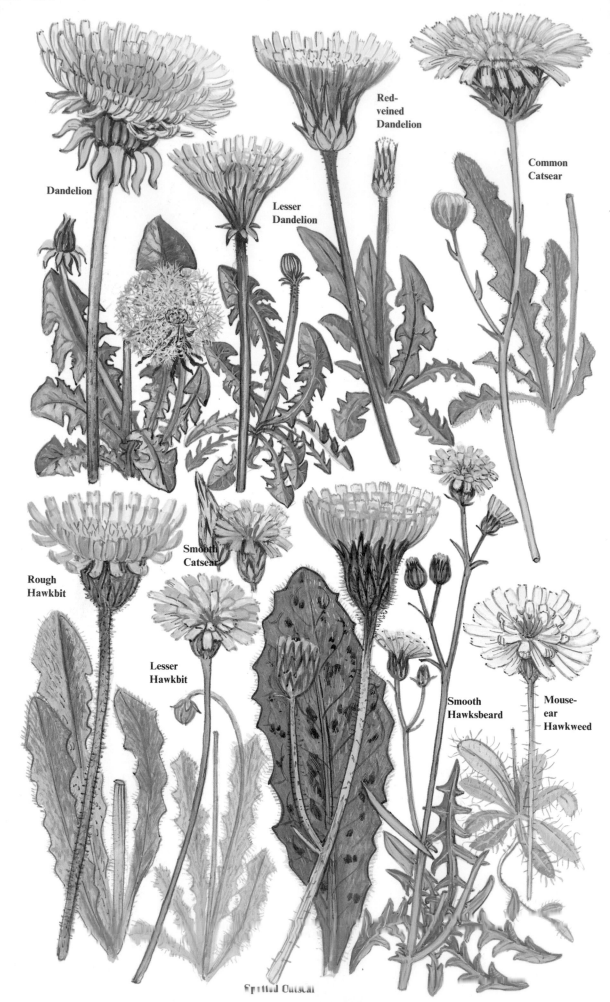

Dandelion

Lesser Dandelion

Red-veined Dandelion

Common Catsear

Rough Hawkbit

Lesser Hawkbit

Smooth Catsear

Smooth Hawksbeard

Mouse-ear Hawkweed

Spotted Catsear

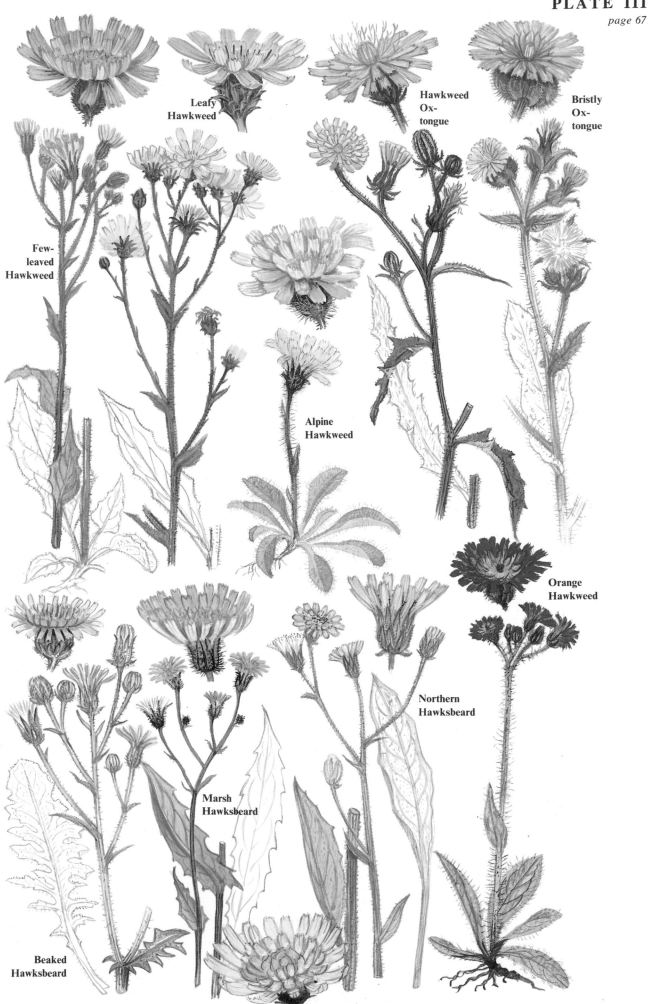

PLATE 111

page 67

Leafy
Hawkweed

Hawkweed
Ox-
tongue

Bristly
Ox-
tongue

Few-
leaved
Hawkweed

Alpine
Hawkweed

Orange
Hawkweed

Northern
Hawksbeard

Marsh
Hawksbeard

Beaked
Hawksbeard

Rough Hawksbeard

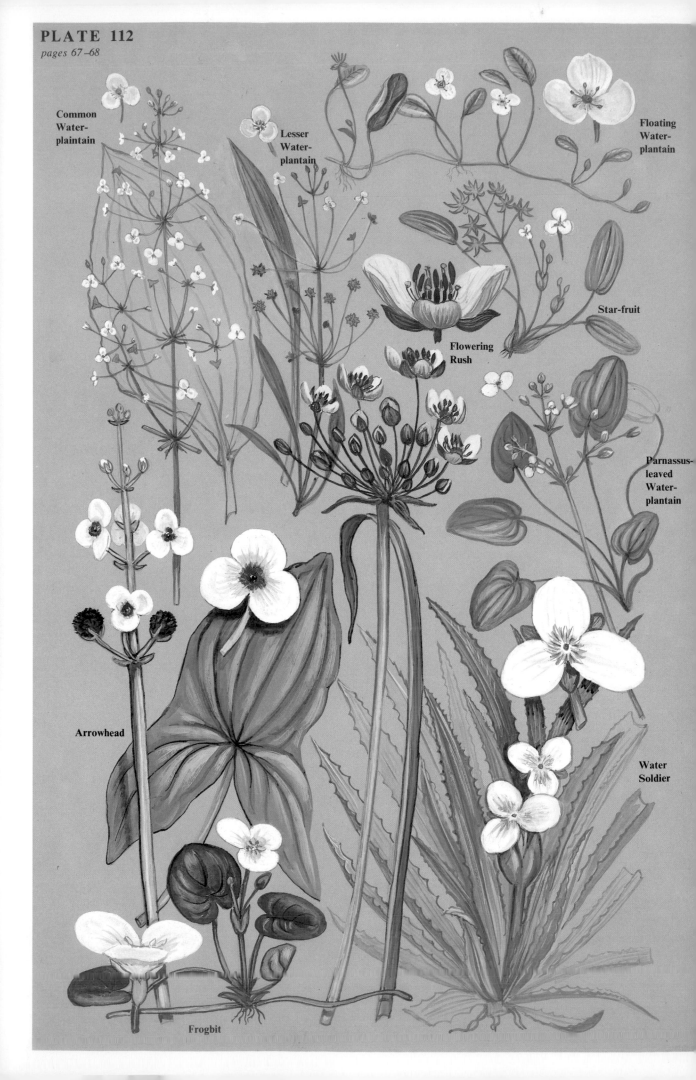

PLATE 112
pages 67–68

Common
Water-
plaintain

Lesser
Water-
plantain

Floating
Water-
plantain

Star-fruit

Flowering
Rush

Parnassus-
leaved
Water-
plantain

Arrowhead

Water
Soldier

Frogbit

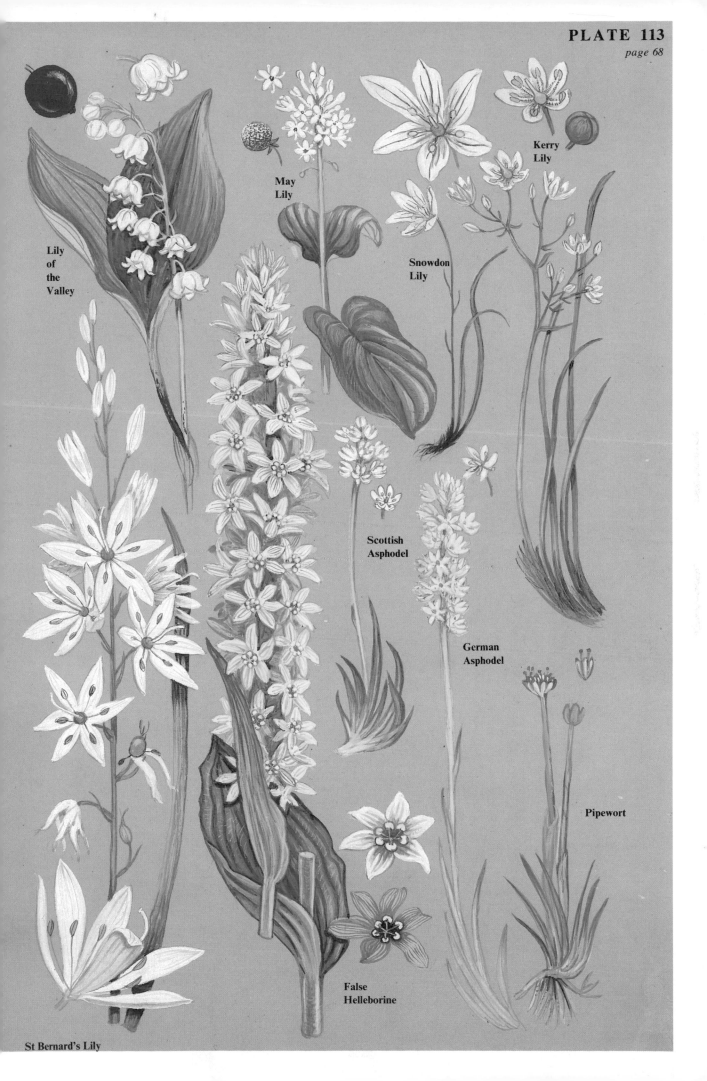

PLATE 113

page 68

Kerry
Lily

May
Lily

Snowdon
Lily

Lily
of
the
Valley

Scottish
Asphodel

German
Asphodel

Pipewort

False
Helleborine

St Bernard's Lily

PLATE 114
pages 68–69

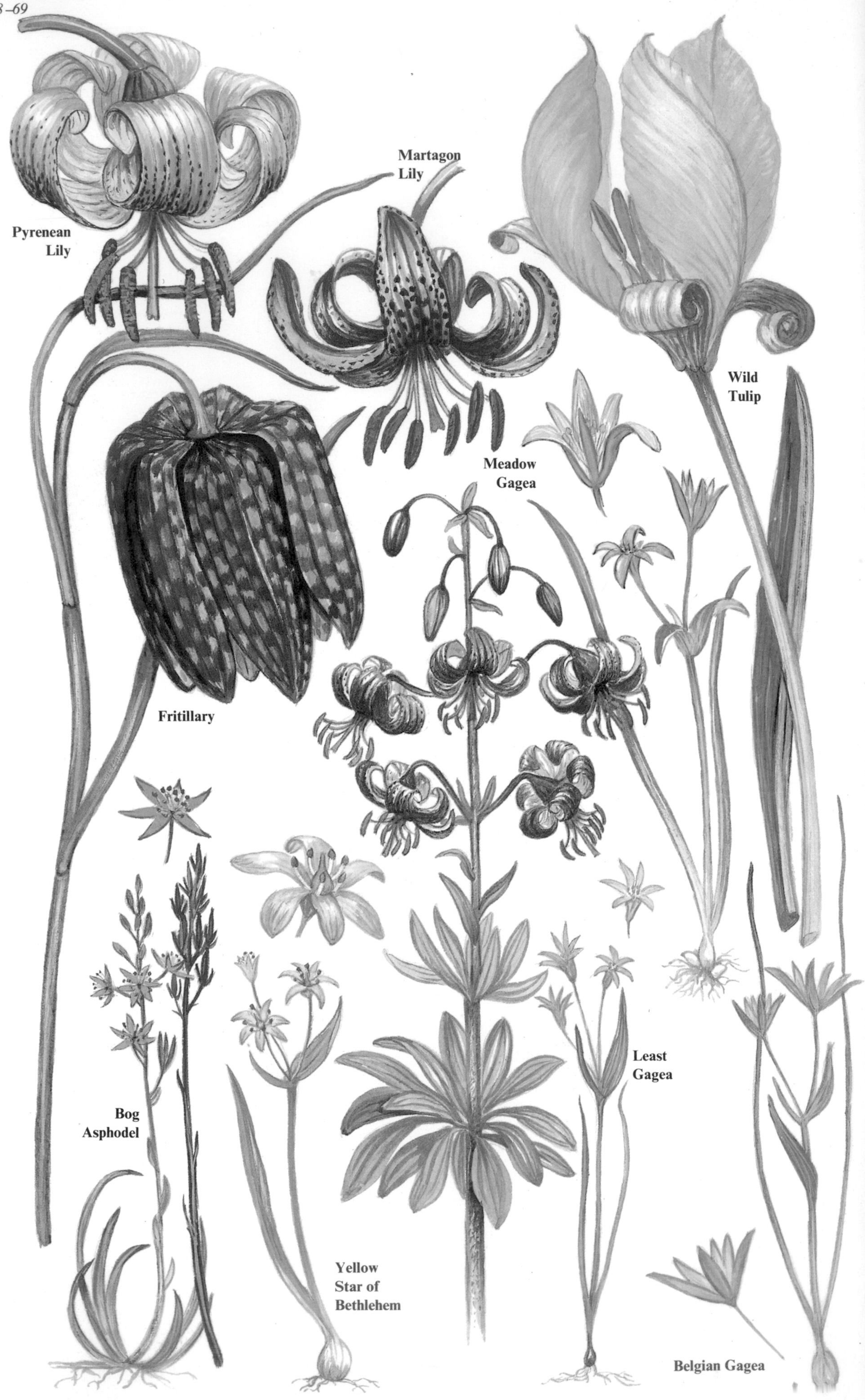

Pyrenean
Lily

Martagon
Lily

Wild
Tulip

Meadow
Gagea

Fritillary

Bog
Asphodel

Yellow
Star of
Bethlehem

Least
Gagea

Belgian Gagea

PLATE 115
page 69

Crow Garlic

Field
Garlic

Keeled
Garlic

Chives

Ramsons

Three-
cornered
Leek

Round-
headed
Leek

Welsh
Onion

Wild
Leek

German
Garlic

Sand
Leek

PLATE 116
pages 69–70, 71

Bluebell

Alpine
Squill

Spanish
Bluebell

Spring
Squill

Autumn
Squill

Grape
Hyacinth

Small
Grape
Hyacinth

Meadow
Saffron

Black Bryony

PLATE 117
page 70

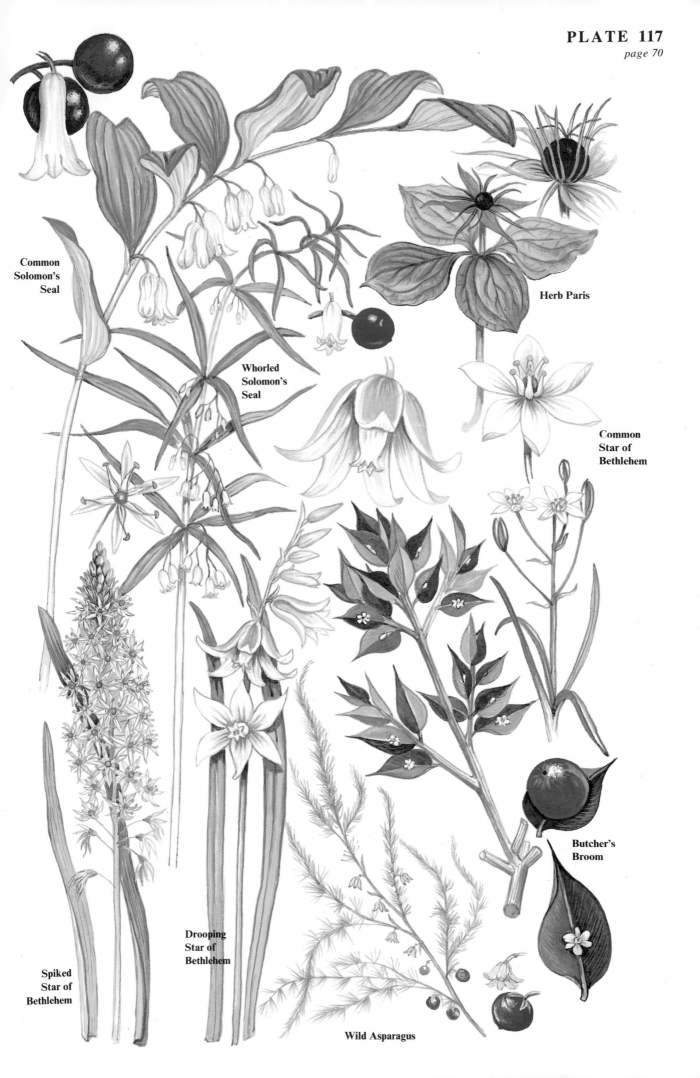

Common
Solomon's
Seal

Herb Paris

Whorled
Solomon's
Seal

Common
Star of
Bethlehem

Spiked
Star of
Bethlehem

Drooping
Star of
Bethlehem

Butcher's
Broom

Wild Asparagus

PLATE 118
page 71

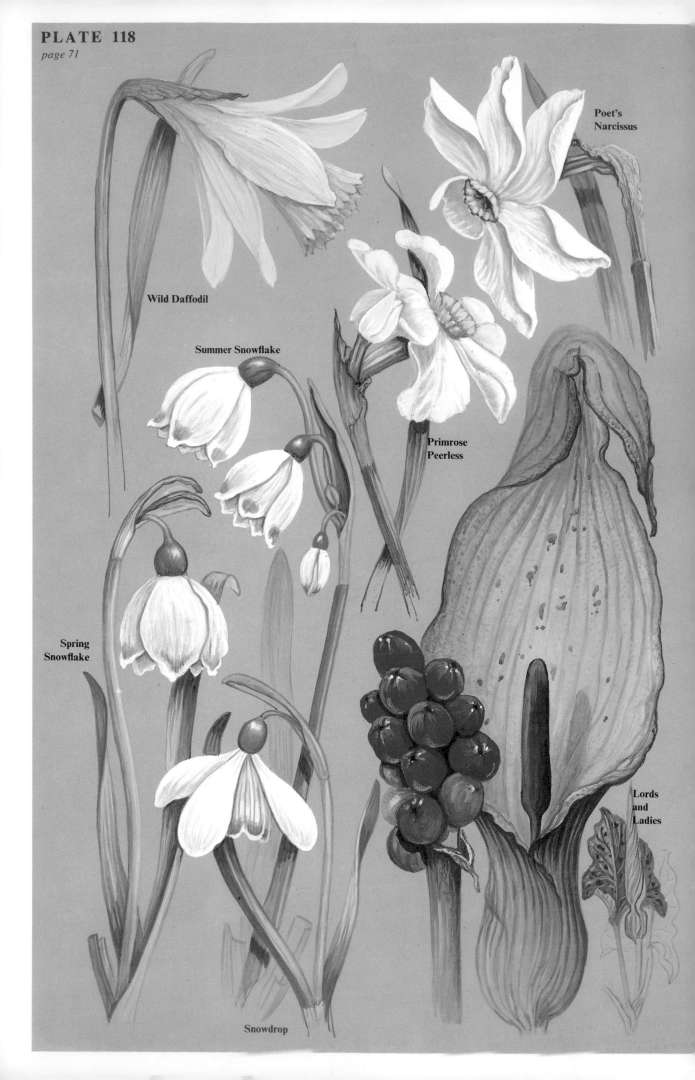

Wild Daffodil

Poet's
Narcissus

Summer Snowflake

Primrose
Peerless

Spring
Snowflake

Lords
and
Ladies

Snowdrop

PLATE 119
pages 71–72

Siberian
Iris

Yellow Iris

Garden
Iris

Purple
Flag

Butterfly
Iris

Gladiolus

Sand
Crocus

Spring Crocus

Blue-
eyed
Grass

Stinking
Iris

PLATE 120
page 72

Late
Spider
Orchid

Bee
Orchid

Wasp
Orchid

Lady's Slipper

Late
Spider
Orchid

Early
Purple
Orchid

Fly
Orchid

Calypso

Black
Vanilla
Orchid

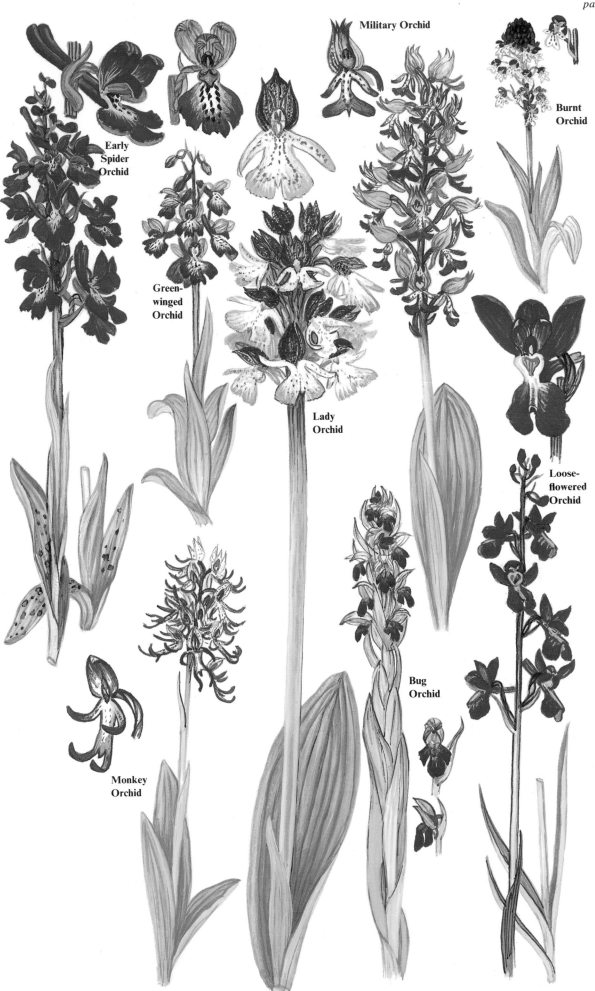

PLATE 121
pages 72–73

Military Orchid

Burnt
Orchid

Early
Spider
Orchid

Green-
winged
Orchid

Lady
Orchid

Loose-
flowered
Orchid

Monkey
Orchid

Bug
Orchid

PLATE 122
page 73

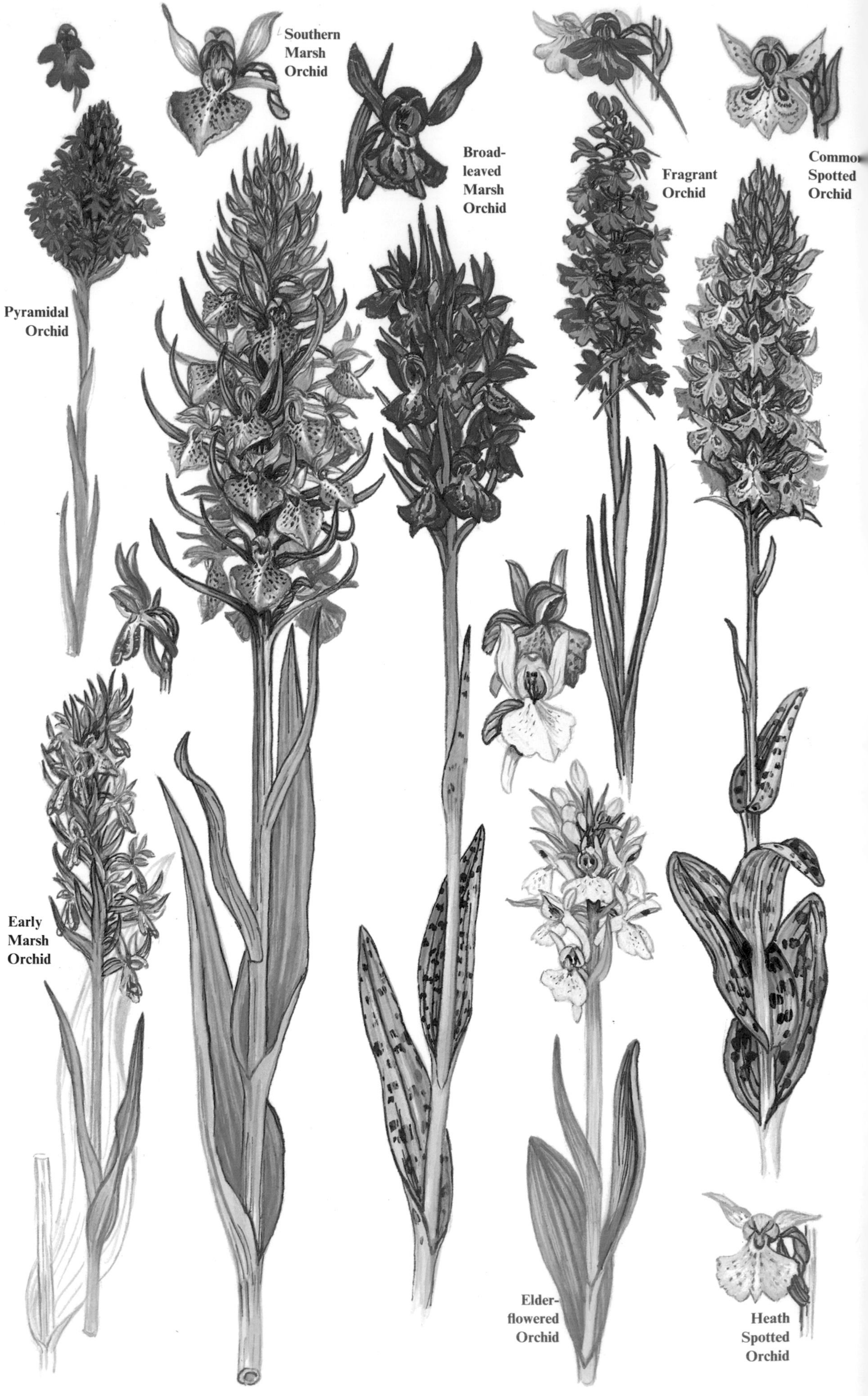

Southern
Marsh
Orchid

Broad-
leaved
Marsh
Orchid

Fragrant
Orchid

Common
Spotted
Orchid

Pyramidal
Orchid

Early
Marsh
Orchid

Elder-
flowered
Orchid

Heath
Spotted
Orchid

PLATE 123
pages 73–74

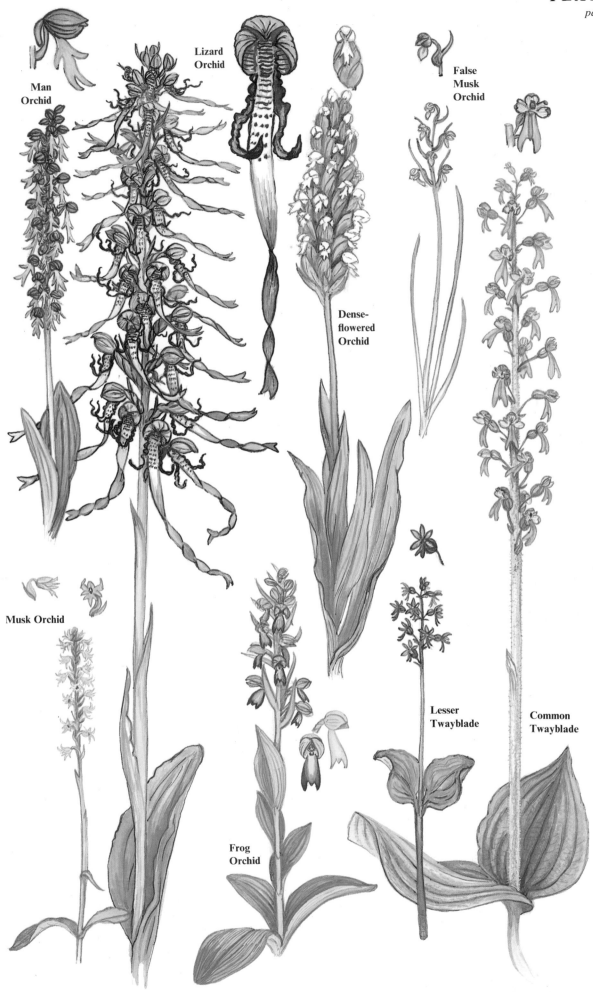

Man Orchid

Lizard Orchid

False Musk Orchid

Dense-flowered Orchid

Musk Orchid

Frog Orchid

Lesser Twayblade

Common Twayblade

PLATE 124
page 74

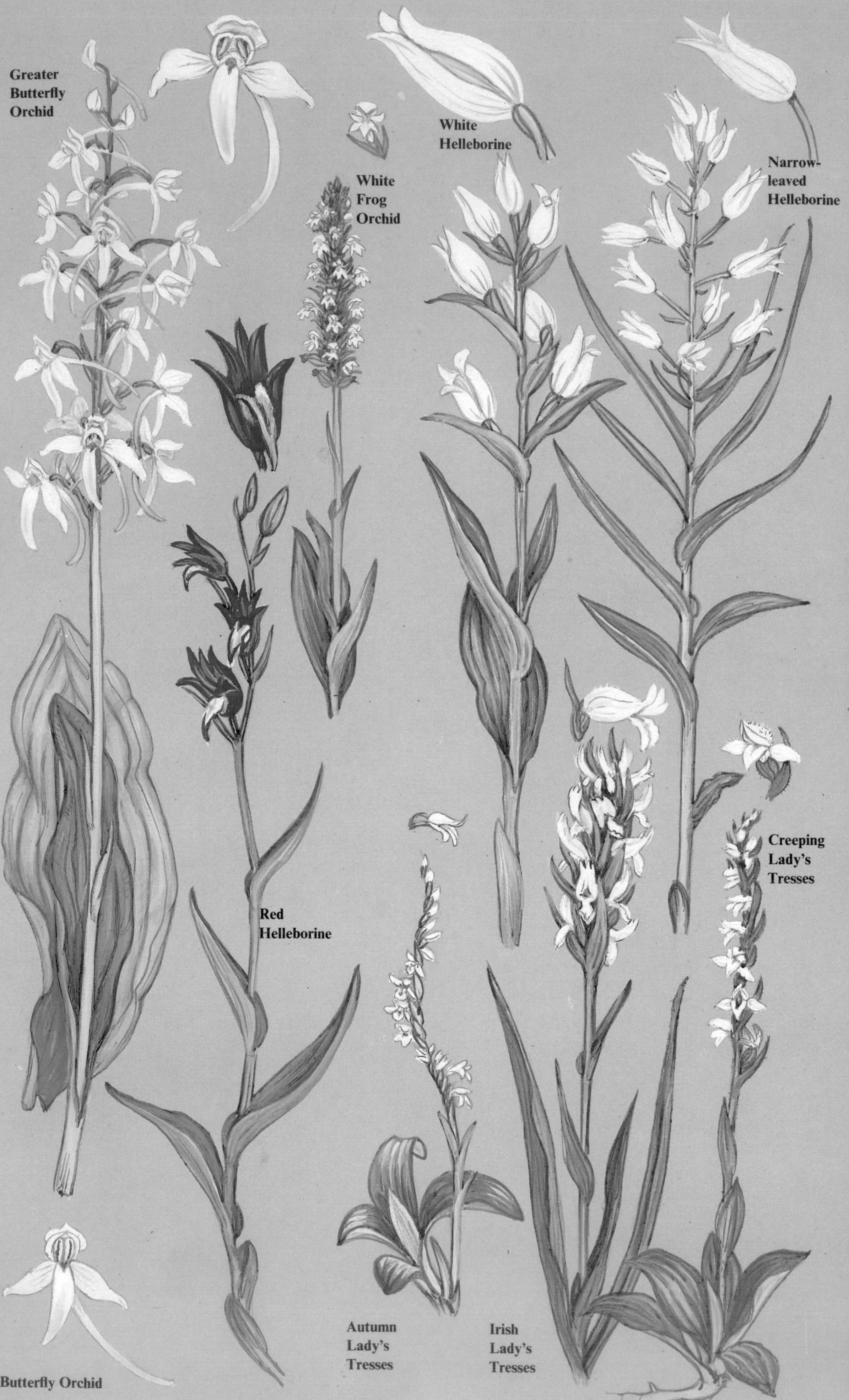

Greater
Butterfly
Orchid

White
Helleborine

White
Frog
Orchid

Narrow-
leaved
Helleborine

Red
Helleborine

Creeping
Lady's
Tresses

Autumn
Lady's
Tresses

Irish
Lady's
Tresses

Lesser Butterfly Orchid

PLATE 125
pages 74–75

Marsh
Helleborine

Dark
Red
Helleborine

Broad-
leaved
Helleborine

Narrow-
lipped
Helleborine

Violet
Helleborine

Dune
Helleborine

Green-
flowered
Helleborine

PLATE 126
page 75

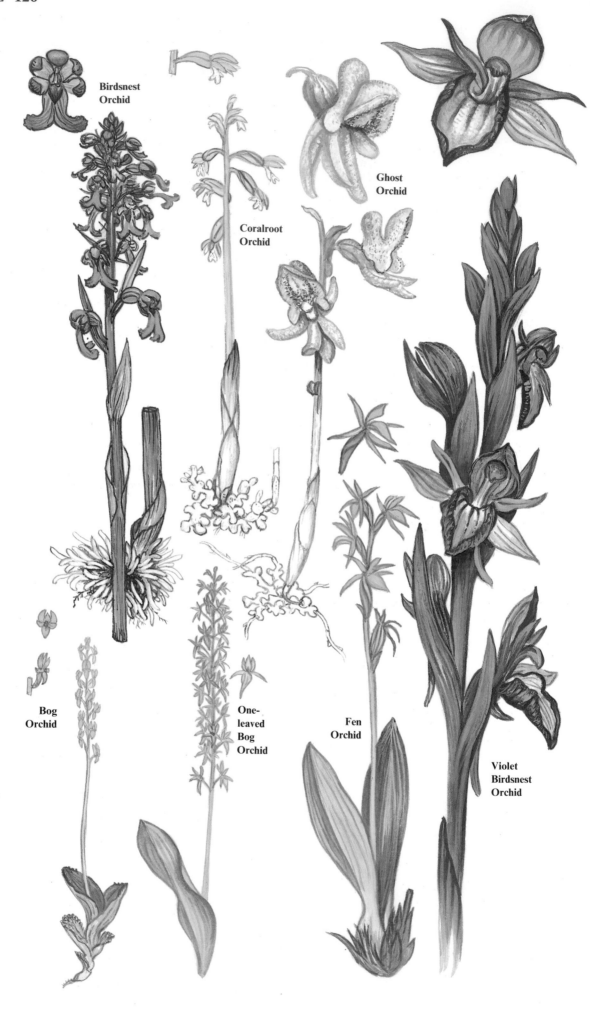

Birdsnest
Orchid

Coralroot
Orchid

Ghost
Orchid

Bog
Orchid

One-
leaved
Bog
Orchid

Fen
Orchid

Violet
Birdsnest
Orchid

PINE FAMILY
Pinaceae

Fruit a woody cone. Widely planted.

1 **Silver Fir*** *Abies alba*
Pyramidal tree to 50 m, branches regularly whorled; bark scaly, greyish. Leaves single, whitish beneath, in two rows, grooved, leaving an *oval scar*. Flowers Apr-May. Cones erect, 10-20 cm, with bracts between the scales. Mainly in mountains. (B), F, G, (S). *A. procera* and *A. grandis* from N America are widely planted.

1 **Douglas Fir*** *Pseudotsuga menziesii*
Similar to Silver Fir but taller, to 100 m, with branches irregularly whorled, bark ridged and red-brown, leaves fragrant when bruised and shorter, hanging cones. (T) from N America.

1 **Norway Spruce*** *Picea abies*
Pyramidal tree to 60 m, branches regularly whorled; bark scaly, red-brown. Leaves single, in two rows, 4-sided, grass-green, falling to leave a *peg-like projection*. Flowers May-June. Cones hanging, 10-18 cm, with no bracts protruding. Forests, especially in mountains. T, but (B).

1 **Western Hemlock*** *Tsuga heterophylla*
Similar to Norway Spruce. Has branches irregularly whorled, leading shoots drooping, flat leaves on cushion-like projections, and much shorter oval cones. (T) from N America.

1 **European Larch*** *Larix decidua*
Pyramidal tree to 35 m; bark rough, grey-brown. Leaves single and tufted, pale green, *deciduous*. Male flowers yellow, female pink; Mar-Apr. Cones short, egg-shaped. Mountain forests. (B), F, G, (S).

1 **Scots Pine*** *Pinus sylvestris*
Dome-shaped tree to 40 mm, but pyramidal when young; bark reddish, flaking. Leaves in *pairs*, greyish, twisted, 30-70 mm; buds sticky, resinous. Male flowers orange-yellow, female pinkish-green; May-June. Cones conical, hanging, 30-60 mm. Forests, moors, heaths. T.

1 **Maritime Pine*** *Pinus pinaster*
Similar to Scots Pine but has more ridged bark, leaves much longer (to 250 mm), curved and greener, buds not sticky and larger, broader cones. (B. F) from S Europe.

CYPRESS FAMILY
Cupressaceae

1 **Lawson's Cypress*** *Chamaecyparis lawsoniana*
Evergreen columnar tree to 65 m; bark red-brown. Leaves *scale-like*, opposite, closely pressed to flattened stems, often greyish, parsley-scented, leading shoots drooping. Male flowers pink, female yellow-brown; Apr. Cones globular, 8 mm. Widely planted, sometimes naturalised. (T) from N America.

1 **Juniper*** *Juniperus communis*
Evergreen shrub or small tree to 6 m, bushy columnar or (ssp. *nana*) prostrate. Leaves greyish, in whorls of three, *spine-tipped*. Flowers yellow, male and female on separate plants; May-June. Fruit berry-like, green at first, blue-black in its second year. Coniferous woods, moors, heaths, scrub; ssp. *nana* on mountains and by sea. T.

YEW FAMILY
Taxaceae

1 **Yew*** *Taxus baccata*
Evergreen tree or shrub to 20 m; bark red-brown, flaking. Leaves dark green, in two rows. Flowers green; male, with many yellow stamens, and female on separate trees; Feb-Apr. Fruit in a fleshy *reddish-pink* cup. Woods, scrub, screes, often on lime; widely planted. T.

JOINT PINE FAMILY
Ephedraceae

1 **Joint Pine** *Ephedra distachya*
Well-branched undershrub with green twigs, appearing leafless because leaves so small. Flowers small, yellow-green, often unstalked; male and female flowers on different plants; May-June. Fruit fleshy, red. Sandy shores, rocks, walls. F, western.

WILLOW FAMILY
Salicaceae

Deciduous trees or shrubs. Leaves usually alternate and finely toothed. Flowers small, petalless but with a scale, in catkins, often appearing before the leaves; male and female on different plants, male usually yellow, female usually green. Fruit woolly with long hairs. Willows and Sallows *Salix* have buds with only one outer scale, catkins usually on leafy shoots, scales untoothed and usually two stamens. Hybrids are frequent.

2 **Bay Willow*** *Salix pentandra*
Shrub or small tree to 7 m, *hairless*; bark grey, rugged; twigs shiny. Leaves usually *broad* elliptical, dark glossy green, sticky and fragrant when young. Catkins slender, stamens five or more, stigmas purple; May-June, with leaves. By fresh water. T.

2 **Crack Willow*** *Salix fragilis*
Spreading tree to 25 m, often pollarded; bark grey, rugged; twigs hairless, easily breaking. Leaves *narrow* elliptical, hairless, paler beneath; stipules soon falling. Catkins slender; Apr-May, with leaves. By fresh water. T.

2 **White Willow*** *Salix alba*
Similar to Crack Willow but less spreading and looks silvery-grey from silky hairs on young leaves

and beneath mature leaves; twigs not fragile; May. Distinct subspecies, often planted, have blue-green leaves (ssp. *coerulea*, the Cricket-bat Willow) and bright orange-yellow twigs (ssp. *vitellina*, the Golden Osier).

plate 2   **Goat Willow** or **Great Sallow*** *Salix caprea*
Small tree or shrub to 10 m; twigs downy at first, later (except in the N) hairless. Leaves *oval with pointed tip*, usually rounded at base, hairless above (except in the N), softly grey downy beneath. Catkins stout, unstalked, the scales black-brown with white hairs, which show silvery white in bud, when known as 'pussy willow' or 'palm'; Mar-Apr, before leaves. Woods, scrub, by fresh water. T.

2   **Grey Willow** or **Grey Sallow*** *Salix cinerea*
Similar to Goat Willow. A shrub to 6 m, with twigs ridged under the bark and often continuing downy, and leaves narrower, tapering to base and either greyish above or with only a few rust-coloured hairs beneath. Usually in damp places.

2   **Eared Willow** or **Eared Sallow*** *Salix aurita*
Similar to Goat Willow. A much smaller shrub, to 2 m, with twigs widely angled and ridged under the bark, more rounded, markedly wrinkled leaves, and green catkin scales.

2   **Purple Willow*** *Salix purpurea*
Shrub to 5 m, with straight slender twigs often purplish at first. Leaves *bluish-green*, lanceolate, often opposite, hairless, blackening when dried. Male catkins with dark, purple-tipped scales and reddish or purplish anthers, female often red-purple; Mar-Apr, before leaves. Fens, by fresh water. T, but (S).

2   **Violet Willow*** *Salix daphnoides*
Similar to Purple Willow. Taller, to 10 m, and may be a tree, with bluish waxy bloom on twigs, narrow, more sharply toothed leaves, not blackening, and yellow anthers, (B, F, G), S.

2   **Osier*** *Salix viminalis*
Shrub or small tree to 5 m; twigs long, straight, flexible, used in basket-making as withies. Leaves very *long and narrow*, to 25 cm, silky white beneath, untoothed, the margins down-turned. Catkins longer than Goat Willow, scales brown with white hairs; Mar-Apr, before leaves. By fresh water. T, but (S). Many hybrids are cultivated and become naturalised.

3   **Dark-leaved Willow*** *Salix nigricans*
Shrub or small tree to 4 m; twigs usually downy. Leaves *pointed oval*, mostly greyish beneath, almost hairless, usually blackening when dried. Catkins short, scales green and black-brown; Apr-May, usually before leaves. By fresh water; in south of range only in the hills. T.

3   **Downy Willow*** *Salix lapponum*
Shrub to 4 m, with *grey down*. Leaves pointed oval, to broad lanceolate, *untoothed*, grey on both sides. Catkin scales brown with white hairs, anthers red-dish at first; May-June, with leaves. Tundra, mountains. B, S, northern.

3   **Woolly Willow*** *Salix lanata*
Shrub to 3 m, twigs *thickly downy*. Leaves broad oval, *untoothed*, yellow-hairy at first, then grey-hairy, finally almost hairless above. Catkins with long yellow hairs; May-July, with leaves. Tundra, mountains. B, S, northern.

3   **Mountain Willow*** *Salix arbuscula*
Shrub to 2 m; twigs hairless, ridged under the bark. Leaves *pointed oval*, shiny above, greyish and often hairless beneath. Catkin scales with rusty hairs, anthers reddish at first, stigmas purple-brown; May-June, with leaves. Mountains. B, S.

3   **Spear-leaved Willow** *Salix hastata*
Similar to Mountain Willow. Has mature leaves larger, sometimes roundish, not shiny or hairy, and stipules much larger and more persistent. S.

3   **Whortle-leaved Willow*** *Salix myrsinites*
Similar to Mountain Willow. Prostrate with twigs downy at first, not ridged, leaves shiny on both sides, hairy only on margins and sometimes untoothed, and anthers purple.

3   **Creeping Willow*** *Salix repens*
Shrub with *creeping* stems up to 2 m high; twigs silky hairy at first. Leaves narrow to broad oval, white usually with *silky hairs* beneath and sometimes above, almost untoothed. Catkins short, scales dark green tipped purple-brown, female green to purple-brown; Apr-May, before leaves. Swamps, bogs, fens, dune slacks. T.

3   **Dwarf Willow*** *Salix herbacea*
Prostrate *patch-forming* undershrub; twigs 2-3 cm long. Leaves *rounded*, toothed, hairless, shiny above. Catkins short, scales yellowish, sometimes tinged red; June, after leaves. Mountains, tundra, B, G, S.

3   **Net-leaved Willow*** *Salix reticulata*
Similar to Dwarf Willow but has larger, darker green, wrinkled, longer-stalked, untoothed leaves, whitish and conspicuously net-veined beneath, and brownish scales with grey hairs; anthers and stigmas purple.

All species of Poplars and members of the next five families are deciduous (except Evergreen Oak) and have alternate leaves and separate male and female flowers – Poplars and Bog Myrtle on separate plants, the others on the same plant.

POPLARS
Populus

Have buds with several unequal outer scales, and catkins, appearing before the *broad* leaves, with toothed scales, the male reddish and with four or more stamens, the female greenish-yellow.

2

4 **Grey Poplar*** *Populus canescens*
Spreading tree to 30 m, with black gashes on smooth grey bark, suckering freely; young twigs and buds *white downy*. Spring leaves pointed oval, broadest above the middle, with large teeth, almost hairless in summer; summer and sucker leaves more sharply lobed and maple-like, always downy. Catkin scales deeply cut; Mar. Damp woods; widely planted. B, F, G.

4 **White Poplar*** *Populus alba*
Similar to Grey Poplar. Young twigs and buds more thickly downy, spring leaves rounder, broadest below middle, always whitely downy beneath, summer and sucker leaves more deeply palmately lobed, and catkin scales less deeply cut. (B, F), G.

4 **Aspen*** *Populus tremula*
Spreading tree to 20 m, suckering freely; bark smooth, grey-brown, twigs and slightly sticky buds almost hairless. Leaves *rounded*, bluntly toothed, soon hairless, swaying in every breeze on thin flattened stalks; sucker leaves very like Grey Poplar. Catkin scales deeply cut; March. Damp woods and heaths, fens, moors, mountains. T.

4 **Black Poplar*** *Populus nigra*
Spreading tree to 30 m, with rugged blackish bark and large bosses on trunk, rarely suckering; twigs and sticky buds hairless. Leaves *ace-of-spades*, shorter and broader on short shoots. Flowers Mar-Apr, before leaves. By fresh water. B, F, G. The tall slender Lombardy Poplar var. *italica* is widely planted.

4 **Balsam Poplar*** *Populus gileadensis*
Has a more fan-shaped crown than Black Poplar, no bosses on trunk, more frequent suckers, and larger leaves. Buds and young leaves balsam-fragrant and leaves without pimples, paler beneath, with hairs on veins, female trees rare. Less widely planted.

BOG MYRTLE FAMILY
Myricaceae

4 **Bog Myrtle** or **Sweet Gale*** *Myrica gale*
Shrub to 2·5 m, *fragrant* from yellow dots on red-brown twigs and narrow oval leaves, downy beneath. Orange male and shorter reddish female catkins on different plants; Apr-May, before leaves. Wet heaths, bogs. T, western.

WALNUT FAMILY
Juglandaceae

4 **Walnut*** *Juglans regia*
Spreading tree to 30 m; bark grey, smooth at first. Leaves pinnate, aromatic. Flowers yellow-green, male in hanging catkins, female in short erect spikes; Apr-May. Fruit a brown nut in a green case. Hedgerows, widely planted, often bird-sown. (B, F, G) from S E Europe.

BIRCH FAMILY
Betulaceae

4 **Silver Birch*** *Betula pendula*
Erect tree to 30 m, with papery peeling *white* bark and dark bosses on trunk; young twigs hairless, with resinous dots. Leaves ace-of-spades, teeth of different depths. Catkins yellowish, male hanging, female erect, shorter; Apr-May, with leaves. Woods, scrub, heaths, moors. T.

4 **Downy Birch*** *Betula pubescens*
Similar to Silver Birch but shorter and may be a shrub, with bark grey or brown no bosses, young twigs downy and without dots, and leaves uniformly toothed. Usually wetter places, not on lime. Northern.

4 **Dwarf Birch*** *Betula nana*
Semi-prostrate shrub to 1 m; twigs hairless. Leaves *rounded,* deeply toothed, downy when young. Catkins as Silver Birch but smaller; June-July, after leaves. Moors, bogs, tundra. B, G, S.

4 **Alder*** *Alnus glutinosa*
Spreading tree or shrub to 20 m; bark dark brown, rugged, twigs hairless. Leaves *roundish*, toothed, blunt-tipped, almost hairless. Male catkins yellowish, female egg-shaped, purplish; Feb-Mar, before leaves. Fruit cone-like. Fens, by fresh water. T.

4 **Grey Alder*** *Alnus incana*
Similar to Alder. Has smooth bark, and young twigs and narrower pointed leaves downy at least when young. Drier places. T, but (B). Hybrids with Alder are found.

HAZEL FAMILY
Corylaceae

5 **Hornbeam*** *Carpinus betulus*
Spreading tree to 25 m; bark smooth, grey, twigs slightly downy. Leaves pointed oval, toothed, scarcely downy. Catkins greenish; Apr-May with leaves. Fruit a nut within *leafy bracts*. Woods; widely planted. T, south-eastern.

5 **Hazel*** *Corylus avellana*
Shrub to 6 m; bark red-brown, peeling. Leaves oval to rounded, with a small point, toothed, downy. Male flowers in hanging catkins, pale yellow; female erect, bud-like, with bright red styles; *Jan-Mar*, before leaves. Fruit a nut, enclosed in a leafy husk. Woods, scrub, hedges. T.

BEECH FAMILY
Fagaceae

5 **Beech*** *Fagus sylvatica*
Spreading tree to 30 m; bark smooth, grey, buds red-brown. Leaves pointed oval, shallowly toothed, veins prominent at edge, silky white beneath at first. Flowers greenish, male in a roundish *tassel*, female erect, in pairs; Apr-May, with leaves. Fruit a warm-

OTHER TREES

brown nut ("mast") enclosed in a bristly husk. Woods, usually in pure stand; widely planted. T, southern.

plate 5 **Sweet Chestnut*** *Castanea sativa*
Spreading tree to 30 m; bark rugged, grey-brown. Leaves *elliptical*, toothed. Catkins yellowish, with a sickly fragrance, male flowers at the top, female below; July. Fruit a brown nut encased in a softly spiny cup. Widely planted, sometimes naturalised. (T) from S Europe.

5 **Evergreen Oak** or **Holm Oak*** *Quercus ilex*
Evergreen tree to 25 m; bark greyish, scaly, twigs grey downy. Leaves pointed oval, untoothed or with holly-like spines, grey downy beneath. Catkins greenish-yellow, male long, female short; May-June. Fruit a nut (acorn) in a cup. (B), F.

5 **Pedunculate Oak*** *Quercus robur*
Spreading tree to 45 m; bark rugged, grey-brown, twigs and leaves almost hairless. Leaves oblong, *lobed*, the basal lobes usually overlapping the very short stalk. Catkins greenish-yellow, male longer than female; Apr-May, with leaves. Fruit a nut (acorn) in a long-stalked scaly cup. Woods, usually in pure stand; widely planted. T.

5 **Sessile Oak** or **Durmast Oak*** *Quercus petraea*
Similar to Pedunculate Oak. Leaves tapering to the unlobed base and acorns scarcely stalked. Less often planted. Southern.

5 **Turkey Oak*** *Quercus cerris*
Similar to Pedunculate Oak. Has downy young twigs, larger, more jaggedly lobed leaves and short-stalked acorns in bristly cups. (B), F, G.

5 **Red Oak*** *Quercus rubra*
Similar to Pedunculate Oak with dark red twigs and much larger leaves turning rich red in autumn is the most frequent of many planted N American oaks.

ELM FAMILY
Ulmaceae

6 **Wych Elm*** *Ulmus glabra*
Spreading tree to 40 m, with rugged bark and no suckers; twigs roughly hairy when young. Leaves broad oval to elliptical, alternate, roughly hairy. Flowers small, unstalked, with a *tuft of reddish stamens*; Mar-Apr, before leaves. Fruit a pale green notched disc, the seed in the centre. Woods, hedges. T.

6 **English Elm*** *Ulmus procera*
Similar to Wych Elm. Suckers freely and has twigs always hairy, leaves smaller and rounder, sometimes almost hairless above, and fruit (rare in B) with seed above middle. Rarely in woods. B, F.

6 **Small-leaved Elm*** *Ulmus minor*
Similar to Wych Elm but has suckers, and hairless twigs, narrower leaves hairless beneath, and fruit with seed above middle. Rarely in woods. B, F, G.

PLANE FAMILY
Platanaceae

6 **London Plane*** *Platanus hybrida*
Spreading tree to 30 m, with smooth grey bark, constantly flaking off. Leaves alternate, sharply palmately lobed. Flowers and fruit in *roundish heads*, flowers green. Widely planted, occasionally self-sown. (B, F, G), of unknown origin.

MAPLE FAMILY
Aceraceae

Trees or shrubs, with long-stalked, palmately-lobed, ivy-like opposite leaves. Flowers small, greenish-yellow, 5-petalled, male and female separate on same tree. Fruit a pair of keys (samara), each with a single long wing.

6 **Sycamore*** *Acer pseudoplatanus*
Spreading tree to 30 m, with smooth grey bark, flaking when old. Leaves 5-lobed to about half-way, well toothed. Flowers in *hanging* clusters; May. Fruit with wings diverging at right angles. Woods, hedges, widely planted. (B), F, G, (S).

6 **Norway Maple*** *Acer platanoides*
Similar to Sycamore. Has leaves with more sharply pointed lobes and fewer, sharper teeth, brighter yellow flowers in erect clusters, appearing in April, before leaves, and fruit as Field Maple. T, but (B).

6 **Italian Maple** *Acer opalus*
Similar to Sycamore. Has rather leathery, much less toothed leaves and fruit with wings diverging more narrowly. F, G.

6 **Field Maple*** *Acer campestre*
Small tree or shrub to 20 m, with roughish grey bark; twigs downy, later corky. Leaves bluntly 5-lobed, untoothed, much smaller than Sycamore, red when young. Flowers in *erect* clusters; May. Fruit with wings diverging horizontally, usually downy. Woods, hedges. T, southern.

6 **Montpelier Maple** *Acer monspessulanus*
Similar to Field Maple. Has leaves 3-lobed, rather leathery, shiny above, flowers sometimes before leaves, and fruit with wings almost parallel. F, G. eastern.

HORSE-CHESTNUT FAMILY
Hippocastanaceae

7 **Horse Chestnut*** *Aesculus hippocastanum*
Tree to 25 m, with grey bark, smooth at first, and sticky buds. Leaves opposite, palmate with *5-7 leaflets*. Flowers white, with a yellow to pink spot, 5-petalled, in conspicuous erect stalked clusters; May. Fruit a large warm-brown nut, in a fleshy

4

green, stoutly but softly spiny case. Widely planted, often self-sown. (B,F,G) from SE Europe.

HOLLY FAMILY
Aquifoliaceae

7 **Holly*** *Ilex aquifolium*
Evergreen tree or shrub to 10 m, with grey bark, smooth at first. Leaves oval, usually *spiny,* leathery, dark green. Flowers 4-petalled, white, often purplish, in clusters, male and female on different trees; May-Aug. Fruit a red berry. Woods, scrub, hedges. T, southern.

LIME FAMILY
Tiliaceae

7 **Small-leaved Lime*** *Tilia cordata*
Spreading tree to 30 m, with smooth dark brown bark and large bosses on trunk; young twigs more or less hairless. Leaves heart-shaped, greyish beneath, with faint side-veins and small tufts of reddish hairs. Flowers 5-petalled, yellowish, *fragrant,* in small clusters, on stalks half-joined to an oblong bract; July. Fruit a globular nut. Woods. T.

7 **Large-leaved Lime*** *Tilia platyphyllos*
Similar to Small-leaved Lime. Has no trunk bosses, young twigs usually downy, larger leaves with all veins prominent and uniformly grey downy beneath, and fewer larger flowers to the cluster. Southern.

OLIVE FAMILY
Oleaceae

7 **Ash*** *Fraxinus excelsior*
Spreading tree to 30 m, with grey bark, becoming rugged; buds *black.* Leaves opposite, *pinnate,* the leaflets unstalked. Flowers petalless, with tufts of purple-black stamens, becoming greenish; Apr-May, before leaves. Fruit a key (samara) with a single wing. Woods, sometimes in pure stand, hedges. T.

QUASSIA FAMILY
Simaroubaceae

7 **Tree of Heaven*** *Ailanthus altissima*
Tree to 20 m, with smooth grey bark; *suckering.* Leaves alternate, pinnate. Flowers 5-petalled, greenish, in stalked clusters; *July.* Fruit a key, reddish at first. Widely planted, frequently naturalised. (B,F,G) from China.

BIRTHWORT FAMILY
Aristolochiaceae

8 **Birthwort*** *Aristolochia clematitis*
Medium/tall hairless stinking perennial. Leaves bluntly heart-shaped, alternate, untoothed. Flowers dull yellow, irregularly *tubular* with a flattened lip, swollen at the base, in small clusters at base of upper leaves; June-Sept. Waste places, often by water. (B),F,G, eastern.

8 **Asarabacca*** *Asarum europaeum*
Low creeping patch-forming downy perennial. Leaves kidney-shaped, shiny, long-stalked. Flowers dull purple, solitary, *bell-shaped,* 3-lobed; Mar-Aug. Woods on lime-rich soils. (B),F,G, southern, scattered.

MISTLETOE FAMILY
Loranthaceae

8 **Mistletoe*** *Viscum album*
Woody, regularly branched parasite on tree boughs (mainly apples and poplars, rarely conifers). Leaves elliptical, in pairs, yellowish, *leathery.* Flowers inconspicuous, green, 4-petalled, stamens and styles on separate plants; Feb-Apr. Fruit a sticky *white berry;* Nov-Feb. T, southern.

SANDALWOOD FAMILY
Santalaceae

8 **Bastard Toadflax*** *Thesium humifusum*
Short, often prostrate, parasitic perennial. Leaves linear, 1-veined, alternate. Flowers dull white inside, yellowish-green outside, in stalked spikes, with three bracts but no sepals; petal tube 5-lobed, persistent and much shorter than fruit; June-Aug. Dry grassland on lime. B,F,G, western.

HEMP FAMILY
Cannabaceae

8 **Hop*** *Humulus lupulus*
Tall, roughly hairy, square-stemmed climbing perennial, twining *clockwise.* Leaves deeply *palmately* lobed, toothed. Flowers green, the branched clusters of males and the cone-like females on separate plants; July-Sept. Often in hedges, also cultivated. T, lowland.

8 **Hemp*** *Cannabis sativa*
Tall, *strong-smelling* annual. Leaves deeply 3-9-lobed, almost to the base. Flowers green, male in a branching cluster, female, on separate plants, in stalked spikes; July-Sept. Casual on waste ground, also illegally sown as a source of marijuana. T, lowland.

5

NETTLE FAMILY
Urticaceae

plate 8   **Nettle*** *Urtica dioica*
Medium/tall perennial, armed with *stinging* hairs. Leaves heart-shaped, toothed, opposite, longer than their stalks. Flowers green with yellow stamens, in catkins, stamens and styles on separate plants; June-Sept. Woods, waste ground, often near houses. T.

8   **Annual Nettle*** *Urtica urens*
Similar to Nettle but is annual and smaller, with sting less powerful, lower leaves shorter than their stalks, and stamens and styles in separate flowers on same plant. Cultivated ground.

8   **Pellitory of the Wall*** *Parietaria judaica*
Short/medium, much-branched, softly hairy perennial; stems reddish. Leaves untoothed, alternate, to 70 mm, not more than three times as long as their stalks. Flowers green with yellow stamens, in small forked clusters, stamens and styles in separate flowers; June-Oct. Walls, banks, rocks. B, F, G, western.

DOCK FAMILY
Polygonaceae

Frequent weeds of waste places and arable land, also wet places. Leaves alternate. Characteristically there is a sheath at the leaf base forming a tube around the stem (the *ochrea*). In bistorts *Polygonum* the usually five sepal-like petals of the small sepal-less flowers persist and enclose the fruit.

9   **Bistort*** *Polygonum bistorta*
Medium patch-forming, unbranched, almost hairless perennial. Leaves narrow *triangular,* their stalks winged in the upper part. Flowers pink, in a dense spike, up to 15 mm broad; June-Oct. Meadows and woods, usually away from lime, often near water. B, F, G, (S).

9   **Amphibious Bistort*** *Polygonum amphibium*
Short/medium creeping perennial with two forms. In water, hairless and floating, rooting at the leaf-junctions, with leaves oblong, not tapering at the base. The terrestrial form is smaller, slightly hairy, the longer, thinner leaves with a rounded base. Both have pink flowers in dense spikes; June-Sept. Near or in still or slow-flowing water or on waste ground. T, lowland.

9   **Redshank*** *Polygonum persicaria*
Medium, sprawling, hairless, branched annual. Leaves lanceolate, usually *dark-spotted,* tapering to the base. Flowers pink or whitish, in densely crowded spikes; June-Oct. Bare ground, often near water. T.

9   **Pale Persicaria*** *Polygonum lapathifolium*
Similar to Redshank but larger and slightly hairy,

with pale dots on leaves and flower-stalks, and stouter spikes of greenish-white or brick-red flowers.

9   **Alpine Bistort*** *Polygonum viviparum*
Short unbranched hairless perennial. Leaves narrow lanceolate, tapering at base. Flower spikes with pale pink or white flowers at top and red *bulbils* at base; June-Aug. Mountain grassland and lowland in the north. B, G, S.

9   **Water-Pepper*** *Polygonum hydropiper*
Medium hairless annual with a *burning taste*; ochreae not fringed. Leaves narrow lanceolate. Flowers white, tinged pink or green, in a narrow, yellow-dotted nodding spike; July-Sept. Damp meadows, wet mud, shallow water. T, lowland.

9   **Knotgrass*** *Polygonum aviculare*
Low hairless annual, with silvery, ragged few-veined ochreae. Leaves lanceolate, larger on main stem than on branches. Flowers pink or white, 1-6 together at base of upper leaves; petals persistent, *enclosing fruit*; June-Nov. Bare ground, including sea-shores. T.

9   **Sea Knotgrass*** *Polygonum maritimum*
Similar to Knotgrass. A perennial with many-veined ochreae, down-rolled leaf-margins, and dead petals shorter than fruit; July-Sept. Atlantic coasts. B(rare), F.

9   **Buckwheat*** *Fagopyrum esculentum*
Medium hairless annual, reddening. Leaves arrow-shaped. Flowers white or pink in branched clusters; June-Sept. Cultivated and naturalised in open places. T, southern.

10   **Black Bindweed*** *Bilderdykia convolvulus*
Tall, climbing annual, with broader leaves and totally different flowers from the true bindweeds (p. 46); twines *clockwise.* Leaves heart-shaped, powdery below. Flowers greenish-pink, in loose spikes; July-Oct. Fruit stalks 2 mm, jointed above the middle; fruit dull black, narrowly winged white. Cultivated and disturbed ground. T, lowland.

10   **Copse Bindweed*** *Bilderdykia dumetorum*
Similar to Black Bindweed but taller and slenderer with whiter flowers, fruit stalks up to 8 mm, jointed below the middle, and fruit shiny black, broadly winged white. Often in hedges, in warm sunny places. T, southern.

10   **Japanese Knotweed*** *Reynoutria japonica*
Tall, vigorous perennial, often forming dense thickets; stems stout, somewhat zigzag. Leaves broad triangular. Flowers whiter in branched spikes; Aug-Oct. Waste ground. (T), from Japan.

10   **Himalayan Knotweed*** *Polygonum polystachyum*
Tall stout patch-forming perennial. Leaves lanceolate, *tapering* at the base, often slightly hairy beneath. Flowers pink or white with red stalks, in long branched spikes; July-Oct, a shy flowerer. Waste places, often by rivers. (B, F, G), from Assam.

10 **Iceland Purslane*** *Koenigia islandica*
Insignificant prostrate annual. Resembles Blinks (below) but has minute *broad* oval unstalked leaves and often reddish stems, whole plant reddening in late summer. Flowers 3-petalled, green, short-stalked, in small clusters; July-Sept. Damp mud and bare ground. B (rare), S, northern.

DOCKS
Rumex

Mostly hairy perennials with alternate leaves and ochreae. Flowers small, green, in whorls (the lower accompanied by a small leaf) in branched spikes, often turning red. Petals and sepals alike, six, the three inner larger, enlarging and becoming the 'valves' around the 3-sided nut. Fruit characters are important for identification. Hybrids are frequent.

11 **Common Sorrel*** *Rumex acetosa*
Short/tall acid-tasting perennial. Leaves arrow-shaped, 2-6 times as long as wide, the lobes at the base pointing backwards, the upper clasping the stem; ochreae with fringed margin. Flower-head little branched, loose; May-Aug. Grassland and woods. T.

11 **Sheep's Sorrel*** *Rumex acetosella* agg.
Slender low/short perennial. Leaves *arrow-shaped,* sometimes very narrow (as illustrated), the basal lobes spreading or pointing *forwards,* the upper stalked. Flower May-Aug. Dry, rather bare places, not on lime. T.

11 **Broad-leaved Dock*** *Rumex obtusifolius*
Tall perennial with broad oblong leaves up to 25 cm long, hairy on veins beneath, the lower *heart-shaped* at the base. Flower-head lax; June-Oct. Fruit valves triangular, toothed, one swollen. Very common on bare and disturbed ground. T.

11 **Clustered Dock*** *Rumex conglomeratus*
Medium/tall perennial with *zig-zag* stem, and branches spreading. Lower leaves oblong with *rounded* base, long-stalked, the upper narrower, rarely red-fringed. Flowers in whorls, leafy nearly to the top, well spread out; June-Aug. Valves untoothed, oblong, all swollen. Woods, grassy and waste places. T, southern.

11 **Fiddle Dock*** *Rumex pulcher*
Short/medium, *spreading* perennial, with leaves often *waisted* like a fiddle. Flowers in whorls; June-Aug. Flower-stems drooping, stiff and tangled in fruit; valves toothed, all swollen. Dry, often waste places. T, southern, scattered.

11 **Water Dock*** *Rumex hydrolapathum*
Very tall perennial reaching 2 m; much branched, the branches erect. Leaves narrow, sometimes *over 1 m* long, 4-5 times as long as wide. Flowers July-Sept. Valves triangular, not toothed, all swollen. Rivers and wet places. T.

11 **Marsh Dock*** *Rumex palustris*
Medium annual/perennial, much branched and turning *yellow-brown* in fruit; stems rather wavy. Root leaves tapering, wavy-edged, about six times

as long as wide. Flowers in leafy whorls, well separated, but more crowded at the tips; June-Sept. Fruit-stalks thick, stiff, shorter than valves; valves toothed, all swollen. Bare ground near water. T, southern.

11 **Mountain Sorrel*** *Oxyria digyna*
Short hairless perennial; stem almost leafless. Leaves fleshy, *kidney-shaped.* Flowers June-Aug. Fruit with *two* valves, not swollen. Damp rock ledges and by streams on mountains; to sea-level in the north. T.

MESEMBRYANTHEMUM FAMILY
Aizoaceae

10 **Hottentot Fig*** *Carpobrotus edulis*
Prostrate perennial with long creeping woody stems, and stout *fleshy* leaves, *triangular* in section. Flowers usually magenta with a yellow centre, sometimes all yellow; May-Aug. Cliffs and dunes. (B, F), western, from S Africa.

PURSLANE FAMILY
Portulacaceae

10 **Blinks*** *Montia fontana*
Very variable, but always insignificant straggling annual/perennial; stems often reddish. Leaves *narrow* oval, tapering into the stalk. Flowers tiny, white, 5-petalled, long-stalked, in loose clusters; Apr-Oct. Bare, usually wet places, avoiding lime. T.

10 **Spring Beauty*** *Montia perfoliata*
Short hairless annual. Leaves pointed oval, long-stalked at base, one pair completely *encircling* the stem. Flowers white, the five petals *not* deeply notched; Apr-July. Acid sandy soils, often in quantity on disturbed ground. (B, F, G), northern, from N America.

10 **Pink Purslane*** *Montia sibirica*
Short annual, hairless and rather fleshy. Stem leaves unstalked, but *not* encircling the stem. Flowers pink, the five petals deeply *notched*; Apr-July. Damp woods. (T), scattered, from N America and N E Asia.

GOOSEFOOT FAMILY
Chenopodiaceae

Goosefoots *Chenopodium* and Oraches *Atriplex* are annuals (except Good King Henry), often mealy, with alternate toothed leaves and spikes of inconspicuous green petalless flowers, with joined sepals (except Red Goosefoot) and yellow anthers. There are few good diagnostic characters for the naked eye. In Goosefoots leaf-shape is important. Oraches are told from Goosefoots by their separate male and

7

female flowers, and by their sepals being enclosed by two triangular bracts. Bare ground, often by the sea.

plate 12 **Good King Henry*** *Chenopodium bonus-henricus*
Medium *perennial,* often reddish. Leaves large to 10 cm, mealy when young, *triangular,* almost untoothed. Flowers in almost leafless spikes; May-Aug. Compare Spear-leaved Orache (below), which has smoother leaves and stamens and styles in separate flowers. Waste places. T, southern.

12 **Fat Hen*** *Chenopodium album*
Medium/tall and deep green under a thick *white mealy* covering; stem often reddish. Leaves variable, lanceolate to diamond-shaped. Flowers June-Oct. Abundant on disturbed ground. T.

12 **Red Goosefoot*** *Chenopodium rubrum*
Variable, medium/tall, hairless, and often red-tinged. Leaves diamond-shaped, irregularly toothed. Sepals *not* joined together; Aug-Oct. Disturbed ground, manure heaps, common near the sea. T, southern.

12 **Maple-leaved Goosefoot*** *Chenopodium hybridum*
Tall and hairless, with leaves usually triangular, heart-shaped at base, conspicuously, though sparsely toothed. Flowers in scattered leafless clusters; July-Oct. Disturbed ground. T, scattered.

12 **Many-seeded Goosefoot*** *Chenopodium polyspermum*
Variable, short, spreading; stems square, often reddish. Leaves oval, *untoothed,* turning purple in Autumn. Flowers July-Oct. Disturbed ground. T.

12 **Common Orache*** *Atriplex patula*
Very variable, medium/tall, much branched, usually mealy. Leaves lanceolate to triangular, the basal lobes pointing forwards, tapering into the stalk. Bracts toothed or not; July-Oct. Disturbed ground, sea-shores. T.

12 **Grass-leaved Orache*** *Atriplex littoralis*
Similar to Common Orache. Has almost linear leaves, the upper unstalked. Salt-marshes.

12 **Spear-leaved Orache*** *Atriplex hastata*
Similar to Common Orache. Often reddens and has ascending branches, triangular leaves, the basal lobes at right angles to the stalk, and bracts always toothed.

12 **Frosted Orache*** *Atriplex laciniata*
Short/medium, sprawling, *silvery*; stems reddish, much branched, rather weak. Leaves diamond-shaped. Bracts 3-lobed; July-Sept. Dunes and beaches near high-tide mark. T, southern.

12 **Sea Beet*** *Beta vulgaris* ssp. *maritima*
Sprawling, hairless, often red-tinged perennial with tall, upright shoots. Leaves dark green, *leathery,* untoothed. Flowers as in Goosefoots (above); June-Sept. Wild subspecies of cultivated beets, mangolds, etc. Coasts. T, southern.

12 **Polycnemum** *Polycnemum majus*
Short, often sprawling hairless annual. Leaves *sharp-tipped,* triangular in section. Flowers greenish, petalless, solitary, at base of upper leaves; July-Oct. Dry places, bare ground. F,G, eastern.

13 **Sea Purslane*** *Halimione portulacoides*
Short/medium silvery *undershrub*; stems brownish. Leaves elliptical, untoothed, the lower opposite. Flowers green, in short branched spikes, stamens and styles in separate flowers; July-Oct. Fruit unstalked. Banks of channels in salt-marshes. B, F, G, southern.

13 **Glasswort*** *Salicornia europaea*
Low/medium fleshy annual, sometimes unbranched, often reddening or yellowing in fruit. Leaves scale-like, opposite, *succulent,* translucent, fused to envelop the stem. Flowers obscure, green with yellow anthers, usually in groups of three; Aug-Sept. Muddy salt-marshes, sometimes on sandy soils inland. T.

13 **Annual Seablite*** *Suaeda maritima*
Variable, short/medium, sometimes prostrate branched annual. Leaves cylindrical, alternate, fleshy with *pointed* tip and tapering base. Flowers small, green, 1-3 in a cluster at base of upper leaves; stigmas two; Aug-Oct. Coasts, especially salt-marshes. T, southern.

13 **Shrubby Seablite*** *Suaeda vera*
Small greyish hairless *shrub* to 120 cm. Leaves cylindrical, rounded at base and *tip.* Flowers like Annual Seablite; stigmas three; June-Oct. Sand and shingle or among rocks above high-tide mark. B, F.

13 **Prickly Saltwort*** *Salsola kali*
Variable, short/medium, prickly, usually semi-prostrate annual, hairless or not; stem often striped. Leaves linear, unstalked, succulent, usually *sharp-tipped.* Flowers green, solitary with leaf-like bracts; flower persisting and covering the fruit; July-Oct. Sandy coasts, in the south sometimes inland. T.

13 **Hairy Seablite** *Bassia hirsuta*
Short/medium, often prostrate, slightly hairy annual. Leaves linear, fleshy. Flowers resembling Annual Seablite, but ripe fruit *spiny.* Meadows near the sea. G.

AMARANTH FAMILY
Amaranthaceae

13 **Green Amaranth*** *Amaranthus hybridus*
Medium/tall yellow-green hairless annual; much branched. Leaves pointed oval, alternate, untoothed. Flowers tiny, 5-petalled, green or red, in very dense erect spikes, often branched, mixed with pointed bracts; July-Oct. Waste places. (B, F, G), from tropical America.

PINK FAMILY
Caryophyllaceae

Leaves in opposite pairs, undivided, usually untoothed. Flowering shoots repeatedly forked; petals 4-5, sepals may be separate or fused into a tube. Flower dry.

SANDWORTS have white flowers (except Cyphel), five *unnotched* petals and three styles.

14 **Thyme-leaved Sandwort*** *Arenaria serpyllifolia*
Variable low/short, prostrate to bushy, hairy greyish annual. Leaves pointed oval, unstalked. Flowers 5-8 mm, petals shorter than sepals; anthers yellowish; Apr-Nov. Dry, bare places and walls. T.

14 **Arctic Sandwort*** *Arenaria norvegica*
Low, *tufted* perennial, almost hairless. Leaves oval, rather fleshy, not clearly veined. Flowers 8-12 mm, petals longer than sepals, anthers yellowish; June-Aug. Bare places, usually on lime. B, S, scattered, northern.

14 **Three-veined Sandwort*** *Moehringia trinervia*
Low/short, downy, rather straggling annual. Leaves pointed oval, with three or five *prominent veins*. Flowers 6 mm, petals shorter than sepals; May-June. Woods on rich soils. T.

14 **Spring Sandwort*** *Minuartia verna*
Low mat-forming perennial; stems usually downy. Leaves stiff, linear, 3-veined in tufts. Flowers 8-9 mm, petals longer than sepals, anthers pink; May-Sept. Dry rocky places, often on lime; old mine-tips. B, F, G, scattered.

14 **Fine-leaved Sandwort*** *Minuartia hybrida*
Low, very slender, erect annual, usually much branched and hairless. Leaves linear, mostly near the base. Flowers 6 mm, petals much shorter than narrow white-edged sepals, anthers pink; May-Sept. Dry stony and sandy places. B, F, G.

14 **Curved Sandwort*** *Minuartia recurva*
Short, tufted perennial, slightly downy with woody stems and dense, somewhat *curved* leaves. Petals slightly longer than sepals; June-Oct. Mountains. Ireland (rare).

14 **Cyphel*** *Minuartia sedoides*
Low, cushion-forming, hairless perennial. Leaves linear, overlapping. Flowers almost flush with the cushion, *yellow-green* often without petals, distinguishing it from Moss Campion (p. 11); June-Aug. Bare, rocky places, usually in mountains. B, F, G.

14 **Sea Sandwort*** *Honkenya peploides*
Creeping, rather yellowish perennial; stems and oval leaves *fleshy*. Flowers 6-10 mm, greenish-white, solitary among the leaves along the stems, petals not longer than sepals; May-Aug. Fruits like small green peas. Sand and shingle by sea. T.

STITCHWORTS and CHICKWEEDS *Stellaria*

Flowers white, petals five, notched or cleft, styles three.

15 **Greater Stitchwort*** *Stellaria holostea*
Short, straggly perennial; stems square. Leaves narrow lanceolate, *unstalked*. Flowers 20-30 mm, petals split to halfway; Apr-June. Woods, hedges, on heavier soils. T.

15 **Lesser Stitchwort*** *Stellaria graminea*
Similar to Greater Stitchwort. Flowers 5-12 mm, petals equalling sepals; May-Aug. Rarely on lime.

15 **Common Chickweed*** *Stellaria media*
Low/short, very variable, often prostrate annual, with a line of hairs down the weak round stem. Leaves *oval,* the lower long-stalked. Flowers 8-10 mm, petals cleft to base, equalling sepals, or absent; all year. Bare and cultivated ground. T.

15 **Wood Stitchwort*** *Stellaria nemorum*
Similar to Common Chickweed. A short perennial with stem hairy all round and petals twice as long as sepals; May-July. Damp woods. Eastern.

15 **Greater Chickweed*** *Stellaria neglecta*
Similar to Common Chickweed. Short and sometimes perennial, with flowers 10 mm, petals slightly longer than sepals; Apr-July. Compare Water Chickweed. Damp shady places. Local.

15 **Lesser Chickweed*** *Stellaria pallida*
Similar to Common Chickweed. Has all leaves short-stalked, and flowers 4-8 mm, always without petals; Mar-May. Sandy places. Southern.

15 **Bog Stitchwort*** *Stellaria alsine*
Similar to Common Chickweed. Has a square stem, unstalked leaves, flowers 4-6 mm, and petals shorter than sepals; May-Aug. Wet places.

15 **Water Chickweed*** *Myosoton aquaticum*
Straggling medium perennial, downy above. Leaves pointed oval, the lower stalked. Flowers 15 mm, petals deeply split, much longer than sepals; differs from Greater Chickweed in having five styles; June-Oct. Wet places. T, southern.

15 **Umbellate Chickweed** *Holosteum umbellatum*
Low greyish annual. Leaves lanceolate. Flowers in umbel-like heads, white; petals ragged, longer than sepals; Mar-May. Dry sandy places, walls. F, G, S, southern; extinct in B.

MOUSE-EARS
Cerastium

Flowers white, five notched petals, five styles (except Starwort Mouse-ear).

15 **Field Mouse-ear*** *Cerastium arvense*
Low perennial, slightly hairy. Leaves narrow lanceolate, not tapering at base. Flowers *12-20 mm,* petals twice as long as sepals; Apr-Aug. Dry open places on lime. T.

plate

15 **Starwort Mouse-ear*** *Cerastium cerastoides*
Is hairless except for line of hairs down stem; flowers 9-12 mm, styles three; July-Aug. Mountains. B, S.

15 **Common Mouse-ear*** *Cerastium fontanum*
Very variable, low/short perennial, slightly hairy, with leafy non-flowering shoots. Leaves lanceolate. Petals deeply notched, equalling sepals; lower bracts leaflike, upper sometimes white-edged; Apr-Nov. Grassland, bare ground. T.

15 **Sticky Mouse-ear*** *Cerastium glomeratum*
Low, yellowish, stickily hairy annual. Flowers in *tight* heads, rarely opening fully, sepals very hairy; Apr-Oct. Bare ground. T.

15 **Upright Chickweed*** *Moenchia erecta*
Low greyish hairless annual. Flowers white with petals not notched, four styles and sepals with broad *white margins*; Apr-June. Bare sandy places. B, F, G.

16 **Corn Spurrey*** *Spergula arvensis*
Short/medium, stickily hairy annual. Leaves linear, blunt-tipped, in whorls, channelled on underside, with small stipule at base. Flowers 4-8 mm, white, petals five, not notched, styles five; May-Sept. Disturbed ground, not on lime. T, lowland.

16 **Lesser Sea Spurrey*** *Spergularia marina*
Low/short, rather fleshy annual. Leaves slightly pointed, with small stipule at base. Flowers 5-8 mm, usually pink, with five pointed petals shorter than sepals; styles five; May-Sept. Dry parts of saltmarshes. T, rare inland.

16 **Greater Sea Spurrey*** *Spergularia media*
Is an almost hairless perennial; flowers 9-12 mm, petals a paler, bluer pink, longer than sepals. Saltmarshes. T, inland in G.

16 **Knotted Pearlwort*** *Sagina nodosa*
Short, tufted perennial. Leaves linear, largest at base, forming stiff *clusters* ("knots") up stem. Flowers white, 5-10 mm, petals five, not notched, much larger than sepals; styles five; July-Sept. Damp, sandy places, mainly on lime. T.

16 **Procumbent Pearlwort*** *Sagina procumbens*
Low hairless tufted perennial, spreading from a non-flowering rosette. Leaves linear, ending in a minute bristle. Flowers tiny, greenish-white, long-stalked, petals usually four, much smaller than sepals, often absent; styles usually four; May-Sept. Sepals spreading when flower ripe. Damp, bare places. T.

16 **Heath Pearlwort*** *Sagina subulata*
Similar to Procumbent Pearlwort but slightly hairy with flowers white, petals five, equalling slightly sticky sepals; styles five. Dry, sandy places. Scattered.

16 **Annual Knawel*** *Scleranthus annuus*
Low, rather spiky-looking annual. Leaves linear, *meeting round stem.* Flowers in clusters, no petals, sepals five, usually pointed, green and narrow white margin; May-Oct. Dry, sandy places. T.

16 **Strapwort*** *Corrigiola litoralis*
Low greyish annual with stems often reddish. Leaves linear, all *alternate.* Flowers white, minute and crowded, petals five, as long as often partly reddish sepals; June-Oct. Damp, sandy and gravelly places. T, southern, scattered, rare in B.

16 **Smooth Rupturewort*** *Herniaria glabra*
Variable prostrate bright green, more or less hairless annual/perennial. Flowers *green,* in clusters at base of oval leaves, petals green, blunt; May-Oct. Flower pointed, longer than sepals. Dry, bare places, often on lime. T, southern, rare in B.

16 **Coral Necklace*** *Illecebrum verticillatum*
Prostrate hairless annual. Resembles Smooth Rupturewort but has *white* flowers with pointed petals; June-Oct. Damp, sandy ground, not on lime. B (rare), F, G, southern.

16 **Four-leaved Allseed*** *Polycarpon tetraphyllum*
Low hairless branching annual. Leaves oval, apparently in *whorls* of four. Flowers in clusters, white, tiny, petals shorter than sepals; June-Aug. Sandy places. B (rare), F, south-western.

CAMPIONS and CATCHFLIES
Silene and *Lychnis*

Mostly have conspicuous flowers with five petals, and sepals joined in a tube.

17 **Bladder Campion*** *Silene vulgaris*
Medium greyish perennial, usually hairless; all shoots flowering, woody at base. Leaves pointed oval, often wavy-edged. Flowers white, petals deeply cleft, sepal-tube inflated to form a bladder; many flowers in each cluster; styles three; May-Sept. Arable, waste, and grassy places, especially on lime. T.

17 **Sea Campion*** *Silene maritima*
Is short, with non-flowering shoots and broader petals; clusters few-flowered. Cliffs and shingle by sea, also on mountains.

17 **Nottingham Catchfly*** *Silene nutans*
Variable medium unbranched perennial, downy below and sticky above. Leaves broader at tip. Flowers white, drooping, opening and fragrant at night, all usually pointing one way, petals *rolled back,* very narrow and deeply cleft; May-Aug. Dry, undisturbed places. T.

17 **White Sticky Catchfly** *Silene viscosa*
Medium biennial/perennial, densely covered with *sticky hairs.* Leaves narrow oval, the lower with wavy margins. Flowers white, 20 mm, in a long spike, petals deeply cleft, sepals hairy; June-July. Dry, grassy places. G, S, northern.

17 **Spanish Catchfly*** *Silene otites*
Medium perennial, stickily hairy near the base. Leaves broadest at tip, in rosettes. Flowers small, 3-4 mm, *yellowish*, apparently in whorls, flower-heads very unlike other catchflies; stamens and styles often on different plants; June-Sept. Dry, sandy places. B (rare), F, G, south-eastern.

17 **Moss Campion*** *Silene acaulis*
Low, hairless, slightly woody perennial, forming characteristic bright green, moss-like *cushions*, often covered with the solitary, pink flowers; June-Aug. Wild Azalea (p. 42) has duller green leaves and very different flowers, and Cyphel (p. 9) has less pointed leaves and yellowish flowers. Bare places in mountains, and near sea-level in north. B, S.

17 **Sweet William Catchfly*** *Silene armeria*
Short hairless annual with all shoots flowering. Leaves lanceolate, greyish, the upper clasping the stem. Flowers bright pink, clustered in rather flat-topped heads, petals only notched; June-Sept. Dry, often shady places, and as a garden escape. F, G, (B, S).

17 **Flaxfield Catchfly** *Silene linicola*
Medium annual; stem *rough*, branching. Leaves linear. Flowers pink, with red-purple stripes, petals deeply cleft, sepals clearly veined, inflated, contracted at tip; June-July. Flax fields. F, G.

17 **Rock Catchfly** *Silene rupestris*
Short, slender, hairless, *greyish* perennial. Leaves lanceolate. Flowers white or pink, on long stalks, petals notched, sepal-tube 10-veined; June-Sept. Dry places, often in mountains. S; rare and southern in F, G.

17 **Northern Catchfly** *Silene wahlbergella*
Short, unbranched, slightly hairy perennial with long, narrow leaves and solitary flowers. Sepal-tube *inflated* and *longer* than the inconspicuous, purplish petals; June-Aug. Mountain meadows on lime. S.

17 **Forked Catchfly*** *Silene dichotoma*
Medium/tall annual, all stems flowering. Leaves lanceolate. Flowers 15 mm, white, occasionally pink, petals *deeply cleft*; sepals hairy, not sticky; May-Aug. Waste places, (B casual), F, G.

18 **Red Campion*** *Silene dioica*
Medium/tall hairy perennial. Leaves pointed oval, the basal ones stalked. Flowers bright *pink*, sometimes much paler as a result of hybridisation with White Campion, giving a complete range of shades; petals cleft; calyx-teeth triangular, pointed; stamens and styles in separate flowers, styles five; Mar-Nov. Teeth on seed-pod rolled back. Rich soils, especially in or near woods or shady hedges. T.

18 **White Campion*** *Silene alba*
Medium/tall, much branched, stickily-hairy perennial, resembling Red Campion but flowers longer and *white*, calyx-teeth narrow lanceolate, blunt, and teeth on seed-pod upright; May-Oct. Roadsides and more or less bare places, often on cultivated ground. T.

18 **Night-flowering Catchfly*** *Silene noctiflora*
Medium, stickily hairy annual. Leaves pointed oval. Flowers pink, opening at night, and petals rolling inwards by mid-morning to show their *yellowish* undersides; styles *three*, in same flowers as stamens. Teeth on seed-pod turned back. Arable fields. T, eastern.

18 **Ragged Robin*** *Lychnis flos-cuculi*
Medium/tall, rough-stemmed perennial. Leaves lanceolate. Flowers bright pink, the characteristic irregularly and narrowly 4-lobed petals giving them a *ragged* appearance; May-Aug. Damp meadows and marshy places. T.

18 **Sticky Catchfly*** *Lychnis viscaria*
Medium tufted perennial with leafy flowering shoots, *sticky* just below each leaf-junction. Leaves lanceolate. Flowers 20 mm, bright rosy red, petals notched, apparently *whorled*, in long spikes; May-Aug. Dry, rock places, rarely on lime. T, upland, rare in B.

18 **Alpine Catchfly*** *Lychnis alpina*
Short tufted perennial with lanceolate leaves and smooth stems ending in a compact cluster of flowers, smaller (6-12 mm) and pinker than Sticky Catchfly and *deeply* notched; June-July. Bare places in mountains. B (rare), S.

18 **Corn Cockle*** *Agrostemma githago*
Tall, hairy annual. Leaves narrow lanceolate. Flowers pale red-purple, petals notched, sepals hairy, forming a tube with five *long*, narrow, spreading teeth, projecting well beyond the petals; May-Aug. Cornfields. T, southern, decreasing.

18 **Soapwort*** *Saponaria officinalis*
Medium/tall, often rather straggling, hairless perennial, with runners. Leaves lanceolate. Flowers soft pink, the petals not notched, apparently stalked, and *standing clear* of the scarcely inflated sepals; styles two; June-Sept. Hedges and woods by streams, waysides. T, lowland, but (B). A double-flowered form is a frequent escape in B.

19 **Small-flowered Catchfly*** *Silene gallica*
Short/medium, stickily hairy annual. Leaves lanceolate, the lower broadest near tip. Flowers 10-12 mm, mostly pointing in one direction; petals notched, white or pink, sometimes with a deep red spot (var. *quinquevulnera*, illustrated); June-Oct. Sandy places. B, F, G.

19 **Sand Catchfly*** *Silene conica*
Short, stickily hairy, greyish annual. Leaves narrow lanceolate. Flowers 4-5 mm, variably pink, the sepal-tube soon *swelling*, clearly veined but shorter than petals; May-June. Sandy places, mostly near the coast. B, F, G, southern.

plate 19 **Berry Catchfly*** *Cucubalus baccifer*
Medium/tall downy perennial with rather brittle branches. Flowers about 18 mm, drooping, greenish-white, petals deeply cleft; July-Sept. Fruit a round, *black berry*. Shady places. (B), F, G, eastern.

19 **Fastigiate Gypsophila** *Gypsophila fastigiata*
Very variable low/tall perennial, hairless below, downy above. Leaves linear, 20-80 mm. Flowers 5-8 mm, *white or lilac*, in a dense, *flat-topped* head, petals notched, less than twice as long as sepals; styles two; June-Sept. Dry rocks. G, S, southern, scattered.

19 **Annual Gypsophila** *Gypsophila muralis*
Low/short, usually hairless annual. Leaves linear, 5-25 mm, greyish. Flowers 4 mm, *pink*, in a *loose cluster*, petals slightly notched, twice as long as sepals; styles two; June-Oct. Damp woods and meadows. F, G, S, southern.

19 **Cow Basil*** *Vaccaria pyramidata*
Medium greyish hairless annual with a regularly branching stem. Leaves oval. Flowers pink, 10-15 mm, long-stalked, with an inflated, *winged* sepal-tube; June-July. Arable fields, often on lime. (B, casual), F, G.

19 **Tunic Flower*** *Petrorhagia saxifraga*
Short/medium, usually hairless perennial. Leaves linear. Flowers pale pink or white, usually solitary, on long stalks, in a *loose head*, petals notched; June-Aug. Dry sandy places and walls. (B, rare), F, G, southern.

19 **Proliferous Pink** *Petrorhagia prolifera*
Short/medium hairless annual. Leaves linear, fused into a sheath at the base, about as long as wide. Flowers pink, in *dense clusters*, each surrounded by several large, *brown, papery bracts*; flowers opening one or two at a time; petals notched; May-Sept. Dry, open places, usually on lime. F, G, S, southern.

PINKS
Dianthus

Perennials (except Deptford Pink) with stiff, greyish linear leaves. Flowers white, pink, or red, with sepals fused into an unribbed tube, surrounded by an epicalyx of 2-6 scales.

20 **Cheddar Pink*** *Dianthus gratianopolitanus*
Short, hairless, densely tufted with *long*, creeping sterile shoots. Leaves *rough-edged*. Flowers 20-30 mm, solitary, fragrant, pale pink, petals shortly toothed; epicalyx with 2-4 short segments, pointed, May-July. Sunny rocks, often on lime. B (rare), F, G, scattered.

20 **Clove Pink*** *Dianthus caryophyllus*
Short/medium, hairless, tufted, with *smooth-edged* leaves; sterile shoots short. Flowers 35-40 mm,

sometimes in loose groups of up to five, fragrant, pink, petals *shortly toothed*; epicalyx as Cheddar Pink; July-Aug. Walls. (T) from S Europe. Also widely cultivated as Carnation.

20 **Wild Pink*** *Dianthus plumarius*
Short, with the habit of Clove Pink but *rough-edged* leaves. Flowers 25-35 mm, fragrant, pink or white, the petals *cut to half-way* into narrow, feathery lobes; epicalyx with 2-4 pointed segments up to one-third as long as sepal tube; June-Aug. Walls. (T, southern) from S E Europe.

20 **Jersey Pink** *Dianthus gallicus*
Short/medium, loosely tufted, *downy*. Leaves stiff, very short, not more than 15 mm. Flowers 20-30 mm, mauve pink, the petals as in Wild Pink, but less deeply lobed; epicalyx as in Cheddar Pink; June-Aug. Coastal sand dunes. F.

20 **Large Pink** *Dianthus superbus*
Medium/tall, branching, hairless. Flowers *30-50 mm*, pink, the petals as in Wild Pink but divided *almost to the base*; epicalyx long, pointed; June-Sept. Dry, often shady places. F, G, S, southeastern.

20 **Maiden Pink*** *Dianthus deltoides*
Short/medium, loosely tufted, with *short*, creeping sterile shoots; flower-stems *roughly hairy*. Leaves short, roughly hairy at the edges. Flowers 15-20 mm, pale pink, spotted, petals toothed; epicalyx usually with two long-pointed scales half as long as the sepal-tube; June-Sept. Dry grassy, usually sandy places. T.

20 **Deptford Pink*** *Dianthus armeria*
Medium stiff hairy *annual*, dark green, not greyish. Leaves shortly sheathed at the base. Flowers 8-15 mm, bright pink or red, in dense 2-10-flowered clusters, surrounded by *long, green, leafy bracts*; epicalyx with two scales as long as the softly hairy sepal-tube; June-Aug. Dry sandy places and tracksides. T, southern.

20 **Carthusian Pink** *Dianthus carthusianorum*
Variable, medium, hairless, with leaf-sheaths several times longer than the diameter of the stem. Flowers about 20 mm, usually bright pink or red, in dense clusters surrounded by *short brown bracts*; epicalyx half as long as dark sepal-tube; May-Aug. Dry grassy places and open woods. F, G, eastern.

WATER-LILY FAMILY
Nymphaeaceae

Hairless perennials of stagnant and slow-flowing fresh water. They root in the mud and have large floating leaves on long stalks, and conspicuous flowers.

21 **Yellow Water-lily*** *Nuphar lutea*
Leaves oval, larger than White Water-lily up to 40 cm, and some thin and *submerged*. Flowers yel-

low, much smaller than White Water-lily to 60 mm held a few cm above the water surface; June-Sept. Fruits roundish, warty. Still or slow-flowing water, sometimes deeper than White Water-lily. T, lowland.

21 **Least Water-lily*** *Nuphar pumila*
Similar to Yellow Water-lily but smaller with flowers to 30 mm and larger gaps between the petals; June-July. Hybridises with Yellow Water-lily and intermediates occur, sometimes in the absence of both parents. Stagnant water, mainly upland.

21 **White Water-lily*** *Nymphaea alba*
All leaves *floating*, almost circular, rather broader than the flowers, the lobes at the base not overlapping. Flowers 50-200 mm, white, fragrant; June-Sept. Fruits carafe-shaped, smooth. Still, shallow water. T, southern in S.

BUTTERCUP FAMILY
Ranunculaceae

Includes a very mixed bag of rather primitive plants, all with many stamens and normally five, usually very prominent, petals or petal-like sepals. The flowers often contain small honey-leaves or nectaries, which secrete nectar.

21 **Stinking Hellebore*** *Helleborus foetidus*
Tall foetid perennial with over-wintering stems. Leaves palmate, simply divided, all *on the stem*, the uppermost undivided. Flowers *bell-shaped*, petalless, sepals yellow-green, purple-tipped, in clusters. Jan-May. Dry woods and scrub, mainly on lime. B, F, G, southern.

21 **Green Hellebore*** *Helleborus viridis*
Short perennial with *two root leaves* that die before winter; all leaves palmately divided, except in the south and east where forms with undivided leaves occur. Flowers spreading, larger than one, petalless, the sepals dull green like the leaves; Feb-Apr. Damp woods in thick leaf-mould. B, F, G, southern.

21 **Love-in-a-mist*** *Nigella damascena*
Short, branched annual. Leaves divided into *thread-like* segments. Flowers solitary, with five pale blue sepals, *surrounded* by feathery leaves; June-July. Dry, open places. (B, casual, F), from Mediterranean.

21 **Winter Aconite*** *Eranthis hyemalis*
Low hairless perennial. Leaves palmately lobed, all from roots and appearing after flower-stem has died down, except for three which form a *ruff* immediately below the solitary flower, sepals yellow, usually six; Jan-Mar. Woods, naturalised from gardens. (B, F, G, scattered), from S Europe.

22 **Globe Flower*** *Trollius europaeus*
Short/medium hairless perennial. Leaves palmate, deeply cut. Flowers large, almost *spherical*, petalless, the ten yellow sepals curving in at the top; May-Aug. Damp, grassy places, mainly upland. T.

22 **Marsh Marigold*** *Caltha palustris*
Short stout hairless perennial; dwarf and creeping on mountains. Leaves large, *kidney-shaped*, toothed, dark green, shiny, and often mottled paler on the upper surface. Flowers variable, 10-50 mm, with five yellow sepals and no petals; Mar-Aug. Fruit rather pod-like, clustered, conspicuous in summer. Wet places. T.

BUTTERCUPS
Ranunculus

Mostly have shiny yellow flowers (except Large White and Glacier, p. 14) and both petals and sepals, distinguishing them from Globe Flower and Marsh Marigold.

22 **Meadow Buttercup*** *Ranunculus acris*
Medium/tall hairy perennial with characteristic 2-7-lobed leaves, rather rounded in outline, the end lobe *unstalked*. Flower-stalks unfurrowed, sepals *erect*, nectaries golden-yellow; Apr-Oct. Meadows, damp grassy places. T.

22 **Bulbous Buttercup*** *Ranunculus bulbosus*
Short, very hairy perennial with stem-base swollen. Leaves like three but less deeply lobed and end lobe *stalked*. Sepals *turned downwards*, flower-stalks furrowed; Mar-June. Drier grassland than Meadow and Creeping Buttercups, and prefers lime. T.

22 **Creeping Buttercup*** *Ranunculus repens*
Short/medium, slightly hairy, creeping perennial, with rooting *runners*. Leaves rather triangular in outline, end lobe *stalked*. Resembles Bulbous more than Meadow Buttercup, but sepals erect. May-Sept. Damp, often bare places. T.

22 **Greater Spearwort*** *Ranunculus lingua*
Tall hairless perennial with long *runners*. Leaves to 25 cm long, *lanceolate*, toothed. Flowers *more than* 20 mm, stalks not furrowed; June-Sept. Marshes and fens, becoming rare. T, scattered.

22 **Lesser Spearwort*** *Ranunculus flammula*
Very variable, usually short/medium, hairless perennial, sometimes creeping and then rooting at some leaf-junctions of the often reddish stem, but with *no* runners. Leaves *lanceolate*, short- or unstalked, to 4 cm, more or less toothed. Flowers *7-20 mm*, stalks furrowed; June-Oct. Wet places. T.

22 **Lesser Celandine*** *Ranunculus ficaria*
Low/short hairless perennial with rather fleshy, dark green, heart-shaped leaves. In shady places may have bulbils at base of leaf-stalk. Usually 8-12 narrow petals, whitening when old; Mar-May. Woods, hedge-banks, bare damp ground. T.

23 **Goldilocks Buttercup*** *Ranunculus auricomus*
Short, slightly hairy perennial with lowest leaves only slightly lobed. Flowers few, sepals purple-tinged, petals 0-5, often *distorted* and sometimes *absent*, otherwise resembling a slender Meadow Buttercup (above); Apr-May. Woods, hedges. T.

13

BUTTERCUP FAMILY

plate 23 **Celery-leaved Buttercup*** *Ranunculus sceleratus*
Medium hairless annual with palmately lobed shiny leaves. Flowers numerous, small, petals *no longer* than down-turned sepals; May-Sept. Fruit head conical, with several hundred seeds. In or near slow or stagnant water. T, lowland.

23 **Corn Buttercup*** *Ranunculus arvensis*
Short/medium hairless annual with small (4-12 mm) pale yellow flowers on unfurrowed stalks, and spreading sepals; May-July. Fruit *spiny*, strongly ridged. Cornfield weed, often in rather damp places on lime. T, southern.

23 **Small-flowered Buttercup*** *Ranunculus parviflorus*
Short hairy, usually sprawling annual. somewhat unbuttercup-like; stem leafy. Root leaves circular. Flowers tiny (3-6 mm), on furrowed stalks, petals no longer than down-turned sepals; May-July. Bare, dry places on lime. B,F. south-western.

23 **Large White Buttercup** *Ranunculus platanifolius*
Tall perennial. Leaves large, shallowly 5-7-lobed. Flowers 20 mm, *white*, on long hairless stalks; May-Aug. Damp woods, mainly lowland. F, G.

23 **Glacier Buttercup** *Ranunculus glacialis*
Low hairless perennial with thick 3-5-lobed leaves. Flowers large, solitary or few, white or pinkish, sepals with purple-brown hairs; June-Aug. Stony ground in mountains near snow-line, not on lime. S.

WATER CROWFOOTS
Ranunculus subgenus *Batrachium*

Grow in all freshwater habitats from mud to swift water. Leaves palmately lobed when floating and/or much divided and feathery when submerged. Flowers white, petals with yellow claw. Most are very similar, and often best identified on habitat and leaf-type.

23 **Common Water Crowfoot*** *Ranunculus aquatilis*
Very variable annual/perennial, with submerged leaves branching in three planes and usually also *toothed* floating leaves. Flowers 10-20 mm, nectaries circular. Fruit-stalk shorter than leaf-stalk; Apr-Sept. Still or slow water to 1 m deep. T.

23 **Ivy-leaved Crowfoot*** *Ranunculus hederaceus*
Creeping annual/perennial, with all leaves ivy-shaped. Flowers 3-6 mm, petals equalling sepals; Apr-Sept. Shallow water, rarely in limestone areas. T, western.

MEADOW-RUES
Thalictrum

Have flowers in clusters with four inconspicuous petals and no sepals but long stamens which give the flowers their colour and rather shaggy appearance. Leaves 2-3-pinnate.

24 **Common Meadow-rue*** *Thalictrum flavum*
Tall, almost hairless perennial. End leaflet *longer* than broad. Flowers erect, densely crowded, with whitish petals and long yellow stamens; June-Aug. Wet meadows. T.

24 **Greater Meadow-rue*** *Thalictrum aquilegifolium*
Tall hairless perennial. Leaflets about as long as broad. Flowers larger than Common and Lesser Meadow-rue, greenish-white petals and very long, *broad* lilac-coloured stamens; June-July. Woods, meadows. (B), G, S, eastern.

24 **Lesser Meadow-rue*** *Thalictrum minus*
Variable medium (in dry places) to tall (in wet places) perennial. End leaflet roughly *as long as broad*. Flowers yellowish or purplish, in loose clusters; June-Aug. Sand dunes, turf, rocks and mountain ledges, and by streams, mainly on lime. T, scattered.

24 **Alpine Meadow-rue*** *Thalictrum alpinum*
The smallest Meadow-rue, a short delicate unbranched perennial. Leaves 2-trefoil, end leaflet rounded. Flowers purple, in an unbranched stalked spike; stamens violet with yellow anthers; May-July. Damp turf, ledges, usually in mountains. B, S, northern.

24 **Baneberry*** *Actaea spicata*
Medium hairless perennial, strong smelling, rather umbellifer-like, with large, long-stalked 2-pinnate or 2-trifoliate root leaves. Flowers white, in stalked spikes; petals short, usually four, stamens long, *white*, conspicuous; May-July. Fruit a large, shiny *black berry*. Woods and limestone pavements. T, eastern, rare in B.

24 **Traveller's Joy*** *Clematis vitalba*
Tall clambering woody perennial, sometimes with immensely long stems. Leaves pinnate, often with twining stalks. Flowers fragrant, with four greenish petals and conspicuous stamens; July-Sept. Fruit with long, grey, hairy *plumes*, in dense clusters, persisting through the winter, giving rise to the name Old Man's Beard. Hedges and scrub on lime, B, F, G, southern.

24 **Alpine Clematis** *Clematis alpina*
A much smaller plant than Traveller's Joy, with 2-pinnate leaves and larger, solitary, showy *violet* flowers; May-July. Fruit with similar hairy plumes. Rocky mountain woods. G, S, rare.

25 **Columbine*** *Aquilegia vulgaris*
Tall, branching perennial with 2-trifoliate leaves, the leaflets rounded, dull green. Flowers characteristic, each sepal with a *long spur*, usually violet, but sometimes pink or white, especially when escaped from gardens; May-July. Woods and scrub, on lime. T.

25 **Monkshood*** *Aconitum napellus*
Tall hairless perennial, with leaves palmately divided almost to the midrib. Flowers large, *violet*

14

or blue, broadly hooded, in long spikes; May-Sept. Damp woods and by streams. B, F, G, southern.

25 **Variegated Monkshood** *Aconitum variegatum*
Similar to Monkshood but has flowers blue, white or variegated, the hood taller, almost conical. Mountain woods. G, southern.

25 **Wolfsbane** *Aconitum vulparia*
Tall hairless perennial with leaves palmately divided to midrib. Flowers pale yellow, narrowly hooded, in branched spikes; June-Aug. Very shady, damp woods. F, G, eastern.

25 **Forking Larkspur*** *Consolida regalis*
Short, downy annual; widely branched. Leaves much divided into many very narrow segments. Flowers deep purple, *long-spurred* in a loose spike; flower-stalks much longer than their leaf-like bracts; June-Aug. Fruit hairless. Arable fields on lime. T, but casual in B.

25 **Yellow Pheasant's-eye** *Adonis vernalis*
Short perennial, stem scaly at base. Leaves 2-3-pinnate, feathery. Flowers large, 40-80 mm across, *yellow*, with more than ten petals; Apr-May. Dry grassland. F, G, S, south-eastern.

25 **Large Pheasant's-eye** *Adonis flammea*
Short/medium annual, like Summer Pheasant's-eye, but flowers larger (25-30 mm) and sepals *hairy* at least at base and pressed against petals; June-July. Arable fields on lime. F, G.

25 **Summer Pheasant's-eye** *Adonis aestivalis*
Short hairless annual with feathery 3-pinnate leaves, the lower stalked. Flowers *red* (or yellow, var. *citrina*) 15-25 mm, with prominent black centres and black anthers; sepals hairless, touching with 5-8 spreading petals; June-July. Arable fields on lime. F, G.

25 **Mousetail*** *Myosurus minimus*
Low hairless annual. Leaves linear, slightly fleshy, all in a basal tuft. Flowers small, solitary, long-stalked, 5-7-petalled, greenish-yellow, with a greatly elongated plantain-like fruit head, fancifully likened to a mouse's tail. Bare, usually damp ground. T.

ANEMONES
Anemone and *Pulsatilla*

Conspicuous, solitary flowers, opening in spring, with brightly coloured sepals and no petals. *Pulsatilla* usually has six, and *Anemone* more than six sepals.

26 **Pasque Flower*** *Pulsatilla vulgaris*
Low hairy perennial. Leaves 2-pinnate, feathery, covered with long hairs. Flowers large, purple, *bell-shaped*, 50-80 mm, erect at first, later drooping, anthers bright yellow; Mar-May. Fruit with long, silky plumes, sometimes persisting into late summer. Dry grassland on lime. T, southern.

26 **Pale Pasque Flower** *Pulsatilla vernalis*
Short hairy perennial. Leaves much less divided than in Pasque Flower, with broader lobes and fewer, shorter hairs. Flowers similar to Pasque Flower, but *white* inside and violet or pink outside, drooping at first, later erect; Apr-June. Stem lengthening in fruit. Meadows, especially in mountains. F, G, S, eastern.

26 **Small Pasque Flower** *Pulsatilla pratensis*
Low hairy perennial, much resembling Pasque Flower, but flowers smaller (40 mm), always *drooping*; dark purple in the north, paler southwards; May. Root leaves very feathery, stem lengthening in fruit. Meadows. G, S.

26 **Eastern Pasque Flower** *Pulsatilla patens*
Differs from Pasque Flower in having broadly lobed root leaves, and *spreading* petals, so that flower is not bell-shaped; Apr-May. Meadows. S.

26 **Wood Anemone*** *Anemone nemorosa*
Low/short hairless perennial. Stem leaves three, long-stalked, deeply palmately lobed, in a whorl just below the flower; root leaves similar, appearing after flowers, few, sometimes absent. Flowers solitary, white, 20-40 mm, sometimes pinkish, especially on the underside of the 6-12 hairless sepals; Mar-May. Deciduous woods, except on very acid soils, mountain meadows. T.

26 **Yellow Anemone*** *Anemone ranunculoides*
Short hairy perennial. Leaves like Wood Anemone, those on the stem very short-stalked. Flowers bright *yellow*, buttercup-like, 15-20 mm, usually solitary and with 5-8 sepals, hairy beneath; Mar-May. Woods. T, but (B).

26 **Snowdrop Windflower** *Anemone sylvestris*
Short/medium hairy perennial. Leaves palmately lobed. Flowers white, to 70 mm, with only *five* sepals, hairy beneath, anthers yellow; Apr-June. Dry woods on lime. F, G, S, southern.

26 **Hepatica** *Hepatica nobilis*
Low/short hairless perennial. Leaves *3-lobed*, untoothed, evergreen and purplish below. Flowers solitary, 15-25 mm, usually blue-purple, occasionally pink or white, with 6-9 sepals and three sepal-like bracts immediately below them; anthers whitish; Mar-Apr. Woods and scrub on lime. F, G, S.

BARBERRY FAMILY
Berberidaceae

27 **Barberry*** *Berberis vulgaris*
Deciduous shrub to 4 m; stem with 3-pointed *spines*. Leaves oval, sharply toothed. Flowers yellow, in drooping spikes; May-June. Fruit a bright red berry. Hedges, dry woods, often on lime. T, southern.

15

FUMITORY AND POPPY FAMILIES

plate 27 **Oregon Grape*** *Mahonia aquifolium*
Much shorter than Barberry, with spineless stem,
leaves pinnate and spine-toothed, flowers fragrant,
in erect spikes, and fruit blue-black; Mar-May.

FUMITORY FAMILY
Fumariaceae

Mostly rather floppy, hairless plants with leaves
several times pinnately divided, and characteristic
tubular, two-lipped, spurred flowers. Fumitories
Fumaria are mostly annual weeds of arable fields
and waste places.

27 **Yellow Corydalis*** *Corydalis lutea*
Short perennial with leafy stems and leaves ending
in a leaflet. Flowers bright *yellow*, in dense spikes
opposite upper leaves; May-Sept. Fruit drooping.
Walls. (B, F, G), from S Europe.

27 **Pale Corydalis*** *Corydalis ochroleuca*
Similar to Yellow Corydalis. Leaf-stalks narrowly
winged, cream-coloured flowers, and an erect fruit.
Walls and rocks.

27 **Bulbous Corydalis*** *Corydalis solida*
Short perennial with only *1-3 leaves* on the stem and
a scale below the lowest leaf; leaflets in threes.
Flowers 18-30 mm long, pink-purple, more than ten
to each rather lax, *terminal* spike; bracts lobed;
Apr-May. Woods, hedges. T but (B).

27 **Climbing Corydalis*** *Corydalis claviculata*
Medium/tall, *climbing* annual, with leaves ending in
a tendril. Flowers 5-6 mm long, creamy, 6-8 in
dense spikes opposite leaves; June-Sept. Rocky,
often wooded places, not on lime. T, western.

27 **Common Fumitory*** *Fumaria officinalis*
Much the commonest species. Weak scrambling
annual. Leaf-segments flattened. Flowers pink,
tipped darker, the largest *7-9 mm* long, sepals more
than ¼ the length of the petals; Apr-Oct. Bracts
shorter than the fruit-stalks. T.

27 **Wall Fumitory*** *Fumaria muralis*
Rather robuster than Common Fumitory, with
larger flowers 9-12 mm, 12 on each spike; spikes
shorter than their stalk; lower petals turned up at the
edges. Fruit stalks *not* curved back. Often on
hedge-banks. T, western.

27 **Ramping Fumitory*** *Fumaria capreolata*
Robust climbing annual, up to 1 m long. Flowers
white, tipped blackish-pink, the largest 10-14 mm,
on short stalks, about 20 in each spike; upper petals
compressed, lower with turned-up edges; May-
Sept. Fruit stalks *turned back*. Often in hedges. T,
southern.

27 **Small Fumitory*** *Fumaria parviflora*
Slender annual. Leaf-segments channelled. Flowers *5-6 mm*, white or pinkish, tipped darker pink in
dense 20-flowered spikes on very short stalks; sepals less than a quarter the length of the petals;
June-Sept. Bracts as long as fruit-stalks. Usually on
chalk. B, F, G, southern.

POPPY FAMILY
Papaveraceae

POPPIES
Papaver

Mostly weeds of cultivated ground with large, solitary, brightly-coloured flowers whose four petals
have a rather creased, silky appearance. They have
two sepals which fall off soon after the buds open.
Juice usually white. Leaves 1-2-pinnate.

28 **Common Poppy*** *Papaver rhoeas*
Medium, usually roughly hairy annual. Flowers
70-100 mm, deep scarlet, often with a *dark centre*,
anthers blue-black; flower-stalks with spreading
hairs; June-Oct. Pod almost *round*, hairless. Arable
fields and disturbed ground. T, southern.

28 **Prickly Poppy*** *Papaver argemone*
Short, stiffly hairy annual with hairs closely pressed
to stem. Flowers 20-60 mm, generally smaller than
Common and Long-headed Poppies, petals *pale
scarlet*, not overlapping; May-July. Pod long and
narrow, with numerous bristles. Arable fields,
especially on sandy soils. T, southern.

28 **Rough Poppy*** *Papaver hybridum*
Resembles Prickly Poppy but with a *rounded* pod,
densely covered with stiff yellow bristles. Flowers
darker, crimson; June-Aug. Arable fields, mainly on
lime. T, southern.

28 **Long-headed Poppy*** *Papaver dubium*
Medium annual, with hairs closely pressed to
stems; juice white. Flowers paler than Common
Poppy, 30-70 mm, *without* dark centres; anthers
violet; June-Aug. Pod much *longer* than wide, hairless. Arable fields and disturbed ground. T.

28 **Opium Poppy*** *Papaver somniferum*
Medium/tall, almost hairless perennial with large,
wavy, greyish leaves, irregular in outline. Flowers
up to 180 mm, from *lilac* with dark centres to white;
June-Aug. Arable fields or waste ground, mainly an
escape from cultivation. (T, southern). Grown since
early times as a source of opium.

28 **Arctic Poppy** *Papaver radicatum*
Low/short tufted hairy perennial with deeply lobed
leaves, juice white or yellow. Flowers yellow,
sometimes very pale, 20-40 mm; June-Aug. Pod
softly hairy, less than twice as long as wide. Bare,
rocky ground in mountains. S.

28 **Yellow Horned-Poppy*** *Glaucium flavum*
Medium/tall, hairless, rather greyish perennial,
with wavy edged leaves clasping the branching
stem. Root leaves more deeply lobed, all leaves
rough to the touch. Flowers 60-90 mm, yellow, variable; June-Sept. Pods *very long* up to 300 mm,
sickle-shaped, hairless. Sea shingle and waste
places inland. T, western.

28 **Welsh Poppy*** *Meconopsis cambrica*
Medium, slightly hairy perennial with long-stalked,

16

deeply lobed root leaves and similar, but short-stalked stem leaves. Flowers usually *more than 50 mm*, yellow; June-Aug. Pod hairless, longer and narrower than Arctic Poppy. Damp woods and rocks. B, F, upland and as a garden escape in B and G.

28 **Greater Celandine*** *Chelidonium majus*
Medium/tall, almost hairless perennial, its branched stems easily broken, revealing an orange juice. Leaves rather greyish, pinnately lobed. Flowers *20-25 mm*, smaller than other poppies, in clusters of 3-8; Apr-Oct. Hedges, walls, waste places, often near houses. T.

CABBAGE FAMILY
Cruciferae

Crucifers get their name from the characteristic cross made by their four, usually well separated petals; sepals four; flowers usually in stalked spikes. Seed pods are important characters and are either long and thin (siliquae), or less than three times as long as broad (siliculae) and of various shapes.

29 **Yellow Whitlow-grass*** *Draba aizoides*
Low tufted hairless perennial with stiff narrow undivided leaves but a *leafless* stem. Petals yellow, much longer than sepals; Mar-May. Pod elliptical. Rocks and walls on lime. B (rare), F, G, southern, scattered.

29 **Annual Wall Rocket*** *Diplotaxis muralis*
Short/medium, hairless annual/biennial, much branched, with stems *leafless* or almost so. Root leaves stalked, deeply pinnately lobed. Flowers 10-15 mm, deep yellow; June-Sept. Pods longer, exceeding their stalks, held at an angle to the stem. Walls, rocks, also a weed of bare and waste places. T, southern.

29 **Small Alison*** *Alyssum alyssoides*
Low/short, downy annual. Leaves small, lanceolate. Flowers tiny, *pale* yellow, 3-4 mm, in dense spikes; style *minute*; Apr-June. Pod almost *round*, the hairy sepals persisting with it. Sandy fields, often on lime. T, eastern, but (B, rare).

29 **Mountain Alison** *Alyssum montanum*. Low/short, hairy, often rather whitish perennial, with broader leaves and slightly larger flowers than Small Alison. Flowers *bright* yellow, style longer; Apr-June. Pod round, sepals not persisting. Sandy places. F, G, southern.

29 **Gold of Pleasure*** *Camelina sativa*
Short/medium, usually hairless annual. Leaves narrowly arrow-shaped, clasping the stem. Flowers 3 mm, yellow; May-July. Pod *oblong*, becoming yellowish. A weed of arable and waste places. T, a rare casual in the north and west.

29 **Ball Mustard*** *Neslia paniculata*
Medium downy annual with lanceolate leaves, sometimes slightly toothed, the lower stalked, the upper clasping the stem. Flowers yellow, 3-4 mm; June-Sept. Pods rounded, often rather flattened, *wrinkled*. Waste places. (B, casual, S), F, G, southern.

29 **Buckler Mustard** *Biscutella laevigata*
Short, slightly hairy perennial, with deeply lobed root leaves. Flowers 5-10 mm, yellow; May-July. Pod much wider than long, flattened, with two almost *circular* lobes. Dry limestone rocks, occasionally in waste places. F, G.

30 **Wallflower*** *Cheiranthus cheiri*
Medium/tall perennial with narrow lanceolate untoothed leaves covered with *flattened* hairs. Flowers *25 mm*, orange-yellow or orange-brown, fragrant; Mar-June. Pods long, flattened. Old walls, dry limestone rocks. (B, F, G), from the Mediterranean.

30 **Hedge Mustard*** *Sisymbrium officinale*
Medium/tall, *stiff*, roughly hairy (occasionally hairless) annual with spreading branches and rosette leaves deeply pinnately lobed. Flowers *3 mm*, pale yellow; May-Sept. Pods 6 20 mm, erect and closely *pressed* to stem. Waste places and hedge banks. T.

30 **Tall Rocket*** *Sisymbrium altissimum*
Tall, branched annual, hairless above. Root leaves pinnate, roughly hairy, soon dying; stem leaves unstalked, with very *narrow*, *deeply cut* lobes. Flowers 10 mm, pale yellow; June-Aug. Pods long, to 100 mm. Waste places. (T), from E Europe.

30 **Flixweed*** *Descurainia sophia*
Similar to Tall Rocket. Leaves 2-pinnate with even narrower lobes, flowers 3 mm, petals shorter than sepals, and pods 10-40 mm. T.

30 **Woad*** *Isatis tinctoria*
Medium/tall, mostly hairless biennial/perennial. Lower leaves narrow, downy; upper greyish, hairless, *arrow-shaped*, clasping the stem. Flowers 4 mm, yellow; June-Aug. Pods dark brown, oblong, *hanging*. Dry places and rocks. (T, southern), from S Europe.

30 **Warty Cabbage*** *Bunias orientalis*
Medium/tall, hairless perennial; stems warty. Leaves pinnately lobed, the topmost unlobed. Flowers sulphur-yellow, 15 mm; May-Aug. Pods rounded, *warty*, shiny, long-stalked. Waste places. (T), from E Europe.

30 **Treacle Mustard*** *Erysimum cheiranthoides*
Short/tall, *square-stemmed* annual covered with flattened branched hairs. Rosette leaves lanceolate, *shallowly* and irregularly toothed, soon dying. Flowers 6 mm, yellow, flower-stalks longer than sepals; June-Sept. Pods long, 10-30 mm, 4-angled. Waste places. T.

30 **Common Wintercress*** *Barbarea vulgaris*
Medium/tall *hairless* perennial. Leaves with 2-5

17

pairs of coarse lobes, end lobe shorter than rest of leaf; upper leaves undivided. Flowers 7-9 mm, bright yellow; May-Aug. Pods long, 15-30 mm, stiffly *erect*. Damp places and roadsides. T.

plate 30 **Great Yellowcress*** *Rorippa amphibia*
Tall hairless perennial with runners. Leaves lanceolate, toothed or pinnately lobed. Flowers 6 mm, bright yellow; June-Aug. Pods *oblong, long-stalked*. Wet places. T.

30 **Creeping Yellowcress*** *Rorippa sylvestris*
Straggling, hairless perennial with runners and short/medium flowering shoots. Leaves pinnately lobed, the upper sometimes unlobed. Flowers 5 mm, yellow, petals longer than sepals; June-Sept. Pods long, 6-18 mm, equalling stalk. Damp and bare places. T.

30 **Marsh Yellowcress*** *Rorippa palustris*
Is similar to Creeping Yellowcress, but erecter and stronger-stemmed; flowers 3 mm, petals not longer than sepals; June-Oct; pod 4-9 mm, oblong, shorter than stalk.

Wild Cabbage, Wild Turnip and Wild Radish are cultivated forms and their wild relatives, so much variability must be expected.

31 **Wild Cabbage*** *Brassica oleracea*
Medium/tall hairless perennial with a thick straggling stem, woody at the base and clearly marked with old *leaf scars*. Leaves *greyish*, pinnately lobed somewhat clasping the stem. Flowers 30-40 mm in a long spike, the unopened *buds above* the flowers; May-Sept. Sea-cliffs in B and F, western; also (T), widely cultivated as cabbage, cauliflower, etc.

31 **Wild Turnip*** *Brassica rapa*
Tall slender annual/biennial. Root leaves pinnately lobed, roughly hairy, bright green, stem leaves clasping. Flowers 20 mm, in a more or less flat-topped spike, the *flowers above* the unopened buds. Apr-Aug. Pods long. Cultivated, and on bare ground, especially by streams. (T).

31 **Black Mustard*** *Brassica nigra*
Tall, rather greyish annual. Flowers yellow, 15 mm; June-Aug. All leaves *stalked*, the lowest pinnately lobed, bristly and bright green. Pods long, pressed against stem. Waste places, sea cliffs, stream banks, woods, also cultivated. T.

31 **Charlock*** *Sinapis arvensis*
Medium/tall roughly hairy annual. Lower leaves large, irregularly lobed and toothed, the upper narrow, with pointed teeth, *unstalked* but not clasping the stem. Flowers 15-20 mm, yellow; Apr-Oct. Pods long, markedly beaded. Arable fields, waste places, most often on lime. T.

31 **Hairy Rocket*** *Erucastrum gallicum*
Short/medium, densely hairy annual. Leaves pinnately lobed, the lower stalked, the upper not clasping the stem. Flowers pale yellow, 10-15 mm, sepals erect; May-Sept. Pods *less than 40 mm long*, beaded. Waste places, dry rocks. T, southern, but (B, rare).

31 **Wallflower Cabbage*** *Rhynchosinapis cheiranthos*
Medium biennial with base of leafy stem hairy. Leaves deeply pinnately lobed. Flowers yellow, 20-25 mm; June-Aug. Pods long, *more than 40 mm*. Dry and waste places, rarely on lime. (B), F, G, south-western.

31 **Bastard Cabbage*** *Rapistrum rugosum*
Medium hairy annual whose stalked leaves have three pairs of lobes. Flowers pale yellow, 10 mm; May-Sept. Pods with *two segments*, the upper large and rounded, with an abrupt beak, the lower narrower, closely pressed to the stem. Waste ground (B, F, G), from the Mediterranean.

31 **Wild Radish*** *Raphanus raphanistrum*
Medium, roughly hairy annual, slightly resembling Charlock but with the teeth of the upper leaves blunt. Flowers larger (25-30 mm), pale yellow or white with lilac veins; May-Sept. Pods long, markedly *beaded*, and breaking easily at the joints. Bare and waste ground. T.

BITTERCRESSES
Cardamine

Have pinnate leaves (except Daisy-leaved Bittercress) and long pods.

32 **Cuckoo Flower*** *Cardamine pratensis*
Medium hairless perennial, sometimes tufted, with root leaves forming a *rosette*; stem leaves dissimilar. Flowers variable, 12-20 mm, lilac or white, anthers yellow; Apr-June. Pods to 40 mm. Damp places. T.

32 **Daisy-leaved Bittercress** *Cardamine bellidifolia*
Similar to Cuckoo Flower but dwarf and tufted, with all leaves undivided, few or none on stems, and very small (7-10 mm) white flowers. S, mountains.

32 **Large Bittercress*** *Cardamine amara*
Medium hairless perennial with basal leaves *not* in a rosette; stem leaves with *broader* leaflets than Cuckoo Flower. Flowers white, 12 mm, anthers violet; Apr-June. Damp or wet places, often in woods. T.

32 **Radish-leaved Bittercress** *Cardamine raphanifolia*
Similar to Large Bittercress but taller with a large, rounded terminal leaflet, deep lilac flowers and yellow anthers. Streamsides. (B, rare), from S Europe.

32 **Coralroot Bittercress*** *Cardamine bulbifera*
Medium hairless perennial with *no root leaves*; upper stem leaves narrow lanceolate, with purple-brown *bulbils* at their base. Flowers 12-18 mm, lilac to purple; Apr-June. Pods 20-35 mm. Woods, often of beech, on lime. T, southern.

18

32 **Nine-leaved Bittercress** *Cardamine enneaphyllos*
Similar to Coralroot Bittercress. Has 2-trefoil leaves, no bulbils and drooping pale yellow or white flowers. Mountain woods. G, southern.

32 **Narrow-leaved Bittercress*** *Cardamine impatiens*
Medium hairless annual/biennial. Leaves with up to 18 *3-lobed leaflets*; leaf-stalks clasping the stem. Flowers white, but petals inconspicuous or absent; anthers greenish-yellow; May-Aug. Pods explosive when ripe. Damp, shady, often rocky places, on lime in the north. T, mainly western.

32 **Garlic Mustard*** *Alliaria petiolata*
Medium hairless biennial with long-stalked leaves, heart-shaped at the base, smelling of *garlic* when crushed. Flowers white; Apr-Aug. Pods long. Hedges and open woods. T.

32 **Dame's Violet*** *Hesperis matronalis*
Medium/tall, hairy perennial, with toothed lanceolate short-stalked leaves. Flowers 15-20 mm, white or violet, very *fragrant*; May-Aug. Pods long, to 100 mm, curving upwards. Hedges, roadsides, a frequent garden escape. (B, G, S), F.

32 **Perennial Honesty*** *Lunaria rediviva*
Tall perennial with a hairy stem. Leaves pointed oval, sharply toothed, the upper stalked. Flowers fragrant, purple, about 20 mm; May-July. Pods long, very *flattened*, elliptical with pointed tip. Damp woods, mainly on lime. T but (B), eastern.

32 **Watercress*** *Nasturtium officinale*
Short/medium *creeping* hairless perennial, with pinnate leaves, green in autumn. Flowers white; May-Oct. Pods less than 18 mm long, with two rows of seeds inside. In and beside shallow, flowing water, often on lime. T, southern.

33 **Sea Rocket*** *Cakile maritima*
Short/medium greyish hairless *succulent* annual. Leaves linear to pinnately lobed. Flowers lilac, sometimes very pale; June-Sept. Pods egg-shaped, angled. Sandy coasts. T.

33 **Sea Kale*** *Crambe maritima*
Stout medium greyish hairless perennial, making large clumps, with thick stems, woody at the base. Leaves large, rounded, fleshy, with *crinkly* lobes or teeth, but narrower up the stem. Flowers 10-15 mm, white, in a rather flat-topped head; June-Aug. Pods globular. Sea shores, on sand and shingle. T.

33 **White Ball Mustard*** *Calepina irregularis*
Medium/tall hairless annual. Stem leaves *clasping*, toothed, arrow-shaped. Flowers 2-4 mm, with unequal petals. May-June. Pods more or less spherical, beaked. Waste places, mainly on lime; not a coastal plant. (B, rare), F, G.

33 **Hoary Stock*** *Matthiola incana*
The garden plant, a medium/tall, grey, stickily hairy annual/perennial; stem leafless and usually woody at the base. Leaves narrow lanceolate, untoothed.

Flowers *30 mm*, *purple*, sometimes very pale, fragrant; May-July. Pods long, stout, hairy. Sea cliffs. B (rare), F, western.

33 **Horse-radish*** *Armoracia rusticana*
Tall hairless perennial with *large* (to 50 cm), very long-stalked, wavy-edged, toothed root leaves and *narrow*, short-stalked stem leaves. Flowers 8-9 mm, white, densely clustered on long-stalked leafy spikes; May-Aug. Pods almost spherical. Cultivated, and naturalised in damp places and waysides. (T, southern) from E Europe.

33 **Dittander*** *Lepidium latifolium*
Tall greyish hairless perennial resembling Horse-radish but with smaller shorter-stalked leaves, not wavy-edged. Flowers 2-3 mm, sepals *white-edged*; July-Aug. Pods rounded, rather flattened. Damp places, usually near the coast. T, southern.

33 **Common Scurvy-grass*** *Cochlearia officinalis*
Very variable, low/medium hairless perennial with *fleshy*, heart-shaped leaves, the upper loosely clasping the stem. Flowers white, 8-10 mm; Apr-Aug. Pod *swollen*, almost spherical. Dry saltmarshes and banks, occasionally inland. T.

33 **Early Scurvy-grass*** *Cochlearia danica*
Very variable, low/short overwintering annual, differing from Common Scurvy-grass especially in its oval pods, often lilac flowers and *stalked* upper leaves; Jan-Sept. Usually sandy places by the sea. T.

34 **Hairy Bittercress*** *Cardamine hirsuta*
Low/short, rather hairy annual, with a compact rosette of pinnate leaves, each with 3-7 pairs of leaflets. Flowers less than 5 mm, with four stamens, less obvious than *long, erect* pods; Feb-Nov. Bare open ground. T.

34 **Northern Rockcress*** *Cardaminopsis petraea*
Short, slightly hairy perennial with *lobed* lower leaves and narrow, toothed stem leaves. Flowers 5-8 mm, white, sometimes lilac; June-Aug. Pods long, strongly *flattened*. Rocks and river shingle in mountains. B, G, S.

34 **Tall Rockcress** *Cardaminopsis arenosa*
Annual/perennial, taller than Northern Rockcress and all leaves more deeply lobed. Flowers larger than Northern Rockcress, white in the north, lilac further south; Apr-June. Pods like Northern Rockcress. Sandy soils, usually lime-rich. F, G, S.

34 **Thale Cress*** *Arabidopsis thaliana*
Short/medium annual with roughly hairy, *elliptical* toothed root leaves, forming a rosette; stem leaves narrower, not stalked or clasping the stem. Flowers 3 mm, white; Mar-Oct. Pods long, only slightly flattened. Dry sandy soils and walls. T.

34 **Hairy Rockcress*** *Arabis hirsuta*
Short/medium hairy biennial/perennial with both stem leaves and long pods *tightly pressed* against

19

CABBAGE FAMILY

stem; stem leaves tapering at base; root leaves in a rosette, long oval, only slightly toothed. Flowers white, 3-5 mm, numerous; May-Aug. Dry grassland, dunes, rocks, walls, on lime. T.

plate 34 **Tower Mustard*** *Arabis glabra*
Tall, almost hairless, *grey-green* biennial with softly hairy, toothed, short-lived root leaves and arrow-shaped stem leaves *clasping* the stem. Flowers 5-6 mm, creamy; May-July. Pods long, numerous, closely pressed to stem. Dry banks, roadsides, open woods. T, eastern.

34 **Alpine Rockcress*** *Arabis alpina*
Low/short creeping hairy perennial, with long *runners*, forming conspicuous grey-green *mats*. Stem leaves deeply toothed, bases bluntly arrow-shaped. Flowers 6-10 mm, white, petals spreading; May-July. Mountain rocks. B (rare), S.

34 **Towercress*** *Arabis turrita*
Medium, softly hairy biennial/perennial with an often reddish stem. Root leaves long-stalked, densely grey-hairy. Flowers yellowish-white; Apr-July. Pods very *long*, up to 150 mm, all *twisted* to one side and downwards. Rocks, walls. (B, F, G), southern, from S Europe.

34 **Annual Rockcress** *Arabis recta*
Short, softly hairy annual with *untoothed* leaves, the oval root ones soon withering, the stem ones clasping with arrow-shaped points. Flowers white, less than 5 mm, petals erect; Apr-June. Pods long, 10-35 mm, spreading. Mountain rocks. F, G.

35 **Wild Candytuft*** *Iberis amara*
Short, slightly downy annual with more or less deeply toothed, hairless leaves scattered up the stem. Flowers 6-8 mm, white or mauve, petals *unequal*; May-Sept. Pods rounded, less than 5 mm long. Bare ground and arable fields, on lime. B, F, G, southern.

35 **Shepherd's Purse*** *Capsella bursa-pastoris*
Very variable, low/medium annual/biennial, hairy or hairless. Leaves lanceolate, pinnately lobed, deeply toothed or untoothed, mainly in a basal rosette. Flowers 2-3 mm, white; all year. Pod an inverted, notched *triangle*. Extremely common weed. T.

35 **Shepherd's Cress*** *Teesdalia nudicaulis*
Low/short, hairless annual with an almost *leafless* stem, and a rosette of pinnately lobed root leaves. Flowers 2 mm, petals unequal, not notched; June-Oct. Open sandy places, not on lime. T, mainly southern.

35 **Hoary Alison*** *Berteroa incana*
Medium hairy annual, grey with hairs. Leaves lanceolate, untoothed. Flowers 5-8 mm, white, petals deeply *cleft*; June-Oct. Pods oval. Casual on waste ground. (B, F, S), G, eastern.

35 **Sweet Alison*** *Lobularia maritima*
Short, densely hairy, greyish perennial, with *narrow* untoothed leaves. Flowers 5-6 mm, fragrant, white, petals not notched; June-Sept. A garden escape, especially near the sea. (T), from S Europe.

35 **Wall Whitlow-grass*** *Draba muralis*
Short hairy annual with sparsely leafy stem. Leaves rounded, toothed, *partly clasping* the stem. Flowers 2-3 mm, white, petals not notched; Apr-June. Pods elliptical, 5 mm, spreading. Rocks and walls, mainly on lime. T, scattered.

35 **Common Whitlow-grass*** *Erophila verna*
Very variable, low, slightly hairy annual with a leafless stem. Leaves lanceolate, in a basal rosette. Flowers white, petals *cleft to base*, 3-6 mm; Mar-May. Pods elliptical or rounded, on long stalks. Bare, often sandy ground, rocks. T.

35 **Hutchinsia*** *Hornungia petraea*
Low hairless annual with a rosette of pinnate leaves and a leafy stem. Flowers minute, greenish-white, petals not notched; Mar-May. Pod elliptical, 2 mm. Bare sandy ground, rocks, mainly on lime. T, southern, scattered.

36 **Hoary Cress*** *Cardaria draba*
Medium, usually hairless perennial with *greyish*, pointed, toothed leaves, clasping the stem. Flowers 5-6 mm, white, stalked, in flat-topped, *umbel-like* clusters; May-June. Pods kidney-shaped, beaked. Roadsides and disturbed ground, forming clumps. T, southern.

36 **Field Pepperwort*** *Lepidium campestre*
Medium greyish annual/biennial, with many spreading hairs. Leaves lanceolate, the upper rather triangular and clasping the stem. Flowers 2-3 mm, white, petals *longer* than sepals, anthers yellow; May-Aug. Pods roundish, flattened, notched, rough, *as long* as their stalks. Dry banks, disturbed ground. T.

36 **Garden Cress*** *Lepidium sativum*
Short hairless, strong-smelling annual, the cress used for salads. Leaves *linear*, not clasping the stem, the lower pinnate. Flowers sometimes reddish, 4-5 mm, petals longer than sepals; June-July. Pod roundish, flattened *longer* than its stalk. Disturbed ground. (T), from W Asia.

36 **Narrow-leaved Pepperwort*** *Lepidium ruderale*
Short/medium, almost hairless annual/biennial, smelling strongly like Garden Cress, with pinnate root leaves and narrow undivided stem leaves. Flowers green, usually petalless; May-Sept. Pods oval, flattened, *shorter* than their stalks. Waste places, commonest near coasts. T.

36 **Field Pennycress*** *Thlaspi arvense*
Short/medium hairless, foetid annual with broad lanceolate toothed leaves clasping the stem, the

20

lower not in a rosette. Flowers 4-6 mm, white, anthers yellow; May-Aug. Pods rounded, with *broad*, almost translucent *wings*, the very short style persisting in a deep notch. Cultivated and waste ground. T.

36 **Alpine Pennycress*** *Thlaspi alpestre*
Very variable short hairless perennial with non-flowering rosettes. All leaves *untoothed*, somewhat clasping the stem. Flowers white or mauve, 4-8 mm, anthers violet; Apr-July. Pods heart-shaped, winged, the style usually projecting beyond the notch. Limestone rocks and lead-mine debris, and in mountain woods away from lime. T, scattered, eastern.

36 **Perfoliate Pennycress*** *Thlaspi perfoliatum*
Is low/short and rather greyish, with all leaf rosettes flowering. Leaves lanceolate, deeply clasping stem. Flowers white, anthers yellow; Apr-May. Pods heart-shaped, winged. Stony and waste ground, on lime. T, southern, rare in B.

36 **Mountain Pennycress** *Thlaspi montanum*
Short hairless mat-forming perennial, with *sparsely leafy* stems. Root leaves long-stalked. Flowers 10-12 mm, anthers yellow; Apr-June. Pods heart-shaped, flattened, broadly winged, style projecting beyond notch. Rocky grassland, on lime. F, G, southern.

36 **Swinecress*** *Coronopus squamatus*
Prostrate annual/biennial. Leaves 1-2-pinnate, leaflets narrow. Flowers 2-3 mm, white, in small clusters opposite leaves; June-Sept. Pods longer than stalks, rounded, clearly 2-lobed, warty, *not* notched, with prominent style. Characteristic weed of paths and *trodden* ground. T, southern.

36 **Lesser Swinecress*** *Coronopus didymus*
More delicate than Swinecress, often *semi-erect*, with a pungent smell and more feathery leaves. Flowers 1-2 mm, white or petalless; June-Sept. Pods shorter than stalks, more obviously 2-lobed than Swinecress, and *notched*, with obscure style. Waste places. T, southern.

MIGNONETTE FAMILY
Resedaceae

37 **Weld*** *Reseda luteola*
Tall hairless unbranched biennial. Leaves lanceolate, *untoothed*, wavy-edged. Flowers 4-5 mm, yellow-green, with *four* sepals and petals; June-Sept. Pods globular, erect. Disturbed ground, often on lime. T, southern.

37 **Wild Mignonette*** *Reseda lutea*
Medium branched biennial/perennial, the stem clothed with small *pinnate* leaves. Flowers 6 mm, yellow-green, with *six* sepals and petals; June-Sept. Pods oblong, erect. Disturbed ground, often on lime. T, southern.

SUNDEW FAMILY
Droseraceae

Insectivorous plants, whose leaves are covered with long sticky hairs which curve inwards to trap insects.

37 **Common Sundew*** *Drosera rotundifolia*
Low/short perennial with a leafless flower-stem more than twice as long as the neat rosette of *round* red leaves with long stalks. Flowers 5 mm, white, 5-petalled, in a shortly stalked spike, arising from the rosette; June-Aug. Hybridises with Great Sundew. Wet heaths and moors, sphagnum bogs, never on lime. T.

37 **Oblong-leaved Sundew*** *Drosera intermedia*
Differs from Common Sundew in its long *narrow* leaves, tapering to their shorter hairless stalks. Flower-stem arising from *below* rosette and curving upwards. Habitat similar. T, rather scattered.

37 **Great Sundew*** *Drosera anglica*
Similar to Oblong-leaved Sundew but with larger longer leaves and flower-stem arising from rosette. Sometimes on lime. Northern.

GRASS OF PARNASSUS FAMILY
Parnassiaceae

37 **Grass of Parnassus*** *Parnassia palustris*
Short hairless tufted perennial with a rosette of heart-shaped, untoothed, stalked leaves and a stem with a *single* leaf and a *solitary* white flower, 15-30 mm, with five clearly veined petals; June-Sept. Wet, marshy places. T.

STONECROP FAMILY
Crassulaceae

Mostly hairless perennials with untoothed, fleshy, un- or short-stalked leaves. Flowers star-like, usually conspicuous, with five petals and sepals. Characteristic of dry rocky places and walls.

37 **Navelwort*** *Umbilicus rupestris*
Low/medium hairless perennial, the *round* fleshy leaves with a 'navel' in the centre, above the leaf-stalk; stem leaves less rounded. Flowers bell-shaped, toothed, greenish or pinkish-white; June-Aug. Rocks, banks, walls, not on lime. B, F, western.

37 **Roseroot*** *Rhodiola rosea*
Short hairless grey perennial, often purple-tinged. Leaves thick, stiff, *succulent*, more or less oval, often hiding the stem. Flowers yellow, 4-petalled, in rather flat-topped heads, stamens and styles on separate plants; anthers purple; May-June. Fruit orange. Mountain rocks, sea-cliffs. B, S, northern, and rare in F.

21

plate 38 **Orpine*** *Sedum telephium*
Very variable, short/tall sometimes greyish perennial, with clusters of erect, often red-tinged leafy
stems. Leaves up to 80 mm long, oblong, *flattened*,
slightly toothed, alternate. Flowers pinkish-red,
whitish, greenish or yellowish, petals spreading, in
flattened heads; July-Sept. Shady places and
woods. T.

38 **Caucasian Stonecrop*** *Sedum spurium*
Similar to Orpine. Shorter and creeping, forming
mats, with erect, downy flowering stems; leaves to
30 mm, more toothed, and larger flowers, usually
pinkish-red, rarely white, petals erect. Garden
escape. (T), from Caucasus.

38 **Biting Stonecrop*** *Sedum acre*
Low creeping evergreen with *peppery* taste. Leaves
3-6 mm, cylindrical, not spreading, yellowish,
broadest at base. Flowers 12 mm, bright yellow;
May-July. Dry, bare places, often on lime. T.

38 **White Stonecrop*** *Sedum album*
Bright green, often red-tinged, mat-forming evergreen, creeping with short, erect flowering stems.
Leaves *6-12 mm*, rarely to 25 mm, alternate, cylindrical, rather flattened on the upper surface. Flowers 6-9 mm, *white*, in a dense, much-branched,
flat-topped head; June-Aug. Rocks, walls. T,
southern.

38 **Reflexed Stonecrop*** *Sedum reflexum*
Short creeping evergreen, with short, erect
flowering shoots and low leafy non-flowering ones.
Leaves 8-20 mm, *cylindrical*, not persisting when
dead. Flowers 15 mm, *yellow*, usually with seven
petals and sepals; June-Aug. Rocks, walls. T,
southern, but (B).

38 **Alpine Stonecrop** *Sedum alpestre*
Low evergreen, somewhat resembling Biting
Stonecrop but not peppery. Leaves rather flattened,
parallel-sided. Flowers 6-8 mm, dull yellow; June-
July. Mountain rocks, not on lime. F, G.

38 **English Stonecrop*** *Sedum anglicum*
Low mat-forming evergreen, greyish but soon
reddening. Leaves *3-5 mm*, cylindrical, alternate.
Flowers 12 mm, *white* (pink below), the flowerhead
much less branched than White Stonecrop; June-
Sept. B, F, S, western, rarely on lime.

38 **Hairy Stonecrop*** *Sedum villosum*
Low, reddish, *downy* biennial. Leaves 6-12 mm,
alternate, flattened on the upper surface. Flowers
6 mm, *pink*, on long stalks; stamens ten; June-Aug.
Wet places and by streams, in mountains. T.

38 **Annual Stonecrop** *Sedum annuum*
Low hairless annual/biennial. Leaves flattened on
both surfaces, 6 mm. Flowers *yellow*, short-
stalked; June-Aug. G, S, only on mountains in the
south.

38 **Mossy Stonecrop*** *Crassula tillaea*
Very low moss-like annual, with tiny crowded

broad opposite leaves pressed against stem. Flowers white, 1-2 mm, petals usually three, shorter than
sepals. June-Sept. Damp sandy places, wet in
winter. B, F, G, western.

38 **Hen-and-Chickens Houseleek** *Jovibarba sobolifera*
Succulent perennial with leaves in roundish rosettes, often tipped red. Flowers pale yellow, bell-
shaped, 6-petalled. July-Aug. Dry, often sandy
grassland. G.

SAXIFRAGE FAMILY
Saxifragaceae

Rather short perennials (except Rue-leaved Saxifrage). Leaves alternate (except Purple Saxifrage).
Stamens ten, petals, sepals, styles five. Fruit a capsule in two parts, often joined at the base.

37 **Opposite-leaved Golden Saxifrage*** *Chrysosplenium oppositifolium*
Low creeping perennial, slightly hairy; stem
square. Leaves roundish, bluntly toothed, opposite;
root leaves as long as stalks. Flowers 3-4 mm,
greenish, *without* petals, sepals four, stamens eight,
anthers bright yellow; Mar-July. Wet places. T,
but western in S.

37 **Alternate-leaved Golden Saxifrage*** *Chrysosplenium alternifolium*
Similar to Opposite-leaved Golden Saxifrage.
Triangular stem, alternate, broader, more toothed
leaves, root leaves on long stalks, and flowers
5-6 mm. Eastern.

39 **Starry Saxifrage*** *Saxifraga stellaris*
Low/short, sparsely hairy, with leafless stem and a
rosette of very short-stalked, *toothed* leaves. Flowers white, in a lax head, 10-15 mm, with conspicuous red anthers; sepals turned down; June-Aug. The
commonest white-flowered mountain saxifrage; in
wet places. T.

39 **St Patrick's Cabbage*** *Saxifraga spathularis*
Loosely tufted, with short, leafless flower-stem.
Leaves spoon-shaped, mostly in rosettes, hairless,
with pointed teeth and a narrow *translucent* margin;
stalks long, flattened. Petals 4-5 mm, white with
several *red spots*, sepals turned down; June-July.
Rocks, not on lime. Ireland.

39 **Arctic Saxifrage*** *Saxifraga nivalis*
Low, with basal rosette of small, thick leaves,
15-30 mm, rounded, coarsely toothed, *purple*
beneath, and sticky at the edges. Flower-stalks
leafless, very hairy. Flowers *whitish*, unstalked, in a
crowded head, petals unspotted; sepals spreading;
July-Aug. B, S, mountains.

39 **Rue-leaved Saxifrage*** *Saxifraga tridactylites*
Low, erect, *stickily hairy* annual, often reddish.
Upper leaves spoon-shaped, 3-5-lobed, the lower
untoothed; all leaves on stem. Flowers about 5 mm,
white, with notched petals; Mar-June. Walls, bare
places, lowland, mainly on lime. T, southern.

39 **Yellow Saxifrage*** *Saxifraga aizoides*
Low/short, very *leafy*, slightly hairy. Leaves
10-20 mm, narrow, *unstalked*, fleshy. Flowers in
loose head, petals *yellow*, well spaced; June-Sept.
Streams and wet places in mountains. B, G, S.

39 **Meadow Saxifrage*** *Saxifraga granulata*
Short/medium, downy, with *bulbils* at leaf-bases,
but no barren shoots. Leaves kidney-shaped, shallowly lobed, mainly basal. Flowers 20-30 mm,
white, not spotted, in loose clusters; Apr-June.
Grassy places, lowland. T.

39 **Highland Saxifrage*** *Saxifraga rivularis*
Very low, hairless, with runners from bulbils at
stem base; stem leafy. Leaves stalked, with *3-5
blunt lobes*. Flowers few, 6-10 mm, dowdy, white;
July-Aug. Wet mountain rocks. B (rare), S.

39 **Mossy Saxifrage*** *Saxifraga hypnoides*
Low/short, hairy, with many long, leafy, *barren*
shoots forming a mat. Leaves long-hairy, usually
3-lobed, clustered at the end of each stem. Flowers
10-15 mm, white, buds nodding; bulbils often present; May-July. Wet, often grassy places in hills.
B, F, S, western.

39 **Purple Saxifrage*** *Saxifraga oppositifolia*
Creeping, with trailing stems covered with small,
unstalked, *opposite* leaves, often lime-encrusted.
Flowers 10-20 mm, *purple*, almost unstalked;
Apr-May, July. Damp places in mountains, often on
lime. B, S.

39 **Livelong Saxifrage** *Saxifraga paniculata*
Short, tufted with long, oblong, finely-toothed
leaves, lime-encrusted, in hemispherical rosettes.
Flower-stem long, mostly leafless, with a *loose
panicle* of white flowers; June-Aug. Mountain
rocks. F, G.

39 **Hawkweed Saxifrage** *Saxifraga hieracifolia*
Low/short, with a rosette of hairy oval leaves.
Flower stem leafless with a spike of small reddish-
green flowers. Mountains, S.

ROSE FAMILY
Rosaceae

Leaves alternate, usually pinnate, with stipules at
base of leaf-stalk. Flowers usually open with five
conspicuous petals, except for the first eight species
below, often with an epicalyx – an outer ring of
sepals below the true sepals.

40 **Meadowsweet*** *Filipendula ulmaria*
Tall hairless perennial with leafy stems. Leaves
long-stalked, pinnate, with 2-5 pairs of toothed
leaflets, each more than 20 mm, and small leaflets in
between, *stipules* green above, downy and pale
beneath. Flowers in *dense clusters*, creamy, fragrant, with five or six petals, 2-5 mm; June-Sept.
Marshes, fens, swamps, wet meadows and woods.
T.

40 **Goatsbeard Spiraea** *Aruncus dioicus*
Tall perennial with very large leaves like
Meadowsweet but *without* stipules, the flowerheads
with many long, *finger-like* branches, held more or
less horizontal; June-Aug. Mountain woods. F, G.

40 **Agrimony*** *Agrimonia eupatoria*
Medium downy perennial with pinnate leaves, not
at all sticky. Flowers 5-8 mm, *yellow*, in a spike;
June-Aug. Fruit grooved, covered with small erect
hooks at its apex. Dry grassy places, often on lime.
T.

40 **Great Burnet*** *Sanguisorba officinalis*
Medium/tall hairless perennial. Leaves pinnate,
with 3-7 pairs of leaflets, 20-40 mm long. Flowers
tiny, on dense *oblong* heads, 10-20 mm long, stamens and styles in the same flower; petals absent,
sepals deep red; June-Sept. Damp grassland. T,
southern.

40 **Salad Burnet*** *Sanguisorba minor*
Short, rather greyish, almost hairless perennial,
similar to Great Burnet, but with 4-12 pairs of
leaflets all less than 20 mm. Flowers in *round* heads,
the *upper with red styles*, the lower with yellow
stamens; sepals green, no petals; May-Sept. Dry,
grassy places, mainly on lime. T, southern.

40 **Lady's Mantle*** *Alchemilla vulgaris*
A variable collection of similar microspecies;
low/medium, usually rather densely hairy, but
sometimes hairless perennials. Leaves palmately
lobed, *not* cut to the base, *green* on both sides.
Flowers 3-5 mm, in loose clusters with an epicalyx
but no petals, sepals green, anthers yellow; May-
Sept. Grassy places. T.

40 **Alpine Lady's Mantle*** *Alchemilla alpina*
Smaller and hairier than Lady's Mantle with leaves
divided *to the base* into 5-7 narrow lobes, *silvery
grey* with hairs beneath. Flowers pale green, 3 mm;
June-Aug. Mountain grassland. T.

40 **Parsley Piert*** *Aphanes arvensis*
More or less prostrate hairy, pale green annual.
Leaves 3-lobed, toothed. Flowers minute, green, in
clusters *opposite* the leaves, surrounded by the
toothed leaf-like stipules; Apr-Oct. Bare ground. T,
southern.

ROSES
Rosa

Shrubs with thin stems armed with thorns. Leaves
pinnate, with stipules. Flowers large, white, pink or
red, with large, floppy petals, easily detached. Fruit
a berry-like hip.

41 **Dog Rose*** *Rosa canina*
Variable; stems arching, to 3 m. Thorns *curved*.
Leaves with 2-3 pairs of toothed leaflets, *hairless* or
sometimes downy beneath. Flowers 45-50 mm,
pink or white, styles not joined; June-July. Sepals

ROSE FAMILY

with narrow lobes, falling before the hips turn red. Hedges, scrub. T, commoner in the south.

plate 41 **Field Rose*** *Rosa arvensis*
Scrambling, forming bushes not more than 1 m tall, unless on other shrubs; stems green, thorns curved. Leaflets hairless, 2-3 pairs on each leaf. Flowers 30-50 mm, *always* white, the styles *joined* into a column; sepals scarcely lobed, soon falling; July-Aug. Hips red. Woods, hedges, scrub. B, F, G, southern.

41 **Burnet Rose*** *Rosa pimpinellifolia*
Suckering stems with *straight* thorns and stiff bristles, forming short bushes to 50 cm. Leaves with 3-5 pairs of small, rounded leaflets. Flowers 20-40 mm, cream, sometimes pink; sepals not lobed; May-July. Ripe hips dark purple or *black*. Dry, open places, often on coastal dunes. T.

41 **Downy Rose*** *Rosa tomentosa*
To 2 m; resembling Dog Rose but leaflets *densely downy*; thorns may be straight. Flowers 30-40 mm, deep pink, sometimes pale; June-July. Sepals pinnate, sometimes persisting till red hips fall or decay. Hedges, scrub, especially in the hills. T, northern.

41 **Bramble*** *Rubus fruticosus*
Very variable scrambling shrub armed with easily detached thorns; over 2000 microspecies have been described. Rather woody, with long biennial, usually angled stems, rooting where they touch the ground. Leaves prickly, with 3-5 leaflets. Flowers 20-30 mm, white or pink; May-Nov. Fruit (blackberry) with several fleshy segments, red at first, *purplish-black* when ripe. Woods, scrub, open and waste ground. T.

41 **Raspberry*** *Rubus idaeus*
Unbranched *erect* perennial with woody, biennial stems, armed with weak prickles. Leaves with 3-7 leaflets. Flowers smaller than Bramble, the petals *erect*, well spaced, *always* white, rather inconspicuous; May-Aug. Fruit *red* when ripe. Shady places. T, and widely cultivated.

41 **Stone Bramble*** *Rubus saxatilis*
Resembles Bramble but smaller, slenderer, prostrate, and spineless; stems annual. Leaves with three leaflets. Flowers smaller than Bramble or Raspberry, 8-10 mm, the narrow petals *no longer than* the sepals; June-Aug. Fruit red when ripe, the segments fewer and larger. Shady, rocky places, often on limestone. T, north-eastern.

41 **Cloudberry*** *Rubus chamaemorus*
Low/short creeping downy perennial with *rounded*, palmately lobed leaves. Flowers always white, conspicuous, solitary, stamens and styles on separate plants; June-Aug, but a shy flowerer in B. Fruit *orange* when ripe. Upland bogs and damp moors. B, G, S, northern.

41 **Arctic Bramble** *Rubus arcticus*
Short spineless creeping perennial. Leaves with

three leaflets, smaller than Stone Bramble. All stems flowering; flowers 15-25 mm, *bright red*, petals sometimes toothed; June-July. Moors. S, probably extinct in B.

42 **Wild Strawberry*** *Fragaria vesca*
Low/short perennial, with long *runners*, rooting at intervals. Leaves trefoil, bright green, with pointed teeth, the leaflets paler beneath and hairy with *flattened* silky hairs, less than 80 mm long; hairs on stalks *not* spreading. Flowers 12-18 mm, white, on a short stalk no longer than the leaves; Apr-July. Fruit the familiar strawberry, but much smaller, covered all over with seeds, the sepals bent back from it. Dry, grassy places and woods, often on lime in the north. T.

42 **Hautbois Strawberry*** *Fragaria moschata*
Similar to Wild Strawberry but larger, usually without runners; leaflets more than 60 mm; flower-stalks longer than leaves; flowers 15-25 mm; fruit without seeds at base. T, but (B), eastern.

42 **Water Avens*** *Geum rivale*
Medium downy perennial with pinnate root leaves, becoming trefoil up the stem, and small stipules, 5 mm, at base of stem leaves. Flowers nodding, *bell-shaped*, petals dull pink, 8-15 mm; sepals purple; Apr-Sept. Fruit with persistent hairy style, hooked. Damp, often shady places. T.

42 **Herb Bennet*** *Geum urbanum*
Medium downy perennial. Leaves pinnate, the smaller with leaf-like stipules up stems. Flowers 8-15 mm, *yellow*, petals erect, sepals green; style as in Water Avens; May-Sept. Woods and shady places on fertile soils. T.

42 **Mountain Avens*** *Dryas octopetala*
Low creeping downy perennial with long stems. Leaves *oblong*, blunt-toothed 5-20 mm, green above, *grey* beneath. Flowers 20-40 mm, white, with *eight or more* petals, and many conspicuous yellow stamens; May-July. Fruit with long, feathery styles. Mountain rocks and to sea-level in the north, on lime. B, S.

CINQUEFOILS
Potentilla

Are usually creeping perennials with compound leaves, conspicuous yellow or white flowers, five petals (except Tormentil), numerous stamens, and an epicalyx.

42 **Barren Strawberry*** *Potentilla sterilis*
Low hairy perennial, usually with runners, and with *spreading* hairs on stem and leaves. Leaves smaller than Wild Strawberry, blunt-toothed, and bluish; leaflets 5-25 mm, toothed. Flowers 10-15 mm, white, with gaps between the slightly notched petals; Feb-May. Fruit dry, *not* strawberry-like. Dry grassland and open woods. T, southern

24

42 **Rock Cinquefoil*** *Potentilla rupestris*
Short/medium hairy perennial without runners. Root leaves *pinnate* with rather rounded leaflets, and simpler, usually trefoil leaves up the stem. Flowers 15-25 mm, *white*; May-June. Rocky slopes. T, scattered, rare in B.

42 **Marsh Cinquefoil*** *Potentilla palustris*
Short/medium hairless perennial with pinnate leaves. Flowers *star-shaped*, erect; petals narrow, deep purple, shorter than the broader spreading, *maroon* sepals, 10-15 mm long; May-July. Lime-free wet places. T.

43 **Shrubby Cinquefoil*** *Potentilla fruticosa*
Small, branched, downy *shrub* up to 1 m high. Leaves deciduous, pinnate; leaflets untoothed, greyish, hairy, narrow, usually five. Flowers about 20 mm, in loose clusters; May-July. Wet hollows, river banks, upland rocks. T, scattered, rare in B.

43 **Tormentil*** *Potentilla erecta*
Creeping and patch-forming, with short, downy flowering stems, not rooting at leaf-junctions. Root leaves in rosette, trefoil, soon withering, stem leaves unstalked, appearing to have five leaflets from conspicuous toothed leaf-like stipules. Flowers 7-11 mm, with *four* petals and sepals, numerous in loose heads; May-Sept. Moors and grassy places, not on lime. T.

43 **Trailing Tormentil*** *Potentilla anglica*
Similar to Tormentil. Stems longer, rooting at leaf-junctions, some leaves with five leaflets, rosette persistent, and short-stalked stem leaves with untoothed stipules; flowers 14-18 mm, solitary, petals 4-5. Often in woods. T, southern.

43 **Creeping Cinquefoil*** *Potentilla reptans*
Similar to Tormentil. Stems to 1 m, rooting at leaf-junctions, all leaves with 5-7 leaflets, stem leaves stalked with untoothed stipules; flowers 17-25 mm, solitary, petals five. Waste places, bare ground, hedges, also on lime.

43 **Spring Cinquefoil*** *Potentilla tabernaemontani*
Low/short, rather hairy, mat-forming, with creeping, *rooting* branches. Root leaves with 5-7 leaflets, each 10-40 mm, and narrow stipules; upper leaves trefoil, unstalked. Flowers 10-20 mm; epicalyx segments blunt, lanceolate; Apr-June. Dry, often rocky limestone grassland. T, southern.

43 **Hoary Cinquefoil*** *Potentilla argentea*
Short/medium, with woolly, usually erect flowering stems. Leaves with five leaflets, dark green above, silvery *white* with dense hairs beneath; leaflets pinnately lobed, except at base, margins inrolled. Flowers 10-15 mm, style rounded at tip; June-Sept. Dry grassy places. T, southern.

43 **Snow Cinquefoil** *Potentilla nivea*
Similar to Hoary Cinquefoil, usually has trefoil leaves. S.

43 **Sulphur Cinquefoil*** *Potentilla recta*
Short/medium, hairy, *stiffly* erect, lower leaves with 5-7 leaflets to 100 mm. Flowers 20-25 mm, petals longer than sepals, pale yellow, in clusters; June-Sept. Dry grassy and waste places. (B, S), F, G, southern.

43 **Grey Cinquefoil** *Potentilla cinerea*
Mat-forming with short, woody stems as Hoary Cinquefoil but all creeping, *densely* covered with grey hairs. Leaves with 3-5 leaflets, grey-green above, green beneath; stipules very narrow. Flowers 10-15 mm, few; Apr-May. Dry grassy and rocky places, mainly upland. F, G, S, south-eastern.

43 **Silverweed*** *Potentilla anserina*
Creeping with long runners, rooting at leaf-junctions. Leaves *pinnate*, often silvery, at least beneath, leaflets toothed. Flowers 15-20 mm, *solitary*, petals twice as long as sepals; May-Aug. Damp grassy places. T.

43 **Sibbaldia*** *Sibbaldia procumbens*
Very low, tufted and covered with stiff hairs. Leaves trefoil, leaflets 3-toothed at tip. Flowers *5 mm*, few; petals shorter than sepals, sometimes absent; July-Aug. Mountain grassland. T.

44 **Crab Apple*** *Malus sylvestris*
Small tree to 10 m, rather spiny. Leaves toothed, pointed oval, hairless when mature. Flowers 30-40 mm, white or pink, in loose clusters; May. Fruit the familiar green apple, sometimes turning red. Woods and hedges. T.

44 **Wild Pear** *Pyrus pyraster*
Deciduous tree to 20 m, usually *spiny*, twigs grey to brown. Leaves roundish to elliptical, slightly toothed, hairless when mature. Flowers white, 5-petalled, in clusters; Apr. Fruit roundish to pear-shaped, not fleshy, yellow, brown or black, surmounted by dead sepals. Woods, scrub. ?B, F, G.

44 **Whitebeam*** *Sorbus aria*
Very variable tree, to 25 m. Leaves to 120 mm, more or less pointed oval, widest below the middle, *silvery white* with short hairs beneath, the teeth pointing to the tip. Flowers 10-15 mm, white, in dense, rather flat heads; May-June. Fruit 8-15 mm long, scarlet. Woods and scrub on lime. B, F, G.

44 **Hawthorn*** *Crataegus monogyna*
Hairless *thorny* deciduous shrub or small tree, 2-10 m. Leaves deeply *3-5-lobed*, more than half-way to midrib. Flowers 8-15 mm, white, in broad dense flattened clusters; one style; May-June. Fruit a *crimson* berry (haw). Hedges, scrub. T.

44 **Blackthorn*** *Prunus spinosa*
Deciduous thorny shrub, 1-4 m, much branched, with black or dark brown twigs. Leaves 20-40 mm, rather *oval*, toothed. Flowers 10-15 mm, white, solitary, in short dense spikes, usually appearing *before* the leaves; Mar-May. Fruit a *bluish-black* berry (sloe). Scrub, hedges. T.

plate

44 Wild Cherry* *Prunus avium*
Deciduous tree to 25 m. Leaves 60-150 mm, pale, often reddish, sparingly *downy* beneath, dull above, on long stalks. Flowers 15-30 mm, white, few in loose clusters appearing with leaves; Apr-May. Fruit a bright *red* bitter cherry, 10 mm across. Woods and hedges. T.

44 Bird Cherry* *Prunus padus*
Deciduous tree to 15 m with leaves 50-100 mm, almost hairless, its long crowded *drooping* flower-spikes quite unlike Wild Cherry; flowers 10-15 mm; May. Fruit *black*. Woods, hedges, mainly upland. T.

44 Wild Cotoneaster* *Cotoneaster integerrimus*
Deciduous shrub rarely more than 1 m, *not* thorny, all but the youngest twigs hairless. Leaves 15-40 mm, oval, *untoothed*, grey with dense long hairs beneath. Flowers pink in groups of 2-4; Apr-June. Fruit a small red berry. Limestone rocks, stony ground, mainly upland. T, eastern, rare in B.

44 Small-leaved Cotoneaster* *Cotoneaster microphyllus*
Similar to Wild Cotoneaster. Evergreen with leaves 5-8 mm long and usually solitary white flowers. Bird sown. (B) from Asia.

44 Amelanchier *Amelanchier ovalis*
Deciduous tree to 12 m, with toothed hairless oval leaves, 30-70 mm. Flowers white in short erect spikes, petals 10-13 mm, *narrow*; Apr. Fruit a small purple-black berry. Woods, scrub. F, G, southern.

PEA FAMILY
Leguminosae

Has highly distinctive 5-petalled flowers, the broad and often erect 'standard' at the top, the two narrower 'wings' at the sides, and the two lowest joined at the 'keel' which conceals the stamens and styles. Fruit a usually elongated pod.

MILK-VETCHES
Astragalus

Leaves pinnate, usually with a terminal leaflet. Flowers in spikes or heads at base of leaves, keel *blunt*-tipped; calyx-teeth short.

45 Purple Milk-vetch* *Astragalus danicus*
Low/short downy perennial. Flowers *violet*; May-July. Pods whitely hairy. Mountain and lime-rich grassland, dunes. T.

45 Alpine Milk-vetch* *Astragalus alpinus*
Similar to Purple Milk-vetch. Much paler flowers and brown hairs on pods. Mountain rocks and grassland. T, but rare in B.

45 Wild Lentil *Astragalus cicer*
Medium/tall hairy perennial. Flowers pale *yellow*,

sepal-tube and pod black-haired; June-July. Grassy places. F, G.

45 Yellow Alpine Milk-vetch *Astragalus frigidus*
Short perennial, almost hairless. Leaves greyish. Flowers yellowish-white; teeth of reddish sepal-tube tipped with black hairs; July-Aug. *Mountain* grassland. F, G, S, northern.

45 Wild Liquorice* *Astragalus glycyphyllos*
Medium/tall straggling perennial, slightly hairy; stems *zigzag*. Flowers greenish-cream; June-Aug. Grassland, scrub, open woods. T.

45 Yellow Milk-vetch* *Oxytropis campestris*
Short hairy perennial. Leaves pinnate, silky, with terminal leaflet. Flowers in rounded heads on leafless stems, creamy white or pale *yellow*, often tinged purple, keel finely *pointed*; June-July. Mountain rocks and grassland, rarely by the sea. B (rare), S.

45 Mountain Milk-vetch* *Oxytropis halleri*
Like Yellow Milk-vetch but flowers *purple*. B (rare), S.

45 Crown Vetch* *Coronilla varia*
Medium/tall straggling hairless perennial. Leaves pinnate, with a terminal leaflet. Flowers in rounded heads, *particoloured* (pink, lilac, keel tipped purple); June-Aug. Pod 4-angled. Grassy places. (B, S), F, G.

45 Goat's Rue* *Galega officinalis*
Medium/tall *erect* hairless perennial. Leaves pinnate, with a terminal leaflet. Flowers in spikes, white or pinkish-lilac. Five *bristle-like* calyx-teeth; July-Sept. Pod rounded. Damp and waste ground. (B), F, G.

46 Gorse* *Ulex europaeus*
Evergreen shrub to 2.5 m, hairy. Leaves as rigid furrowed *spines*. Flowers rich golden-yellow, in leafy-stalked spikes, almond scented, wings longer than keel and standard longer still; sepals yellowish, with spreading hairs as long as petals; all year. Heaths, grassland. B, F, G, western.

46 Western Gorse *Ulex gallii*
Similar to Gorse. Shorter with harder yellow flowers, wings as long as keel, and sepals nearly as long as petals. July-Nov. B, F.

46 Broom* *Cytisus scoparius*
Tall deciduous *spineless shrub*, sometimes prostrate by the sea; almost hairless; stems ridged. Leaves lanceolate and *trefoil*. Flowers yellow in leafy stalked spikes; Apr-June. Heaths, open woods. T.

46 Dyer's Greenweed* *Genista tinctoria*
Medium deciduous *spineless* undershrub, sometimes prostrate, slightly hairy. Leaves *lanceolate*. Flowers yellow, standard equalling keel, in leafy

stalked spikes; June-Aug. Pods hairless. Grassland, heaths, open woods. T.

46 **Petty Whin*** *Genista anglica*
Slender short/medium undershrub, almost hairless, *spiny* (rarely spineless). Leaves small, pointed oval. Flowers yellow in leafy stalked spikes, standard shorter than keel; Apr-June. Heaths, moors. T, western.

46 **Laburnum*** *Laburnum anagyroides*
Deciduous *tree* to 7 m, bark smooth. Leaves trefoil. Flowers yellow in drooping stalked spikes. May-June. Woods and scrub in mountains; widely planted. (B), F, G.

46 **Bladder Senna*** *Colutea arborescens*
Deciduous shrub to 3 m, hairy. Leaves *pinnate*. Flowers in stalked spikes, deep yellow, sometimes marked red; June-Aug. Pods papery, inflated. Open woods, scrub, also naturalised on waste ground in N and W. (B), F, G.

46 **Tree Lupin*** *Lupinus arboreus*
Evergreen shrub to 3 m, hairy. Leaves *palmate*. Flowers in a stalked spike, *yellow* or white, sometimes tinged mauve, scented. Sandy soils. (B), from California; May-Aug.

46 **Wild Lupin*** *Lupinus nootkatensis*
Medium/tall perennial, hairy. Leaves *palmate*, leaflets 6-8. Flowers in stalked spikes, *blue* and purple; May-July. River shingle, moors. (B, S), from N America.

46 **False Acacia*** *Robinia pseudacacia*
Deciduous tree to 25 m, suckering, bark grey-brown, deeply furrowed, shoots *thorny*. Leaves pinnate. Flowers in drooping stalked spikes, white; June. Sandy soils. (T), from N America.

46 **Scorpion Senna** *Coronilla emerus*
Deciduous shrub to 3-4 m. Leaves pinnate, *greyish*. Flowers in heads, pale yellow often tipped red; Apr-June. Pods 50-100 mm. Scrub. F, G, S.

VETCHES
Vicia

Mostly climbing or clambering plants. Leaves pinnate ending (except Upright Vetch) in a tendril, usually branched. Flowers usually in heads, on stalks from base of leaves. Pods long, more or less flattened. All except Bithynian Vetch differ from Peas. *Lathyrus* (below) in not having stems winged or angled.

47 **Tufted Vetch*** *Vicia cracca*
Clambering perennial to 1.5 m, slightly downy. Leaflets 8-12 pairs. Flowers *10-40* in one-sided spikes, *blue*-violet, 10-12 mm; June-Aug. Pods brown. Hedges, bushy places. T.

47 **Fodder Vetch*** *Vicia villosa*
Similar to Tufted Vetch. A variable annual with 6-8

pairs of leaflets, often larger flowers, sometimes with white or yellow wings, and sepal-tube swollen at base. June-Nov. Bare and waste ground. T, but (B).

47 **Wood Vetch*** *Vicia sylvatica*
Clambering hairless perennial to 2 m. Leaflets 5-12 pairs. Flowers *5-20* in one-sided spikes, white or *pale* lilac, with purple veins. 12-20 mm. June-Aug. Pods black. Open woods, rarely on sea cliffs and shingle. T.

47 **Bush Vetch*** *Vicia sepium*
Medium/tall clambering downy perennial. Leaflets 3-9 pairs. Flowers 2-6 in a short spike, *blue*-purple, rarely yellow. 12-15 mm. Apr-Nov. Pods black. Hedges, bushy places. T.

47 **Upright Vetch*** *Vicia orobus*
Medium *erect* perennial, slightly downy; stems *unwinged*. Leaves ending in a minute *point*, not a tendril. Flowers pink-lilac; May-June. Pods yellowish-brown. Scrub, rocks. T, western.

47 **Common Vetch*** *Vicia sativa*
Variable short/medium clambering downy annual. Leaflets 3-8 pairs, varying from almost linear to oval, tendrils sometimes unbranched; usually a *dark spot* on toothed stipules at base. Flowers 1-2, reddish-purple, *10-30 mm*; Apr-Sept. Pods downy or hairless, black to yellow-brown. Bare or grassy ground; large forms are cultivated. T.

47 **Spring Vetch*** *Vicia lathyroides*
Similar to Common Vetch. A prostrate downy annual, with 2-4 pairs of narrow leaflets, tendrils always unbranched, untoothed unspotted stipules, solitary deep lilac 5-8 mm flowers and black hairless pods. Apr-May. Sandy ground, especially near sea.

47 **Hairy Tare*** *Vicia hirsuta*
Slender short annual, almost hairless. Leaflets 4-10 pairs, tendrils sometimes unbranched. Flowers 1-8 in spike, pale *lilac, 4-5 mm,* sepal-teeth longer than tube. May-Aug. Pods downy. Grassy places. T.

47 **Smooth Tare*** *Vicia tetrasperma*
Similar to Hairy Tare. 3-6 leaflet pairs, 1-2 larger (4-8 mm) deep lilac flowers and hairless pods.

47 **Slender Tare*** *Vicia tenuissima*
Similar to Hairy Tare. 2-5 leaflet pairs, 2-5 still larger (6-9 mm) deep lilac flowers, and pods downy or hairless; June-Aug. B, F, G, southern. Both Smooth and Slender Tare have calyx-teeth shorter than tube and tendrils usually unbranched.

47 **Yellow Vetch*** *Vicia lutea*
More or less prostrate downy annual. Leaflets 3-10 pairs, tendrils branched or not. Flowers 1-3, *yellowish-white*, often tinged purple, 20-35 mm; June-Sept. Pods usually downy, B, F, G.

47 **Bithynian Vetch*** *Vicia bithynica*
Medium clambering hairy annual, stems 4-angled.

27

PEA FAMILY

Leaflets 2-3 pairs, large, *broad*. Flowers 1-3, purple, wings and keel *creamy white*, 16-20 mm. May-June. Pods brown or yellow, downy. Grassy places, hedges. B, F, western.

PEAS
Lathyrus

Differ from all Vetches (above), except Bithynian Vetch, in their winged or angled stems. Most have fewer leaflets, but some have more. Pods usually brown.

plate 48 **Broad-leaved Everlasting Pea*** *Lathyrus latifolius*
Climbing perennial to 3 m, hairless or downy; stems winged. Leaflets *one* pair, large, *broad*. Flowers 5-15, bright magenta-pink, 20-30 mm; July-Sept. Scrub, widespread garden escape. (B), F, G.

48 **Narrow-leaved Everlasting Pea*** *Lathyrus sylvestris*
Similar to Broad-leaved Everlasting Pea. Narrower leaves and stipules, and smaller muddy pink flowers; June-Aug. Woods, scrub, hedges. T.

48 **Meadow Vetchling*** *Lathyrus pratensis*
Short/tall clambering perennial, hairless or downy; stems angled. Leaflets one, occasionally two, pairs. Flowers 4-12, *yellow;* May-Aug. Pods black. Grassy places. T.

48 **Spring Pea** *Lathyrus vernus*
Short *erect* hairless perennial, stems angled. Leaflets 2-4 pairs, *no* tendrils. Flowers 3-10, red-purple, fading blue, 13-20 mm; Apr-June. Pods brown. Woods, scrub. F, G, S.

48 **Bitter Vetchling*** *Lathyrus montanus*
Short erect perennial, hairless; stems *winged*. Leaflets 2-4 pairs, sometimes very narrow (var. *tenuifolius,* illustrated), leaves ending in a *point* not a tendril. Flowers 2-6, red-purple fading blue, 10-16 mm; Apr-July. Pods red-brown. Woods, scrub, heaths. T.

48 **Sea Pea*** *Lathyrus japonicus*
Prostrate fleshy perennial, hairless or downy; stems angled. Leaflets 2-5 pairs, greyish, sometimes no tendril. Flowers 2-12, purple fading blue, 14-22 mm; June-Aug. Shingle and dunes *by sea*. B, G, S.

48 **Marsh Pea*** *Lathyrus palustris*
Medium/tall clambering perennial, slightly downy. Leaflets 2-5 pairs, tendril branched. Flowers 2-8, bluish-purple, 12-20 mm; June-July. Pods black. *Marshes*, fens. T. northern.

48 **Tuberous Pea*** *Lathyrus tuberosus*
Medium/tall clambering perennial, more or less hairless; stems angled. Leaflets one pair. Flowers 2-7, bright *crimson*, slightly fragrant, 12-20 mm; June-July. Grassy and cultivated ground. (B), F, G.

48 **Hairy Vetchling*** *Lathyrus hirsutus*
Medium/tall clambering annual, slightly downy; stems winged. Leaflets one pair, tendrils branched. Flowers 1-3, pale red-purple, fading blue, keel *creamy*, 7-15 mm; June-Aug. Pods brown, downy. Grassy and bare places. (B), F, G, eastern.

48 **Grass Vetchling*** *Lathyrus nissolia*
Short/tall erect annual, hairless or slightly downy. Unique among peaflowers of region for long narrow *grasslike* 'leaves', (actually modified stems) with no tendrils, very hard to detect among the grass. Flowers 1-2, long-stalked, crimson; May-July. Pods pale brown. Grassy places. B, F, G.

48 **Yellow Vetchling*** *Lathyrus aphaca*
Medium/tall hairless clambering annual. Unique among peaflowers for its leaves having become unbranched *tendrils* direct from the stems and its stipules developed into *triangular* greyish apparent leaves, *joined* around the stem. Flowers usually solitary, yellow; May-Aug. Dry grassy places. B, F, G.

49 **Sainfoin*** *Onobrychis viciifolia*
Short/medium erect, rarely prostrate, downy perennial. Leaves *pinnate*. Flowers in stalked spikes, bright *pink*; June-Sept. Pods warty, pitted. Dry grassy and waste places; widely cultivated. (T), from E Europe.

49 **Rest-harrow*** *Ononis repens*
Short/medium semi-erect hairy undershrub; stem hairy all round, sometimes with soft *spines*. Leaves *trefoil* or oval, blunt or slightly notched. Flowers in leafy stalked spikes, pink, wings equalling keel; July-Sept. Dry grassy places. T.

49 **Spiny Rest-harrow*** *Ononis spinosa*
Similar to Rest-harrow. Erect with sharper spines, stem with two lines of hairs, leaflets never notched and sometimes pointed, and reddish-pink flowers with wings shorter than keel.

49 **Large Yellow Rest-harrow** *Ononis natrix*
Medium erect undershrub, stickily hairy. Leaves trefoil, variable. Flowers in branched spikes, *deep yellow*, often veined red or purple; May-Aug. Pods short. Dry open places. F, G, southern.

49 **Small Rest-harrow*** *Ononis reclinata*
Low semi-prostrate annual, stickily hairy, with shiny dots. Leaves trefoil. Flowers in leafy spikes, pink, 5-10 mm; May-June. Pods hang straight down when ripe. Sandy turf and cliffs by sea. B (rare), F.

49 **Kidney Vetch*** *Anthyllis vulneraria*
Very variable, low/short, semi-prostrate/erect, annual/perennial, silkily hairy. Leaves *pinnate*, the lowest sometimes lanceolate. Flowers in heads, sometimes paired, yellow, orange, red, purple, whitish or particoloured; two leafy bracts at base; Apr-Sept. Dry grassland, often by sea and on mountains. T.

49 **Ribbed Melilot*** *Melilotus officinalis*
Medium/tall hairless biennial. Leaves trefoil.

28

Flowers in stalked *spikes*, yellow, keel shorter than wings and standard; June-Sept. Pods hairless, brown when ripe. Bare and waste ground. T, but (B).

49 **White Melilot*** *Melilotus alba*
Tall hairless biennial. Leaves trefoil. Flowers in stalked spikes, *white*: July-Oct. Pods hairless, netveined, brownish when ripe. Bare and waste ground; grown as Bokhara Clover. T, but (B).

49 **Classical Fenugreek** *Trigonella foenum-graecum*
Short/medium annual, almost hairless. Leaves trefoil, toothed. Flowers *1-2* at base of upper leaves, yellowish-white, tinged purple at base; Apr-May. Pods hairless, slightly curved, beaked. Bare and waste ground; widely cultivated. F, G, southern.

49 **Lucerne*** *Medicago sativa*
Medium hairless perennial. Leaves *trefoil*. Flowers in short spikes, of varying shades of violet (ssp. *sativa*), yellow (ssp. *falcata*), green and livid black (hybrids between the two); June-Oct. Pods sometimes curved or spiral. Grassy, waste and cultivated places; widely grown as Alfalfa. T.

50 **Birdsfoot Trefoil*** *Lotus corniculatus*
More or less prostrate perennial, downy or hairless. Leaves with five leaflets, lowest pair bent back so that leaves appear *trefoil*. Flowers 2-7 in a head, yellow, often tinged orange or red, 10-16 mm; sepal-teeth erect in bud, an obtuse angle between the two upper; May-Sept. Pods straight, in a head resembling a bird's foot, 15-30 mm. Grassy places. T.

50 **Narrow-leaved Birdsfoot Trefoil*** *Lotus tenuis*
Similar to Birdsfoot Trefoil but slenderer, with narrower leaflets, fewer and smaller yellow flowers in each head, and the rear sepal-teeth converging June-Aug.

50 **Hairy Birdsfoot Trefoil*** *Lotus subbiflorus*
Prostrate *hairy* annual. Leaves like Birdsfoot Trefoil. Flowers 2-4 in a head, on stalks much longer than leaves, orange-yellow, 5-10 mm; June-Sept. Pods 6-12 mm. Grassy places. B, F.

50 **Dragon's Teeth*** *Tetragonolobus maritimus*
Prostrate patch-forming perennial, hairless or downy. Leaves trefoil. Flowers *solitary*, pale yellow, sometimes red-veined, 25-30 mm; May-Sept. Pods 4-angled, dark brown, 30-60 mm. Grassy places, often damp. T, but (B, rare).

50 **Horseshoe Vetch*** *Hippocrepis comosa*
Prostrate downy perennial. Leaves *pinnate*, ending in a leaflet. Flowers 5-12 in a head, yellow, 6-10 mm; May-July. Pods curved, with horseshoe-like segments, 15-30 mm. Dry grassland, often on limy soils. B, F, G.

50 **Birdsfoot*** *Ornithopus perpusillus*
Prostrate downy annual. Leaves *pinnate*, ending in a leaflet. Flowers 3-8 in a head, yellowish-white or pink, veined red, 3-5 mm; bracts pinnate, leaf-like; May-Aug. Pods beaded, 10-18 mm, in a head resembling a bird's foot. Bare and grassy places. T, southern.

50 **Orange Birdsfoot*** *Ornithopus pinnatus*
Similar to Birdsfoot. 1-5 orange-yellow flowers with no leaf-like bract. B (rare), F.

50 **Black Medick*** *Medicago lupulina*
Low, often prostrate annual, usually downy. Leaves trefoil, leaflets with a minute *point*. Flowers yellow, 10-50 in a short-stalked rounded head, 3-8 mm; Apr-Oct. Pods curved, *black* when ripe, not covered by dead flowers. Bare and grassy places, widely cultivated as Nonsuch. T.

50 **Lesser Trefoil*** *Trifolium dubium*
Similar to Black Medick. Almost hairless; leaflets very slightly notched, not pointed, the middle one longer-stalked; flowers 3-15 in the head, pods straight, covered by dead brown flowers; May-Sept.

50 **Slender Trefoil*** *Trifolium micranthum*
Is like Lesser Trefoil with all leaflets unstalked, flowers 1-6 in a head with long hairlike stalks, 2-3 mm. Southern.

50 **Spotted Medick*** *Medicago arabica*
Prostrate annual, hairless or slightly downy. Leaves trefoil, usually with a *dark spot* on each leaflet, stipules toothed. Flowers 1-4 in a head, yellow, 5-7 mm. Apr-Sept. Pods spiny, spirally coiled, faintly netted. Bare and grassy places. B, F, G, southern.

50 **Hop Trefoil*** *Trifolium campestre*
Low/short annual, hairy. Leaves trefoil, leaflets with *no* point, the middle one longer-stalked. Flowers *20-30* in rounded stalked 10-15 mm heads, yellow; May-Sept. Pods covered by pale brown dead flowers. Grassy places. T.

CLOVERS
Trifolium

Leaves trefoil. Flowers small, usually in a dense rounded head, wings longer than keel, sepal-tube 5-toothed. Pods covered by dead flowers. Grassy places.

51 **Red Clover*** *Trifolium pratense*
Variable erect low/tall hairy perennial. Leaflets often with a whitish crescent; stipules triangular, bristle-pointed. Flowerheads globular or eggshaped, sometimes paired, usually unstalked, with two leaves closely beneath, 20-40 mm; flowers of varying shades of *pink-purple*, rarely creamy or white; May-Oct. Widely cultivated. T.

51 **Mountain Clover** *Trifolium montanum*
Short/medium hairy perennial. Flowerheads often paired, well stalked, 15-30 mm; flowers *yellowish-white*, rarely pink, turning brownish; May-July. Especially in mountains. F, G, S.

plate 51 **Sulphur Clover*** *Trifolium ochroleucon*
Similar to Mountain Clover. Two leaves closely below the larger (20-40 mm) un- or short-stalked flowerheads. Lowlands, B, F, G.

51 **White Clover*** *Trifolium repens*
Creeping perennial, more or less hairless, stems rooting at leaf-junctions. Leaflets usually with a whitish mark. Flowerheads globular, long-stalked, 15-30 mm; flowers *white*, pink, or rarely purple, turning brown, scented, angles between sepal-teeth acute; May-Oct. Widely cultivated as Wild White, Dutch or Kentish Clover. T.

51 **Alsike Clover*** *Trifolium hybridum*
Similar to White Clover. Short/medium and erect, with unmarked leaves and shorter-stalked heads of more often pink flowers, angles between sepal-teeth blunt; June-Sept. Often on waste ground; also widely cultivated. (B, S), F, G.

51 **Strawberry Clover*** *Trifolium fragiferum*
Creeping hairy perennial; stems often rooting at leaf-junctions. Flowerheads globular, 10-14 mm, *swelling* in fruit to appear like miniature pale pink strawberries; flowers pink; June-Sept. T.

51 **Knotted Clover*** *Trifolium striatum*
Low, more or less erect downy annual. Leaves downy on *both* sides. Flowerheads egg-shaped, unstalked at base of leaves, 10-15 mm; flowers pink, sepal-teeth swollen in fruit, with erect teeth; June-July. Dry places. T, southern.

51 **Haresfoot Clover*** *Trifolium arvense*
Low/short hairy annual/biennial. Leaflets narrow. Flowerheads *egg-shaped*, stalked, 10-20 mm; flowers whitish or pale pink, much shorter than sepal-tube; June-Sept. Scarce on lime. T.

51 **Upright Clover*** *Trifolium strictum*
Similar to Haresfoot Clover. Larger but still narrower leaflets, and smaller (7-10 mm), more globular, longer-stalked heads of larger bright pink flowers, much longer than calyx; June. B (rare), F.

51 **Crimson Clover*** *Trifolium incarnatum*
Short/medium hairy annual. Flowerheads elongated, 10-40 mm; flowers *bright* crimson, pink or creamy white, sepal-teeth spreading in fruit; June-July. Widely cultivated. Pale-flowered subsp. *molinerii*. Long-headed Clover, is native on clifftops by the sea. B, F (G, S), southern.

51 **Fenugreek*** *Trifolium ornithopodioides*
Prostrate hairless annual. Flowers 2-4 in short-stalked heads, white or pale pink, 6-8 mm; June-July. Pods much longer than sepal-tube. Bare dry places, often damp in winter. B, F, G, southern.

51 **Burrowing Clover*** *Trifolium subterraneum*
Similar to Fenugreek. Larger (8-14 mm) flowers and fruit heads buried in the ground; May-June.

51 **Suffocated Clover*** *Trifolium suffocatum*
Prostrate hairless annual. Flowerheads unstalked, tightly packed, 5-6 mm; flowers white, almost *hidden* by green calyx-teeth, recurved in fruit; July-Aug. Dry places. B, F.

WOOD-SORREL FAMILY
Oxalidaceae

Downy. Leaves trefoil, often closing up at night. Flowers 5-petalled, cup-shaped. Fruit a capsule.

52 **Wood-sorrel*** *Oxalis acetosella*
Low creeping perennial. Flowers *white*, usually veined mauve, sometimes tinged purple; Apr-May. Woods, shady places, also on mountains. T.

52 **Yellow Oxalis*** *Oxalis corniculata*
Low/short creeping annual/perennial, stems rooting at leaf-junctions. Leaves often purplish, stipules tiny. Flowers *yellow*, 4-7 mm; May-Oct. Fruit stalks bent right back. Bare, especially cultivated, ground. T, southern, but (B).

52 **Pink Oxalis*** *Oxalis articulata*
Low/short tufted perennial. Leaves spotted pale orange beneath. Flowers in a cluster, *rose-pink*; May-Sept. Garden escape. (B, F), from S America.

52 **Bermuda Buttercup*** *Oxalis pes-caprae*
Low/short tufted perennial. Leaflets sometimes with a pale brown blotch. Flowers in an umbel-like cluster, *yellow*. 20-25 mm. Mar-June. Naturalised weed. (B, rare, F), from S Africa.

FLAX FAMILY
Linaceae

Slender, hairless. Leaves undivided, untoothed; no stipules. Flowers 5-petalled (except Allseed), open. Fruit a capsule.

52 **Perennial Flax*** *Linum perenne*
Short/medium hairless perennial. Leaves more or less linear, alternate, 1-veined or obscurely 3-veined. Flowers in a cluster, on erect stalks, pale to bright blue, 25 mm; anthers and stigmas unequal; inner sepals often blunt, much shorter than fruit; May-Aug. Dry grassland. B, F, G.

52 **Pale Flax*** *Linum bienne*
Similar to Perennial Flax. 1-3 veined leaves, pale bluish-lilac flowers that drop early, and all sepals pointed, nearly as long as the more pointed fruit. B, F.

52 **Common Flax*** *Linum usitatissimum*
Similar to Perennial Flax. Annual with leaves always 3-veined and sepals like Pale Flax. June-Oct. Widely cultivated. (T).

52 **Purging Flax*** *Linum catharticum*
Low annual. Leaves oblong, opposite, 1-veined. Flowers in a loose cluster, white, 4-6 mm; May-Sept. Grassland, fens, especially on lime. T.

52 **Yellow Flax** *Linum flavum*
Variable medium hairless perennial, sometimes woody at base. Leaves lanceolate, the lower broader at tip. Flowers yellow, about 30 mm, in a cluster. Dry grassy places. G.

30

52 Allseed* *Radiola linoides*
A tiny (rarely above 5 cm) annual, with repeatedly branching thread-like stems. Leaves oblong, opposite, 1-veined. Flowers 4-petalled, white, 1 mm, equalling sepals; July-Aug. Bare damp places, not on lime. T, western.

GERANIUM FAMILY
Geraniaceae

Hairy or downy. Leaves deeply palmately lobed or cut, with stipules. Flowers 5-petalled, sepals often bristle-tipped, stamens prominent. Fruit ends in long straight pointed beak, whence "cranesbill".

52 Common Storksbill* *Erodium cicutarium*
Low/medium annual/biennial, hairy, sometimes stickily so; often strong-smelling. Leaves *2-pinnate*, stipules lanceolate. Flowers in umbel-like heads with five, easily shed, often unequal petals, purplish-pink to white, sometimes with a blackish spot at base of two upper petals, 4-11 mm; Apr-Sept. Fruit with a long twisted beak. Bare and grassy places, frequent by the sea. T.

52 Sea Storksbill* *Erodium maritimum*
Low, often prostrate, downy annual/biennial. Leaves oval, toothed, often in a rosette. Flowers usually solitary, pale pink or white, the five petals dropping very soon; May-Aug. Fruit with a long twisted beak. Bare ground, short turf, usually near the sea. B, F.

53 Meadow Cranesbill* *Geranium pratense*
Medium/tall perennial. Leaves cut nearly to base. Flowers *blue*, 25-30 mm; petals not notched; June-Sept. Flower stalks bent down after flowering, becoming erect when fruit ripe. Grassy places, usually on lime. T.

53 Wood Cranesbill* *Geranium sylvaticum*
Similar to Meadow Cranesbill. Less deeply cut leaves, generally smaller, more reddish-mauve flowers and flower stalks always erect. Also in woods and on mountains. Northern.

53 Bloody Cranesbill* *Geranium sanguineum*
Short/medium tufted perennial. Leaves cut nearly to base. Flowers *bright* purple-crimson, very rarely pink, 25-30 mm. June-Aug. Dry grassy places, usually on lime. T.

53 French Cranesbill* *Geranium endressii*
Medium perennial. Leaves cut to more than half-way. Flowers *pink*, unveined, 25 mm; petals not notched; June-Aug. Garden escape (B, F), from S W France.

53 Pencilled Cranesbill* *Geranium versicolor*
Similar to French Cranesbill. Paler pink flowers, pencilled with violet veins, and notched petals. From Italy and Balkans.

53 Dusky Cranesbill* *Geranium phaeum*
Similar to French Cranesbill but less deeply cut leaves, smaller drooping maroon flowers and unnotched wavy-edged petals. Damp and shady places; garden escape in the West. (B), F, G.

53 Marsh Cranesbill *Geranium palustre*
Medium/tall perennial. Leaves cut to more than half-way. Flowers pale *purple* or lilac, 30 mm; petals not or very slightly notched; July-Aug. Fruit stalks bent down. Damp grassy places. F, G, S, eastern.

53 Hedgerow Cranesbill* *Geranium pyrenaicum*
Medium perennial. Leaves cut to about half-way. Flowers pink-purple to lilac, often *mauve-pink*, 15 mm; petals well notched; May-Sept. Fruit stalks bent down. Grassy places, open woods. T, southern, but (B).

53 Bohemian Cranesbill *Geranium bohemicum*
Similar to Hedgerow Cranesbill. Annual/biennial, with smaller, bright violet-blue flowers, less deeply notched petals and erect fruit stalks. Eastern.

53 Herb Robert* *Geranium robertianum*
Medium annual/biennial, strong-smelling, often reddening. Leaves triangular, 1-2-pinnate. Flowers *pink*, 20 mm; petals scarcely notched, pollen orange; Apr-Nov. Fruit slightly wrinkled. Shady places, rocks, shingle. T.

53 Little Robin* *Geranium purpureum*
Similar to Herb Robert. Much smaller flowers, yellow pollen and strongly wrinkled fruit. B, F.

53 Shining Cranesbill* *Geranium lucidum*
Short annual, almost hairless, often reddening. Leaves *glossy*, rounded, cut to half-way. Flowers pink, 15 mm; petals not notched; May-Aug. Fruit wrinkled. Shady rocks and hedge-banks. T.

53 Dovesfoot Cranesbill* *Geranium molle*
Short semi-prostrate annual, with long hairs on stems. Root leaves cut to less than half-way, stem leaves to half-way or more, all rounded. Flowers dark or pale pinkish-purple, 10 mm; petals well notched; Apr-Sept. Fruit hairless, usually wrinkled. Bare and grassy places. T.

53 Small-flowered Cranesbill* *Geranium pusillum*
Similar to Dovesfoot Cranesbill but has only short hairs on stem, stem leaves more narrowly cut to more than half-way, smaller lilac flowers, half the stamens without anthers, and fruit downy, not wrinkled.

53 Cut-leaved Cranesbill* *Geranium dissectum*
Short/medium straggling annual/biennial. Leaves cut almost to base. Flowers pink-purple, 8 mm; petals notched; May-Sept. Fruit downy. Bare and sparsely grassy places. T.

53 Long-stalked Cranesbill* *Geranium columbinum*
Similar to Cut-leaved Cranesbill. Sometimes reddens and has larger longer-stalked flowers, petals not notched and fruit hairless. Dry grassy places.

31

SPURGE FAMILY
Euphorbiaceae

SPURGES
Euphorbia
Stems with milky juice. Leaves undivided, usually alternate and untoothed. Flowers in usually broadening umbel-like clusters, yellowish-green; no petals or sepals, but a solitary 3-styled female flower, surrounded by several 1-anthered male flowers is cupped by a calyx-like bract, with 4-5 glands on its lip, and 2-3 small leaflike bracts at its base. Fruit rounded, stalked.

plate 54 **Wood Spurge*** *Euphorbia amygdaloides*
Medium/tall unbranched perennial, downy, often tinged red. Leaves lanceolate. Flowers yellow, glands horned, bracts joined together; Apr-May. Woods, scrub. B, F, G.

54 **Cypress Spurge*** *Euphorbia cyparissias*
Similar to Wood Spurge. Shorter and hairless, with much narrower leaves, turning bright red, and bracts not joined; May-Aug. Bare and grassy places. T, but (B).

54 **Sea Spurge*** *Euphorbia paralias*
Short/medium greyish hairless perennial; unbranched. Leaves fleshy, oval, midrib *not* prominent beneath, overlapping up the stem. Flowers with short-horned glands; June-Sept. Sands by the *sea*. B, F, G, southern.

54 **Portland Spurge*** *Euphorbia portlandica*
Short greyish hairless perennial; branched from the base, often reddening. Leaves oval, *midrib* prominent below. Flowers with long-horned glands; Apr-Sept. Sands and short turf by the sea. B, F.

54 **Caper Spurge*** *Euphorbia lathyris*
Tall greyish hairless biennial. Leaves narrow, opposite. Flowers with horned glands; June-Aug. Fruit large, *3-sided*, resembling a green caper. Bare and cultivated ground. B(rare), F, G.

54 **Irish Spurge*** *Euphorbia hyberna*
Medium little-branched perennial, almost hairless; often in clumps. Leaves untoothed, downy beneath, reddening. Flowers with yellow bracts and *kidney-shaped* yellow glands; Apr-July. Fruit with long and short warts. Damp or shady places. B, F, southern.

54 **Sun Spurge*** *Euphorbia helioscopia*
Short, usually unbranched, hairless annual. Leaves oval, finely toothed. Flowers in a broad umbel, bracts often yellowish, glands green, oval; Apr-Nov and through mild winters. Fruit smooth. Common weed of cultivation. T.

54 **Petty Spurge*** *Euphorbia peplus*
Low/short, often branched hairless annual. Leaves oval, untoothed. Flowers green, glands horned; Apr-Nov and through mild winters. Fruit with wavy ridges. Common weed of cultivation. T.

54 **Broad-leaved Spurge*** *Euphorbia platyphyllos*
Similar to Petty Spurge. Taller and may be downy, with longer leaves finely toothed at the tip, larger yellower flowers with rounded glands and fruit with rounded warts; June-Sept. B, F, G.

54 **Dwarf Spurge*** *Euphorbia exigua*
Low slender greyish annual, hairless. Leaves linear. Flowers yellowish, glands horned; May-Oct. Fruit smooth. Weed of cultivation, especially cornfields. T.

54 **Purple Spurge*** *Euphorbia peplis*
Prostrate fleshy hairless annual; stems crimson. Leaves oblong, greyish, opposite. Flowers stalked, along stems, 1-2 mm; July-Sept. Sandy shores. B (rare), F, southern.

54 **Dog's Mercury*** *Mercurialis perennis*
Low/short unbranched downy foetid perennial. Leaves broad lanceolate, opposite. Flowers in stalked tassels, petalless, green, 4-5 mm, stamens and styles on separate plants; Feb-May. Woods, shady places, often carpeting the ground; also on mountains. T.

BALSAM FAMILY
Balsaminaceae

BALSAMS *Impatiens*
Hairless annuals, stems fleshy. Leaves oval, stalked, slightly toothed. Flowers in long-stalked spikes from base of leaves, 5-petalled, with a broad lip, a small hood and a spur, often curved. Fruit cylindrical, exploding when ripe.

55 **Himalayan Balsam*** *Impatiens glandulifera*
Tall, stems often reddish. Leaves opposite or in threes, with small red teeth. Flowers large, pale to dark pink-purple, with short bent spur; July-Oct. Bare places, especially by streams. (T).

55 **Touch-me-not Balsam*** *Impatiens noli-tangere*
Medium/tall, leaves alternate. Flowers *yellow*, sometimes spotted red-brown, spur curved downwards; July-Sept. Damp shady places. T.

55 **Orange Balsam*** *Impatiens capensis*
Similar to Touch-me-not Balsam. Red-spotted orange flowers with spur bent into a crook; July-Sept. By rivers and canals. (B, F), from N America.

55 **Small Balsam*** *Impatiens parviflora*
Short/medium, leaves alternate. Flowers *pale* yellow, spur short and straight, 3-5 mm; June-Sept. Shady or bare places. (T), from C Asia.

MILKWORT FAMILY
Polygalaceae

Hairless perennials. Leaves unstalked, usually alternate, no stipules. Flowers 5-sepalled, the two inner large and petal-like on either side of the three true petals, which are joined at the base. Stamens also petal-like, in two Y-shaped bundles of four. Fruit flat, heart-shaped, slightly winged.

55 **Common Milkwort*** *Polygala vulgaris*
Low perennial. Leaves lanceolate, pointed, broadest at or below the middle, the lower shorter and broader than the upper. Flowers in stalked spikes, usually blue, also often mauve, pink, white or white tipped mauve or blue, 4-7 mm; May-Sept. Fruit shorter than inner sepals. Grassy places. T.

55 **Heath Milkwort*** *Polygala serpyllifolia*
Has at least the lower leaves opposite and more crowded than Common Milkwort, and shorter spikes of usually dark blue or dark pink flowers. Not on lime. Southern.

55 **Shrubby Milkwort** *Polygala chamaebuxus*
More or less prostrate evergreen undershrub. Leaves oval to lanceolate, rather leathery. Flowers usually yellow tipped purple, also red, pink or white; Apr-Sept. Woods, grassy places, especially on mountains. F, G, south-eastern.

DAPHNE FAMILY
Thymelaeaceae

Hairless or almost so. Leaves untoothed, shortly stalked, usually alternate, no stipules. Flowers in clusters at base of leaves, petalless with four petal-like sepals joined at base.

55 **Mezereon*** *Daphne mezereum*
Deciduous shrub to 2 m. Leaves lanceolate, pale green. Flowers strongly scented, *pinkish-purple*; Feb-Apr, before the leaves. Fruit a *red* berry. Woods on lime. T.

55 **Spurge Laurel*** *Daphne laureola*
Evergreen shrub to 1 m. Leaves lanceolate, dark green, rather leathery. Flowers slightly scented, *yellow-green*; Jan-Apr. Fruit a *black* berry. Open woods, often on lime. B, F, G.

55 **Annual Thymelaea** *Thymelaea passerina*
Medium annual. Leaves almost linear, pointed. Flowers 1-3 together, greenish, tiny; July-Oct. Fruit a downy nut. Dry bare uncultivated places. F, G.

RUE FAMILY
Rutaceae

55 **Burning Bush** *Dictamnus albus*
Medium/tall bushy hairy perennial, pungent from aromatic oil, which may burst into flame if a match is held near it in still summer weather. Leaves pinnate. Flowers 5-petalled, white or pink with purple streaks and prominent purple stamens, in stalked spikes. Dry places. G.

CURRANT FAMILY
Grossulariaceae

Small deciduous shrubs, to 1.5 m. Leaves alternate, palmately lobed. Flowers 5-petalled, green. Fruit a berry.

56 **Red Currant*** *Ribes rubrum*
Stems erect. Leaves hairless or downy beneath, *not* aromatic. Flowers purple-edged, in drooping stalked spikes; Apr-May. Fruit red, acid. Damp woods, fens, by fresh water; widely cultivated. T.

56 **Black Currant*** *Ribes nigrum*
Similar to Red Currant. Aromatic leaves and black fruit.

56 **Mountain Currant*** *Ribes alpinum*
Similar to Red Currant. Bushier, with smaller, more deeply lobed leaves, flowers in erect clusters, male and female on different bushes, each with a conspicuous green bract, and tasteless fruit. Upland woods, often on lime; rarely cultivated.

56 **Gooseberry*** *Ribes uva-crispa*
Stems spreading, *spiny*. Leaves smaller than Red Currant. Flowers purple-edged, petals turned back, 1-3 together; Mar-May. Fruit egg-shaped, green, often tinged red or yellow, usually hairy. Woods, scrub, hedges; widely cultivated. T.

SPINDLE-TREE FAMILY
Celastraceae

56 **Spindle-tree*** *Euonymus europaeus*
Deciduous shrub, rarely a small tree, to 6 m, with 4-sided green twigs. Leaves elliptical, opposite, scarcely toothed. Flowers small, greenish-white, 4-petalled, in small clusters; May-June. Fruit a bright *coral-pink* berry. Woods, scrub, hedges, often on lime. T.

BOX FAMILY
Buxaceae

56 **Box*** *Buxus sempervirens*
Evergreen shrub or small tree, to 5 m, twigs green. Leaves oval, shiny, *leathery*, opposite. Flowers petalless, greenish-yellow, in small clusters at base of upper leaves; Mar-May. Fruit dry. Dry hillsides, widely planted. B (rare), F, G.

BUCKTHORN FAMILY
Rhamnaceae

56 **Buckthorn*** *Rhamnus catharticus*
Deciduous shrub or small tree to 6 m, often thorny. Leaves broad elliptical, finely toothed, *opposite*, with *conspicuous* veins. Flowers small, green, 4-petalled, in small clusters at base of upper leaves; male and female separate; May-June. Fruit a black berry. Scrub, hedges, fens, usually on lime. T.

56 **Alder Buckthorn*** *Frangula alnus*
Deciduous shrub or small tree to 5 m, thornless. Leaves broad elliptical, untoothed, *alternate*. Flowers small, green, usually 5-petalled, in small clusters at base of upper leaves; May-June. Fruit a black berry, red at first. Damp heaths and woods, fens, usually not on lime. T.

33

OLEASTER FAMILY
Elaeagnaceae

plate 56 **Sea Buckthorn*** *Hippophaë rhamnoides*
Deciduous shrub or small tree to 11 m, *thorny*, suckering freely and forming thickets. Brown twigs and untoothed narrow lanceolate alternate leaves both covered with *silvery scales*, the older leaves brownish. Flowers tiny, green, petalless, male and female on different plants; Apr-May, before leaves. Fruit a bright orange berry. Coastal dunes, sea cliffs, mountain river beds. T.

TAMARISK FAMILY
Tamaricaceae

56 **Tamarisk*** *Tamarix gallica*
Evergreen shrub to 3 m, hairless; twigs reddish. Leaves minute, *scale-like*, overlapping, alternate, often greyish, producing a feathery foliage. Flowers pink, 5-petalled, in stalked spikes; July-Sept. By salt and fresh water, often planted. (B), F.

BLADDER-NUT FAMILY
Staphyleaceae

56 **Bladder-nut*** *Staphylea pinnata*
Deciduous shrub to 5 m. Leaves pinnate, opposite. Flowers white, 5-petalled, in hanging stalked clusters; May-June. Fruit *inflated*. Woods on lime; often planted. (B, F), G.

MALLOW FAMILY
Malvaceae

Downy or softly hairy. Leaves rounded, palmately lobed, toothed, stalked, alternate, with stipules. Flowers in whorls at base of leaves, open, with five notched petals; calyx in two rings, the outer smaller; stamens numerous, prominently bunched together. Fruit a flat disc.

57 **Musk Mallow*** *Malva moschata*
Medium/tall perennial, stem hairs often purple-based. Leaves deeply and *narrowly* cut. Flowers 40-60 mm, solitary, *rose-pink*; hairs on stalks unbranched, outer sepal-ring 3-lobed, hairless or almost so; July-Aug. Fruit hairy. Grassy places, scrub. T.

57 **Dwarf Mallow*** *Malva neglecta*
More or less prostrate annual. Flowers 3-6 together, pale lilac or whitish, 10-15 mm; petals twice as long as sepals; June-Sept. Waste places. T.

57 **Least Mallow*** *Malva parviflora*
Short/medium annual, sometimes hairless. Flowers 2-4 together, pale lilac-blue, 4-5 mm; petals slightly longer than short-haired or hairless sepals, which greatly enlarge in fruit; June-Sept. Fruit segments net-veined, winged on angles. Waste places. (B), F.

57 **Common Mallow*** *Malva sylvestris*
Variable, often sprawling, medium/tall annual/perennial. Leaves often with a small *dark spot*. Flowers two or more together, pale to dark pink-purple, 25-40 mm; outer sepal-ring not joined at base; June-Oct. Fruit segments with sharp angles. Waste places, waysides. T.

57 **Tree Mallow*** *Lavatera arborea*
Tall biennial to 3 m, softly downy, *woody* at base. Flowers pink-purple, veined purple; outer sepal-ring 3-lobed, cup-shaped; Apr-Sept. Rocks and bare ground by sea. B, F.

57 **Smaller Tree Mallow*** *Lavatera cretica*
Medium/tall annual/biennial, differing from Common Mallow especially in its less deeply lobed leaves, paler and pinker flowers, outer sepal lobes broader and joined at base, and fruit segments with rounded angles; Apr-July. Bare places. B (rare), F.

57 **Marsh Mallow*** *Althaea officinalis*
Tall perennial, covered with velvety down, whose roots are used to make the sweetmeat. Flowers pink, 25-30 mm; outer sepal-ring 6-9-lobed; Aug-Sept. Damp saline places, especially near sea. B, F, G.

57 **Rough Mallow*** *Althaea hirsuta*
Short/medium, sometimes semi-prostrate annual. Leaves becoming more deeply cut up the stems. Flowers pale pink, becoming bluer; outer sepal-ring with 6-9 narrow lobes; May-July. Fruit rough, hairless. Cf. 1. Grassy and bare places, weed of cultivation; likes lime. (B), F, G.

ST JOHN'S WORT FAMILY
Guttiferae

Hairless, except Hairy and Marsh St John's Worts. Leaves opposite, untoothed, with translucent veins. Flowers in branched, usually leafy, clusters (except Rose of Sharon), open, yellow, with five petals and sepals and many stamens. Fruit a dry capsule, except Tutsan.

58 **Tutsan*** *Hypericum androsaemum*
Medium/tall half-evergreen undershrub, stems 2-winged, often reddish. Leaves broad oval, faintly aromatic when crushed. Flowers 20 mm; sepals oval, unequal; June-Aug. Fruit a fleshy *berry*, green, then red, finally purplish-black. Woods, shady places, cliff ledges. B, F.

58 **Rose of Sharon*** *Hypericum calycinum*
Creeping medium evergreen undershrub. Leaves elliptical. Flowers solitary, *70-80 mm*, anthers red; June-Oct. Banks, shrubberies. (B, F), from S E Europe.

58 **Perforate St John's Wort*** *Hypericum perforatum*
Medium perennial, with two raised lines down stem. Leaves oval to linear, with *translucent dots*. Flowers 20 mm, petals black-dotted, especially on margins; pointed sepals sometimes also black-dotted; July-Sept. Grassy and bushy places. T.

58 **Hairy St John's Wort*** *Hypericum hirsutum*
Medium/tall *downy* perennial. Leaves elliptical, with translucent dots. Flowers pale yellow, sometimes red-veined, 15-20 mm; sepals edged with black dots; July-Sept. Woods, scrub, hedge-banks. T.

58 **Square-stalked St John's Wort*** *Hypericum tetrapterum*
Medium/tall perennial; stems *4-winged*. Leaves with translucent dots, almost clasping the stem. Flowers pale yellow, 10 mm; sepals pointed, usually not black-dotted; July-Sept. Damp places, often by streams. T, southern.

58 **Slender St John's Wort*** *Hypericum pulchrum*
Slender short/medium perennial. Leaves with translucent dots and often inrolled margins. Flowers rich yellow, tinged *red* beneath, 15 mm; petals and sepals with black dots, petals also red-dotted; July-Sept. Heaths, scrub, open woods; not on lime. T, western.

58 **Trailing St John's Wort*** *Hypericum humifusum*
Slender, usually prostrate perennial. Leaves with translucent dots, often also with black dots on margins beneath. Flowers 10 mm, sepals sometimes black-dotted at margins; July-Oct. Open woods, heathy places; not on lime. T, southern.

58 **Irish St John's Wort*** *Hypericum canadense*
Low/short annual/perennial; stems with four raised lines. Leaves narrow, 1-3-veined. Flowers with no black dots, 6 mm; July-Sept. Damp places. B (Ireland), G.

58 **Marsh St John's Wort*** *Hypericum elodes*
Creeping low/short *greyish* perennial, conspicuously hairy. Leaves rounded. Flowers less open than other St John's Worts, 15 mm; sepals red-dotted at margins; June-Sept. Shallow fresh water, damp mud. B, F, G, western.

VIOLET FAMILY
Violaceae

VIOLETS AND PANSIES
Viola

Leaves alternate, toothed, with stipules. Flowers solitary, open, with five unequal petals, the lowest spurred; sepals with short appendages. Fruit an ovoid capsule. Hybrids frequent. Violets are perennials, with more or less heart-shaped leaves and inconspicuous stipules. Pansies may be annual and have more deeply toothed, more or less broad lanceolate leaves, with conspicuous leaflike stipules, and flatter flowers.

59 **Sweet Violet*** *Viola odorata*
Low creeping perennial, downy, with rooting runners. Leaves in a tuft, rounded, enlarging in summer. Flowers 15 mm, *fragrant*, blue-violet or white, rarely lilac, pink or yellow; sepals *blunt*; Mar-May, Aug-Sept. Woods, scrub, hedgebanks. T.

59 **Common Dog Violet*** *Viola riviniana*
Low perennial, almost hairless. Leaves in a tuft, heart-shaped, stipules usually toothed. Flowers 15-25 mm, blue-violet, *unscented*; spur stout, curved, pale, often creamy, notched at tip; sepals *pointed*, appendages enlarging in fruit; Mar-May, July-Sept. Woods, grassy places, mountains. T.

59 **Early Dog Violet*** *Viola reichenbachiana*
Similar to Common Dog Violet. Narrower leaves, paler 12-18 mm flowers with narrower petals and an unnotched violet spur and sepal appendages less prominent in fruit. Shady places. Southern.

59 **Heath Dog Violet*** *Viola canina*
Low/short perennial, hairless or slightly downy. Leaves not in a tuft, broad to narrow. Flowers 15-25 mm, bluer than Common Dog Violet, sometimes white, with spur yellowish or whitish. Sepals *pointed*, appendages not enlarging in fruit; Apr-June. Heaths, open woods, fens. T.

59 **Pale Dog Violet*** *Viola lactea*
Similar to Heath Dog Violet. Erecter, with narrower leaves, not heart-shaped, and pale bluish-white flowers with a short greenish spur; May-June. Heaths. B, F.

59 **Meadow Violet** *Viola pumila*
Low/short perennial, hairless. Leaves *narrow*. Flowers 15 mm, roundish, *pale blue*, spur greenish, short; May-June. Grassland. F, G, S, eastern.

59 **Northern Violet** *Viola selkirkii*
Low perennial, almost hairless. Leaves tufted, heart-shaped. Flowers 15 mm, pale violet, long-spurred, sepals pointed; Apr-May. *Coniferous* woods, damp places. S.

59 **Marsh Violet*** *Viola palustris*
Low perennial, usually hairless. Leaves kidney-shaped. Flowers 10-15 mm, pale lilac veined purple, short-spurred, bracts at or below middle of stalks; Apr-July. Bogs, marshes. T.

59 **Yellow Wood Violet** *Viola biflora*
Low creeping perennial, sparsely hairy. Leaves in a tuft, kidney-shaped. Flowers 15 mm, bright yellow; June-Aug. Damp, shady places, mainly in mountains. F, G, S.

59 **Wild Pansy*** *Viola tricolor*
Variable low/short annual/biennial, hairless or downy. Leaves oval to broad lanceolate; stipules leafy, pinnately lobed, the end lobe longer. Flowers 10-25 mm, violet, yellow or both, petals longer than sepals, spur longer than appendages; Apr-Nov. Grassy and bare places, dunes. T.

plate 59 **Mountain Pansy*** *Viola lutea*
Similar to Wild Pansy: a creeping perennial with longer flower stalks and 15-30 mm flowers, the end stipules not larger than the others; May-Aug. Mountain grassland.

59 **Field Pansy*** *Viola arvensis*
Variable low/short annual, shortly hairy. Leaves broad to narrow; stipules leafy, semi-pinnate, end segment lanceolate. Flowers 10-15 mm, cream-coloured, sometimes tinged yellow or violet, petals usually shorter than sepals, spur equalling appendages; Apr-Nov. Weed of cultivation. T.

59 **Dwarf Pansy*** *Viola kitaibeliana*
Similar to Field Pansy. Smaller, and downy, with more rounded lower leaves and stipule lobes, and 4-8 mm flowers never violet-tinged; Apr-July. Dry bare ground. B (rare), F, G, southern.

ROCK-ROSE FAMILY
Cistaceae

Downy. Leaves untoothed. Flowers 5-petalled, open, sepals unequal, stamens numerous. Fruit egg-shaped.

60 **Common Rock-rose*** *Helianthemum nummularium*
Variable, more or less prostrate undershrub. Leaves lanceolate to roundish, 1-veined, usually downy *white* beneath, opposite, with leaflike stipules. Flowers 20-25 mm, yellow, rarely white, cream, orange or pink; May-Sept. Grassy and rocky places on lime. T, southern.

60 **White Rock-rose*** *Helianthemum apenninum*
Similar to Common Rock-rose. Narrow leaves with markedly inrolled margins and smaller stipules, and flowers white with yellow centre. T, rare in B.

60 **Hoary Rock-rose*** *Helianthemum canum*
Similar to Common Rock-rose. Smaller, with narrower leaves, sometimes downy grey above, and 10-15 mm flowers; May-June.

60 **Spotted Rock-rose*** *Tuberaria guttata*
Low annual. Leaves elliptical, 3-veined, opposite. Flowers 10-20 mm, yellow, often with a *red spot*, petals dropping by mid-morning, sepals black-dotted; May-Aug. Dry, rather bare places, often on lime. B (rare), F, G.

60 **Common Fumana** *Fumana procumbens*
Spreading undershrub to 40 cm. Leaves alternate, linear, no stipules. Flowers yellow, usually with a deeper yellow spot; May. Dry, bare, often rocky places. F, G, S, southern.

SEA-HEATH FAMILY
Frankeniaceae

60 **Sea-heath*** *Frankenia laevis*
Prostrate mat-forming heather-like undershrub, variably downy. Leaves opposite, margins inrolled, sometimes with a white crust. Flowers 5-petalled, open, pink, purplish or whitish; July-Aug. Fruit a capsule. Sands, shingle and salt-marshes by sea. B, F.

GOURD FAMILY
Cucurbitaceae

60 **White Bryony*** *Bryonia cretica*
Climbing perennial to 4 m, hairy. Leaves *ivy-shaped*, not glossy, with unbranched tendrils opposite the stalks. Flowers 10-18 mm, 5-petalled, greenish-white with darker veins; stamens and styles on different plants, stigma downy; May-Sept. Fruit a *red* berry. Hedges, scrub. B, F, G.

WILLOWHERB FAMILY
Onagraceae

60 **Enchanter's Nightshade*** *Circaea lutetiana*
Short/medium patch-forming downy perennial. Leaves pointed oval, sometimes slightly heart-shaped, opposite. Flowers 4-8 mm, in leafless spikes which elongate before flowers fall; 2-petalled, white; June-Sept. Fruit covered with hooked bristles. Woods, shady places, sometimes a garden weed. T.

60 **Large-flowered Evening Primrose*** *Oenothera erythrosepala*
Medium/tall hairy biennial, with conspicuous red spots on stem. Leaves alternate, lanceolate, with finely toothed crinkled margins. Flowers 80-100 mm, 4-petalled, open, pale yellow, with red or red-striped sepal-tube; June-Sept. Fruit an elongated capsule. Bare and waste places, dunes. (B, F, G), of garden origin.

60 **Fragrant Evening Primrose*** *Oenothera stricta*
Differs from Large-flowered Evening Primrose in having no red spots and smaller (40-90 mm) flowers, fragrant at night and soon turning red; June-Sept. (B, F, G), from S America.

WILLOWHERBS
Epilobium

More or less hairy perennials. Leaves lanceolate (except New Zealand Willowherb), toothed. Flowers in stalked spikes (except New Zealand Willowherb), with four notched petals and eight stamens; June-Aug. Fruit a long narrow 4-sided pod, splitting when ripe to reveal the silky plume of hairs attached to each seed. Hybrids are very frequent.

61 **Rosebay Willowherb*** *Epilobium angustifolium*
Tall, patch-forming, almost hairless. Leaves alternate. Flowers 20-30 mm, bright pink-purple, petals slightly *unequal*. Open woods, heaths, mountains, waste ground. T.

61 **Great Willowherb*** *Epilobium hirsutum*
Tall, softly hairy. Leaves mostly opposite, the upper half-clasping stem. Flowers 15-25 mm, purplish-pink, stigma 4-lobed. Damp places. T.

61 **Hoary Willowherb*** *Epilobium parviflorum*
Similar to Great Willowherb but smaller, with woolly hairs on lower stem, upper leaves alternate and not clasping stem, and much smaller (6-9 mm) flowers.

61 **Broad-leaved Willowherb*** *Epilobium montanum*
Short/medium perennial, stem rounded. Leaves broad lanceolate, opposite, very shortly stalked. Flowers 6-9 mm, pinkish-purple, petals well notched, stigma 4-lobed. Shady and waste plates. T.

61 **Square-stemmed Willowherb*** *Epilobium tetragonum*
Similar to Broad-leaved Willowherb. Has four raised lines on stem, unstalked strap-shaped leaves, a club-shaped stigma and less notched petals.

61 **Pale Willowherb*** *Epilobium roseum*
Similar to Broad-leaved Willowherb. Has four raised lines on stem, mostly alternate long-stalked leaves and flowers white becoming pink with a club-shaped stigma. The latest to flower, Aug-Sept.

61 **American Willowherb*** *Epilobium adenocaulon*
Similar to Broad-leaved Willowherb. Has four raised lines on stem, mostly alternate leaves and smaller, paler flowers with a club-shaped stigma. (T), from N America.

61 **Marsh Willowherb*** *Epilobium palustre*
Slender short/medium perennial, with thread-like runners. Leaves unstalked, narrow, not or scarcely toothed. Flowers 4-6 mm, pink to white, stigma club-shaped. Wet places. T.

61 **Alpine Willowherb*** *Epilobium anagallidifolium*
Low creeping perennial, almost hairless, with runners above ground. Leaves little toothed. Flowers 4-5 mm, reddish-pink, sepals red. Pods red when ripe. Wet places on mountains. T.

61 **New Zealand Willowherb*** *Epilobium brunnescens*
Prostrate creeping perennial, almost hairless. Leaves stalked, rounded, weakly toothed, often bronzy. Flowers 4 mm, long-stalked, very pale pink, petals deeply notched. Bare damp places. (B, F), from New Zealand.

LOOSESTRIFE FAMILY
Lythraceae

61 **Purple Loosestrife*** *Lythrum salicaria*
Tall perennial, variably downy; stems with four raised lines. Leaves opposite or in whorls of three, untoothed, unstalked, lanceolate. Flowers 10-15 mm, in whorled spikes, *6-petalled*, bright red-purple; June-Aug. Fruit egg-shaped. Damp places, especially by rivers. T.

61 **Grass Poly*** *Lythrum hyssopifolia*
Low/short hairless annual. Leaves alternate, linear to oblong. Flowers tiny, 5-6-petalled, pale pink, unstalked at base of leaves; July-Sept. Bare damp ground, especially winter-wet hollows. T, southern.

DOGWOOD FAMILY
Cornaceae

Leaves opposite, untoothed, pointed oval. Flowers 4-petalled, in an umbel. Fruit a berry.

62 **Dogwood*** *Cornus sanguinea*
Deciduous shrub to 4 m, with *red* twigs, conspicuous in winter. Leaves with 3-5 pairs of prominent veins, reddening in autumn. Flowers *white*; May-July. Fruit black. Scrub, hedgerows, on lime. T.

62 **Cornelian Cherry*** *Cornus mas*
Deciduous shrub or small tree to 8 m, with greenish-yellow twigs. Umbels unstalked with four yellow-green sepal-like bracts, flowers *yellow*; Feb-Mar, *before leaves*. Fruit red. Woods, scrub, widely planted. (B), F, G.

62 **Dwarf Cornel*** *Cornus suecica*
Short creeping perennial. Leaves unstalked, rounded to elliptical. Umbels with four conspicuous *white petal-like* bracts, flowers purplish-black; June-Aug, shy flowerer. Fruit red. Heaths, moors, mountains; not on lime. B, G, S.

IVY FAMILY
Araliaceae

62 **Ivy*** *Hedera helix*
Evergreen woody climber, carpeting the ground or ascending by means of tiny roots. Leaves glossy, often bronzy, 3-5-lobed (ivy-shaped) on non-flowering shoots, pointed oval on flowering shoots. Flowers in an *umbel*, green with yellow anthers; Sept-Nov. Berries black. Woods, hedgerows, rocks, walls. T.

CARROT FAMILY
Umbelliferae

Leaves alternate, no stipules (except Marsh Pennywort). Flowers small, 5-petalled, in umbels, usually in turn arranged in an umbel. The whole flowerhead thus looks like a flat-topped umbrella, whose spokes (rays) are the stalks of the secondary umbels. Flowers of white-flowered species often tinged pink. The strap-like upper and lower bracts at the base of the primary and secondary umbels respectively, and the dry, usually ridged fruit, are both important in identification.

The first five species are untypical, all having their flowers in simple umbels.

62 **Marsh Pennywort*** *Hydrocotyle vulgaris*
Prostrate creeping perennial. Leaves almost *circular*, shallowly lobed, erect on long stalks. Flowers tiny, pinkish-green, in one or more whorls from base of leaves, often hard to detect among vegetation. June-Aug. Fruit rounded. Damp, often grassy places, shallow fresh and brackish water. T.

62 **Sanicle*** *Sanicula europaea*
Short/medium hairless perennial. Leaves long-stalked, shiny, *palmately* 3-5-lobed, toothed. Flowers pale pink or greenish-white, in clusters of tight umbels; May-July. Fruit roundish with hooked spines. Woods, often on lime. T.

CARROT FAMILY

plate 62 **Astrantia*** *Astrantia major*
Medium/tall perennial. Leaves long-stalked, pal-mately lobed, toothed. Flowers white, scented, in umbels with pinkish *petal-like* bracts; June-Sept. Woods, mountain meadows. (B, rare), F, G.

62 **Sea Holly*** *Eryngium maritimum*
Short/medium hairless perennial. Leaves leathery, rounded, spiny, blue-green with whitish veins and edges. Flowers powder-blue, in tight umbels with spiny leaflike bracts; June-Sept. Fruit egg-shaped. Sand and shingle by sea. T.

62 **Field Eryngo*** *Eryngium campestre*
Similar to Sea Holly. Much branched and greener, with smaller heads of usually greenish-white flowers. Bare, dry places. B (rare), F, G.

63 **Cow Parsley*** *Anthriscus sylvestris*
Medium/tall perennial, slightly hairy, stems often purple. Leaves 2-3-pinnate. Flowers white, no lower bracts; Apr-June. Fruit oblong, beaked, black, *smooth*. Hedge-banks, shady places. T.

63 **Sweet Cicely*** *Myrrhis odorata*
Similar to Cow Parsley. Aromatic when crushed, with leaves flecked whitish and much longer ribbed fruit. Waysides. (T), from S Europe.

63 **Rough Chervil*** *Chaerophyllum temulentum*
Medium/tall hairy biennial; stem *purple or purple-spotted*. Leaves 2-3-pinnate, turning purple. Flowers white, no lower bracts; May-July. Fruit long, ridged, narrowed to tip. Hedge-banks, shady places. T, southern.

63 **Bur Chervil*** *Anthriscus caucalis*
Medium annual, slightly hairy; stem often purplish below. Leaves 2-3-pinnate, finely cut. Flowers white, umbels *opposite* leaves, no lower bracts; May-June. Fruit with hooked bristles. Bare, often sandy places. T, southern.

63 **Upright Hedge Parsley*** *Torilis japonica*
Medium/tall hairy annual; stems *stiff*. Leaves 1-3-pinnate, narrowly triangular. Flowers white or pink, petals slightly unequal, lower bracts 4-6; July-Sept. Fruit egg-shaped, with purple *hooked* bristles. Hedge-banks, shady places. T.

63 **Knotted Bur Parsley*** *Torilis nodosa*
More or less prostrate annual, roughly hairy. Leaves 1-2-pinnate. Flowers white or pink, umbels few-flowered, *opposite* leaves; no lower bracts; upper bracts longer than flowers; May-July. Fruit with warts and *straight* bristles. Dry, sparsely grassy places. B, F, G.

63 **Coriander*** *Coriandrum sativum*
Short hairless, *foetid* annual. Leaves 1-2-pinnate, the lower with broader segments. Flowers white or pink, outer petals longer, no lower bracts; June-Aug. Fruit globular, ridged, red-brown, *aromatic* when ripe. Bare places. (B, F, G), from W Asia.

63 **Greater Bur Parsley*** *Turgenia latifolia*
Medium annual, roughly hairy. Leaves *1-pinnate*. Flowers pink, red-purple or white, with lower bracts 2-3, upper bracts broad with pale edges; May-Aug. Fruit ridged, with 2-3 rows of *hooked* bristles on each ridge. A weed of cultivation. (B, rare)' F, G.

63 **Caraway*** *Carum carvi*
Medium hairless biennial. Leaves 2-3-pinnate. Flowers white, usually no bracts; June-July. Fruit oblong, ridged, *aromatic*, the familiar caraway seed. Grassy places. T, but (B).

63 **Whorled Caraway*** *Carum verticillatum*
Medium/tall hairless perennial. Leaves oblong, with numerous *whorled* threadlike segments, recalling Yarrow (p. 62). Flowers white, with both upper and lower bracts; July-Aug. Fruit egg-shaped, ridged. Damp grassland, marshes. B, F, G, western.

63 **Wild Carrot*** *Daucus carota*
Medium hairy biennial. Leaves 3-pinnate. Flowers white, the centre one of the umbel often red, petals often unequal, *lower bracts conspicuously pinnate or 3-forked*; June-Sept. Fruit flattened, with often hooked bristles; fruit umbels become hollowly concave. Grassy places; near the sea often fleshy and more luxuriant. T.

64 **Pignut*** *Conopodium majus*
Short/medium perennial, almost hairless; root tuberous, edible. Leaves 2-3-pinnate, the upper with almost *thread-like* lobes. Flowers white, lower bracts 0-2; May-July. Fruit oblong, obscurely ridged, with erect styles. Open woods, shady grassland. B, F, S.

64 **Burnet Saxifrage*** *Pimpinella saxifraga*
Variable medium perennial, downy; stems slightly ridged. Leaves 1-2-pinnate, the lower usually *1-pinnate* with broader leaflets, the upper usually 2-pinnate with narrow leaflets. Flowers white, no bracts; May-Sept. Fruit egg-shaped. Dry grassland, especially on lime. T.

64 **Shepherd's Needle*** *Scandix pecten-veneris*
Short annual, almost hairless. Leaves 2-3-pinnate, lobes linear. Flowers white, umbels often simple but sometimes with 2-3 rays, *opposite* leaves; no lower bracts, upper bracts broad, deeply toothed; May-Aug. Fruit conspicuously *long* (15-80 mm). Weed of cultivation. T, southern.

64 **Ground Elder*** *Aegopodium podagraria*
Creeping, *patch-forming* short/medium perennial. Leaves 1-2-trefoil. Flowers white, usually no bracts; June-Aug. Fruit egg-shaped, ridged. Shady and waste places, and a tenacious garden weed. T.

64 **Moon Carrot*** *Seseli libanotis*
Variable medium/tall perennial, downy or hairless; stems ridged. Leaves 1-3-pinnate, lobes narrow. Flowers white or pink, umbels many-rayed, bracts numerous; July-Sept. Fruit egg-shaped. Dry grassland, especially on lime. T, but rare in B.

38

64 **Fool's Parsley*** *Aethusa cynapium*
Low/medium annual, hairless; stems ribbed. Leaves 2-3-pinnate, dark green. Flowers white, with long upper bracts making umbels look *bearded*; June-Oct. Fruit egg-shaped, ridged. Weed of cultivation. T. Ssp. *cynapioides* is taller; woods, eastern.

64 **Spignel*** *Meum athamanticum*
Short/medium perennial, hairless, *aromatic*. *Leaves 3-4 pinnate, lobes thread-like*. Flowers white, often tinged yellow or purple, lower bracts 0-2; June-Aug. Mountain grassland. B, F, G.

64 **Bladderseed*** *Physospermum cornubiense*
Medium/tall perennial, almost hairless. Leaves 2-trefoil, *dark green*. Flowers white, bracts lanceolate; July-Aug. Fruit globular, ridged. Woods. B (rare), F.

64 **Honewort*** *Trinia glauca*
Low *greyish* hairless perennial; stems angled, much branched. Leaves 2-3-pinnate, lobes narrow. Flowers white, stamens and styles on different plants, no bracts; May-June. Fruit egg-shaped, ridged. Grassland, especially on lime. B (rare), F, G.

65 **Hogweed*** *Heracleum sphondylium*
Very variable tall *stout* biennial/perennial, to 3 m, hairless or roughly hairy. Leaves 1-3-pinnate, with very broad toothed leaflets and stalks expanded to a sheath. Flowers white or pink, umbels up to 20 cm across, petals of outer flowers *larger*, usually no lower bracts; Apr-Nov. Fruit flattened, elliptical to rounded. Grassy places, open woods. T.

65 **Angelica*** *Angelica sylvestris*
Tall perennial, almost hairless, stems often purplish. Leaves 2-3-pinnate, with broad, toothed leaflets and *inflated* sheathing stalks. Flowers white or pink, sepals untoothed, often no lower bracts, upper bracts thread-like; July-Sept. Fruit egg-shaped, flattened, winged. Damp grassy places and woods, cliffs. T.

65 **Hemlock*** *Conium maculatum*
Tall hairless, foetid, very poisonous biennial; stems *purple-spotted*. Leaves 2-4-pinnate, finely cut. Flowers white, upper bracts only on *outer edge* of umbel; June-Aug. Fruit globular, with wavy ridges. Damp, sparsely grassy places. T.

65 **Hemlock Water Dropwort*** *Oenanthe crocata*
Tall hairless parsley-scented, very poisonous perennial; stems grooved. Leaves 3-4-pinnate, with broad *wedge-shaped* toothed leaflets. Flowers white, sometimes no lower bracts; June-Aug. Fruit cylindrical, long-styled. Damp grassy places. B, F.

65 **Greater Water-parsnip*** *Sium latifolium*
Tall hairless perennial; stems ridged. Leaves *1-pinnate* with about five pairs of leaflets; also submerged 2-3-pinnate leaves. Flowers white, lower bracts large, *leafy*; June-Sept. Fruit egg-shaped, ridged, short-styled. In and by fresh water, fens, marshes. T.

65 **Pleurospermum** *Pleurospermum austriacum*
Tall biennial/perennial, slightly hairy; stems ridged. Leaves 2-3-trefoil, *triangular*, lobes wedge-shaped, toothed. Flowers white, upper bracts unequal, down-turned, June-Sept. Fruit egg-shaped, ridged. Mountain grassland. F, G, S, eastern.

65 **Cowbane*** *Cicuta virosa*
Tall, hairless, very poisonous perennial, stems sometimes half-floating. Leaves 2-3-pinnate, lobes toothed. Flowers white, no lower bracts; July-Aug. Fruit globular, ridged. In and by fresh water. T.

65 **Longleaf*** *Falcaria vulgaris*
Medium/tall patch-forming annual/perennial; stems much branched. Leaves 1-2-trefoil with long *straplike*, finely toothed leaflets. Flowers white, umbels rather open, bracts linear; July-Sept. Fruit oblong, ridged. Grassy and waste places. T but (B, S).

65 **Cambridge Milk-parsley*** *Selinum carvifolia*
Tall perennial, almost hairless, parsley-scented, stems ridged. Leaves 2-3-pinnate, with winged ridges. July-Oct. Damp grassland and open woods. T, eastern, rare in B.

66 **Lesser Water-parsnip*** *Berula erecta*
Medium, often sprawling hairless perennial. Leaves 1-pinnate with 7-10 pairs of toothed leaflets; also 3-4 pinnate submerged leaves with linear lobes. Flowers white, umbels *opposite* leaves, bracts usually leaflike, often *3-cleft* or more or less pinnate; July-Sept. Fruit globular, almost divided in two, faintly ridged, long-styled. Wet places. T.

66 **Fool's Watercress*** *Apium nodiflorum*
More or less prostrate perennial; stems rooting at lower leaf-junctions. Leaves 1-pinnate, leaflets oval to lanceolate, toothed. Flowers white, umbels not or very shortly stalked, *opposite* leaves; *no* lower bracts; June-Sept. Fruit egg-shaped, ridged. Wet places. B, F, G.

66 **Wild Celery*** *Apium graveolens*
Medium/tall yellow-green biennial, hairless, *celery-scented*. Leaves 1-2-pinnate, shiny, with large toothed leaflets. Flowers white, umbels shortly or not stalked, often opposite leaves; no bracts; June-Aug. Fruit egg-shaped. Damp grassy places near sea, saline meadows inland. T.

66 **Tubular Water Dropwort*** *Oenanthe fistulosa*
Medium greyish hairless perennial, little branched. Leaves 1-2-pinnate, the upper with linear lobes and *inflated* stalks. Flowers white, umbels few-rayed, becoming globular in fruit; usually no lower bracts; June-Sept. Fruit cylindrical, long-styled. Wet places, shallow fresh water. T, southern.

66 **Parsley Water Dropwort*** *Oenanthe lachenalii*
Medium/tall perennial. Leaves 2-pinnate, the upper with narrower pointed lobes and sometimes 1-pinnate. Flowers white, umbel rays not thickened in fruit, sometimes no lower bracts; June-Sept. Fruit egg-shaped, ridged, short-styled. Damp grassland, fens. T, western.

39

CARROT FAMILY

plate 66 **Fine-leaved Water Dropwort*** *Oenanthe aquatica*
Medium/tall, pale green hairless perennial; much branched. Leaves 3-4-pinnate, upper with pointed lobes, lower with lobes linear to thread-like. Flowers white, umbels *opposite* leaves as well as terminal, rays not thickened in fruit; usually no lower bracts; June-Sept. Fruit oblong, often curved, short-styled. Slow or still fresh water. T.

66 **Corn Parsley*** *Petroselinum segetum*
Medium greyish hairless biennial, *parsley-scented*. Leaves 1-pinnate, leaflets broad, toothed. Flowers white, umbels few-rayed and few-flowered, bracts thread-like; Aug-Oct. Fruit egg-shaped. Dry, sparsely grassy places. B, F, G, western.

66 **Stone Parsley*** *Sison amomum*
Medium/tall perennial, hairless, *foetid*, pale green turning purple; much branched. Leaves and flowers like Corn Parsley. Fruit globular. Hedge-banks, grassy places. B, F.

67 **Hog's Fennel*** *Peucedanum officinale*
Tall dark green hairless perennial. Leaves 2-6-trefoil, the repeatedly divided linear lobes making a *tangled mass*. Flowers *yellow*, umbels many-rayed, often no lower bracts; July-Sept. Fruit egg-shaped, flattened, ridged. Grassy places. B (rare), F, G.

67 **Milk Parsley*** *Peucedanum palustre*
Tall perennial, almost hairless; stems often purplish. Leaves 2-4-pinnate, lobes blunt. Flowers white, bracts unequal, sometimes *forked*, down-turned; July-Sept. Fruit egg-shaped, flattened, ridged. Marshes, damp grassland. T.

67 **Masterwort*** *Peucedanum ostruthium*
Medium/tall perennial, almost hairless. Leaves 2-trefoil, with broad, toothed leaflets and *inflated* sheathing stalks. Flowers white or pink, no lower bracts; June-July. Fruit rounded, flattened, ridged. Grassy places in hills and mountains. F, G, (B, S).

67 **Hartwort*** *Tordylium maximum*
Medium/tall, coarsely hairy annual/biennial; stems with *down-turned* hairs. Leaves 1-pinnate, root leaves with broader leaflets. Flowers white, outer petals *larger*; June-Aug. Fruit rounded, flattened, ridged, bristly. Grassy and waste places. (B, rare), F, G.

67 **Sermountain** *Laserpitium latifolium*
Tall greyish perennial, almost hairless. Leaves 2-pinnate, stalks of upper leaves *inflated*, lobes heart-shaped. Flowers white, lower bracts numerous, *down-turned*; June-Aug. Fruit egg-shaped with wavy ridges. Mountain woods and rocks. F, G, S.

67 **Cnidium** *Cnidium dubium*
Medium/tall perennial, almost hairless. Leaves 2-3-pinnate, lobes with somewhat *recurved* edges and pointed whitish tip; stalks often purplish, sheathing the stem. Flowers white, umbels with numerous narrowly winged rays, few or no lower bracts;

July-Oct. Fruit globular, ridged. Damp woods, disturbed ground, often near sea. G, S.

67 **Scots Lovage*** *Ligusticum scoticum*
Medium/tall hairless perennial, *celery-scented*; stems often purple. Leaves 2-trefoil, glossy, with broad, toothed lobes and *inflated* stalks sheathing the stem. Flowers white, bracts narrow; June-July. Fruit egg-shaped, ridged. Cliffs, rocks and shingle by sea. B, G, S.

68 **Wild Parsnip*** *Pastinaca sativa*
Medium/tall biennial, roughly hairy, pungent. Leaves 1-pinnate with broad, toothed leaflets. Flowers yellow, few or no bracts; June-Sept. Fruit egg-shaped, winged. Grassy and bare places. T

68 **Alexanders*** *Smyrnium olusatrum*
Tall hairless pungent biennial. Leaves 3-trefoil, dark green, *glossy*, with broad, toothed leaflets. Flowers yellow, few or no bracts; Apr-June. Fruit globular, black. Hedge-banks and waste ground near sea. (B), F, G.

68 **Rock Samphire*** *Crithmum maritimum*
Short/medium greyish hairless perennial. Leaves 1-2-pinnate, with narrow *fleshy* lobes. Flowers yellow, bracts eventually down-turned; July-Oct. Fruit egg-shaped. Cliffs, rocks and sands by sea. B, F, G, southern.

68 **Fennel*** *Foeniculum vulgare*
Tall greyish strong-smelling biennial/perennial. Leaves 3-4-pinnate, feathery, with long *thread-like* lobes. Flowers yellow, no bracts; July-Sept. Fruit egg-shaped. Bare and waste ground, often by the sea. (B), F, G.

68 **Pepper Saxifrage*** *Silaum silaus*
Medium/tall hairless perennial. Leaves 2-4-pinnate, lobes linear, pointed. Flowers yellow, few or no lower bracts; June-Sept. Fruit egg-shaped, short-styled. Grassland. T, southern.

68 **Lovage** *Levisticum officinale*
Tall pungent perennial. Leaves 2-3-pinnate, *glossy*, with broad, toothed lobes. Flowers greenish-yellow, lower bracts numerous, upper bracts joined at base; June-Aug. Fruit egg-shaped, yellow brown. Grassy places in mountains. (F, G, S), from S W Asia.

67 **Slender Hare's-ear*** *Bupleurum tenuissimum*
A most atypical umbellifer, hard to detect among long grass. Medium greyish hairless annual. Leaves undivided, more or less *linear*. Flowers *yellow*, very small, in head-like umbels with 1-3 rays; no lower bracts; Aug-Sept. Fruit globular. Grassy places by the sea, saline meadows inland. T, southern.

68 **Thorow-wax*** *Bupleurum rotundifolium*
Short/medium, greyish or purplish annual, looking quite unlike most umbellifers. Leaves undivided, roundish, the upper narrower and *joining* round the stem, the lower short- or unstalked. Flowers yel-

40

low, umbels with 5-10 rays, secondary umbels *cupped* by enlarged upper bracts, no lower bracts; June-Aug. Fruit oblong, smooth, blackish. Weed of cultivation, bare ground. (B), F, G.

68 **Small Hare's-ear*** *Bupleurum baldense*
Low hairless greyish annual; another very untypical umbellifer, often hard to detect in short turf. Leaves undivided, *narrower*. Flowers yellow, in tiny 3-9-rayed head-like umbels, *enfolded* by the enlarged greyish, yellowish or brownish *bracts*; June-July. Fruit egg-shaped, smooth. Dry bare and grassy places; likes lime. B (rare), F.

68 **Sickle Hare's-ear*** *Bupleurum falcatum*
Medium/tall hairless perennial. Leaves *undivided*, variable, often *curved*. Flowers yellow, umbels with thread-like rays, lower bracts unequal; July-Oct. Fruit egg-shaped. Grassy and bare places. (B, rare), F, G.

WINTERGREEN FAMILY
Pyrolaceae

Evergreen creeping hairless perennials with 5-petalled flowers and fruit a dry capsule.

69 **One-flowered Wintergreen*** *Moneses uniflora*
Low perennial. Leaves rounded, toothed, pale green, opposite, tapering to the stalk. Flowers white, *solitary*, open, 15 mm; style long, straight; May-July. Woods, especially coniferous, in hill and mountain districts. T, but rare in B.

69 **Toothed Wintergreen*** *Orthilia secunda*
Low perennial. Leaves in rosettes, pointed oval, toothed, rather pale green. Flowers greenish-white, globular, 5 mm, in a nodding *one-sided* spike; style straight, protruding conspicuously from flower; June-Aug. Woods and rock ledges in hill and mountain districts. T.

69 **Common Wintergreen*** *Pyrola minor*
Low/short perennial. Leaves in a rosette, rounded, toothed. Flowers white or pale pink, globular, 6 mm, in a stalked spike, style *straight*, shorter than stamens, *not* protruding from flower; June-Aug. Woods, scrub, marshes, moors, mountains. T.

69 **Intermediate Wintergreen*** *Pyrola media*
Similar to Common Wintergreen. Flowers 10 mm, in longer spikes, with style protruding from flower and slightly curved.

69 **Round-leaved Wintergreen*** *Pyrola rotundifolia*
Short perennial. Leaves like Common Wintergreen but more rounded. Flowers pure white, larger (12 mm) and more *open* than Common Wintergreen with a much longer and *S-shaped* style; June-Sept. Woods, short turf, rock ledges, dune slacks. T.

69 **Norwegian Wintergreen** *Pyrola norvegica*
Similar to Round-leaved Wintergreen but shorter, with even more rounded leaves. Bare places in mountains. S.

69 **Yellow Wintergreen** *Pyrola chlorantha*
Short perennial. Leaves in a rosette, roundish, toothed. Flowers greenish- or yellowish-white, in a stalked spike, with style protruding, curved; June-July. Woods, rocks. F, G, S, eastern, but only on mountains in the south.

69 **Umbellate Wintergreen** *Chimaphila umbellata*
Short perennial. Leaves in *whorls*, narrowly oval, toothed, dark green, leathery. Flowers pink open, in *umbel-like* head, style not protruding; June-July. Woods, rocks. F, G, S.

69 **Yellow Birdsnest*** *Monotropa hypopitys*
Low perennial with no green colouring matter but stems and scale-like leaves *yellow*, turning brown; a saprophyte feeding on decaying organic matter. Flowers yellow, tubular, 4-5-petalled, in nodding spikes, erect in fruit; June-Aug. Fruit egg-shaped. Compare Birdsnest Orchid (p. 76). Woods, in Britain especially of beech and pine, and dunes. T.

DIAPENSIA FAMILY
Diapensiaceae

69 **Diapensia*** *Diapensia lapponica*
Low evergreen hairless undershrub, forming *cushions*. Leaves oval, untoothed, shiny, leathery. Flowers white, 5-petalled, stigma 3-lobed, sepals reddening in fruit. May-June. Fruit a dry capsule. Bare mountains and tundra. B (rare), S.

HEATH FAMILY
Ericaceae

Undershrubs or small shrubs with leaves undivided, usually alternate, untoothed and evergreen, and with margins inrolled downwards in many species, including all *Ericas*. Flowers globular, bell-shaped or flask-shaped (except Cranberry), the petals usually joined with 4-5 lobes. Fruit usually a dry capsule, but sometimes a berry.

70 **Heather*** *Calluna vulgaris*
Short/medium carpeting undershrub, sometimes downy. Leaves in opposite rows, linear. Flowers *pale* purple, in leafy stalked spikes; July-Sept. Heaths, moors, bogs, open woods, fixed dunes, often dominating extensive tracts. T.

70 **Bell Heather*** *Erica cinerea*
Short hairless undershrub. Leaves in whorls of three, linear, dark green, often bronzy. Flowers *red-purple*, in stalked spikes; May-Sept. Drier heaths and moors, open woods. T, western.

70 **Cross-leaved Heath*** *Erica tetralix*
Short greyish downy undershrub. Leaves in whorls of four, linear. Flowers *pink*, globular, 6-7 mm, in compact heads; June-Oct. Fruit downy. Wet heaths and moors, bogs. T, eastern.

41

plate 70 **Dorset Heath*** *Erica ciliaris*
Similar to Cross-leaved Heath. May be taller and more straggly, with leaves in whorls of three and broader; flowers larger (8-10 mm), more elongated and in spikes; and fruit hairless; Apr-Oct; hybridises with Cross-leaved Heath; B (rare), F.

70 **Cornish Heath*** *Erica vagans*
Short/medium hairless undershrub. Leaves in whorls of 4-5, linear. Flowers pink, lilac or white, in leafy stalked spikes, *chocolate-brown* anthers protruding; July-Sept. Drier heaths. B (rare), F.

70 **Irish Heath*** *Erica erigena*
Medium/tall hairless shrub *to 2 m*. Leaves in whorls of four, linear. Flowers pale pink-purple, in leafy stalked spikes, *reddish* anthers protruding; Mar-May and occasionally in winter. Wet moors, bogs. Ireland (rare), F.

70 **St Dabeoc's Heath*** *Daboecia cantabrica*
Short hairy undershrub. Leaves narrowly elliptical, *whitish* beneath, the margins inrolled downwards. Flowers pink-purple, in stalked spikes, calyx-teeth 4; May-Oct. Heaths, moors, open woods. B (Ireland), F.

70 **Mountain Heath*** *Phyllodoce caerulea*
Low/short undershrub. Leaves linear, rough-edged, flat, *green* beneath. Flowers purple, in head-like clusters of 1-6, calyx-teeth five; June-July. Moors. B (rare), S.

70 **Bog Rosemary*** *Andromeda polifolia*
Low/short hairless undershrub. Leaves narrowly elliptical, greyish and shiny above, whitish beneath. Flowers pink or white, in a terminal cluster; May-June. Bogs, wet heaths. T.

70 **Arctic Rhododendron** *Rhododendron lapponicum*
Low shrub. Leaves oval, leathery, dark green, reddish hairy beneath. Flowers tubular, violet; May-June. Mountain heaths. S.

71 **Bilberry*** *Vaccinium myrtillus*
Short/medium erect *deciduous* hairless undershrub; stems angled, green. Leaves oval, bright green, slightly toothed. Flowers pink or greenish-pink, solitary or paired; Apr-July. Fruit an edible *black* berry with characteristic purplish bloom. Hybridises with Cowberry. Heaths, moors, open woods, not on lime. T.

71 **Northern Bilberry*** *Vaccinium uliginosum*
Similar to Bilberry. Rounded brownish stems, bluish-green untoothed leaves, clusters of 1-4 pale pink flowers, and bluer berries. Mainly higher moors.

71 **Cowberry*** *Vaccinium vitis-idaea*
More or less prostrate creeping *evergreen* undershrub; twigs rounded, slightly downy when young. Leaves oval, broadest in the *middle*, untoothed, rather leathery, glossy, margins inrolled downwards. Flowers white or pink, open-mouthed, in clusters; May-July. Fruit an edible *red* berry. Hybridises with Bilberry. Moors, heaths, mountains, open woods. T.

71 **Cranberry*** *Vaccinium oxycoccos*
Low slender creeping evergreen undershrub. Leaves dark green, oval, whitish beneath. Flowers pink, with four spreading or *down-turned* petals and prominent stamens, slightly downy, 1-4 in stalked spikes; June-Aug. Fruit an edible round or pear-shaped red berry, spotted white or brown. Bogs, T.

71 **Alpine Bearberry*** *Arctostaphylos uva-ursi*
Prostrate *mat-forming* evergreen undershrub to 2 m, almost hairless. Leaves dark green, untoothed, broadest at *tip*, rather leathery, margins flat. Flowers pink, in clusters; Apr-July. Fruit a shiny edible *red* berry. Moors, mountains, rocks, open woods, scrub. T.

71 **Labrador Tea*** *Ledum palustre*
Evergreen bush to 1 m, with *rust-coloured* down on stems and under the oblong leathery dark green leaves. Flowers creamy white, in umbels, with five free petals. May-July. Fruit dry. Bogs. (B), G, S.

71 **Wild Azalea*** *Loiseleuria procumbens*
Prostrate mat-forming undershrub, hairless. Leaves *opposite*, oblong. Flowers small, pink, in umbels; May-July. Mountain tops, Arctic heaths. T, northern.

71 **Cassiope** *Cassiope hypnoides*
Prostrate mat-forming undershrub. Leaves scale-like, unstalked, *overlapping* up the stems. Flowers bell-shaped, with white and pink petals and *deeper pink* sepals, solitary, long-stalked, drooping; June-Aug. Mountain tops, Arctic heaths. S.

71 **Leatherleaf** *Chamaedaphne calyculata*
Short shrub. Leaves leathery, pointed oval. Flowers white, rim yellow, bell-shaped in a stalked spike; June. Damp places, S, northern.

71 **Strawberry Tree*** *Arbutus unedo*
Small evergreen *tree* or shrub, to 12 m, with roughish red-brown bark. Leaves elliptical, leathery, dark green, shiny, slightly toothed, alternate. Flowers creamy-white, bell-shaped, in drooping clusters; Aug-Dec. Fruit a warty berry, 2 cm across reddening the following autumn, and supposedly strawberry-like. Rocks, scrub. Ireland (rare), F, western.

CROWBERRY FAMILY
Empetraceae

71 **Crowberry*** *Empetrum nigrum*
Prostrate mat-forming or erecter tufted evergreen undershrub, resembling the Heath Family. Leaves oblong, dark green, shiny, margins *inrolled* downwards, alternate. Flowers pink, 6-petalled, very small, at base of leaves, stamens and styles usually on separate plants.; Apr-June. Fruit a *berry*, green, then pink, then purple, finally *black*. Moors, bogs. T.

PRIMROSE FAMILY
Primulaceae

Leaves undivided. Flowers 5-petalled (except Chickweed Wintergreen). Fruit a capsule. *Primula* has elongated oval leaves, all from the roots, and open flowers in an umbel (except Primrose) on leafless stalks.

72 **Primrose*** *Primula vulgaris*
Low hairy perennial. Leaves *tapering* to stalk. Flowers pale yellow, 20-23 mm, *solitary* on long hairy stalks; rarely the common stalk rises just above ground to make a long-stalked umbel; Mar-May and sporadically in autumn and winter. Hybridises with Oxlip and Cowslip. Woods, scrub, grassy banks, sea cliffs, mountains, often in quantity. T, southern.

72 **Oxlip*** *Primula elatior*
Low hairy perennial. Leaves *abruptly* narrowed at base. Flowers pale yellow, 15-20 mm, not fragrant, 1-20 in a nodding one-sided cluster; Apr-May. Hybridises with Primrose and Cowslip. Woods, scrub, grassland, usually in quantity. T, eastern.

72 **False Oxlip*** *Primula veris × vulgaris*
Is the not uncommon hybrid between Primrose and Cowslip, with leaves more gradually tapered to base, flowers deeper yellow and umbels not one-sided; grows singly, usually near one or both parents.

72 **Cowslip*** *Primula veris*
Low/short hairy perennial. Leaves *abruptly* narrowed at base. Flowers deeper yellow than Primrose and Oxlip, with orange spots in centre, 10-15 mm, *fragrant*, 1-30 in an often nodding one-sided cluster; Apr-May. Hybridises with Primrose and Oxlip. Grassland, open scrub and woods, often in quantity, on lime. T.

72 **Birdseye Primrose*** *Primula farinosa*
Low perennial, mealy white on young stems and beneath leaves. Leaves broadest near *tip, toothed*, in a basal rosette. Flowers lilac-pink with a yellow eye; sepal-teeth pointed; May-July. Grassy places in hills and mountains. T.

72 **Scottish Primrose*** *Primula scotica*
Low biennial, mealy white on stems and leaves. Leaves broadest in the *middle, untoothed*, in a basal rosette. Flowers purple with a yellow eye, sepal-teeth blunt; May-June and again in July-Aug. Short coastal turf and dunes. N Scotland.

72 **Yellow Loosestrife*** *Lysimachia vulgaris*
Medium/tall downy perennial. Leaves broad lanceolate, often black-dotted, very short-stalked, in whorls of 2-4. Flowers yellow, *15-20 mm*, in leafy branched clusters, sepal-teeth with reddish margins; July-Aug. Wet places and by fresh water. T.

72 **Tufted Loosestrife*** *Lysimachia thyrsiflora*
Medium perennial, almost hairless. Leaves lanceolate, unstalked, opposite. Flowers yellow, 5 mm, with prominent stamens, in *globular clusters* at base of middle leaves, top of stem having leaves only; June-July, a shy flowerer. Fens, marshes, by fresh water. T.

72 **Creeping Jenny*** *Lysimachia nummularia*
Prostrate creeping hairless perennial. Leaves rounded, opposite. Flowers yellow, *bell-like*, 15-25 mm, with broad sepal-teeth; June-Aug. Fruit uncommon in B. Damp shady and grassy places. T.

72 **Yellow Pimpernel*** *Lysimachia nemorum*
Is smaller than Creeping Jenny, with narrower pointed leaves and longer-stalked open 12 mm flowers with narrow sepal-teeth, and fruit frequent; May-Aug.

72 **Alpine Snowbell** *Soldanella alpina*
Low perennial, slightly hairy. Leaves thick, kidney-shaped, long-stalked. Flowers blue or white, bell-like, 2-3 together on leafless stems, the petals deeply cut to form a fringe. Mountains. G, southern.

73 **Water Violet*** *Hottonia palustris*
Pale green *aquatic* perennial, almost hairless, with short erect leafless stems above surface. Leaves *pinnate*, submerged. Flowers pale lilac with yellow eye, in a whorled cluster; May-July. Still fresh water. T, southern.

73 **Cyclamen** *Cyclamen purpurascens*
Low perennial, almost hairless. Leaves long-stalked, all arising direct from a corm, rounded, heart-shaped, not angled or lobed, sometimes finely toothed, pale-blotched above, reddish-purple beneath. Flowers carmine-pink, petals *turned back*, throat rounded; June-Oct, with the leaves. Woods, scrub. F, G, eastern.

73 **Sowbread*** *Cyclamen hederifolium*
Similar to Cyclamen. Sharply angled or lobed leaves, and longer-stalked paler pink or white flowers with 5-sided throat; Aug-Nov, before the leaves. (B), F.

73 **Chickweed Wintergreen*** *Trientalis europaea*
Low/short hairless perennial. Leaves lanceolate, in a *single whorl* near the top of the slender stem. Flowers white, star-like, 5-9-petalled, usually solitary; May-Aug. Conifer woods, moors, heaths. T.

73 **Brookweed*** *Samolus valerandi*
Low/short hairless perennial, often unbranched. Leaves oval, in a basal rosette, and alternate up the stems. Flowers white in a stalked spike, petals *joined half-way*; June-Aug. Fruit globular. Damp places, especially near sea. T, southern.

73 **Scarlet Pimpernel*** *Anagallis arvensis*
Prostrate annual, almost hairless, stems square. Leaves pointed oval, black-dotted beneath, unstalked, paired or whorled. Flowers usually pale scarlet, but sometimes pink, lilac or blue, *star-like*, solitary at base of leaves, opening in sunshine; petals blunt, often finely toothed at tip, with hairs along margins; May-Oct. Weed of cultivation, dunes. T.

plate 73 **Blue Pimpernel*** *Anagallis foemina*
Similar to Scarlet Pimpernel. Flowers always blue with narrower pointed hairless petals.

73 **Bog Pimpernel*** *Anagallis tenella*
Delicate, often mat-forming hairless perennial. Leaves oval or rounded, short-stalked, opposite. Flowers pink, *bell-like*, opening in sunshine; May-Sept. Boggy, peaty and marshy places, fens. B, F, G, western.

73 **Chaffweed*** *Anagallis minima*
One of the tiniest European plants, rarely over 5 cm high, often *under 2 cm*; a hairless annual. Leaves oval, with a thin *black line* round the underside, mostly alternate. Flowers pink, hidden at base of leaves, June-Aug. Fruit pink. Bare damp sandy places on heaths and in open woods. T.

73 **Northern Androsace** *Androsace septentrionalis*
Low/short downy annual/biennial. Leaves lanceolate, toothed, all in a basal rosette. Flowers white or pink, 5 mm, long-stalked, in an *umbel*; May-July. Dry grassy places, mountains. F, G, S, northern.

73 **Sea Milkwort*** *Glaux maritima*
More or less prostrate creeping hairless perennial. Leaves elliptical, almost unstalked, opposite. Flowers pale pink, petal-less, unstalked, solitary at base of leaves; May-Sept. *Saltmarshes*, on saline soils inland. T.

SEA-LAVENDER FAMILY
Plumbaginaceae

Perennials. Leaves undivided. Flowers 5-petalled, with *papery* bracts. Often in saline habitats. *Limoniums* are hairless and have leaves all basal and flowers in one-sided spikes in a branched cluster.

74 **Thrift*** *Armeria maritima*
Low/short downy cushion-forming perennial. Leaves linear, 1-veined, all basal. Flowers dark to pale pink, in *roundish* heads, with a brown bract; sepal-teeth with short bristles; Apr-Aug. Coastal cliffs, rocks and saltmarshes, also inland on mountains; ssp. *elongata* in sandy grassland. T.

74 **Common Sea-lavender*** *Limonium vulgare*
Low/short carpeting perennial, stems rounded. Leaves elliptic to broad lanceolate, long-stalked, with *pinnate* veins. Flowers lilac-lavender, tightly packed in flat-topped clusters, at the end of the stalks, which usually start branching well above the middle; July-Sept. Coastal saltmarshes. T, western.

74 **Matted Sea-lavender*** *Limonium bellidifolium*
Low perennial, with stems branched almost from the base into numerous *zigzag* branches, rough to the touch. Leaves oblong. Flowers pink-lavender, with whitish bracts, only on the uppermost branches; June-Aug. Coastal saltmarshes. B (rare), F.

74 **Rock Sea-lavender*** *Limonium binervosum*
Variable low/short perennial; stems branched from near base. Leaves oval to lanceolate, not pinnately veined, with a winged 3-veined stalk. Flowers lilac-lavender, on all but the lowest branches, spikes curved; July-Sept. Coastal cliffs and rocks, less often shingle and sand. B, F.

OLIVE FAMILY
Oleaceae

74 **Wild Privet*** *Ligustrum vulgare*
Half-evergreen shrub to 4 m. Leaves lanceolate, untoothed, opposite, rather leathery, often bronzing. Flowers white, strong-smelling, in short spikes, with four joined petals; May-June. Fruit a shiny *black* berry. Scrub, open woods. T.

BOGBEAN FAMILY
Menyanthaceae

74 **Bogbean*** *Menyanthes trifoliata*
Short hairless aquatic or creeping perennial. Leaves *trefoil*, held conspicuously above surface. Flowers pink and white, in spikes, petal-tube with five lobes, *fringed* with long white hairs; Apr-June. Fruit globular. Shallow fresh water, marshes, fens, bogs. T.

74 **Fringed Water-lily*** *Nymphoides peltata*
Hairless aquatic perennial. Leaves rounded, shallowly toothed, floating, purple beneath and sometimes purple-spotted above; much smaller than true water-lilies (p. 12). Flowers yellow, with five *fringed* petal-lobes; June-Sept. Fruit egg-shaped. Still and slow-moving fresh water. B, F, G.

PERIWINKLE FAMILY
Apocynaceae

74 **Lesser Periwinkle*** *Vinca minor*
More or less prostrate evergreen undershrub, almost hairless; stems rooting. Leaves elliptic, opposite, short-stalked, rather leathery. Flowers *blue-violet*, 25-30 mm, solitary, with five joined petals; Feb-May. Fruit elongated, forked. Woods, hedge-banks, rocks. (B), F, G.

74 **Greater Periwinkle*** *Vinca major*
Similar to Lesser Periwinkle. Quite hairless and has stems rooting only at tip, much broader longer-stalked leaves, and larger (40-50 mm) flowers with fringed sepals.

MILKWEED FAMILY
Asclepiadaceae

74 **Vincetoxicum** *Vincetoxicum hirundinaria*
Variable medium/tall perennial, slightly hairy. Leaves *heart-shaped*, sharply pointed, opposite

44

Flowers greenish, or yellowish-white, in clusters at base of upper leaves, with five joined petals; June-Sept. Fruit elongated, forked. Woods, rocks, bare ground; on lime. F, G, S.

GENTIAN FAMILY
Gentianaceae

Hairless. Leaves undivided, untoothed, opposite, usually unstalked; no stipules. Flowers in a branched cluster, with joined petals, often opening only in sunshine. Fruit a dry capsule.

75 **Common Centaury*** *Centaurium erythraea*
Variable low/short annual. Leaves elliptical, 3-7-veined, mostly in a basal *rosette* but a few narrower stem leaves. Flowers pink, 5-petalled, almost *unstalked* in tightly packed stalked clusters, but occasionally solitary; June-Sept. Grassy places, dunes. T.

75 **Lesser Centaury*** *Centaurium pulchellum*
Slender low/short annual, varying from unbranched to well branched. Leaves elliptical, with *no* basal rosette. Flowers reddish-pink, with five (rarely four) rather narrow petals, *stalked*, in loose, widely spreading clusters; June-Sept. Damp grassy places, drier salt-marshes. T.

75 **Perennial Centaury*** *Centaurium scilloides*
Low/short perennial; stems numerous, semiprostrate, some *not* flowering. Leaves roundish and stalked on the non-flowering stems. Flowers pink, larger than Common Centaury in heads of 1-6, 5-petalled; July-Aug. Grassy sea cliffs. B (rare), F.

75 **Yellow-wort*** *Blackstonia perfoliata*
Short/medium greyish annual. Leaves of basal rosette oblong, stem leaves more or less triangular and *joined* round stem. Flowers yellow, 6-8-petalled, petals longer than sepals, in a loose branched cluster; ssp. *serotina* has leaves not completely joined, flowers paler and sepals equalling petals. June-Oct. Grassy places, dunes, on lime. B, F, G.

75 **Yellow Centaury*** *Cicendia filiformis*
Low annual, sometimes only 2 cm high, often little branched. Leaves linear. Flowers yellow, solitary, 4-petalled; June-Oct. Fruit egg-shaped. Bare damp places, often near sea. B, F, G, western.

75 **Guernsey Centaury** *Exaculum pusillum*
A minute low annual, sometimes only 1 cm high, well branched, very hard to detect in short turf. Leaves linear, greyish. Flowers pink, pale yellow or white, 4-petalled, minute; sepal-teeth long, narrow; June-Oct. Bare damp places. F.

75 **Great Yellow Gentian** *Gentiana lutea*
Medium/*tall* perennial. Leaves pointed oval, up to 30 cm, bluish-green, the upper clasping the stem, the lower stalked. Flowers yellow, 5-9-petalled, in tight whorls at base of upper leaves; June-Aug. Grassy places in mountains. F, G.

75 **Northern Gentian** *Gentianella aurea*
Short biennial, branched from the base. Leaves oval, the upper unstalked. Flowers in a leafy spike, the leaves almost concealing the dull blue-violet flowers, dull yellow at the base; sepals 4-5; July-Aug. Near coast. S. northern.

76 **Spring Gentian*** *Gentiana verna*
Low tufted perennial. Leaves oval to elliptical, mostly in a basal rosette. Flowers bright blue, *solitary*, petal-tube 5-lobed, 15-25 mm long; Apr-June. Short, often stony turf in hills and mountains. B, F, G.

76 **Alpine Gentian*** *Gentiana nivalis*
A slenderer annual, often unbranched, with flowers half the size (10-15 mm) of Spring Gentian. Also on Arctic heaths. T, but rare in B.

76 **Marsh Gentian*** *Gentiana pneumonanthe*
Low/short perennial. Leaves linear. Flowers bright blue, striped *green* outside, trumpet-shaped. 25-40 mm long, often solitary, petal-tube 5-lobed; July-Sept. Wet heaths, bogs. T.

76 **Cross Gentian** *Gentiana cruciata*
Medium perennial. Leaves oval to broad lanceolate, rather leathery, the upper clasping the stem, the lower stalked. Flowers *dull* blue, oblong, in tight clusters up the stem, petal-tube 4-lobed; June-Sept. Dry grassy places, open woods. F, G, eastern.

76 **Purple Gentian** *Gentiana purpurea*
Short/medium perennial. Leaves elliptical, greyish, the lower stalked. Flowers bright *red-purple*, yellow at base and with green stripes and spots, bell-shaped, petal-tube 5-8-lobed; sepal-tube split to base on one side; July-Aug. Grassy and rocky places in mountains. F, G, S.

76 **Field Gentian*** *Gentianella campestris*
Short annual/biennial, variably branched. Leaves oval and blunt at base, narrower and pointed on stem. Flowers bluish-mauve, bell-shaped, 15-30 mm long, in small clusters up the stem, *petal-tube 4-lobed*; sepal-tube with two outer lobes much larger and *overlapping* the inner ones; June-Oct. Grassy places, dunes. T.

76 **Autumn Gentian*** *Gentianella amarella*
Low/short biennial. Leaves elliptical to lanceolate. Flowers dull purple, sometimes whitish, bell-shaped, 12-22 mm long, in small clusters up the stem, petal-lobes four or five; sepal-teeth equal; July-Sept. Hybridises with Chiltern Gentian. Grassy places, dunes, often on lime. T.

76 **Chiltern Gentian*** *Gentianella germanica*
Similar to Autumn Gentian but larger with broader leaves and longer (25-35 mm) flowers wider at the mouth. Always on lime. B (rare), F, G.

76 **Slender Gentian** *Gentianella tenella*
Slender low annual, often unbranched. Leaves oblong, the lower *broader* at the tip. Flowers dull

blue-violet, 8-12 mm long, *long-stalked*, with usually four petal-lobes; July-Aug. Grassy places in mountains. F, G, S.

plate 76 **Fringed Gentian** *Gentianella ciliata*
Slender low/short perennial. Leaves linear, not in a rosette. Flowers blue, in small clusters at base of upper leaves, the four spreading oval petal-lobes 40 mm across and *fringed* with hairs; Aug-Oct. Dry grassy, rocky places. F.

76 **Marsh Felwort** *Swertia perennis*
Medium perennial, unbranched. Leaves lanceolate, yellowish-green, the upper clasping the stem, the lower long-stalked. Flowers purple, 5-petalled, *star-like*, 25-35 mm across; July-Sept. Wet grassy places in mountains. F, G.

BINDWEED FAMILY
Convolvulaceae

Often climbers, twining anticlockwise. Leaves alternate, no stipules. Fruit a capsule. *Convolvulus* and *Calystegia* have flowers open trumpet-shaped.

77 **Hedge Bindweed*** *Calystegia sepium*
Creeping or climbing perennial to 3 m, more or less hairless. Leaves arrow-shaped. Flowers white, rarely pink, unscented, *30-35 mm* across; two large but not overlapping sepal-like bracts enclosing the five narrower sepals; June-Sept. Fruit a capsule. Bushy and waste places, woods, fens. T.

77 **Great Bindweed*** *Calystegia silvatica*
Similar to Hedge Bindweed but larger (60-75 mm) flowers, occasionally pink or pink-striped, and larger, almost inflated overlapping bracts, hiding the sepals. (T) from S Europe, often commoner in and around human settlements.

77 **Sea Bindweed*** *Calystegia soldanella*
Prostrate creeping hairless perennial. Leaves *kidney-shaped*, fleshy. Flowers pink with white stripes, 40-50 mm across, bracts shorter than sepals; June-Sept. Coastal sand, less often on shingle. B, F, G, western.

77 **Field Bindweed*** *Convolvulus arvensis*
Creeping or climbing perennial to 2 m, slightly downy when young. Leaves arrow-shaped. Flowers pink and/or white, *15-30 mm* across, faintly scented; June-Sept. Weed of cultivation, waste places. T.

77 **Common Dodder*** *Cuscuta epithymum*
Slender *climbing* annual, parasitic on Gorse (p. 26), Heather (p. 41) and many smaller plants; stems red. Leaves reduced to *scales*. Flowers pale pink, scented, bell-shaped with five pointed petal-lobes, stamens and styles slightly protruding, sepals pointed, in tight heads; June-Oct. Heaths, grassy places. T.

PHLOX FAMILY
Polemoniaceae

77 **Jacob's Ladder*** *Polemonium caeruleum*
Medium/tall perennial, slightly downy. Leaves *pinnate*, alternate. Flowers in a cluster, purplish-blue, open, with five petal-lobes; June-Aug. Fruit a capsule. Grassy places and open woods in hill and mountain districts, also as a garden escape. B (rare), F, G.

BEDSTRAW FAMILY
Rubiaceae

Stems *square*, weak, often scrambling over other vegetation. Leaves usually elliptical or lanceolate, unstalked, in *whorls*, with often leaflike stipules. Flowers in clusters or loose heads, small, open, with usually four petal-lobes. Only Field Madder has sepals. Fruit a 2-lobed nutlet, a berry in Wild Madder.

77 **Field Madder*** *Sherardia arvensis*
More or less prostrate annual, hairy. Leaves in whorls of 4-6, elliptical. Flowers *pale purple*, in heads surrounded by leaflike bracts; May-Sept. Fruit globular, surrounded by enlarged sepal-teeth. Bare and cultivated ground. T.

77 **Squinancywort*** *Asperula cynanchica*
Slender, more or less prostrate hairless perennial. Leaves *linear*, sometimes unequal, in whorls of four. Flowers pale pink outside, white inside, in terminal clusters, petal-lobes four, bracts lanceolate; June-Sept. Dry grassland, dunes; on lime. B, F, G.

77 **Blue Woodruff*** *Asperula arvensis*
Slender short annual, hairless. Leaves linear, blunt, in whorls of 6-9. Flowers bright *blue*; in heads; Apr-June. Weed of cultivation. (B, rare), G.

78 **Wild Madder*** *Rubia peregrina*
Scrambling evergreen perennial to 2 m; stems rough on angles with down-turned prickles. Leaves lanceolate, dark green, shiny, *prickly*, rather leathery, in whorls of 4-6. Flowers yellowish-green, petal-lobes 5, in small stalked clusters at base of leaves. June-Aug. Fruit a black *berry*. Woods, scrub, rocks; in Britain near the sea. B, F.

78 **Crosswort*** *Cruciata laevipes*
Short perennial, *softly* hairy. Leaves elliptical, yellowish-green, in whorls of four. Flowers *pale yellow*, scented, with bracts on stalks, in whorls at base of leaves; Apr-June. Fruit blackish. Grassy places, open woods; on lime. B, F, G.

77 **Woodruff*** *Galium odoratum*
Short *carpeting* perennial, almost hairless; unbranched. Leaves elliptical, in whorls of 6-9, edged with tiny forward-pointing prickles. Flowers *white*, in loose heads; Apr-June. Fruit covered with hooked bristles. Woods. T.

78 **Hedge Bedstraw*** *Galium mollugo*
Variable medium/tall, often scrambling perennial, sometimes downy; stems *smooth*, square. Leaves elliptical, *1-veined*, ending in a point, in whorls of 6-8. Flowers white, petal lobes pointed, in loose branched clusters; June-Sept. Fruit black. Hybridises with Lady's Bedstraw. Grassy places, hedge-banks. T.

78 **Northern Bedstraw*** *Galium boreale*
Short, rather stiff perennial, sometimes downy. Leaves dark green, rough-edged, *3-veined*, in whorls of four. Flowers white, in clusters; June-Aug. Fruit covered with hooked bristles. Grassy, bushy and rocky places. T.

78 **Heath Bedstraw*** *Galium saxatile*
More or less prostrate hairless perennial. Leaves elliptical, sharply pointed, in whorls of 4-6, edged with forwardly directed prickles. Flowers white, with a sickly fragrance, in short-stalked clusters along the stems; June-Aug. Fruit with very pointed warts. Dry grassy and heathy places; not on lime. T.

78 **Marsh Bedstraw*** *Galium palustre*
Variable, rather straggling, short/medium hairless perennial; stems *rough* at angles. Leaves elliptical, blunt, in whorls of 4-5. Flowers white, anthers red, in loose stalked clusters; June-Aug. Fruit black. Wet places. T.

78 **Lady's Bedstraw*** *Galium verum*
Low/short sprawling perennial, almost hairless. Leaves linear, dark green, shiny, with margins in-rolled beneath, in whorls of 8-12. Flowers *bright yellow*, in leafy clusters; June-Sept. Fruit black. Hybridises with Hedge Bedstraw. Dry grassy places. T.

78 **Common Cleavers*** *Galium aparine*
Straggling medium/tall annual, *clinging* to animal fur and human clothing by numerous tiny down-turned prickles on stems, leaves and fruit. Leaves lanceolate, in whorls of 6-8. Flowers *dull* white, in small stalked clusters at base of and longer than leaves; May-Sept. Fruit green or purplish, bristles with white swollen bases, on straight spreading stalks. Hedge-banks, fens, disturbed and waste ground, shingle. T.

BORAGE FAMILY
Boraginaceae

Hairy (except Oyster Plant), often roughly hairy. Leaves undivided, alternate. Flowers often pink in bud, later turning blue, five joined petals, usually in *one-sided* stalked spikes, which at first are tightly coiled. Fruit four nutlets.

79 **Common Comfrey*** *Symphytum officinale*
Tall stout perennial, softly hairy; well branched. Leaves broad lanceolate, *running down* on to winged stems, root leaves largest, to 25 cm. Flowers creamy white or mauve, bell-like, in forked clus-

ters; sepal-teeth pointed, at least equalling tube; May-June. Fruit black, shiny. By fresh water, fens. T.

79 **Russian Comfrey*** *Symphytum* × *uplandicum*
Is a hybrid between Common Comfrey and Rough Comfrey (*S. asperum*), is stiffly hairy and has stem wings narrower and not reaching next leaf-junction, and blue or purple-blue flowers. Dry waysides, waste places, a widespread escape from cultivation. (T).

79 **Houndstongue*** *Cynoglossum officinale*
Medium/tall greyish biennial, softly downy, *smelling of mice*. Leaves lanceolate. Flowers *maroon*, open, in clusters; May-Aug. Fruit flattened, covered with short hooked spines and so adhering to fur and clothing, with a thickened flange. Dry grassy places, dunes. T.

79 **Amsinckia*** *Amsinckia intermedia*
Short/medium annual, rather bristly. Leaves lanceolate. Flowers *orange-yellow*, on upper side of coiled spikes. Apr-Aug. Fruit wrinkled. Bare or disturbed ground. (B, G), from America.

79 **Yellow Alkanet*** *Anchusa ochroleuca*
Medium perennial, roughly hairy. Leaves lanceolate. Flowers creamy yellow, open, in clusters; *white-edged* blunt sepals cut to less than half-way; July-Aug. Waste places. (B, F, G), from Caucasus.

79 **Nonea** *Nonea pulla*
Short/medium greyish perennial. Leaves oblong to lanceolate, hairy but not rough, the upper clasping the stem. Flowers dark brown, in a loose leafy one-sided spike, sepals enlarging in fruit; Apr-Aug. Fruit egg-shaped, beaked. Dry grassy, stony places. (F, S), G.

79 **Common Gromwell*** *Lithospermum officinale*
Medium/tall perennial, *well* branched. Leaves lanceolate, unstalked, with prominent side veins. Flowers creamy white, in leafy clusters; May-July. Fruit white, shiny, smooth. Woods, scrub. T.

79 **Corn Gromwell*** *Buglossoides arvensis*
Short/medium annual; *little* branched. Leaves strap-shaped to lanceolate, without prominent side veins, the lower shortly stalked. Flowers creamy white, in clusters; Apr-Sept. Fruit grey-brown, warty. A weed of cultivation. T.

79 **Purple Gromwell*** *Buglossoides purpuro-caerulea*
Short/medium perennial, downy, unbranched. Leaves narrow lanceolate, dark green. Flowers reddish-purple turning *blue*, in leafy terminal clusters; Apr-June. Fruit white, shiny. Woods, scrub, on lime. B (rare), F, G.

80 **Lungwort*** *Pulmonaria officinalis*
Low/short perennial, downy. Leaves lanceolate, *pale spotted*, abruptly narrowed at base, those from roots greatly enlarging after flowering, to 40-60 cm. Flowers pink and blue, bell-shaped, sepals with short broad teeth, in leafy clusters; Mar-May. Fruit egg-shaped, pointed. Shady places. T, but (B).

47

plate 80 **Blue-eyed Mary*** *Omphalodes verna*
Low/short creeping perennial, slightly downy. Leaves *pointed oval*, often heart-shaped, long-stalked. Flowers bright blue, 10 mm across, in a loose cluster; Mar-May. Fruit with a hairy border. Woods. (B, F, G).

FORGETMENOTS
Myosotis

Leaves oblong, usually unstalked. Flowers usually pink in bud, later blue, open. Fruit shiny, on usually elongated spikes.

80 **Wood Forgetmenot*** *Myosotis sylvatica*
Short perennial, softly hairy. Flowers *sky-blue*, 6-10 mm, flat, sepal-tube with spreading hooked hairs; Apr-July. Fruit dark brown, on spreading stalks longer than sepal-tube. Woods, grassland, mountains. T.

80 **Field Forgetmenot*** *Myosotis arvensis*
Low/short, softly hairy annual/biennial. Lower leaves stalked, in a rosette. Flowers *grey-blue*, 3-5 mm across, cup-shaped, sepal-tube with numerous hooked hairs; Apr-Oct. Fruit dark brown, shiny, on stalks longer than sepal-tube. Dry bare or disturbed ground, shady places, dunes. T.

80 **Changing Forgetmenot*** *Myosotis discolor*
Slender low/short annual. Flowers creamy or pale *yellow* at first, turning blue, smaller, almost unstalked; May-June. Fruit dark brown, shiny, on stalks shorter than sepal-tube, which has *incurved teeth*. Bare places, usually on light soils. T.

80 **Water Forgetmenot*** *Myosotis scorpioides*
Low/short creeping perennial; hairs closely *pressed* to stems and sepal-tube. Flowers sky-blue, occasionally pink or white, flat, petals notched, 4-10 mm across, sepal-teeth short, cut up to one-third; June-Sept. Fruit black, on stalks 1-2 times as long as sepal-tube. *Wet* places. T.

80 **Creeping Forgetmenot*** *Myosotis secunda*
Similar to Water Forgetmenot. Spreading hairs on lower stem, flowers 4-6 mm, sepal-tube narrowly cut to at least half-way, and fruit dark brown on stalks 3-5 times as long as sepal-tube, down-turned. B, G, S.

80 **Tufted Forgetmenot** *Myosotis laxa*
Similar to Water Forgetmenot. May be hairless and has flowers 2-4 mm, petals not notched, sepal-teeth cut up to ¾, and fruit dark brown on stalks 2-3 times as long as sepal-tube.

80 **Jersey Forgetmenot** *Myosotis sicula*
Similar to Water Forgetmenot but smaller with flowers pale blue and 2-3 mm, petals not notched, blunt sepal-teeth half as long as sepal-tube, and brown fruit on stalks 1-3 times as long as sepal-tube. F.

80 **Madwort*** *Asperugo procumbens*
Prostrate annual, very bristly; stems *angled*. Flowers blue, 3 mm across, 1-3 together on short down-turned stalks much shorter than the elliptical leaves; May-Nov. Fruit *surrounded* by enlarged sepals. Bare and disturbed ground. T, but (B, rare).

80 **Bur Forgetmenot** *Lappula squarrosa*
Short, greyish annual/biennial, roughly hairy; well branched. Leaves lanceolate, unstalked. Flowers blue, 2-4 mm, in a loose leafy spike; June-July. Fruit with *hooked* spines, surrounded by *star-like* sepal-teeth. Dry bare places, dunes. F, G, S.

81 **Viper's Bugloss*** *Echium vulgare*
Short/medium perennial, roughly hairy. Leaves lanceolate, with no prominent side veins, the upper unstalked. Flowers pink turning vivid blue, 15-20 mm. in a branched spike, with all stamens *protruding*; May-Sept. Fruit hidden by sepal-teeth which give fruit spike a mossy appearance. Dry bare and waste places. T.

81 **Green Alkanet*** *Pentaglottis sempervirens*
Medium perennial, roughly hairy. Leaves pointed oval, the lower stalked. Flowers bright blue, *white-eyed*. 10 mm. in long-stalked leafy clusters, sepal-teeth blunt; Apr-July. Woods, hedge-banks. T, western, but (B).

81 **Borage*** *Borago officinalis*
Medium annual, roughly hairy, with cucumber-scented juice. Leaves pointed oval with wavy margins, the lower stalked. Flowers bright blue, 20-25 mm. in loose leafy clusters, with narrow petal and sepal lobes and a prominent column of purple stamens; May-Sept. Fruit rough. Waysides, waste places. (B, F, G), from S Europe.

81 **Alkanet*** *Anchusa officinalis*
Medium biennial/perennial, *softly* hairy, well branched. Leaves lanceolate, the lower narrowed to a stalk. Flowers blue-purple, 10 mm. in an elongating coiled cluster; June-Aug. Fruit conical, unstalked. Grassy places. T. but (B).

81 **Bugloss*** *Anchusa arvensis*
Short annual, roughly hairy. Leaves lanceolate, *wavy-edged*. Flowers blue 5-6 mm. in elongating often forked clusters, the petal-tube bent; Apr-Sept. Fruit unstalked. Bare, often sandy or cultivated places. T.

81 **Oyster Plant*** *Mertensia maritima*
Prostrate mat-forming greyish *hairless* perennial. Leaves oval, *fleshy*, oyster-tasting. Flowers pink turning blue-purple, in leafy clusters; June-Aug. Fruit smooth, fleshy. Coastal shingle. B. S. northern.

VERBENA FAMILY
Verbenaceae

81 **Vervain*** *Verbena officinalis*
Short/medium perennial, roughly hairy, stems stiff, square. Leaves pinnately lobed, toothed, opposite,

the upper unstalked. Flowers lilac, more or less *2-lipped*, petals 5-lobed, in long slender leafless spikes; June-Oct. Dry bare or sparsely grassy places. T. southern.

LABIATE FAMILY
Labiatae

Often *aromatic*. Stems *square*. Leaves usually undivided, in *opposite* pairs. Flowers with both petals and sepals, normally *2-lipped* and open-mouthed (except Mints, p. 51) though *Ajuga* and *Teucrium* both have upper lip absent or very short, but lower lip 3-lobed and 5-lobed respectively. Fruit four nutlets.

82 **Bugle*** *Ajuga reptans*
Low/short creeping perennial; runners *rooting*, stems hairy on two sides. Leaves oblong, scarcely toothed, hairless, often bronzy, the lower long-stalked. Flowers powder-blue, rarely pink or white, in a leafy, often purplish, spike; Apr-June. Damp woods, grassland. T.

82 **Ground-pine*** *Ajuga chamaepitys*
Low greyish annual, faintly *aromatic* of pine resin. Looks somewhat like a bushy pine seedling with its narrowly *linear* 3-lobed leaves. Flowers yellow, red-dotted, 1-2 together up the leafy stems; May-Sept. Bare, stony, sparsely grassy places. B, F, G.

82 **Skullcap*** *Scutellaria galericulata*
Short creeping perennial, often downy. Leaves lanceolate, bluntly toothed, short-stalked. Flowers bright *blue*, in *pairs* up the leafy stem; petal-tube slightly curved; June-Sept. Hybridises with Lesser Skullcap. Wet grassy places, by fresh water. T.

82 **Spear-leaved Skullcap** *Scutellaria hastifolia*
Similar to Skullcap but slenderer, with untoothed arrow-shaped leaves, purple beneath, and larger flowers in a denser, less leafy spike, with petal-tube strongly curved. Rare in B.

82 **Lesser Skullcap** *Scutellaria minor*
Low/short creeping perennial, sometimes downy. Leaves lanceolate to oval, scarcely toothed. Flowers pale *pinkish-purple*, spotted darker, in *pairs* up the leafy stems, petal-tube almost straight; July-Oct. Damp *heathy* places. T, southern.

82 **Wood Sage*** *Teucrium scorodonia*
Short/medium perennial, downy. Leaves heart-shaped, bluntly toothed, *wrinkled*, sage-like. Flowers *greenish-yellow*, in pairs in leafless stalked spikes, with prominent maroon stamens; July-Sept. Open woods, scrub, heaths, fixed dunes, screes; not on lime. T, western.

82 **Mountain Germander** *Teucrium montanum*
Low/short spreading undershrub. Leaves linear/lanceolate, *white* beneath, margins inrolled. Flowers yellowish-white, in rounded clusters; May-Aug. Rocky places in mountains. F, G.

82 **Wall Germander*** *Teucrium chamaedrys*
Short tufted perennial, slightly hairy. Leaves pointed oval, *shiny*, dark green, rather leathery, with rounded teeth. Flowers dark pinkish-purple, in short leafy whorled spikes; May-Sept. Dry bare places, including walls. (B, rare), F, G.

82 **Water Germander*** *Teucrium scordium*
Low/short sprawling perennial, softly hairy. Leaves oblong, toothed, unstalked. Flowers pinkish-purple, in whorls up leafy stems; June-Aug. Damp places, by *fresh water*, dune slacks. T, rare in B.

82 **Cut-leaved Germander*** *Teucrium botrys*
Low/short downy annual/biennial. Leaves oval, *deeply cut*, almost pinnate. Flowers pink or pinkish-purple, in whorls along leafy stems; June-Oct. Bare, stony ground; on lime. B (rare), F, G.

83 **Self-heal*** *Prunella vulgaris*
Low creeping perennial, downy, not aromatic. Leaves pointed oval, *scarcely toothed*, the lower stalked. Flowers *violet*, rarely pink or white, 10-15 mm long, in *oblong* or square purplish heads; June-Nov. Flowerheads with leaves at base. Hybridises with Large and Cut-leaved Self-heals. Grassy places, bare ground. T.

83 **Large Self-heal** *Prunella grandiflora*
Similar to Self-heal but larger, with flowers 20-25 mm long. Flowerheads with no leaves at base. F, G, S.

83 **Cut-leaved Self-heal*** *Prunella laciniata*
Low creeping perennial, downy, not aromatic; stems with white hairs. Leaves pointed oval, the upper *pinnate* or pinnately lobed. Flowers creamy *white*, occasionally tinged violet (indicating hybridisation with Self-heal), in oblong or square heads; June-Oct. Dry grassy and bare places. (B), F, G.

83 **Ground Ivy*** *Glechoma hederacea*
Low creeping, often purplish perennial, softly hairy, aromatic; runners long, rooting. Leaves *kidney-shaped*, blunt-toothed, long-stalked. Flowers blue-violet, rarely pink, in loose whorls at base of leaves; Mar-June. Woods, hedge-banks, sparsely grassy and bare places, sometimes carpeting. T.

83 **White Horehound*** *Marrubium vulgare*
Medium perennial, *white* with down, *thyme-scented*. Leaves roundish, bluntly toothed, wrinkled, stalked. Flowers white, in dense whorls up leafy stems; sepal-teeth 10, hooked; June-Sept. Dry bare and waste places. T, rare in B.

83 **Catmint*** *Nepeta cataria*
Short/medium perennial, *grey* with down, *mint-scented*. Leaves heart-shaped, more markedly toothed than White Horehound, stalked. Flowers white, red-dotted, in whorls up leafy stems; sepal-teeth five, straight; June-Sept. Hedge-banks, waysides, rocks. T.

LABIATE FAMILY

83 **Hairless Catmint** *Nepeta nuda*
Medium perennial, almost *hairless*. Leaves oblong, toothed. Flowers violet, in branched spikes; June-Sept. Open woods, scrub, grassy and rocky places. F, G.

83 **Bastard Balm*** *Melittis melissophyllum*
Medium perennial, hairy, *strong smelling*. Leaves pointed oval, toothed, stalked. Flowers pink, or white with pink spots, *large* (35-45 mm long), in few-flowered whorls at base of leaves; May-July. Woods, hedge-banks, shady rocks. B, F, G.

83 **Black Horehound*** *Ballota nigra*
Medium, rather straggly perennial, hairy, *strong smelling*. Leaves pointed oval, toothed, stalked. Flowers pinkish-purple, in whorls at base of upper leaves, sepal-teeth *curved* back in fruit; June-Sept. Waste places, waysides. T.

83 **Winter Savory*** *Satureja montana*
Short half-evergreen undershrub, almost hairless, pleasantly aromatic; a culinary herb. Leaves narrow lanceolate, *pointed*, untoothed, rather leathery, hairy on margins, *shiny-dotted*, unstalked and joined at base. Flowers pale pink or white, in clusters. July-Oct. Old walls. (B, rare) from S Europe; cultivated T.

83 **Hyssop*** *Hyssopus officinalis*
Medium perennial, almost hairless, pleasantly aromatic; a culinary herb. Leaves linear oblong, *blunt*. Flowers violet-blue in few-flowered whorls making a long narrow spike. July-Sept. Old walls, dry banks. (B, F, G, rare), from S Europe.

84 **White Dead-nettle*** *Lamium album*
Short creeping perennial, hairy, faintly aromatic; unbranched. Leaves heart-shaped, toothed, stalked, resembling benign Nettle (p. 6) leaves. Flowers *white* with greenish streaks on lower lip, 20-25 mm long in whorls at base of leaves; Mar-Nov. Waysides, waste places. T.

84 **Spotted Dead-nettle*** *Lamium maculatum*
Similar to White Dead-nettle. Strong smelling and has leaves often pale-spotted and flowers usually pink-purple. T, but (B).

84 **Red Dead-nettle*** *Lamium purpureum*
Low/short, often purplish annual, downy, aromatic. Leaves heart-shaped, bluntly toothed, wrinkled, *all stalked*. Flowers pale to dark pinkish-purple, 10-15 mm long; all year. A weed of cultivation. T.

84 **Cut-leaved Dead-nettle*** *Lamium hybridum*
Has more deeply toothed leaves and smaller flowers than Red Dead-nettle.

84 **Henbit Dead-nettle*** *Lamium amplexicaule*
Low/short annual, downy, little branched. Leaves rounded, bluntly toothed, the topmost usually *unstalked* and often half-clasping the stem. Flowers pink-purple, 15 mm long, often also smaller and unopened; in whorls at base of upper leaves; Mar-Oct. A weed of cultivation. T.

84 **Motherwort*** *Leonurus cardiaca*
Medium/tall perennial, slightly downy, strong smelling; unbranched. Leaves *palmately* 3-7-lobed, whitely downy beneath, stalked. Flowers pinkish-purple or white, the lower lip spotted purple, furry outside, 12 mm long, in whorls up the leafy stems; July-Sept. Waysides, waste places. T, but (B).

84 **Common Hemp-nettle*** *Galeopsis tetrahit*
Short/medium annual, roughly hairy; well branched, stems *swollen* at leaf-junctions. Leaves broad lanceolate, toothed, stalked. Flowers pinkish-purple, less often yellow or white, 10-20 mm long, in whorls at base of upper leaves; July-Sept. Open woods, heaths, fens, also a weed of cultivation. T.

84 **Red Hemp-nettle*** *Galeopsis angustifolia*
Short/medium annual, softly hairy; well branched, stems *scarcely* swollen at leaf-junctions. Leaves narrow to broad lanceolate, sparsely toothed, stalked. Flowers *deep* pink, white-flecked on lip, 15-25 mm long, in whorls at base of upper leaves; July-Sept. A weed of cultivation, bare stony places. T, southern.

84 **Large-flowered Hemp-nettle*** *Galeopsis speciosa*
Medium/tall annual, roughly hairy; well branched, stems *swollen* at leaf-junctions. Leaves broad lanceolate, toothed, stalked. Flowers pale *yellow*, lower lip *purple*, 20-45 mm long, in whorls at base of upper leaves; July-Sept. A weed of cultivation, waste places. T.

84 **Downy Hemp-nettle*** *Galeopsis segetum*
Short/medium annual, *softly* hairy; well branched, stems *not* swollen at leaf-junctions. Leaves lanceolate, toothed, stalked. Flowers pale *yellow*, 20-30 mm long, in whorls at base of upper leaves; July-Sept. A weed of cultivation. (B, rare), F, G. Hybridises with Red Hemp-nettle.

84 **Yellow Archangel*** *Lamiastrum galeobdolon*
Short/medium creeping perennial, hairy, strong smelling; *runners* long, leafy, not rooting. Leaves narrow to broad lanceolate, dark green, stalked. Flowers *butter* yellow, usually streaked red-brown on lower lip, in whorls at base of upper leaves; May-June. Woods. T.

85 **Meadow Clary*** *Salvia pratensis*
Medium perennial, hairy, slightly aromatic. Leaves broad lanceolate, the few on the stem narrower and unstalked, bluntly toothed, wrinkled. Flowers *brilliant blue*, in whorled leafless spikes; June-July. Grassland on lime. T.

85 **Wild Sage*** *Salvia nemorosa*
Short/tall hairy perennial. Leaves heart-shaped, much longer than broad, pointed, the upper and middle ones unstalked. Flowers blue, in purplish leafy whorled and branched spikes; June-Aug. Bare and waste places. (B, rare, G), from S Europe.

85 **Wild Clary*** *Salvia verbenaca*
Variable medium perennial, hairy, little branched, purplish on upper leaves and stems. Leaves oval, *jaggedly* toothed, sometimes almost pinnately lobed, the upper unstalked. Flowers blue-violet, often white-spotted on lower lip, 5-15 mm long, in whorled spikes, often not opening and so appearing much smaller than bracts; June-Sept. Dry grassy places. B, F.

85 **Balm*** *Melissa officinalis*
Medium hairy perennial, *lemon-scented* when crushed, a culinary and medicinal herb. Leaves pointed oval, the lowest heart-shaped, toothed, stalked, yellow-green. Flowers *white*, in leafy whorled spikes; July-Sept. An escape from cultivation. (B, F, G), from S Europe.

85 **Hedge Woundwort*** *Stachys sylvatica*
Medium creeping perennial, roughly hairy, *strong smelling*. Leaves heart-shaped, toothed, stalked. Flowers dark *beetroot-purple* with whitish blotches, in leafless whorled spikes; June-Oct. Hybridises with Marsh Woundwort. Hedge-banks, shady places. T.

85 **Marsh Woundwort*** *Stachys palustris*
Similar to Hedge Woundwort but only faintly aromatic and has narrower short- or unstalked leaves and pale pinkish-purple flowers. Damp places, by fresh water.

85 **Downy Woundwort*** *Stachys germanica*
Medium/tall perennial, thickly covered with a *felt of white hairs*. Leaves pointed oval, toothed, the upper short- or unstalked. Flowers pale pinkish-purple, in a leafy whorled spike; July-Sept. Bare ground; on lime. B (rare), F, G.

85 **Limestone Woundwort*** *Stachys alpina*
Similar to Downy Woundwort but less thickly hairy.

85 **Yellow Woundwort*** *Stachys recta*
Variable short/medium hairy perennial, pleasantly aromatic. Leaves toothed, oval to oblong, stalked, the upper much narrower and unstalked. Flowers *pale yellow* with purple streaks, in leafless whorled spikes, the stamens protruding; June-Sept. Dry rocky or waste places. (B, rare). F, G.

85 **Field Woundwort*** *Stachys arvensis*
Low/short, often sprawling hairy annual. Leaves heart-shaped, bluntly toothed, the upper unstalked. Flowers dull purple, *scarcely* exceeding sepals; Apr-Oct. A weed of cultivation; not on lime. T.

85 **Betony*** *Stachys officinalis*
Variable short/medium hairy perennial, usually unbranched. Leaves oblong, slightly toothed, all but the topmost stalked. Flowers reddish-purple, in tight *oblong* spikes; June-Oct. Grassy and heathy places. T.

MINTS
Mentha

Aromatic perennials, each with a distinctive scent. Leaves stalked, except Spear Mint. Flowers small, usually lilac or pale purple, bell-shaped, with four more or less equal petal-lobes, in *tight whorls* at base of leaves; sepal-tube 5-toothed, stamens four, protruding except in the numerous hybrids.

86 **Water Mint*** *Mentha aquatica*
Variable short/medium, often purplish hairy perennial, pleasantly aromatic. Leaves pointed oval, toothed. Flowers lilac or pinkish-lilac, with a *round* terminal head; sepal-tube hairy, long-toothed; July-Sept. Hybridises with Corn Mint and with Spear Mint, from which the resultant hybrid is the often escaping culinary herb Peppermint *M.* × *piperita*, with narrower, more sharply toothed leaves, reddish-lilac flowers, flower stalks and sepal-tube usually hairless and stamens not protruding. Wet places. T.

86 **Corn Mint*** *Mentha arvensis*
Low/medium hairy perennial, rather acridly aromatic. Leaves pointed oval, toothed. Flowers lilac, with *no* terminal head; sepal-tube hairy, short-toothed; July-Sept. Hybridises with Water Mint, the resulting *M.* × *verticillata* having no terminal head but longer sepal-teeth and stamens not protruding. Damp places, and as a weed of cultivation. T.

86 **Spear Mint*** *Mentha spicata*
Short/medium perennial, hairy or hairless; the most commonly grown garden mint. Leaves lanceolate, almost *unstalked*, either green, shiny and hairless or greyish, wrinkled and downy. Flowers lilac, with a *pointed* terminal spike; July-Oct. Hybridises with Water Mint. Damp and waste places. T, southern.

86 **Pennyroyal*** *Mentha pulegium*
Prostrate, sometimes erect and short, perennial, downy, strongly aromatic. Leaves oval, scarcely toothed. Flowers lilac, with *no* terminal head; sepal-tube hairy, well ribbed, the two lower teeth narrower; July-Oct. Damp places. B, F, G.

86 **Gypsywort*** *Lycopus europaeus*
Medium/tall perennial, slightly hairy, *not* aromatic; unbranched. Leaves lanceolate, deeply toothed or lobed, short-stalked. Flowers small, white spotted purple, bell-shaped, in tight whorls at base of upper leaves; July-Sept. By fresh water, marshes. T.

86 **Common Calamint*** *Calamintha sylvatica*
Short/medium hairy perennial, *mint scented*. Leaves oval, slightly toothed, stalked, dark green. Flowers lilac-purple spotted darker, 10-15 mm, in short-stalked opposite clusters at base of leaves; sepal-tube often purple with no hairs protruding from throat after flowering; July-Sept. Dry grassy places, on lime. In open woods or scrub flowers may be 17-22 mm. B, F, G.

51

plate 86 **Wild Basil*** *Clinopodium vulgare*
Short/medium perennial, softly hairy, faintly aromatic; little branched. Leaves pointed oval, slightly toothed, stalked. Flowers pinkish-purple, in whorls at base of upper leaves; bristle-like bracts and purplish sepal-tube covered with *white hairs*; July-Sept. Dry grassy places, scrub, on lime. T.

86 **Marjoram*** *Origanum vulgare*
Medium downy perennial, pleasantly aromatic; a culinary herb, Leaves oval, often slightly toothed, stalked. Flowers purple, darker in bud and with *dark purple* bracts, in loose clusters; July-Sept. Dry grassland, scrub, screes; on lime. T.

86 **Basil Thyme*** *Acinos arvensis*
Low sprawling hairy annual, not aromatic. Leaves oval, slightly toothed, stalked. Flowers *violet* with *white* patch on lower lip, in whorls at base of upper leaves; June-Sept. Dry bare and sparsely grassy places; on lime. T.

86 **Wild Thyme*** *Thymus serpyllum*
Variable prostrate hairy *mat-forming* undershrub, aromatic; with runners. Leaves oval, sometimes quite woolly, short-stalked. Flowers pinkish- or reddish-purple, in *rounded* heads, sometimes also in whorls below; June-Sept. Dry grassy and heathy places, dunes. T.

NIGHTSHADE FAMILY
Solanaceae

Often poisonous. Leaves alternate, normally stalked. Flowers 5-petalled, joined at base.

87 **Bittersweet*** *Solanum dulcamara*
Clambering, sometimes prostrate downy perennial, to 2 m. Leaves pointed oval, often with two lobes at base. Flowers in loose clusters, bright *purple*, petals turning down, yellow anthers in a conspicuous *column;* May-Sept. Fruit a poisonous egg-shaped berry, green then yellow then *red*. Woods, scrub, hedges, waste and damp places, shingle. T.

87 **Black Nightshade*** *Solanum nigrum*
Variable low/short annual, hairless or downy; stems often blackish. Leaves pointed oval, often toothed or lobed. Flowers in loose clusters, *white*, petals turning down, with prominent column of yellow anthers; July-Oct. Fruit a poisonous berry, green then *black*. A weed of cultivation, waste places. T.

87 **Hairy Nightshade** *Solanum luteum*
Short hairy annual. Leaves pointed oval, more deeply lobed than Black Nightshade. Flowers like Black Nightshade but larger. Fruit *orange* or yellowish-brown. Bare and waste places. F, G.

87 **Deadly Nightshade*** *Atropa bella-donna*
Tall stout perennial, sometimes downy; well branched. Leaves pointed oval, up to 20 cm long. Flowers dull purple or greenish, *bell-shaped*, soli-

tary, 25-30 mm; June-Sept. Fruit a glossy *black* berry, extremely poisonous. Woods, scrub, rocky places; on lime. B, F, G. NB: Bittersweet is often miscalled Deadly Nightshade.

87 **Henbane*** *Hyoscyamus niger*
Medium/tall annual/biennial, *stickily* hairy, unpleasantly foetid, very poisonous. Leaves oblong, sometimes with a few teeth, up to 20 cm long, the upper unstalked, clasping the stem. Flowers dull creamy yellow with purple veins, bell-shaped, in a leafy cluster; May-Sept. Fruit a capsule. Bare and disturbed ground, especially by sea. T.

87 **Apple of Peru*** *Nicandra physalodes*
Medium/tall annual, often hairless, foetid, very poisonous. Leaves pointed oval, toothed or lobed. Flowers blue or pale *violet* with white throat, bell-shaped, solitary, 30-40 mm across, opening only for a few hours; June-Oct. Fruit a brown berry, encased in the net-veined *bladder-like* swollen sepals. Bare and waste places, waysides. (B, F, G), from Peru.

87 **Thorn-apple*** *Datura stramonium*
Stout medium/tall hairless annual, foetid and poisonous. Leaves pointed oval, jaggedly toothed. Flowers white, rarely purple, *trumpet-shaped*, solitary, 60-80 mm across; July-Oct. Fruit egg-shaped, *spiny*. Bare, cultivated and waste ground. (T).

87 **Small Tobacco Plant** *Nicotiana rustica*
Medium/tall annual, stickily hairy, strong smelling and poisonous. Leaves *heart-shaped*, shiny, with unwinged stalks. Flowers greenish-yellow, bell-shaped, in clusters; June-Aug. Fruit a capsule. An escape from cultivation. (F, G, southern), from N America.

FIGWORT FAMILY
Scrophulariaceae

Leaves with no stipules. Flowers either open and more or less flat with four or five joined petals (Mulleins and Speedwells), or two-lipped with the lips either open or closed. Fruit a capsule.

MULLEINS
Verbascum
Biennials, usually tall. Leaves in a basal rosette and alternate up stems. Flowers flat, 5-petalled, in spikes; anthers orange. Fruit egg-shaped.

88 **Great Mullein*** *Verbascum thapsus*
Tall, stout, to 2 m, covered with *thick* white woolly down, stem round, usually unbranched. Leaves broad lanceolate, bluntly toothed, running down on to the *winged* stems. Flowers yellow, almost flat, 15-30 mm, with three whitely hairy and two hairless stamens; June-Aug. Dry grassy and bare places, open scrub. T.

88 **Large Mullein*** *Verbascum densiflorum*
Has yellowish-grey down, more pointed and coarsely toothed leaves, and sometimes branched spikes of larger (30-50 mm), completely flat flowers. (B), G.

52

88 Dark Mullein* *Verbascum nigrum*
Medium/tall, hairy, stem ridged, usually unbranched, often purplish. Leaves heart-shaped,
toothed, dark green, stalked. Flowers yellow with
purple hairs on all stamens; June-Sept. Dry grassy
places. T.

88 White Mullein* *Verbascum lychnitis*
Medium/tall, downy; stems angled at top, *branched*
like a candelabrum. Leaves lanceolate, bluntly
toothed, shortly stalked, dark green and almost hairless above, *white* with down beneath. Flowers yellow or white, 15-20 mm, with all stamens whitely
hairy; June-Sept. Dry bare and sparsely grassy
places. T.

88 Moth Mullein* *Verbascum blattaria*
Medium/tall, hairless below but with sticky hairs
above; stems angled, usually unbranched. Leaves
lanceolate, *shiny*, toothed, gradually narrowed to
base. Flowers yellow, 20-30 mm, solitary, *long-
stalked*; stamens with *purple* hairs; June-Aug. Bare
and waste places. B, F, G.

88 Purple Mullein *Verbascum phoeniceum*
Similar to Moth Mullein but with purple flowers.
(F), G.

FIGWORTS
Scrophularia
Square-stemmed perennials. Leaves opposite,
stalked, toothed. Flowers two-lipped, open-
mouthed, with five small blunt lobes; in a branched
terminal cluster.

88 Common Figwort* *Scrophularia nodosa*
Medium/tall, almost hairless, foetid, stems not
winged. Leaves *pointed oval*, not lobed. Flowers
red-brown, sepals *all green*; June-Sept. Woods,
shady places. T.

88 Balm-leaved Figwort* *Scrophularia scorodonia*
Medium/tall, *downy* all over. Leaves *heart-shaped*,
double-toothed, wrinkled. Flowers red-brown, sepals *white-edged*; June-Sept. Dry shady places near
sea. B, F.

88 French Figwort* *Scrophularia canina*
Medium/tall, hairless; well branched. Leaves
pinnately lobed, the lobes toothed. Flowers
purplish-black, upper lip sometimes white, with
purple stamens and orange anthers; June-Aug. Bare
and waste places. (B, rare), F, G.

88 Yellow Figwort* *Scrophularia vernalis*
Medium/tall biennial/perennial, softly hairy.
Leaves heart-shaped, wrinkled, well toothed,
yellowish-green. Flowers pale *greenish-yellow*.
Apr-June. Woods, scrub, bare places, old walls. T,
but (B).

The next 14 plants have 2-lipped flowers, with
mouth closed, except Small Toadflax, and spurred,
except Snapdragon and Lesser Snapdragon. Some
are semi-parasitic on the roots of other plants.

89 Snapdragon* *Antirrhinum majus*
Short/medium perennial, downy, woody at base;
well branched. Leaves narrow lanceolate,
untoothed. Flowers very variable, most commonly
red-purple, less often pale yellow, with a *pouch*
instead of a spur, *30-40 mm*; on stalked spikes;
May-Oct. Dry bare places, rocks, walls. (B), F, G.

89 Lesser Snapdragon* *Misopates orontium*
Short annual, usually downy. Leaves linear,
untoothed. Flowers pink-purple. *10-15 mm,
pouched*, scarcely stalked, at base of upper leaves;
July-Oct. A weed of cultivation, bare sandy places.
T.

89 Common Toadflax* *Linaria vulgaris*
Short/medium greyish hairless perennial. Leaves
linear, untoothed, numerous up stems. Flowers
yellow, with orange spot on lower lip, and long
straight spur 15-30 mm in stalked spikes; June-Oct.
Bare and waste places. T.

89 Sand Toadflax* *Linaria arenaria*
Low annual, stickily hairy; well branched. Leaves
linear, untoothed. Flowers yellow with short spur
often *violet*. 4-6 mm in stalked spikes. May-Sept.
Coastal dunes. (B, rare), F.

89 Pale Toadflax* *Linaria repens*
Short greyish hairless perennial. Leaves linear,
untoothed, numerous up stems. Flowers pale *lilac*,
veined violet, with orange spot on lower lip and
short curved spur, 7-14 mm in stalked spikes;
June-Sept. Dry bare and sparsely grassy places. T.
Hybridises with Common Toadflax.

89 Field Toadflax *Linaria arvensis*
Similar to Pale Toadflax but has lower leaves
whorled in fours and smaller (4-8 mm) blue-lilac
flowers with a white spot. F, G, decreasing.

89 Alpine Toadflax *Linaria alpina*
Similar to Pale Toadflax but has broader whorled
leaves and larger (20 mm) violet flowers with an
orange spot. Mountain screes and river beds. F, G.

89 Purple Toadflax* *Linaria purpurea*
Medium greyish hairless perennial, often unbranched. Leaves linear, untoothed, numerous
up stems. Flowers bright *violet*, occasionally pink,
8 mm with long curved spur, in stalked spikes;
June-Aug. Walls, bare ground. F, (B, G, S).

89 Jersey Toadflax *Linaria pelisseriana*
Shorter than Purple Toadflax and annual, with
lower leaves whorled and larger (10-20 mm) bluer
flowers with a white spot and a straight spur. Bare
and disturbed ground. F.

89 Ivy-leaved Toadflax* *Cymbalaria muralis*
Trailing, often purplish hairless perennial. Leaves
palmately lobed, ivy-like, long-stalked. Flowers
lilac with yellow spot, 8-10 mm, with a short curved
spur, solitary on long stalks at base of leaves; Apr-
Nov. *Walls*, rocks, (B, F, G), from S Europe.

plate 89 **Sharp-leaved Fluellen*** *Kickxia elatine*
More or less prostrate annual, stickily hairy. Leaves all *pointed*, almost triangular, stalked. Flowers with upper lip and throat *purple* and *lower lip yellow*. 8-11 mm, spur straight; solitary on almost hairless stalks at base of leaves; July-Oct. A weed of cultivation, bare places. T.

89 **Round-leaved Fluellen*** *Kickxia spuria*
Similar to Sharp-leaved Fluellen. Leaves oval or roundish, flowers with upper lip maroon, spur curved, stalks hairy.

89 **Small Toadflax*** *Chaenorhinum minus*
Slender low downy annual. Leaves linear, untoothed, greyish, scarcely stalked. Flowers pale purple, mouth *slightly* open, 6-8 mm, with a short blunt spur, solitary on long stalks at base of leaves; May-Oct. A weed of cultivation, railway tracks, bare places. T, southern.

89 **Daisy-leaved Toadflax** *Anarrhinum bellidifolium*
Medium/tall hairless biennial/perennial. Leaves in basal rosette oval to narrowly elliptic, toothed, those up stems narrowly *palmately lobed*. Flowers blue or violet, 3-5 mm. in long slender leafless spikes, spur slender, curved; Mar-Aug. Dry, rather bare places, rocks, walls, coniferous woods. F, G, southern.

90 **Monkey Flower*** *Mimulus guttatus*
Short creeping perennial, downy above, hairless below. Leaves oblong to roundish, toothed, opposite, the upper clasping the stem. Flowers bright yellow with small red *spots*, 2-lipped, open-mouthed, 25-45 mm in leafy stalked spikes; June-Sept. Hybridises freely with Blood-drop Emlets. Wet places. T. from N America.

90 **Blood-drop Emlets*** *Mimulus luteus*
Similar to Monkey Flower but smaller and almost hairless, and has large red blotches on flowers. Less widely naturalised, from Chile.

90 **Musk*** *Mimulus moschatus*
Similar to Monkey Flower but smaller and stickily hairy all over, and has much smaller (10-20 mm) all yellow flowers. Less widely naturalised.

90 **Foxglove*** *Digitalis purpurea*
Tall perennial to 1.5 m, downy; unbranched. Leaves broad lanceolate, wrinkled, *soft* to the touch. Flowers *pink-purple*, occasionally white, tubular, 2-lipped, in long tapering spikes; June-Sept. Woods, scrub, heaths, mountains. T.

90 **Large Yellow Foxglove** *Digitalis grandiflora*
Medium/tall hairy perennial; unbranched. Leaves lanceolate, toothed, hairless above. Flowers pale *yellow* with purple-brown veins, tubular, 2-lipped, hairy outside, 30-40 mm long, in a long slender spike; June-Sept. Open woods, rocks in mountains. F, G.

90 **Small Yellow Foxglove** *Digitalis lutea*
Similar to Large Yellow Foxglove. Leaves hairless on both sides, and smaller (15-20 mm) plain yellow flowers hairless outside. Woods, stony hillsides, mainly on lime.

90 **Gratiola** *Gratiola officinalis*
Medium hairless perennial. Leaves lanceolate, opposite, unstalked, toothed near the tip. Flowers white or pale pink, tubular, scarcely 2-lipped, long-stalked at base of upper leaves; May-Oct. Wet places. F, G.

90 **Fairy Foxglove*** *Erinus alpinus*
Low tufted hairy perennial. Leaves oval, broadest at tip, toothed, mostly in rosettes. Flowers purple, with five *notched* petal-lobes, in short stalked spikes; May-Oct. Rocks, screes, walls, mainly in mountains. (B), F.

90 **Red Bartsia*** *Odontites verna*
Low/short semi-parasitic, often purplish downy annual; well branched. Leaves lanceolate, toothed, unstalked, opposite. Flowers *pink*, 2-lipped, open-mouthed, lower lip 3-lobed, in leafy one-sided spikes; June-Sept. Bare and disturbed ground. T.

90 **Yellow Odontites*** *Odontites lutea*
Short/medium semi-parasitic annual, almost hairless; *well branched*. Leaves narrow lanceolate, toothed, unstalked, opposite, with margins inrolled. Flowers 6 mm, bright yellow, 2-lipped, open-mouthed, lower lip 3-lobed, with stamens protruding, in one-sided spikes; July-Sept. Dry bare or sparsely grassy places, often on lime. (B, rare), F, G.

90 **Alpine Bartsia*** *Bartsia alpina*
Low semi-parasitic downy perennial; unbranched. Leaves oval, toothed, unstalked, opposite. Flowers dark *purple*, 2-lipped, open-mouthed, upper lip hooded, lower 3-lobed, in a short spike with *purple* bracts; July-Aug. Rocks, grassland in hills and mountains. T, but rare in B.

90 **Yellow Bartsia*** *Parentucellia viscosa*
Short semi-parasitic annual, *stickily* hairy; usually *unbranched*. Leaves lanceolate, toothed, opposite, unstalked. Flowers yellow, 2-lipped, open-mouthed, lower lip 3-lobed, upper hooded, in leafy spikes; June-Sept. Damp grassy and sandy places, dune slacks. B, F.

SPEEDWELLS
Veronica
Leaves opposite, usually toothed. Flowers blue, with four joined petals and (except Large Speedwell) four sepals. Fruit flattened, 2-lobed or notched.

91 **Spiked Speedwell*** *Veronica spicata*
Short/medium downy perennial, unbranched. Leaves oval, stalked, often in a rosette, the upper narrower and unstalked. Flowers bright blue, 5 mm, with prominent stamens and blunt sepals, in

long dense *leafless* spikes; July-Oct. Dry grassland, rocks, often on lime. T, but rare in B.

91 **Large Speedwell** *Veronica austriaca*
Short/medium hairy perennial. Leaves oblong, well toothed, un- or short-stalked. Flowers bright blue, 10 mm, *5-sepalled*, in stalked spikes at base of upper leaves; June-Aug. Grassy places. F, G.

91 **Germander Speedwell*** *Veronica chamaedrys*
Low/short sprawling hairy perennial, with two *opposite* lines of hairs on stems. Leaves pointed oval, short- or unstalked. Flowers bright blue with a *white eye*. 10 mm, in opposite stalked spikes at base of upper leaves; Apr-June. Grassy places. T.

91 **Wood Speedwell*** *Veronica montana*
Similar to Germander Speedwell. Stems hairy all round, longer-stalked paler green leaves, purplish beneath and smaller (7 mm) paler blue flowers. Damp woods.

91 **Rock Speedwell*** *Veronica fruticans*
Similar to Germander Speedwell. Almost hairless and has much less toothed leaves and flowers with a red eye; July-Aug. Mountains.

91 **Common Field Speedwell*** *Veronica persica*
Low sprawling hairy annual. Leaves oval, short-stalked, pale green. Flowers sky-blue with darker veins, the lowest petal usually *white*, 8-12 mm, solitary on long stalks at base of upper leaves, all year. Fruit with widely diverging lobes. A weed of cultivation. (T). from W Asia.

91 **Green Field Speedwell*** *Veronica agrestis*
Similar to Common Field Speedwell but smaller, with paler 4-8 mm flowers on shorter stalks, and fruit only notched; Mar-Nov. T.

91 **Grey Field Speedwell*** *Veronica polita*
Similar to Common Field Speedwell but smaller and greyish, with darker and uniformly blue 4-8 mm flowers on shorter stalks and fruit only notched; Mar-Nov.

91 **Smooth Speedwell** *Veronica opaca*
Like Green Field Speedwell but has spoon-shaped sepals and hairless fruit. F, G, S.

91 **Slender Speedwell*** *Veronica filiformis*
Similar to Common Field Speedwell. A mat-forming perennial with rounder leaves, mauver flowers on very long slender stalks, and rounded fruit; Apr-June. Increasing on lawns and in grassy places. (B, F, G) from W Asia.

91 **Ivy-leaved Speedwell*** *Veronica hederifolia*
Low sprawling downy annual. Leaves palmately lobed, *ivy-like*, stalked. Flowers blue or *purple-lilac* to white, rather small, stalked, solitary at base of leaves; Mar-Aug. A weed of cultivation. T.

91 **Thyme-leaved Speedwell*** *Veronica serpyllifolia*
Low creeping perennial, almost hairless. Leaves oval, shiny, *scarcely* toothed, short- or unstalked. Flowers pale blue or white with purple veins, 5-6 mm (larger on mountains, ssp *humifusa*), stalked, in *leafy* spikes; Apr-Oct. Bare and sparsely grassy places. T.

91 **Alpine Speedwell*** *Veronica alpina*
Similar to Thyme-leaved Speedwell but scarcely creeping and has bluish-green leaves and deep blue flowers with a white eye. July-Aug. Mountains, Arctic heaths.

91 **Heath Speedwell*** *Veronica officinalis*
Low creeping hairy perennial. Leaves oval, short-stalked. Flowers *lilac* with darker veins, in stalked spikes at base of leaves. May-Aug. Dry grassy and heathy places. T.

91 **Wall Speedwell*** *Veronica arvensis*
Low *erect* annual, hairy. Leaves pointed oval, toothed, short-stalked. Flowers blue, tiny, shorter than sepals, in dense leafy spikes; Mar-Oct. Dry bare places, walls. T.

91 **Brooklime*** *Veronica beccabunga*
Low creeping rooting hairless fleshy perennial. Leaves *oval*, stalked. Flowers blue, 7-8 mm, in opposite stalked spikes at base of upper leaves; May-Sept. Wet places. T.

91 **Water Speedwell*** *Veronica anagallis-aquatica*
Short creeping rooting hairless fleshy perennial. Leaves *lanceolate*, slightly toothed, unstalked. Flowers pale blue, 5-6 mm, in opposite stalked spikes at base of upper leaves; June-Aug. Fruit rounded. Wet places. T.

91 **Pink Water Speedwell*** *Veronica catenata*.
Similar to Water Speedwell. Stems often purplish and flowers pink.

92 **Eyebright*** *Euphrasia officinalis*
Variable low/short, often bronzy green semi-parasitic hairy annual; often well branched. Leaves more or less oval, deeply toothed, the upper sometimes alternate. Flowers *white*, often tinged violet or with purple veins or a yellow spot, 2-lipped, open-mouthed, the lower lip 3-lobed in leafy spikes with broad, toothed bracts; June-Oct. Fruit hairy. Grassy places, mountains. T.

92 **Yellow Rattle*** *Rhinanthus minor*
Variable low/medium semi-parasitic annual, usually almost hairless. Leaves oblong to linear, toothed, unstalked, opposite. Flowers *yellow*, 2-lipped, usually open-mouthed, often with two purple teeth, in loose leafy spikes. May-Sept. Fruit *inflated*, the seeds rattling inside when ripe. Grassy places, cornfields. T.

LOUSEWORTS
Pedicularis

Semi-parasites, especially on grasses. Leaves pinnately cut, toothed, short-stalked, alternate.

Flowers 2-lipped, open-mouthed, in leafy spikes. Sepal-tube inflated in fruit.

plate 92 **Marsh Lousewort*** *Pedicularis palustris*
Short/medium biennial, almost hairless; stem *single*, branched, often purplish. Flowers reddish-pink, the lips equal, sepal-tube *downy*; May-Sept. Wet grassy and heathy places. T.

92 **Lousewort*** *Pedicularis sylvatica*
Low perennial, almost hairless, stems *numerous*, unbranched. Flowers pink, the upper lip longer, sepal-tube usually *hairless*. Apr-July. Moors, damp heaths, bogs. T.

92 **Moor-king** *Pedicularis sceptrum-carolinum*
Stout medium/tall perennial. Leaves with *oval lobes*, mostly in a basal rosette. Flowers yellow, *30-35 mm*, mouth often closed but if not lower lip purplish, in almost leafless spikes; July-Aug. Damp grassy places and scrub. G, S.

92 **Leafy Lousewort** *Pedicularis foliosa*
Stout medium perennial. Leaves *2-pinnate*, with pointed *triangular* lobes. Flowers pale yellow, 15-20 mm, in dense leafy spikes; June-Aug. Mountain grassland. F, G.

92 **Common Cow-wheat*** *Melampyrum pratense*
Variable short semi-parasitic annual, slightly downy. Leaves lanceolate, untoothed, unstalked, opposite. Flowers yellow, sometimes pinkish-purple, 2-lipped, with mouth *shut*, in pairs facing the same way at base of toothed leafy bracts; May-Sept. Woods, heaths, grassland. T.

92 **Small Cow-wheat*** *Melampyrum sylvaticum*
Similar to Common Cow-wheat but slenderer with smaller, always deep yellow open-mouthed flowers and less toothed bracts; June-Aug. Woods. T, rare in B.

92 **Wood Cow-wheat** *Melampyrum nemorosum*
Similar to Common Cow-wheat. Leaves stalked, much broader at base and slightly toothed, rather larger flowers with orange lower lip and upper bracts purple. Heaths, woods. F, G, S.

92 **Crested Cow-wheat*** *Melampyrum cristatum*
Short/medium semi-parasitic annual, slightly downy. Leaves narrow lanceolate, untoothed, unstalked, opposite. Flowers yellow and purple, 2-lipped, mouth almost closed, in a short *squarish* spike with conspicuously *purple* short-toothed bracts; June-Sept. Dry grassy, rocky places, wood margins. T.

92 **Field Cow-wheat*** *Melampyrum arvense*
Similar to Crested Cow-wheat. Longer looser flower spike with bracts magenta, broader and much longer-toothed. T, rare in B.

92 **Cornish Moneywort*** *Sibthorpia europaea*
Prostrate *mat-forming* perennial, hairy; stems thread-like. Leaves *kidney-shaped*, palmately lobed with very blunt lobes, long-stalked, alternate. Flowers 5-petalled, the two upper pale yellow, the

three lower pale pink, tiny, short-stalked at base of leaves; June-Oct. Damp shady places. B, F.

BROOMRAPE FAMILY
Orobanchaceae

Parasitic on roots of other plants. *No* green pigment. Leaves replaced by *scales*, more or less pointed oval, on stems. Flowers usually coloured as rest of plant, 2-lipped, in spikes. Fruit a capsule, usually egg-shaped. Broomrapes *Orobanche* are a difficult group, with the host often the best clue to identity. Their erect stems persist rigid and brown with the dead flowers through the winter. Grassy places.

93 **Toothwort*** *Lathraea squamaria*
Low/short creamy perennial, slightly downy. Flowers pale *pink*, short-stalked, in a drooping one-sided spike; Apr-May. Woods, hedges; hosts: Hazel (p. 3) and various trees. T.

93 **Purple Toothwort*** *Lathraea clandestina*
Similar to Toothwort but much shorter and hairless, with longer-stalked purple flowers. (B), F.

93 **Greater Broomrape*** *Orobanche rapum-genistae*
Medium/tall perennial, honey-brown tinged purple. Flowers 20-25 mm, upper lip hooded *not lobed*, stamens hairless below and stigma lobes yellow; only one bract; June-July. Hosts: shrubby peaflowers, especially Broom and Gorse (p. 26). B, F, G.

93 **Common Broomrape*** *Orobanche minor*
Variable short/medium annual, purplish, reddish or yellowish. Flowers 10-18 mm, shorter than or equalling their single bract, stamens hairless, stigma lobes purple; June-Sept. Hosts: peaflowers (pp. 26-30) and composites (pp. 60-7). B, F, G.

93 **Purple Broomrape*** *Orobanche purpurea*
Short/medium annual, bluish-purple; rarely branched. Flowers large (18-30 mm), with *three* bracts to each flower, petal lobes pointed; June-July. Host: composites (pp. 60-7), especially Yarrow (p. 62). T, southern, rare in B.

93 **Clove-scented Broomrape*** *Orobanche caryophyllacea*
Short annual, yellowish tinged purple. Flowers *fragrant*, large (20-35 mm), much longer than their single bract, stamens hairy below; June-July. Host: bedstraws (p. 47). B (rare), F, G.

GLOBULARIA FAMILY
Globulariaceae

93 **Globularia** *Globularia vulgaris*
Low/short perennial. Leaves oval, untoothed, the larger often *notched* or 3-lobed at tip, stalked, in a basal rosette; lanceolate, unstalked up stems. Flowers blue, rarely lilac or white, 2-lipped, the upper lip very short, the lower 3-lobed, in a *globular* head; Apr-June. Dry grassy or stony places. F, G, S, southern.

BUTTERWORT FAMILY
Lentibulariaceae

Butterworts *Pinguicula*. Low perennials, stickily hairy. Leaves oblong, untoothed, all in a starfish-like basal rosette, the margins rolling inwards to trap and digest insects. Flowers 2-lipped, spurred, solitary on long leafless stalks.

93 **Common Butterwort*** *Pinguicula vulgaris*
Leaves yellow-green. Flowers *violet* with a *white* throat-patch, spur pointed, 10-15 mm; May-July. Bogs, fens, wet heaths and moors. T.

93 **Large-flowered Butterwort*** *Pinguicula grandiflora*
Similar to Common Butterwort but much larger (25-30 mm) flowers with a stouter spur. B, F.

93 **Pale Butterwort*** *Pinguicula lusitanica*
Leaves olive green with red-brown veins. Flowers pale *lilac* with *yellow* throat and down-turned cylindrical spur, 6-7 mm; June-Oct. Bogs, wet heaths. B, F, western.

PLANTAIN FAMILY
Plantaginaceae

Leaves strongly veined or ribbed, all in a basal rosette (except Branched Plantain). Flowers tiny, 4-petalled, in dense spikes or heads, on long *leafless* stalks (except Branched Plantain), with prominent *stamens* providing most of the colour. Fruit a capsule.

94 **Greater Plantain*** *Plantago major*
Low/short perennial, hairless or downy. Leaves *broad oval*. Flowers pale greenish-yellow and pale brown, in long greenish spikes about equalling the unfurrowed stalks; anthers pale purple then yellowish-brown; June-Oct. Waste and well trodden places, paths, lawns. T.

94 **Hoary Plantain*** *Plantago media*
Similar to Greater Plantain. Always downy and greyish, with longer, often narrower leaves, and shorter long-stalked spikes of fragrant whitish flowers with a fuzz of pinkish-lilac stamens; May-Aug. Grassy places; on lime. T.

94 **Ribwort Plantain*** *Plantago lanceolata*
Low/medium perennial, hairless or downy. Leaves *lanceolate*, slightly toothed. Flowers brown, in short blackish spikes on furrowed stalks, anthers pale yellow; Apr-Oct. Grassy and waste places, one of the commonest European plants. T.

94 **Sea Plantain*** *Plantago maritima*
Low/short perennial, usually hairless. Leaves *linear*, fleshy, 3-5-veined, sometimes slightly toothed. Flowers brownish-pink with yellow anthers, in greenish spikes on unfurrowed stalks; June-Sept. Coastal saltmarshes, occasionally on mountains inland. T.

94 **Branched Plantain*** *Plantago arenaria*
Short downy annual, much branched. Leaves linear, sometimes obscurely toothed, not in a rosette, the lower with short leafy shoots at their base. Flowers pale brown, in long-stalked *egg-shaped* heads up the leafy stems; May-Aug. Waste and sandy places, dunes. T, but (B).

94 **Buckshorn Plantain*** *Plantago coronopus*
Low biennial, usually downy. Leaves variable, usually *pinnately lobed*, less often linear and deeply toothed, 1-veined. Flowers yellow-brown with yellow anthers, in short greenish spikes on unfurrowed stalks; May-Oct. Dry bare, often sandy places, most frequent on the coast. T.

ARROW-GRASS FAMILY
Juncaginaceae

A monocotyledonous family (See p. 67)

94 **Marsh Arrow-grass*** *Triglochin palustris*
Short slender hairless perennial. Leaves linear, deeply furrowed to appear almost *cylindrical*. Flowers green, purple-edged, 3-petalled, tiny, short-stalked, in an interrupted spike, the style showing as a white tuft; May-Aug. Fruit narrow, opening arrow-shaped when ripe. *Marshes* fens, damp grassland. T.

94 **Sea Arrow-grass*** *Triglochin maritima*
Short/medium hairless perennial. Leaves linear, fleshy, *flat*, not veined. Flowers green, 3-petalled, tiny, short-stalked, in a long plantain-like spike. May-Sept. Fruit egg-shaped. Coastal *saltmarshes*. T.

RANNOCH RUSH FAMILY
Scheuchzeriaceae

94 **Rannoch Rush*** *Scheuchzeria palustris*
Has flat leaves with inflated sheathing bases, longer than the small cluster of yellower flowers; bog pools. T. Scattered, rare in B.

MOSCHATEL FAMILY
Adoxaceae

94 **Moschatel*** *Adoxa moschatellina*
Low carpeting hairless perennial. Leaves 2-trefoil, lobed, long-stalked. Flowers greenish, in tight heads of five, at *right angles* to each other; Mar-May. Fruit a green berry. Woods, shady places, also on mountains. T.

VALERIAN FAMILY
Valerianaceae

Leaves opposite, no stipules. Flowers with five joined petals, small, in clusters.

95 **Common Valerian*** *Valeriana officinalis*
Variable short/tall perennial, hairy mainly below; usually unbranched. Leaves *pinnate*, the lower stalked leaflets lanceolate, toothed. Flowers pale

57

pink, pouched at base, in more or less rounded clusters; June-Aug. Woods, grassy places, both damp and dry. T.

plate 95 **Marsh Valerian*** *Valeriana dioica*
Short perennial, almost hairless with creeping *runners*. Root leaves *oval*, untoothed, long-stalked; stem leaves more or less pinnate, unstalked. Flowers pale pink, pouched at base, in rounded clusters; stamens and styles on different plants; May-June. Marshes, fens. T.

95 **Red Valerian*** *Centranthus ruber*
Medium/tall greyish tufted hairless perennial. Leaves pointed oval or *lanceolate*, the lower stalked and untoothed. Flowers red, pink or sometimes white, fragrant, spurred, in rounded clusters; May-Sept. Cliffs, rocks, quarries, walls, steep banks. (B), F, G.

95 **Cornsalad*** *Valerianella locusta*
Low/short annual, almost hairless, well branched. Leaves oblong, unstalked. Flowers pale lilac, *tiny*, in flat-topped umbel-like clusters; Apr-Aug. Fruit flattened. Bare and cultivated ground, dunes, walls. T.

HONEYSUCKLE FAMILY
Caprifoliaceae

Leaves opposite. Flowers with five joined petals.

95 **Dwarf Elder*** *Sambucus ebulus*
Stout tall foetid patch-forming perennial to 1 m. Leaves *pinnate*, leaflets lanceolate, sharply toothed, with leafy stipules. Flowers white, often tinged pink, in a flat-topped umbel-like cluster; anthers violet; July-Aug. Fruit a black berry. Waysides, waste places, scrub. T, but (B).

95 **Guelder Rose*** *Viburnum opulus*
Deciduous shrub or small tree to 4 m, scarcely downy. Leaves palmately 3-5-lobed, *ivy-like*. Flowers white, slightly fragrant, in flat umbel-like clusters, outer petals of outer flowers *much larger*; May-July. Fruit a shiny *red* berry. Damp woods, fens, scrub, hedges. T.

95 **Wayfaring Tree*** *Viburnum lantana*
Downy deciduous shrub to 4 m. Leaves *oval*, minutely toothed, wrinkled. Flowers creamy white, in a flat-topped umbel-like cluster, fragrant; Apr-June. Fruit a berry, red then *black*. Scrub, open woods, hedges; on lime. T.

95 **Twinflower*** *Linnaea borealis*
Delicate prostrate mat-forming downy evergreen undershrub. Leaves oval, toothed, stalked. Flowers pink, *bell-shaped*, drooping, fragrant, in pairs; June-Aug. Fruit egg-shaped. Coniferous woods. T, northern.

95 **Honeysuckle*** *Lonicera periclymenum*
Deciduous woody *climber* to 6 m, hairless or downy; twining clockwise. Leaves oval, untoothed, short- or unstalked, appearing in midwinter. Flowers creamy becoming orange-buff, often reddish outside, tubular, 2-lipped, very fragrant, in a *head*; June-Oct. Fruit a red berry. Woods, scrub, hedges. T.

95 **Fly Honeysuckle*** *Lonicera xylosteum*
Deciduous shrub to 2 m, downy. Leaves pointed oval, short-stalked, greyish. Flowers yellowish, tubular, 2-lipped, *in pairs* at base of upper leaves; May-June. Fruit a red berry. Woods, scrub. T, rare in B.

TEASEL FAMILY
Dipsacaceae

Leaves opposite. Flowers small, 4-5-petalled, tightly packed into a composite-like (p. 60) head, but with four stamens projecting from each flower. Each head cupped by sepal-like bracts. Fruit small, with one seed.

96 **Field Scabious*** *Knautia arvensis*
Medium/tall hairy perennial. Leaves *pinnately lobed*, the upper sometimes undivided. Flowers bluish-lilac, in rather *flat* heads, 30-40 mm, outer petals of outer flowers much larger; bracts in two rows, shorter than flowers; anthers pink; June-Oct. Dry grassy places, cornfields. T.

96 **Small Scabious*** *Scabiosa columbaria*
Variable short/medium hair perennial; little branched. Leaves *pinnate* with narrow lobes, basal leaves sometimes undivided. Flowers like Field Scabious, but heads smaller (15-25 mm) with *dark bristles* among the flowers, and only one row of bracts; June-Oct. Dry grassland; on lime. T, southern.

96 **Yellow Scabious** *Scabiosa ochroleuca*
Similar to Small Scabious. Annual/biennial, with upper leaves more but lower leaves less deeply cut than Small Scabious, and flowers yellow. G.

96 **Grey Scabious** *Scabiosa canescens*
Similar to Small Scabious. Basal leaves always lanceolate and anthers bright purple. F, G, S, southern.

96 **Devilsbit Scabious*** *Succisa pratensis*
Medium/tall hairy perennial. Leaves *elliptical*, untoothed, stalked, often blotched purplish, narrower and sometimes toothed up stems. Flowers dark blue-purple, occasionally pink, in *rounded* heads, 15-25 mm; June-Oct. Damp grassy places. T.

96 **Small Teasel*** *Dipsacus pilosus*
Medium/tall biennial, hairy above, *prickly* on stems and leaves. Leaves oblong, stalked, the upper narrower, all often with a pair of leaflets at base. Flowers *white*, in woolly spiny *globular* heads, anthers violet; July-Sept. Woods, scrub, streamsides. T, but (S).

58

96 **Teasel*** *Dipsacus fullonum*
Tall hairless perennial, *prickly* on stems and leaves; dead stems and flowerheads persist through winter. Leaves lanceolate, covered with white *pimples*, in a basal rosette that withers before flowering; narrower up stems, often cupped at base. Flowers pale *purple*, in a *conical* spiny head; July-Aug. Bare and sparsely grassy places, often damp. B, F, G.

BELLFLOWER FAMILY
Campanulaceae

Leaves undivided, alternate, no stipules. Petals joined, with five lobes. Fruit a capsule. Bellflowers *Campanula* have more or less bell-shaped flowers.

97 **Round-headed Rampion*** *Phyteuma orbiculare*
Low/short perennial, usually hairless, unbranched. Root leaves variable, toothed, broad lanceolate, sometimes heart-shaped; stem leaves lanceolate to linear, unstalked. Flowers *dark* blue, in globular heads, petal lobes narrow; bracts short, triangular to lanceolate; July-Aug. Dry grassland; on lime. B, F, G.

97 **Spiked Rampion*** *Phyteuma spicatum*
Short/medium hairless perennial. Root leaves heart-shaped, toothed, long-stalked; stem leaves narrower, less stalked. Flowers yellowish-white, small, in *elongated* heads, petal lobes narrower; May-July. Woods, grassy places. T, rare in B and S.

97 **Sheepsbit Scabious*** *Jasione montana*
Low/short biennial, slightly hairy; no dead leaves at base. Leaves narrow oblong, untoothed but sometimes *wavy*, the upper unstalked. Flowers blue, in globular heads, petal lobes narrow; May-Sept. Dry grassy places, heaths, sea cliffs, shingle, not on lime. T.

97 **Harebell*** *Campanula rotundifolia*
Slender short/medium hairless perennial. Root leaves *roundish*, withering early; stem leaves *linear*, the upper unstalked. Flowers blue, 15 mm, on long thin stalks, in loose clusters; petal lobes short; July-Oct. Dry grassland, heaths. T.

97 **Clustered Bellflower*** *Campanula glomerata*
Variable stiff low/medium hairy perennial. Lower leaves oval, sometimes heart-shaped, stalked, upper leaves narrower, unstalked. Flowers deep violet, in tight *heads*; sepal lobes *pointed*; June-Oct. Grassland; on lime. T.

97 **Nettle-leaved Bellflower*** *Campanula trachelium*
Medium/tall hairy perennial; stems sharply angled, unbranched. Leaves broad lanceolate, long-pointed, irregularly toothed. Flowers violet-blue, 30-40 mm long, 1-3 together in a leafy spike, opening from the top; petal lobes short, triangular; July-Sept. Woods, scrub, hedges. T.

97 **Spreading Bellflower*** *Campanula patula*
Medium/tall biennial/perennial, rough to the touch; stems angled. Leaves oblong, the upper narrower and unstalked. Flowers violet-blue, 15-25 mm, in a spreading cluster, on stalks with a small bract in the middle; petal-lobes long, sepal-teeth linear; June-July. Woods, grassy places. T.

97 **Peach-leaved Bellflower*** *Campanula persicifolia*
Medium/tall *hairless* perennial. Lower leaves oblong, stalked; upper leaves linear/lanceolate, unstalked. Flowers violet-blue, *30-40 mm*, in a stalked spike, petal-lobes broadly triangular; May-Aug. Woods, scrub, also naturalised from gardens. T.

97 **Bearded Bellflower** *Campanula barbata*
Short perennial, hairy; unbranched. Leaves oblong, wavy, mainly in a basal rosette. Flowers pale blue, with long *white hairs* inside the bell, in a one-sided cluster; sepals in two rows, like a Canterbury Bell (*C. medium*); June-Aug. Woods, grassy places, in mountains. F, G, S.

97 **Ivy-leaved Bellflower*** *Wahlenbergia hederacea*
Low creeping rather delicate hairless perennial. Leaves palmately lobed, *ivy-like*, stalked. Flowers pale blue, bell-shaped with short petal lobes, on hairlike stalks at base of leaves; July-Aug. Damp woods, heaths and moors. B, F, G.

97 **Venus's Looking Glass*** *Legousia hybrida*
Low/short hairy annual. Leaves oblong, wavy, unstalked. Flowers purple, in clusters, petal lobes only 8-12 mm across, *shorter* than sepal teeth, closing in dull weather and then hard to detect; May-Aug. A weed of cultivation, bare sandy or stony places. B, F, G.

97 **Large Venus's Looking Glass** *Legousia speculum-veneris*
Short annual. Leaves oblong, wavy, unstalked. Flowers violet, opening *wide* to 20 mm, in clusters; May-July. Bare, waste and cultivated ground. F, G.

97 **Heath Lobelia*** *Lobelia urens*
Short/medium perennial, more or less hairless; juice *milky*, acrid. Leaves oblong, toothed. Flowers purple-blue, *2-lipped*, upper lip 2-lobed, lower lip 3-lobed, in a stalked spike; Aug-Sept. Damp woods and heaths; not on lime. B (rare), F.

DAISY FAMILY
Compositae

The Composites are the largest and most versatile family of flowering plants. Flowers tiny, closely packed into a compound head, surrounded by sepal-like bracts. Petals are joined in a tube, and are of two kinds, with the tube ending either in five short teeth, *disc florets*, or in a conspicuous flat flap, *ray florets*. Composite flowerheads are thus of three kinds, *rayless*, with disc florets only, like thistles; *rayed*, with disc florets in the centres and ray florets round the edge, like daisies; and *dandelion-like*, with all ray florets. Fruit tiny, often surmounted by a feathery pappus on which it floats away in the wind. Sometimes the pappuses form a rounded 'clock'.

59

plate 98 **Hemp Agrimony*** _Eupatorium cannabinum_
Medium/tall perennial, downy stems often reddish, usually branched. Leaves _palmate_, the segments lanceolate, toothed, the upper undivided. Flowerheads whitish pink to reddish mauve, _rayless_, in dense, rather flat-topped clusters; July-Sept. Damp woods, marshes, fens, by fresh water, and on waste ground. T.

98 **Golden-rod*** _Solidago virgaurea_
Variable short/medium perennial, hairless or downy, little branched. Leaves bluntly oval or lanceolate, toothed, stalked, narrower, untoothed and unstalked up stems. Flowerheads bright yellow, _shortly_ rayed in branched spikes; June-Sept. Woods, scrub, heaths, grassy and rocky places. T.

98 **Canadian Golden-rod*** _Solidago canadensis_
Tall downy perennial; unbranched. Leaves lanceolate, toothed, 3-veined. Flowerheads yellow, _very shortly_ rayed, in one-sided spikes in a branched cluster; July-Sept. Waste places, streamsides (T), from N America.

98 **Goldilocks*** _Aster linosyris_
Short/medium hairless perennial, unbranched. Leaves _linear_, 1-veined, numerous up stems. Flowerheads yellow, _rayless_, in a flat-topped umbel-like cluster; Sept-Nov. Woods, grassy places, on rocks, often by the sea, on lime. T, southern, rare in B.

98 **Canadian Fleabane*** _Conyza canadensis_
Low/tall annual, slightly hairy, branched above. Leaves narrow lanceolate, sometimes toothed. Flowerheads with yellow disc florets and _short_ whitish rays, in loose branched spikes; June-Oct. Bare and waste places. (T), from N America.

98 **Ploughman's Spikenard*** _Inula conyza_
Short/tall perennial, downy; stems purplish, branched above. Leaves broad lanceolate, _foxglove-like_, slightly toothed. Flowerheads dull yellow with no, or obscure, rays and purplish inner bracts, in a flat-topped umbel-like cluster; July-Sept. Open woods, scrub, dry grassy and rocky places; on lime. B, F, G.

98 **Golden Samphire*** _Inula crithmoides_
Tufted short/medium hairless perennial. Leaves linear, _fleshy_, sometimes 3-toothed at tip. Flowerheads yellow, _rayed_, in a loose flat-topped cluster; July-Oct. Coastal cliffs, shingle and saltmarshes. B, F.

98 **Ragweed*** _Ambrosia artemisiifolia_
Medium/tall annual, hairy; stems branched, often reddish, angled. Leaves oval, deeply pinnately cut, _greyish_ beneath, mostly opposite. Flowerheads greenish-yellow, rayless, those with stamens in spikes, those with styles solitary at base of leaves; June-Sept. Fruit prickly. Bare and waste ground. (B, F, G), from N America.

98 **Spiny Cocklebur*** _Xanthium spinosum_
Stiff short/medium annual, hairless or not. Leaves diamond-shaped, 3-5-lobed, dark shiny green above, downy white beneath, with 1-2 sharp 3-forked orange _spines_ at their base. Flowerheads greenish, rayless, covered with hooked spines, globular male heads with stamens above egg-shaped female heads with styles; July-Oct. Fruit covered with hooked spines. A weed of cultivation, waste places. (B, F, G), from N America.

99 **Daisy*** _Bellis perennis_
Low hairy perennial. Leaves spoon-shaped, slightly toothed, in a basal rosette. Flowerheads with disc florets yellow and rays white, often tipped red, _solitary_ on leafless stalks; all year. Lawns, short turf. T.

99 **Scentless Mayweed*** _Matricaria perforata_
Variable short half-prostrate hairless annual/biennial, _not_ aromatic. Leaves 2-3-pinnate with hairlike segments. Flowers with yellow disc florets and white rays. 15-40 mm, solitary; sepal-like bracts bordered brown; Apr-Oct. Bare and disturbed ground. T.

99 **Pineapple Mayweed*** _Chamomilla suaveolens_
Low/short hairless annual, _pineapple_-scented; well branched. Leaves 2-3-pinnate with thread-like segments. Flowerheads yellowish-green, _rayless_, solitary; sepal-like bracts pale-edged; May-Nov. Bare and waste, especially well trodden places. (T), from N E Asia.

99 **Sea Aster*** _Aster tripolium_
Short/medium hairless, _fleshy_ perennial; often well branched. Root leaves bluntly oval, untoothed, dark green; stem leaves narrow lanceolate. Flowers with yellow disc florets and pale purple or whitish rays, but frequently _rayless_, in loose clusters; sepal-like bracts blunt; July-Oct. Coastal _saltmarshes_, cliffs. T.

99 **Michaelmas Daisy*** _Aster novi-belgii_
Variable, medium/tall perennial, almost hairless; well branched. Leaves lanceolate, untoothed, the upper unstalked, numerous up stems. Flowers with yellow disc florets and purple, violet or whitish rays, in a widely branched cluster; outer sepal-like bracts half as long as the inner, _pointed_; Aug-Nov. Damp and waste places, streamsides. (B, F, G), from N America.

99 **Blue Fleabane*** _Erigeron acer_
Low/medium roughly hairy annual/biennial; stems often purple. Leaves lanceolate, untoothed, the upper unstalked. Flowerheads with yellow disc florets and short _erect_ dingy purple rays, 10-15 mm, solitary or in loose clusters; sepal-like bracts dull purple; June-Sept. Dry bare and sparsely grassy places, walls, mountains. T.

99 **Alpine Fleabane*** _Erigeron alpinus_
Low/short perennial, hairy, unbranched. Leaves spoon-shaped in basal rosette, narrower and fewer

up stems. Flowerheads with yellow disc florets and spreading pinkish-purple rays. *20-30 mm*, usually *solitary*, bracts *shortly* hairy, grey-violet; July-Sept. Grassy places and rock-ledges in mountains. T, rare in B.

99 **Shaggy Soldier*** *Galinsoga ciliata*
Low/short annual, whitely hairy. Leaves pointed oval, toothed, dark green, opposite, narrowing up the stem. Flowerheads with yellow disc florets and 4-5 flat *white* trifid rays, in open clusters; June-Oct. Bare and disturbed ground. (T), from S America.

100 **Mountain Everlasting*** *Antennaria dioica*
Low/short creeping perennial with rooting runners. Leaves whitely woolly *beneath*, those in basal rosette broadest near tip. Flowerheads rayless, pink or red, with sepal-like bracts pink or white, in umbels; stamens and styles on separate plants; June-July. Heaths, moors, mountain grassland. T.

100 **Common Cudweed*** *Filago vulgaris*
Low/short annual, covered with silvery, sometimes yellow, hairs; widely branched. Leaves narrow oblong, *wavy-edged*, blunt or pointed, spirally up stems. Flowerheads rayless, white tipped red, but appearing yellow from tips of sepal-like bracts; in globular clusters overtopping upper leaves; July-Aug. Heaths, sandy places. T.

100 **Small Cudweed*** *Logfia minima*
Slender low/short annual, covered with silvery hairs. Leaves linear, spirally up stems. Flowerheads rayless, white tinged red, but appearing yellow from tips of sepal-like bracts, which spread *star-like* in fruit; in narrow conical clusters, overtopping leaves; June-Sept. Heaths, sandy places. T.

100 **Marsh Cudweed*** *Filaginella uliginosa*
Low/short silvery grey annual; well branched. Leaves narrow oblong, green above, alternate. Flowerheads rayless, yellow-brown, in clusters overtopped by upper leaves; July-Oct. Damp bare places. T.

100 **Jersey Cudweed*** *Gnaphalium luteoalbum*
Short/medium annual, thickly covered with white woolly hairs; little branched. Leaves narrow lanceolate, margins inrolled, the upper *wavy-edged*, hairy on both sides. Flowerheads rayless, yellow, with red stigmas, egg-shaped, in umbels; July-Sept. Sandy places. T, but rare in B.

100 **Heath Cudweed*** *Omalotheca sylvatica*
Short/medium perennial, grey with wool; unbranched. Leaves linear, 1-veined, green above, white-felted beneath, alternate. Flowerheads reddish or yellowish, hidden by brown sepal-like bracts, solitary or in small clusters in a *long leafy spike*; July-Sept. Heaths, open woods, dry grassland. T.

100 **Helichrysum** *Helichrysum arenarium*
Short perennial, grey with woolly hairs. Leaves oblong, *flat*, alternate. Flowerheads *bright* yellow, rayless, in a cluster. July-Sept. Bare ground, often sandy. F, G.

100 **Micropus** *Bombycilaena erecta*
Short annual, covered with woolly hairs. Leaves short, narrow, alternate, numerous up stems. Flowerheads straw yellow, rayless in a *tight* cluster; June-July. Grassy places. F, G, southern.

100 **Small Fleabane*** *Pulicaria vulgaris*
Low/short downy annual; much branched. Leaves oblong, *wavy-edged*, alternate. Flowerheads yellow, *shortly* rayed, rays no longer than sepal-like bracts, solitary in loose clusters; Aug-Sept. Damp bare places, especially where water stands in winter. T, southern, rare in B.

101 **Common Fleabane*** *Pulicaria dysenterica*
Medium hairy perennial. Leaves lanceolate, *wavy-edged*, the upper clasping the stem. Flowerheads daisy-like, yellow, *15-30 mm*, in a loose flat-topped cluster; July-Sept. Damp grassy places. T, southern.

101 **Irish Fleabane*** *Inula salicina*
Medium perennial, more or less hairless; stems brittle. Leaves *narrow* elliptical, the upper unstalked and half-clasping the stem. Flowers daisy-like, yellow, 25-40 mm, solitary or in small clusters; sepal-like bracts lanceolate; July-Aug. A shy flowerer in Ireland. Marshes, scrub, rocky slopes. B (Ireland), F, G, S.

101 **Elecampane*** *Inula helenium*
Tall hairy perennial. Leaves elliptical, toothed, basal ones up to *40 cm* long, the rest unstalked, alternate, clasping the stem. Flowerheads daisy-like, rays *narrow*, yellow, 60-80 mm, in small clusters; June-Sept. Grassy places, woods. T, but (B).

101 **Yellow Ox-eye** *Buphthalmum salicifolium*
Medium/tall hairy perennial; little branched. Leaves oblong-lanceolate, feebly toothed, alternate, clasping the stem. Flowerheads daisy-like, rays *broad*, yellow, 30-60 mm, *solitary*; July-Aug. Woods, rocks, in hills and mountains. F, G.

101 **Cone Flower*** *Rudbeckia laciniata*
Tall perennial, almost hairless. Leaves lanceolate, mostly *lobed*, sometimes toothed, alternate. Flowerheads daisy-like, rays broad and downturned, yellow, disc florets blackish-brown, making a conspicuous *cone*. 70-120 mm, solitary or in small clusters: June-Oct. Damp woods, waste places. (B, F, G), from N America.

101 **Perennial Sunflower*** *Helianthus rigidus*
Tall patch-forming perennial to 2 m, *rough* to the touch. Leaves broad lanceolate, scarcely toothed, opposite, very shortly stalked. Flowerheads daisy-like, rays long and broad, yellow, disc florets turning dark *purple*, 60-100 mm, long-stalked; Aug-Oct. Waste places, (B, F, G), from N America.

plate 101 **Arnica** *Arnica montana*
Short/medium downy *aromatic* perennial. Leaves lanceolate, mainly in a basal *rosette*, a few opposite on stems. Flowerheads daisy-like, rays long, yellow, 40-80 mm, solitary; June-Aug. Grassy places in *hills and mountains*. F, G, S.

101 **Yellow Chamomile*** *Anthemis tinctoria*
Short/medium perennial, *grey* with woolly down. Leaves *2-pinnate*, downy beneath. Flowerheads daisy-like or sometimes rayless, yellow, 25-40 mm, solitary, long-stalked; July-Aug. Dry bare and waste places. T, but (B).

101 **Leopardsbane*** *Doronicum pardalianches*
Medium patch-forming hairy-perennial. Leaves broad *heart-shaped*, toothed, the upper unstalked. Flowerheads daisy-like rays long, yellow, 40-60 mm, in small clusters; May-July. Woods, shady places. (B), F, G.

102 **Butterbur*** *Petasites hybridus*
Low/medium patch-forming perennial, downy. Leaves *very large*, to 1 m across, heart-shaped, toothed, downy grey beneath, long-stalked, all from roots, appearing after flowers. Flowerheads rayless, brush-like, lilac-pink, unscented, in spikes; stalks with strap-like bracts; stamens and styles *on separate plants*; Mar-May. Damp places, roadsides, streamsides. T.

101 **Winter Heliotrope*** *Petasites fragrans*
Similar to Butterbur but shorter, and its much smaller leaves appear with the fewer fragrant flowers; Nov-Mar. (B), F.

102 **Yarrow*** *Achillea millefolium*
Short/medium perennial, downy, *aromatic*. Leaves 2-3-pinnate, *feathery*, dark green. Flowerheads shortly rayed, rays white or pink, disc florets creamy, in flat umbel-like clusters; June-Nov. Grassy places. T.

102 **Sneezewort*** *Achillea ptarmica*
Medium hairy perennial, *not aromatic*. Leaves *linear*, minutely saw-toothed, dark green, half-clasping stem. Flowerheads shortly rayed, white, with creamy disc florets, in a loose umbel-like cluster; July-Sept. Damp grassy places, on acid soils. T

102 **Mugwort*** *Artemisia vulgaris*
Medium/tall downy perennial, *slightly* aromatic. Leaves 1-2-pinnate, the upper unstalked, dark green and almost hairless above, silvery downy beneath. Flowerheads rayless, egg-shaped, yellowish- or purplish-brown, numerous in branched spikes; July-Sept. Waste places, roadsides. T.

102 **Sea Wormwood*** *Artemisia maritima*
Short greyish perennial, downy, *pungently* aromatic. Leaves 2-pinnate. Flowerheads rayless, egg-shaped, yellow or orange-yellow, in branched spikes; Aug-Oct. *Saltmarshes*, occasionally inland. T.

102 **Trifid Bur Marigold*** *Bidens tripartita*
Short/medium annual, almost hairless. Leaves lanceolate, with two smaller *lobes at base*, toothed, opposite, on winged stalks. Flowerheads normally unrayed, button-like, yellow, *erect*, often solitary; July-Oct. Fruit flattened, adhering to clothing with two barbed bristles. Damp places, by fresh water. T.

102 **Cottonweed*** *Otanthus maritimus*
Short creeping perennial, covered with *thick* white down. Leaves oblong, toothed. Flowerheads rayless, button-like, yellow, in small clusters; Aug-Nov. Coastal sand and shingle. B (Ireland) (rare), F.

102 **Buttonweed*** *Cotula coronopifolia*
Low/short yellow-green hairless fleshy *aromatic* annual. Leaves variable, linear to pinnate, alternate, sheathing the stem. Flowerheads very shortly rayed, appearing rayless and button-like, yellow, long-stalked, *solitary*, always facing the sun. July-Oct. Sandy places, especially on *coast* (B, F, S), from S Africa.

103 **Ox-eye Daisy*** *Leucanthemum vulgare*
Medium perennial, slightly hairy, little branched. Leaves dark green, variable, the lower rounded or spoon-shaped, toothed or lobed, the upper narrower, clasping the stem. Flowerheads daisy-like, rays white, disc florets yellow, 25-50 mm, *solitary*; May-Sept. Grassy places. T.

103 **Feverfew*** *Tanacetum parthenium*
Short/medium perennial, downy, highly *aromatic* Leaves yellowish, 1-2-pinnate. Flowerheads daisy-like, rays white (occasionally absent), disc florets yellow (a "double" garden form often escapes), 10-25 mm, in an umbel-like *cluster*; June-Sept. Walls, waste places. (T), from S E Europe.

103 **Tansy*** *Tanacetum vulgare*
Medium/tall perennial, almost hairless, strongly *aromatic*; unbranched. Leaves pinnate, toothed. Flowers rayless, *button-like*, yellow, in large umbel-like clusters; July-Oct. Grassy and waste places. T.

103 **Corn Marigold*** *Chrysanthemum segetum*
Short/medium greyish hairless perennial. Leaves fleshy, oblong, toothed or lobed, the upper clasping the stem. Flowers daisy-like, bright *yellow*, 35-55 mm, solitary; June-Oct. A weed of cultivation. T.

103 **Coltsfoot*** *Tussilago farfara*
Low/short creeping downy perennial; unbranched. Leaves heart-shaped with pointed teeth, from roots only, appearing after flowers, much smaller than Butterbur (p. 62). Flowers yellow, with narrow rays, solitary on stems covered with purplish scales; *Feb*-Apr. Fruit a white "clock". Bare and waste ground. T.

103 **Purple Coltsfoot*** *Homogyne alpina*
Low/short creeping hairy perennial; unbranched.

Leaves kidney-shaped, dark green, shiny, purplish beneath, all from roots, much smaller than five. Flowers purple, *rayless*, solitary, on stems with narrow scales; June-Sept. Fruit a white "clock". Damp grassy places in mountains. B (rare), S.

103 **Garden Marigold*** *Calendula officinalis*
Short/medium perennial, roughly hairy. Leaves oblong, often broadest at tip. Flowers daisy-like, *orange*, 40-50 mm, solitary; May-Oct. Waste ground, a frequent garden escape. (B, F, G), from Mediterranean.

RAGWORTS and GROUNDSELS
Senecio

Flowerheads normally rayed (except Groundsel), daisy-like, all yellow, in branched clusters. Fruit pappus with simple hairs, not forming a clock. Hybrids not infrequent.

104 **Ragwort*** *Senecio jacobaea*
Medium/tall biennial, often hairless; little branched. Leaves pinnately lobed, end lobe *small*, blunt. Flowerheads 15-25 mm, in dense flat-topped clusters; outer sepal-like bracts few, much shorter than *dark-tipped* inner bracts; June-Nov. Dry grassy places. T.

104 **Oxford Ragwort*** *Senecio squalidus*
Medium perennial, almost hairless; well branched. Leaves lanceolate to pinnately lobed, the end lobe *sharply* pointed, the upper unstalked. Flowerheads 15-20 mm, sepal-like bracts black-tipped, the outer row much shorter; Apr-Nov. Walls, bare and waste ground. (B, F), from S Italy.

104 **Marsh Fleawort** *Senecio congestus*
Medium/tall annual/perennial, covered with *white* woolly hairs. Leaves *lanceolate*, toothed or not. Flowerheads pale yellow, 20-30 mm; June-July. Marshes. T, but extinct in B.

104 **Fen Ragwort*** *Senecio paludosus*
Medium/tall hairy perennial. Leaves lanceolate, *coarsely* saw-tooth, unstalked, shiny above, cottony *white* beneath. Flowerheads 30-40 mm, in a flat-topped cluster; July-Aug. Wet places. T, but rare in B.

104 **Alpine Ragwort*** *Senecio nemorensis*
Medium/tall perennial, almost hairless. Leaves lanceolate, *finely* saw-toothed, short-stalked Flowerheads with *few* rays, 15-25 mm, in a flat-topped cluster; July-Sept. Woods and rocks, mainly in hills and mountains. T, but (B).

104 **Groundsel*** *Senecio vulgaris*
Low/short annual, often downy, not foetid. Leaves pinnately lobed, hairless above. Flowerheads usually *rayless*, brush-like, but occasionally rayed, yellow, in loose clusters; sepal-like bracts *black-tipped*, the outer very short; all year. A weed of cultivation, disturbed ground. T.

104 **Silver Ragwort*** *Senecio bicolor*
Medium undershrub, covered with a dense *silvery* white felt; well branched. Leaves oval to oblong, toothed to pinnately lobed, green above. Flowerheads 8-12 mm; June-Aug. Cliffs and rocks by sea. (B, F), from Mediterranean.

104 **Field Fleawort*** *Senecio integrifolius*
Low/short perennial, often whitely downy; *unbranched*. Leaves oval, wrinkled, toothed or not, mainly in a basal rosette, narrower up stems. Flowerheads *few*. 15-25 mm, in a loose cluster; May-June. Short dry turf. T.

105 **Globe Thistle*** *Echinops sphaerocephalus*
Medium/tall thistle-like perennial, to 2 m, stickily hairy and white-woolly. Leaves lanceolate, pinnately lobed, spiny. Flowerheads rayless, *globular*, pale blue, spiny; June-Sept. Dry bare stony places. T, but (B)

105 **Carline Thistle*** *Carlina vulgaris*
Low/short *erect* biennial, spiny. Leaves thistle-like, oblong, pinnately lobed, prickly, the lower cottony, not in a rosette. Flowerheads rayless, yellow-brown, but the conspicuous spreading *yellow* sepal-like bracts appear like rays, folding up in wet weather; July-Sept. Dead plants survive through winter. Grassland, dunes, on lime. T.

105 **Stemless Carline Thistle** *Carlina acaulis*
Low biennial/perennial, spiny. Leaves all in a *rosette*, pinnately lobed, more or less prostrate. Flowerheads rayless, whitish, but appearing rayed from the conspicuous spreading *silvery* sepal-like bracts, solitary, unstalked; May-Sept. Grassy, rocky places in mountains. F, G, S.

105 **Alpine Sawwort*** *Saussurea alpina*
Short stout hairy perennial. Leaves lanceolate, more or less *toothed*, silvery white beneath, spineless. Flowerheads rayless, purple, fragrant, in compact clusters; Aug-Sept. Mountain grassland. B, G, S.

105 **Lesser Burdock*** *Arctium minus*
Medium/tall stout downy spineless biennial, stems arching. Leaves broadly heart-shaped, to 30 cm, longer than broad, with hollow stalks. Flowerheads 15-30 mm, rayless, egg-shaped, purple, in short-stalked spikes; hooked bracts forming *burs* when dried and lasting through winter; July-Sept. Shady and waste places. T.

105 **Cotton Thistle*** *Onopordum acanthium*
Tall spiny biennial, to 1.5 m, *white* with cottony down; stems *broadly* winged. Leaves oblong, spiny. Flowerheads rayless, pale purple, solitary, sepal-like bracts cottony at base, ending in yellow spines; July-Sept. Bare and waste ground, often sandy. T.

105 **Milk Thistle*** *Silybum marianum*
Medium/tall spiny annual/biennial; stems downy, unwinged. Leaves oblong, wavy-edged, dark green with conspicuous *white veins*, spiny. Flowerheads

63

rayless, purple, solitary; sepal-like bracts ending in sharp yellow spines; June-Aug. Bare and waste places. (B), F, G.

THISTLES
Carduus and *Cirsium*

Stems usually winged and spiny. Leaves oblong or lanceolate, and usually pinnately lobed, spiny and wavy-edged. Flowerheads rayless, brush-like purple (except Cabbage Thistle); sepal-like bracts usually spine-tipped. Fruit with a pappus, feathery in *Cirsium* but undivided in *Carduus*, not forming a clock.

plate   106 **Cabbage Thistle*** *Cirsium oleraceum*
Medium/tall perennial, more or less hairless. Leaves lanceolate, pinnately lobed to toothed. Flowerheads rayless, egg-shaped, *straw-yellow*, with narrow spiny sepal-like bracts in dense clusters almost hidden by topmost leaves; July-Aug. Damp places. T, but (B, rare).

106 **Creeping Thistle*** *Cirsium arvense*
Short/tall *creeping* perennial, usually *hairless*; little branched, stems spineless. Leaves sometimes cottony beneath. Flowerheads *lilac*, 15-25 mm, fragrant, in clusters; bracts purplish, scarcely spiny; June-Sept. Grassy and waste places, a weed of cultivation. T.

106 **Spear Thistle*** *Cirsium vulgare*
Medium/tall biennial, downy. *sharply* spiny. Leaves deeply pinnately lobed. Flowerheads 20-40 mm across, often *solitary*: bracts often hairless, with yellow-tipped spines; July-Sept. Bare and waste places. T.

106 **Woolly Thistle*** *Cirsium eriophorum*
Tall stout biennial, very spiny, covered with *white wool*, stem unwinged. Leaves almost pinnate. Flowerheads red-purple, *globular*, 40-70 mm across, usually solitary, bracts covered with cobwebby wool; July-Sept. Bare and grassy places, on lime. B, F, G.

106 **Meadow Thistle*** *Cirsium dissectum*
Medium perennial, cottony all over but *scarcely* spiny, little branched, stems unwinged; has creeping runners. Leaves whiter beneath, the upper undivided but clasping the stem. Flowerheads red-purple, 20-25 mm across, usually solitary; June-Aug. Damp grassy places, fens. B, F, G.

106 **Dwarf Thistle*** *Cirsium acaule*
Low/short, usually prostrate perennial, almost hairless. Leaves all in a basal *rosette*, rather spiny. Flowerheads red-purple, 20-50 mm across, usually *unstalked* but occasionally stalked to 15 cm, usually solitary; bracts purplish, scarcely spiny; June-Sept. Dry grassland, on lime. T.

106 **Musk Thistle*** *Carduus nutans*
Medium/tall biennial, with cottony white hairs. Leaves deeply pinnately lobed. Flowerheads bright red-purple, 35-50 mm, often solitary, slightly *nodding*, on spineless upper stalks, bracts conspicuous, purple; June-Sept. Bare and grassy places on lime. T.

106 **Slender Thistle*** *Carduus tenuiflorus*
Short/tall slender annual/biennial, with cottony white hairs. Leaves cottony white beneath. Flowerheads pinkish, *8 mm* across, in clusters; May-Aug. Grassy and waste places, often by sea. B, F, G.

106 **Great Marsh Thistle** *Carduus personata*
Tall perennial, to 2 m, with cottony white hairs. Leaves *softly* spiny, the upper undivided, white beneath. Flowerheads red-purple, 15-20 mm, unstalked, in tight clusters; bracts *not* spine-tipped, the outer recurved, often blackish; July-Aug. Damp places in mountains. F, G.

106 **Welted Thistle*** *Carduus acanthoides*
Tall biennial, to 2 m. Leaves *weakly* spined, cottony white beneath. Flowerheads red-purple. 10-15 mm across, in a cluster, with stalks spineless *at top*; bracts weakly spined; June-Sept. Grassy places, hedge-banks. T.

KNAPWEEDS and STAR-THISTLES
Centaurea

Spineless (except Yellow and Red Star-thistles). Stems stiff, downy. Leaves spirally arranged. Flowerheads rayless but with enlarged sterile outer florets often giving appearance of rays, deeply lobed to appear star-like. Sepal-like bracts with toothed or cut appendages. Pappus not forming a clock. Numerous hybrids also occur.

107 **Black Knapweed*** *Centaurea nigra*
Short/medium perennial. Leaves *lanceolate*, the lower sparsely toothed. Flowerheads more often brush-like than apparently rayed. Solitary, *20-40 mm* across; sepal-like bracts blackish-brown with long fine teeth; June-Sept. Grassy places. T.

107 **Greater Knapweed*** *Centaurea scabiosa*
Medium perennial. Leaves *pinnately lobed*, sparsely bristly. Flowerheads apparently rayed, solitary, *30-50 mm* across; sepal-like bracts *green*, edges and long slender teeth blackish. June-Sept. Grassy places, on lime. T.

107 **Perennial Cornflower*** *Centaurea montana*
Medium creeping downy perennial. Leaves *lanceolate*, unstalked. Flowerheads apparently rayed, blue, solitary, *60-80 mm* across; May-Aug. Grassy places, (B), F, G.

107 **Cornflower*** *Centaurea cyanus*
Medium annual, grey with down. Leaves *pinnately lobed*, stalked, the upper lanceolate, unstalked. Flowerheads apparently rayed, bright blue, solitary, *15-30 mm* across; June-Aug. A weed of cultivation, especially cornfields. T.

107 **Yellow Star-thistle*** *Centaurea solstitialis*
Medium/tall annual, grey-white with down; well branched. Leaves pinnately lobed, the upper linear. Flowerheads rayless, pale *yellow*, solitary; sepal-like bracts ending in a long stiff yellow *spine*, with smaller spines below; July-Sept. Bare and waste ground. (T, casual), from S Europe.

107 **Red Star-thistle*** *Centaurea calcitrapa*
Short/medium perennial, almost hairless; widely branched. Leaves pinnately lobed, the lobes *bristle-pointed*. Flowerheads rayless, thistle-like, red-purple, solitary, 8-10 mm across; sepal-like bracts ending in a long stout yellow *spine*, with shorter spines below; July-Sept. Dry bare places. (B), F, G.

107 **Sawwort*** *Serratula tinctoria*
Slender medium perennial, hairless, thistle-like but *spineless*; stems stiff. Leaves pinnately lobed, lobes *finely* saw-toothed. Flowerheads rayless, purple, in a branched cluster; sepal-like bracts purplish; July-Oct. Pappus yellowish. Damp grassy places. T.

108 **Goatsbeard*** *Tragopogon pratensis*
Medium hairless annual/perennial; little branched. Leaves *linear*, grass-like. Flowerheads yellow, solitary, florets either shorter or longer than sepal-like bracts, opening fully only on sunny mornings, whence folk-name of Jack-go-to-bed-at-noon; May-Aug. Pappus makes a large clock. Grassy places. T.

108 **Salsify*** *Tragopogon porrifolius*
Resembles Goatsbeard but has much larger dull purple flowerheads, whose florets are about as *long* as sepal-like *bracts*; Apr-June. Grassy places, formerly cultivated. (T), from Mediterranean.

108 **Purple Viper's Grass** *Scorzonera purpurea*
Short/medium hairless perennial; little branched. Leaves *linear*, keeled. Flowerheads *lilac-purple*, solitary, florets much longer than sepal-like bracts; May-June. Grassy and rocky places. F, G.

108 **Viper's Grass*** *Scorzonera humilis*
Low/short perennial, almost hairless; little branched. Leaves narrow *lanceolate*, untoothed, becoming small and scale-like up stems. Flowerheads pale *yellow*, solitary, florets much longer than sepal-like bracts; May-July. Damp grassy places. T, southern, rare in B.

108 **Chicory*** *Cichorium intybus*
Medium/tall perennial, hairy or not; stems stiff, well branched, *no* milky juice. Leaves pinnately lobed, the upper undivided. Flowerheads *clear* blue, 25-40 mm, in leafy spikes; June-Sept. Grassy and waste places. T.

108 **Alpine Sow-thistle*** *Cicerbita alpina*
Medium/tall perennial, stems unbranched, with *reddish* hairs. Leaves pinnately lobed, hairless, clasping the stem. Flowerheads mauvish blue, 20 mm, in leafy spikes; July-Sept. Grassy places in *mountains*. T, rare in B.

108 **Blue Lettuce*** *Lactuca perennis*
Medium hairless perennial. Leaves pinnately lobed, the upper clasping the stem, greyish. Flowerheads 30-40 mm, blue-purple or white, long-stalked from *arrow-shaped* bracts, in a loose cluster; May-Aug. Bare and grassy places. F, G.

108 **Purple Lettuce** *Prenanthes purpurea*
Medium/tall greyish perennial, not unlike Wall Lettuce (p. 66), but with purple flowers. Leaves oblong, often *waisted* or lobed, clasping the stem. Flowerheads occasionally white, each with very few florets, 20 mm, in a loose cluster; July-Sept. Pappus white. *Shady places*. F, G.

109 **Smooth Sow-thistle*** *Sonchus oleraceus*
Short/tall greyish annual, hairless. Leaves pinnately lobed, the end lobe the largest, with *softly* spiny margins, clasping the stem with arrow-shaped points. Flowerheads pale yellow, *20-25 mm*, in a loose cluster; May-Nov. Pappuses making a clock. Bare and waste ground, a weed of cultivation. T.

109 **Perennial Sow-thistle*** *Sonchus arvensis*
Tall patch-forming perennial, almost hairless. Leaves pinnately lobed, greyish beneath, softly spiny on margins, clasping the stem with rounded lobes. Flowerheads *40-50 mm*, rich yellow, in clusters; stalks and sepal-like bracts with numerous sticky yellow hairs; July-Sept. Bare and waste places. T.

109 **Marsh Sow-thistle*** *Sonchus palustris*
Very tall, to 3 m, tufted perennial, hairless below. Leaves *deeply* pinnately lobed, greyish, edged with softly spiny teeth, clasping the stem with arrow-shaped lobes. Flowerheads pale yellow, *30-40 mm*, in tight clusters; stalks and sepal-like bracts with numerous sticky blackish-green hairs; July-Sept. Fresh and brackish marshes, ditches. T, southern, rare in B.

109 **Wall Lettuce*** *Mycelis muralis*
Slender short/tall hairless perennial, often purple-tinged. Leaves pinnately lobed, toothed, the end lobe large, *triangular* and sharply cut, clasping the stem with rounded toothed lobes. Flowerheads 7-10 mm, with only five florets, in a loose cluster; June-Sept. Shady places, walls, rocks. T.

109 **Prickly Lettuce*** *Lactuca serriola*
Tall foetid biennial, hairless, stems prickly. Leaves greyish, oblong, sometimes irregularly lobed, alternate, weakly spiny on margins, *prickly* on midrib beneath, clasping the stem with arrow-shaped points; in the sun the upper leaves are held in the vertical plane and oriented north/south, whence name Compass Plant. Flowerheads 11-13 mm, numerous, in branched spikes; sepal-like bracts often purplish; July-Sept. Fruit pale brown to *grey-green*. Bare and waste ground. T, southern.

109 **Least Lettuce*** *Lactuca saligna*
Medium/tall hairless, *spineless* annual/biennial; little branched. Leaves greyish, pinnately lobed, the lobes curved *backwards*, with a white midrib, the

upper narrow, undivided and held almost vertically against the stem, which they clasp with arrow-shaped points. Flowerheads 10 mm, in a slender stalked spike, sepal-like bracts green; July-Aug. Fruit with beak white. Bare grassy or shingly places, often near the sea. B, F, G.

plate 109 **Nipplewort*** *Lapsana communis*
Short/tall hairy annual; *no* milky juice. Leaves pointed oval, toothed, often pinnately lobed *at base*. Flowerheads 10-20 mm, in branched clusters, not opening in dull weather; June-Oct. Shady, bare and waste places. T.

109 **Lamb's Succory*** *Arnoseris minima*
Low/short hairless annual; *no* milky juice. Leaves all from roots, lanceolate, toothed. Flowerheads very shortly rayed, 7-10 mm, solitary, on leafless stems much *swollen* at top; June-Aug. No pappus. Bare places, especially sandy. T, southern, rare in B.

109 **Chondrilla** *Chondrilla juncea*
Medium/tall biennial, hairy only on lower stem. Lower leaves lanceolate, lobed, withering before flowering time; upper leaves narrower, not lobed, sometimes finely toothed. Flowerheads 10 mm, unstalked, in small clusters up stems, sepal-like bracts *downy*; July-Sept. Dry sandy or stony places. F, G.

DANDELIONS
Taraxacum

A variable, difficult group divided into eight Sections, each with many microspecies, typical examples of three being shown here. Perennials, mostly hairless, with *milky juice*. Leaves usually well lobed. Flowerheads solitary, on hollow leafless stalks, often downy at top. Pappus makes a clock.

110 **Dandelion*** *Taraxacum* Sect *Vulgaria*
Low/short perennial. Flowerheads 35-50 mm, outer florets usually *grey-violet* beneath, sometimes purple, never red sepal-like bracts broader than Lesser but narrower than Red-veined Dandelion, erect or *recurved*; all year, but especially Apr-June. Fruit colour variable, but not purplish-red. Grassy and waste places. T.

110 **Lesser Dandelion*** *Taraxacum* Sect *Erythrosperma*
Low delicate perennial. Flowerheads 15-25 mm, sepal-like bracts narrow, appressed, tips of inner ones appearing *forked*; Apr-June. Fruit usually *purplish-red*. Dry grassy and bare places especially on lime. T.

110 **Red-veined Dandelion** *Taraxacum* Sect. *Spectabilia*
Low/short perennial. Leaves often dark-spotted and with reddish stalk and midrib. Flowerheads 20-35 mm, outer florets sometimes reddish or purplish beneath, and sepal-like bracts broader and often closely pressed but not recurved. Apr-Aug. Moist and wet places, often in mountains. T.

110. **Common Catsear*** *Hypochaeris radicata*
Short/medium perennial, little branched. Leaves usually roughly hairy, the end lobe blunt. Flowerheads solitary, on leafless stems, with scattered *scale-like* bracts. June-Sept. Drier grassy places. T.

110 **Rough Hawkbit*** *Leontodon hispidus*
Short/medium perennial, shaggily hairy; unbranched. Leaves shallowly lobed, the end lobe rounded. Flowerheads solitary, 25-40 mm, outer florets often *reddish* or orange beneath, stalks leafless but with *0-2* small scale-like bracts; June-Oct. Pappus making a clock. Grassland; on lime. T.

110 **Lesser Hawkbit*** *Leontodon taraxacoides*
Low/short perennial, hairy or not unbranched. Leaves shallowly lobed. Flowerheads solitary, 12-20 mm, outer florets *grey-violet* beneath, stalks leafless, *bractless* and often hairless; June-Oct. Pappus forming a clock. Dry grassy places, dunes. T, southern

110 **Smooth Catsear*** *Hypochaeris glabra*
Similar to Lesser Hawkbit. A usually hairless annual, with shiny leaves and smaller (12-15 mm) flowerheads, opening fully only in bright sunshine, the florets no longer than the sepal-like bracts; stalks with a few scale-like bracts, especially on sandy soils.

110 **Spotted Catsear*** *Hypochaeris maculata*
Short/medium hairy perennial. Leaves lanceolate, usually heavily spotted purplish-black. Flowerheads pale yellow, 40-50 mm, on stalks with a few tiny leaves; June-Aug. Grassland, especially on lime. T, but rare in B.

110 **Smooth Hawksbeard*** *Crepis capillaris*
Short/medium perennial, mostly hairless; *branched*. Leaves shiny, not all in a basal rosette, the upper narrower and clasping the stem with arrow-shaped points. Flowerheads 10-15 mm, in loose clusters, outer florets often *reddish* beneath; outer sepal-like bracts *half-spreading*, June-Nov. Grassy and waste places. T.

HAWKWEEDS
Hieracium

An exceptionally variable and difficult group, with some hundreds of microspecies. Here only five major groupings can be illustrated. Milky juice stems unbranched, more or less leafy. Leaves lanceolate, toothed, often sparsely, alternate. Pappus hairs usually pale brownish.

110 **Mouse-ear Hawkweed*** *Hieracium pilosella*
Low/short creeping perennial, shaggy with *white* hairs, unbranched, with leafy runners. Leaves elliptical, untoothed, whitish beneath. Flowerheads lemon yellow, solitary, 20-30 mm, outer florets often *reddish* beneath, on leafless, bractless stalks; May-Oct. Bare and grassy places. T.

111 **Few-leaved Hawkweed*** *Hieracium murorum*
Short/leaved perennials, hairy. Leaves *few*, both on stems and at base. Flowerheads 20-30 mm, rather *few* in the cluster, June-Aug. Grassy places, walls, rocks. T.

111 **Leafy Hawkweed*** *Hieracium umbellatum*
Medium/tall perennials, softly hairy. Leaves *numerous*, all up stems. Flowerheads 20-30 mm, *numerous*, in clusters. June-Nov. Grassy and heathy places. T.

111 **Alpine Hawkweed*** *Hieracium alpinum*
Low/short perennials, shaggily hairy. Leaves mostly in a basal *rosette*, few and very small up stems. Flowerheads usually *solitary*. 25-35 mm. July-Aug. Grassy and rocky places in mountains. T.

111 **Orange Hawkweed*** *Hieracium aurantiacum*
Short/medium perennials, covered with *blackish* hairs. Leaves mainly in a basal rosette. Flowerheads *orange-red*. 15 mm, in a tight cluster; June-Aug. Grassy and waste places. T.

111 **Hawkweed Ox-tongue*** *Picris hieracioides*
Medium perennial, roughly hairy, *branched*. Leaves lanceolate, *wavy-edged*. Flowerheads 20-35 mm, in a cluster, sepal-like bracts *narrow*, the outer spreading, covered with blackish hairs; July-Oct. Pappus creamy. Grassy and bare places. T.

111 **Bristly Ox-tongue*** *Picris echioides*
Medium perennial, covered with rough *bristles*; well branched. Leaves oblong, wavy-edged, covered with *whitish pimples*. Flowerheads pale yellow, 20-25 mm, in a cluster; sepal-like bracts *broadly* triangular. June-Nov. Pappus white. Rough grassy places. B, F, G.

HAWKSBEARDS
Crepis

Distinguished from other dandelion-like flowers by the outer row of sepal-like bracts being *much shorter* and usually spreading. Pappus usually white.

111 **Beaked Hawksbeard*** *Crepis vesicaria*
Medium downy biennial. Leaves *pinnately lobed*, dandelion-like, clasping the stem with pointed lobes. Flowerheads 15-25 mm, erect in bud, in a cluster, outer florets usually *orange* beneath; May-July. Grassy and waste places. B, F, G.

111 **Rough Hawksbeard*** *Crepis biennis*
Similar to Beaked Hawksbeard but taller and hairier, with fewer, larger (25-35 mm) richer yellow flowerheads with outer florets yellow beneath. T.

111 **Marsh Hawksbeard*** *Crepis paludosa*
Medium perennial, almost hairless, stems leafy. Leaves lanceolate, *sharply* toothed, clasping the stem with *pointed* bases. Flowerheads dull orange-yellow. 15-25 mm, rather few to the cluster; sepal-

like bracts downy, with numerous sticky *blackish* hairs; July-Sept. Pappus *brownish white*. *Damp* grassy places, stream-sides. T.

111 **Northern Hawksbeard*** *Crepis mollis*
Slender medium perennial, hairy or not. Leaves lanceolate, toothed or not, clasping the stem with *rounded* bases. Flowerheads 20-30 mm, rather few in the cluster; July-Aug. Pappus *pure white*. Woods, streamsides, in hill districts. B (rare), F, G.

WATER-PLANTAIN FAMILY
Alismataceae

The first of the Monocotyledon families (see p. 57). Hairless aquatic plants, with leaves all from roots, 3-petalled flowers and fruit (nutlets) in a rounded head.

112 **Common Water-plantain*** *Alisma plantago-aquatica*
Medium/tall perennial, with *broad* lanceolate leaves, rounded or heart-shaped at base. Flowers in whorls, pale *lilac*, 8-10 mm; June-Sept. Fruiting head a close ring of nutlets with long beak arising at or below middle. By fresh water. T.

112 **Lesser Water-plantain*** *Baldellia ranunculoides*
Low/short perennial, with *narrow* lanceolate leaves. Flowers pale *pink*, 10-15 mm, in whorls of 10-20; June-Sept. In and by shallow, often peaty, fresh water. T, western.

112 **Floating Water-plantain*** *Luronium natans*
Floating perennial, with elliptical leaves also narrow tapering submerged ones. Flowers *white* with a yellow spot, 12-15 mm; May-Aug. Still and slow fresh water. T, western.

112 **Star-fruit*** *Damasonium alisma*
Low/short annual, with blunt oval leaves, heart-shaped at base, floating or submerged. Flowers white, 6 mm; June-Sept. Fruit heads with long-beaked nutlets spreading like a 6-pointed *star*. In or by shallow fresh water. B (rare), F.

112 **Parnassus-leaved Water-plantain**
Caldesia parnassifolia
Medium/tall perennial, with conspicuously *heart-shaped* long-stalked leaves. Flowers white, in whorls; July-Sept. By fresh water. F, G.

112 **Arrowhead*** *Sagittaria sagittifolia*
Medium/tall perennial, with leaves *arrow-shaped* and in fast streams also oval or lanceolate (floating) or ribbon-like (submerged). Flowers white with a large purple spot, 20 mm; July-Aug. Still and flowing shallow fresh water. T.

FLOWERING RUSH FAMILY
Butomaceae

112 **Flowering Rush*** *Butomus umbellatus*
Tall hairless perennial. Leaves long, rush-like, *three-cornered*, all from roots. Flowers 3-petalled,

67

bright pink, in an umbel; July-Aug. Fruit egg-shaped, purple when ripe. In and by shallow fresh water. T, southern.

FROG-BIT FAMILY
Hydrocharitaceae

plate 112 **Frogbit*** *Hydrocharis morsus-ranae*
Hairless floating perennial, with bronzy-green, *kidney-shaped* leaves. Flowers 3-petalled, white with a yellow spot, 20 mm; July-Aug. Still fresh water. T.

112 **Water Soldier*** *Stratiotes aloides*
Floating perennial, submerged except at flowering time, when rosettes of *spine-toothed* lanceolate leaves rise to surface to reveal 3-petalled white 30-40 mm flowers, stamens and styles on separate plants; June-Aug. Still fresh water. T.

PIPEWORT FAMILY
Eriocaulaceae

113 **Pipewort*** *Eriocaulon aquaticum*
Short/medium hairless aquatic perennial; un-branched. Leaves *all submerged* at base of stem, narrow, pointed, translucent. Flowers white, with *grey* bracts, in flat button-like heads, on leafless stems projecting a few centimetres out of the water. July-Sept. Shallow still fresh water, bare wet ground. B (W Ireland, Inner Hebrides).

LILY FAMILY
Liliaceae

Leaves undivided. Flowers with three petals and three sepals, often the same colour and so appearing 6-petalled.

113 **Lily of the Valley*** *Convallaria majalis*
Low/short patch-forming hairless perennial. Leaves *broad* elliptical, two on each stem, nearly opposite. Flowers creamy white, *fragrant*, bell-shaped, drooping in a one-sided spike; May-June. Fruit a red berry. Drier woodland. T.

113 **May Lily*** *Maianthemum bifolium*
Low/short patch-forming hairless perennial, un-branched. Leaves *heart-shaped*, shiny, two on each stem, not opposite. Flowers white, very small, frag-rant, with prominent stamens, in a spike. May-July. Fruit a red berry. Woods. T, rare in B.

113 **Snowdon Lily*** *Lloydia serotina*
Low, slender, hairless perennial; unbranched. Leaves grasslike, almost thread-like. Flowers white, *purple-veined*, 20 mm, bell-shaped, *solitary;* May. Grassy places, rocks in hills or mountains. B, rare.

113 **Kerry Lily*** *Simethis planifolia*
Low/short hairless perennial. Leaves narrow grass-like, often *curled*, greyish, all at the base. Flowers white, purplish outside, 20 mm 6-petalled, in a loose head; May-June. Heathy and rocky places. B (Ireland) (rare), F.

113 **St Bernard's Lily** *Anthericum liliago*
Slender medium hairless perennial, *little branched*. Leaves all at base, long and grasslike. Flowers white, starlike, with conspicuous yellow stamens, 30-50 mm, 6-petalled, in a loose *elongated* cluster; bracts long, lanceolate; May-June. Dry grassland, especially in hills. F, G, S.

113 **False Helleborine** *Veratrum album*
Medium/tall stout hairy perennial. Leaves broad elliptical, *pleated* lengthwise, unstalked, arranged in *threes*. Flowers yellowish-green, often white inside, starlike, 6-petalled, unstalked, in branched spikes; July-Aug. Grassy places in hills and mountains. F, G, S.

113 **Scottish Asphodel*** *Tofieldia pusilla*
Low/short, rather slender hairless perennial, unbranched. Leaves flat, sword-shaped, usually *all at base*, occasionally a few small up stem. Flowers greenish-yellow, with a *green* 3-lobed bract, in a *short* spike. June-Aug. Wet places on mountains and in tundra. B, F, S.

113 **German Asphodel** *Tofieldia calyculata*
Short hairless perennial. Leaves flat, sword-shaped, both at base and smaller *up stem*. Flowers greenish-yellow, occasionally reddish, with both a green lanceolate and a *papery* 3-lobed bract in an *elongated* or tight cluster; July-Aug. Damp grassy places, bogs. G, S (Gotland).

114 **Fritillary*** *Fritillaria meleagris*
Short hairless perennial. Leaves grass-like, greyish, up the stem. Flowers *bell-like*, solitary, nodding, *varying* from dull purple to creamy white, chequered with darker blotches; Apr-May. Damp meadows, forming extensive colonies when these are not ploughed. T southern, scattered.

114 **Bog Asphodel*** *Narthecium ossifragum*
Low/short hairless perennial. Leaves sword-shaped, iris-like, all from roots, in rather flattened tufts, often tinged orange. Flowers *orange*-yellow, starlike, 6-petalled, in spikes on leafless stems; July-Aug. Fruit deep orange. Bogs, wet heaths. T, western.

114 **Martagon Lily*** *Lilium martagon*
Medium/tall hairless perennial, stem red-spotted. Leaves elliptical, dark green, in whorls up stem. Flowers in a close cluster, dull pink spotted dark purple, with petals *curled back*, making the pinkish stamens prominent; June-July. Woods, scrub, mountain grassland. T, southern but (B).

114 **Pyrenean Lily*** *Lilium pyrenaicum*
Similar to Martagon Lily but shorter and foetid, with narrower alternate leaves and larger dark-spotted yellow flowers. (B), from the Pyrenees.

114 **Yellow Star of Bethlehem*** *Gagea lutea*
Low slender perennial, almost hairless. Leaves like Bluebell (p. 70), but solitary, yellower green, more hooded at tip, and with 3-5 prominent ridges on the

68

back, 5-12 mm broad. Flowers yellow, 6-petalled, with a *green band* on the outer side of each petal, starlike, in an umbel-like cluster with a pair of large leaflike bracts at its base on an otherwise leafless stem. Mar-May. Open woods, scrub, grassland. T.

114 **Least Gagea** *Gagea minima*
Like Yellow Star of Bethlehem, but has a very delicate root-leaf *1-2 mm* wide, and flowers long-stalked, 1-7 in a head; Mar-May. Woods, grassy places, on lime. F, G, S, eastern.

114 **Meadow Gagea** *Gagea pratensis*
Low slender hairy perennial. Leaves linear, *2-5 mm* broad, *greyish*, sharply keeled, solitary. Flowers pale greenish-yellow, starlike in a long-stalked umbel-like cluster with a pair of broad leaflike bracts on an otherwise leafless stem; Mar-Apr. Grassy places. F, G.

114 **Belgian Gagea** *Gagea spathacea*
Short perennial with two very narrow leaves. Flowers yellow-green, 2-5 on each spike with hairless stalks and very broad bracts. Apr-May. Damp grassy places in woods. F, G.

114 **Wild Tulip*** *Tulipa sylvestris*
Slender short/medium hairless perennial. Leaves linear, grass-like, hooded at tip, with *no* prominent veins, grooves or ridges, all from roots. Flowers yellow, tinged green or red outside, like a slender garden tulip, fragrant, solitary on leafless stalk; Apr-May. Dry grassy and bare places. (B), F, G.

LEEKS and GARLICS
Allium
Hairless unbranched bulbous perennials, smelling *strongly* of garlic or onion. Flowers usually bell-shaped, often mixed with bulbils, in a head or loose umbel, enclosed by one or more papery bracts, which may fall before flowers open.

115 **Ramsons*** *Allium ursinum*
Short/medium *carpeting* perennial; stem triangular. Leaves *broad* elliptical, all from roots, recalling Lily of the Valley (p. 68), but brighter green and garlic-smelling. Flowers white, *starlike*, in an umbel; Apr-June. Woods, shady banks. T.

115 **Three-cornered Leek*** *Allium triquetrum*
Short/medium perennial, stem 3-sided. Leaves linear, sharply keeled, all at base. Flowers white, with a narrow *green line* on the back of each petal, no bulbils, in a drooping one-sided umbel-like head; Apr-June. Hedge-banks, stream-sides, shady places. (B), from Mediterranean.

115 **Crow Garlic*** *Allium vineale*
Medium stiff perennial. Leaves semi-cylindrical, grooved, hollow. Flowers greenish or pinkish, stamens *protruding*, bract shorter than flowers; either long-stalked in a loose umbel, usually mixed with bulbils, or in a tight head of bulbils only; June-Aug. Grassy and cultivated places. T.

115 **Field Garlic*** *Allium oleraceum*
Similar to Crow Garlic but has flatter leaves, looser umbels of flowers with unequal stalks and stamens not protruding; form with bulbils only is rare. T.

115 **Chives*** *Allium schoenoprasum*
Short/medium *tufted* perennial; a herb used for flavouring. Leaves cylindrical, hollow, greyish, *all from roots*. Flowers purple-pink, short-stalked, in a head, stamens not protruding, papery bract short; June-Aug. Grassy places, rocks. T, rare in B.

115 **Keeled Garlic*** *Allium carinatum*
Medium perennial. Leaves linear, grooved, keeled beneath, up to middle of stem. Flowers pink-purple, *blunt*-petalled, with *protruding* purple stamens and long bracts; long-stalked in a loose umbel, usually mixed with bulbils; July-Aug. Open woods, rocks, grassy places. T, but (B).

115 **Welsh Onion*** *Allium fistulosum*
Medium/tall perennial. Leaves cylindrical, hollow. Flowers yellowish-white, numerous, in umbel on stem swollen and hollow *above middle*; June-Sept. Escape from cultivation, occasionally naturalised. (T).

115 **Sand Leek*** *Allium scorodoprasum*
Tall stiff perennial. Leaves linear, rough-edged. Flowers red-purple, stamens *not* protruding, long-stalked in an umbel, mixed with *bulbils*; June-Aug. Sandy, grassy and cultivated places, hedge-banks. T.

115 **Wild Leek*** *Allium ampeloprasum*
Tall stout perennial, *to 2 m*. Leaves linear, greyish, keeled, finely toothed. Flowers pale purple to whitish, with yellow anthers, slightly protruding stamens, and papery bract falling before flowering; in large compact umbels *50-70 mm* across, sometimes with a few small bulbils; July-Aug. Hedge- and other banks, rocks, often near the sea. B (rare), F.

115 **German Garlic** *Allium senescens*
Short/medium perennial; stem angled. Leaves variable, linear, sometimes *twisted*, all from roots. Flowers rose-pink, numerous in a dense umbel on a leafless stem; June-July. Dry, often grassy or sandy places. F, G, S, south-eastern.

115 **Round-headed Leek*** *Allium sphaerocephalon*
Medium perennial. Leaves semi-cylindrical, grooved, hollow. Flowers pink-purple, with *protruding stamens*, no bulbils and short papery bracts; in *globular heads*; June-Aug. Grassy places, rocks, dunes. B (rare), F, G.

116 **Bluebell*** *Endymion non-scriptus*
Short hairless carpeting perennial. Leaves linear, keeled, with a hooded tip, all from roots. Flowers azure blue, occasionally white, elongated bell-shaped, fragrant, in a *long* one-sided spike, drooping at the tip, on a leafless stem; anthers creamy; Apr-June. Fruit egg-shaped, seeds black. Woods, scrub, hedge-banks, also on sea cliffs and mountains. B, F, G.

69

plate 116 **Spanish Bluebell*** *Endymion hispanicus*
Similar to Bluebell but stouter, with broader leaves, larger paler flowers in an erect not one-sided spike, and blue anthers; rather later flowering. (B, F), from S W Europe.

116 **Spring Squill*** *Scilla verna*
Low/short hairless perennial. Leaves narrow, grass-like, often curly, *all from roots*, appearing before flowers. Flowers sky-blue, rarely white. 6-petalled, starlike, with bluish *bracts*, in a cluster on a leafless stem; *Apr-June*. Grassy places, especially near the sea. B, F, S.

116 **Alpine Squill** *Scilla bifolia*
Low/short hairless perennial. Leaves narrow lanceolate, usually two, less often 3-5, *all on stems*. Flowers bright blue, rarely pink or white, 6-petalled, starlike, with *no* bracts, in a loose cluster; Mar-Aug. Woods, scrub, grassland, also on mountains. F, G.

116 **Autumn Squill*** *Scilla autumnalis*
Low/short hairless perennial. Leaves narrow, grass-like, *all from roots*, appearing *after* flowers. Flowers purplish-blue, starlike, with *no* bracts, in a cluster on a leafless stem; *Aug-Oct*. Dry grassy places, often near the sea. B, F.

116 **Grape Hyacinth*** *Muscari atlanticum*
Short hairless perennial. Leaves *1-3 mm* wide, grass-like, *grooved* and semi-cylindrical rather limp, all from roots. Flowers dark blue, *egg-shaped*, with small whitish petal-lobes, in a tight elongated head on a leafless stem; Apr-May. Dry grassy and cultivated places. B (rare), F, G.

116 **Small Grape Hyacinth** *Muscari botryodes*
Short hairless perennial. Leaves 3-7 mm wide, grass-like, broader *at tip*, all from roots. Flowers pale blue-violet, *globular*, with small whitish petal-lobes, in a loose, more conical head than Grape Hyacinth, on a leafless stem; Mar-May. Grassy places, woods. F, G, S.

116 **Meadow Saffron*** *Colchicum autumnale*
Short hairless perennial. Leaves *oblong-lanceolate*, bright green, in clumps, appearing in spring and dying *before* flowering time. Flowers pale rosy mauve, rarely white, *crocus-like*, on long weak white stalks (which are actually tubular and part of the flower), solitary; anthers orange, stamens six; *Aug-Sept*. Fruit egg-shaped, appearing in spring. Woods, damp meadows. T, southern.

117 **Common Solomon's Seal*** *Polygonatum multiflorum*
Medium patch-forming hairless perennial; stems rounded, arching. Leaves elliptical, alternate, along the stems. Flowers greenish-white, bell-shaped, waisted, unscented, in hanging *clusters* of 1-3 at base of leaves; May-June. Fruit a *blue-black* berry. Woods, scrub. T.

117 **Whorled Solomon's Seal*** *Polygonatum verticillatum*
Medium/tall hairless perennial. Leaves narrow lanceolate, in *whorls* of 4-5 up the stem. Flowers white, tipped green, bell-shaped, unscented, 1-3 together at each whorl; June-July. Fruit a *red* berry. Woods in hill and mountain districts. T, rare in B.

117 **Herb Paris*** *Paris quadrifolia*
Low/short hairless colonial perennial. Leaves pointed oval, unstalked, in a *whorl* of usually four (less often 3-8) together at top of otherwise leafless stem. Flowers yellow-green, 4-6-petalled, starlike, with prominent stamens, solitary; May-June. Fruit a black berry. Woods, on lime, T.

117 **Spiked Star of Bethlehem*** *Ornithogalum pyrenaicum*
Medium/tall hairless perennial; unbranched. Leaves linear, grass-like, greyish, all from roots, usually withered by flowering time. Flowers *greenish-white* or yellowish, 6-petalled, starlike, in a *stalked spike* on a leafless stem; May-July. Woods, hedge-banks, grassland. B, F, G.

117 **Drooping Star of Bethlehem*** *Ornithogalum nutans*
Short/medium hairless perennial. Leaves linear, grass-like, grooved and with a central *white stripe*, all from roots. Flowers white, with a green stripe on the back of each petal, bell-shaped, nodding, in a one-sided spike on a leafless stem; Apr-May. Grassy and cultivated places. (T), southern, from S Europe.

117 **Common Star of Bethlehem*** *Ornithogalum umbellatum*
Low/short hairless perennial. Leaves linear, grass-like, limp, grooved and with a central *white stripe*, all from roots. Flowers white, with a green stripe on the back of each petal, 6-petalled, starlike, in an *umbel-like* cluster, on a leafless stem; May-June. Grassy and cultivated places. T, southern.

117 **Wild Asparagus*** *Asparagus officinalis*
Medium/tall perennial, hairless, well branched. Leaves (actually reduced stems) short, *needle-like*, in tufts. Flowers yellowish or greenish-white, bell-shaped, 1-2 together at base of branches; stamens and styles on separate plants; June-Aug. Fruit a red berry. Grassy and waste places; often by the sea, when may be prostrate, with fleshy greyish 'leaves' and male flowers tinged red at base. Widely cultivated. T.

117 **Butcher's Broom*** *Ruscus aculeatus*
Medium evergreen hairless bush. Leaves (actually flattened branches) oval, ending in a sharp *spine*. Flowers whitish or greenish, tiny, 6-petalled, solitary or paired on upper surface of 'leaves'; stamens and styles on separate plants; Jan-Apr. Fruit a red berry. Woods, scrub, hedge-banks. B, F.

70

YAM FAMILY
Dioscoreaceae

116 **Black Bryony*** *Tamus communis*
Hairless perennial climber to 4 m, twining clock-wise; no tendrils (unlike the completely unrelated White Bryony (p. 36). Leaves *heart-shaped*, dark green, shiny, alternate. Flowers yellow-green, tiny, *6-petalled*, in loose, sometimes branched spikes, stamens and styles on separate plants; May-Aug. Fruit a red berry. Woods, scrub, hedges. B, F, G.

DAFFODIL FAMILY
Amaryllidaceae

Bulbous perennials, hairless. Leaves linear, all from roots. Flower buds enclosed in a sheath (spathe), which splits at flowering; petals in two rings, each usually of three petals or petal-like sepals each. Fruit a capsule.

118 **Wild Daffodil*** *Narcissus pseudonarcissus*
Medium perennial. Leaves greyish, grooved. Flowers yellow, the erect *trumpet-like* inner ring as long as but darker yellow than the spreading outer ring, nodding, solitary on leafless stem; Mar-Apr. Woods, grassland; numerous garden forms, including double ones, escape and appear on waysides and waste ground. T, southern.

118 **Primrose Peerless*** *Narcissus × medioluteus*
Probably originally a natural hybrid between Wild Daffodil and Poet's Narcissus. Flowers *paired*, fragrant, the short trumpet deep yellow with a whitish crisped margin, the outer petals creamy or whitish; Apr-May. Widely naturalised in grassy places. (B, F).

118 **Poet's Narcissus*** *Narcissus poeticus*
Medium perennial. Leaves greyish, grooved. Flowers with a short yellow trumpet, the margin *red and crisped*, and white outer petals, fragrant, nodding, solitary; Apr-May. Grassy places. (B, F, G), from Mediterranean.

118 **Spring Snowflake*** *Leucojum vernum*
Short perennial. Leaves *bright* green. Flowers white tipped green, bell-shaped, nodding, petals 20-25 mm, *solitary* or occasionally paired on leafless stems; anthers orange; Feb-Mar. Damp woods, copses, meadows. B (rare), F, G.

118 **Summer Snowflake*** *Leucojum aestivum*
Short/medium *tufted* perennial. Leaves bright green. Flowers like Spring Snowflake but smaller (petals 15-20 mm) and 3-6 in a *cluster* on unequal stalks; Apr-May. Damp grassy places, by fresh water. B (rare), F.

118 **Snowdrop*** *Galanthus nivalis*
Low/short perennial. Leaves *greyish*, narrower than Spring and Summer Snowflakes, grooved, keeled. Flowers white, inner petals tipped green, outer row green on the back, bell-shaped, nodding, petals 20-25 mm long, *solitary* on leafless stems,

anthers green; Jan-Mar. Damp woods, shady streamsides, meadows, and extensively naturalised. B, F, G.

ARUM FAMILY
Araceae

118 **Lords and Ladies*** *Arum maculatum*
Low/short hairless perennial. Leaves bluntly *arrow-shaped*, dark green, often *dark-spotted*, all from roots, appearing in January. Flowers tiny, male above female, in dense whorls topped by the conspicuous purple finger-like spadix, flowers and spadix both being enveloped by the even more conspicuous pale green hooded spathe, whose base conceals the flowers; Apr-May. Fruit a spike of bright orange berries. Woods, copses, shady banks, B, F, G.

IRIS FAMILY
Iridaceae

IRISES
Iris
Hairless perennials, often showing conspicuous rhizomes (underground stems) above ground. Leaves sword-shaped (except Butterfly Iris), flat, mostly from roots. Flowers showy, with three spreading, sometimes bearded, outer petals (falls), three more or less erect and twisted inner ones (standards), all narrow at the base, and three large, almost petal-like stigmas with branched tips (crests). Flower buds enclosed in a sheath (spathe) which splits at flowering time. Fruit a 3-sided capsule.

119 **Siberian Iris** *Iris sibirica*
Slender tufted perennial. Leaves narrow, grass-like. Flowers blue-violet, 60 mm, with an *all-brown* spathe. Grassy places. F, G, (S), south-eastern.

119 **Purple Flag*** *Iris versicolor*
Medium/tall, little branched. Leaves broader than Yellow Iris, slightly greyish and without raised mid-rib. Flowers pale *pinkish*-purple, blade of falls as long as haft, crests nearly *white*, 1-3 together; June-July. Seeds dark brown. Wet places. (B, rare), from N America.

119 **Yellow Iris*** *Iris pseudacorus*
Tall; stems branched. Leaves with a raised midrib. Flowers *yellow*, 80-100 mm across. 1-3 together; June-Aug. Seeds brown. Marshes, by fresh water. T.

119 **Garden Iris*** *Iris germanica*
Stout medium/tall, branched. Leaves *greyish*. Flowers fragrant, falls blue-violet with *yellow* beard, standards deep lilac, up to 100 mm across, 2-3 together; spathe green and brown; May-June. Grassy places, waysides. (T), from Mediterranean.

119 **Butterfly Iris*** *Iris spuria*
Medium; little branched. Leaves rather narrow, *unpleasant*-smelling when crushed. Flowers pale

71

blue-violet, falls with rounded blade half as long as haft and keel of haft *yellow*, crests violet, 40-50 mm across, unstalked, 1-3 together; May-June. Damp grassland and chalk downs. (B, rare), F, G.

plate 119 **Stinking Iris*** *Iris foetidissima*
Medium, tufted. Leaves dark green, smelling *sickly sweet* when crushed. Flowers *grey-purple*, occasionally yellowish, 80 mm across, 2-3 together; May-July. Seeds bright orange. Open woods, scrub, hedge-banks, sea cliffs and dunes. B, F.

119 **Gladiolus*** *Gladiolus illyricus*
Medium/tall hairless perennial. Leaves sword-shaped, all from roots. Flowers red-purple, 6-petalled, 3-8 in a spike on a leafless stem; June-July. Grassy and heathy places, scrub, marshes. B (rare), F. Several similar species occur as garden escapes.

119 **Sand Crocus*** *Romulea columnae*
Low hairless perennial, to 5 cm. Leaves threadlike, *curly*, all from roots. Flowers pale purple, greenish outside, much smaller than 9 (*10 mm* across) and opening only in full sunshine; Apr. Sandy grassland, dunes. B (rare), F.

119 **Spring Crocus*** *Crocus albiflorus*
Low hairless, perennial. Leaves linear, grooved, keeled, with a *white midrib*, tufted. Flowers like garden crocuses, purple white or both, solitary on leafless stalk; styles orange; Mar-Apr. Grassy places. (B, F), G.

119 **Blue-eyed Grass*** *Sisyrinchium bermudiana*
Low/short hairless perennial. Leaves linear, tufted, all from roots. Flowers blue with a yellow centre, 6-petalled, *starlike*, 2-4 together on a *winged* leafless stem, opening only in sunshine; July. Grassy places. B, (F, G).

ORCHID FAMILY
Orchidaceae

Unbranched perennials, hairless or almost so, except *Epipactis*. Leaves undivided, untoothed, often linear/lanceolate, keeled and rather fleshy. Flowers of rather diverse shape, but two-lipped, the lower lip often developed to appear the predominant part of the flower; often spurred; in a stalked spike with a leaflike bract at base of each flower. Fruit egg-shaped to cylindrical.

120 **Lady's Slipper*** *Cypripedium calceolus*
Short/medium perennial. Leaves broad lanceolate, strongly ribbed, pale green. Flowers maroon with a large hollow *yellow lip*, spotted red inside, solitary, the largest orchid flower of the region; May-June. Woods, scrub, in hill and mountain districts; mainly on lime. T, rare in B.

120 **Bee Orchid*** *Ophrys apifera*
Short/medium perennial. Leaves elliptical, pointed. Flowers with sepals *pink*, petals *green* and

lip red-brown, *rounded at tip*, patterned to appear like the rear of a small bumblebee apparently visiting the flower; June-July. Grassland, open scrub, dunes; only on lime. B, F, G.

120 **Wasp Orchid*** *Ophrys apifera* var. *trollii*
Similar to Bee Orchid. Has a point to the lip (in Bee Orchid this point is bent back under the lip) and also lacks the pale U-shaped mark usually found on the Bee Orchid's lip.

120 **Late Spider Orchid*** *Ophrys fuciflora*
Shorter than Bee Orchid and differs in having both petals and sepals pink and a more elaborate pattern on the lip, supposedly resembling a spider, also a *heart-shaped* appendage at the tip; June-July. Grassy places; on lime. B (rare), F, G.

120 **Early Spider Orchid*** *Ophrys sphegodes*
Shorter than Bee Orchid and differs in having both sepals and petals *yellow-green*, and an *H-* or *X-shaped* mark on the lip, sometimes also likened to the Greek letter pi (π); Apr-June. Grassy places; on lime. B, F, G.

120 **Fly Orchid*** *Ophrys insectifera*
Slender short/medium perennial. Leaves narrow elliptical, shiny. Flowers brown with green sepals, the narrow lip 3-lobed, the middle lobe forked, and with a *bluish patch* at its base; May-June. Woods, scrub, fens, grassy places; on lime. T.

120 **Black Vanilla Orchid** *Nigritella nigra*
Low/short perennial. Leaves linear, pointed. Flowers *blackish-purple*, rarely pink, spurred, *vanilla-scented*, in a tight head; June-Aug. Mountain meadows. F, G, S.

120 **Calypso** *Calypso bulbosa*
Low/short perennial. Leaf elliptical, markedly veined, *solitary*. Flowers purplish-pink with a large *hollow* yellow-blotched pale pink lip, solitary; May. Marshes, marshy woodland. S, a high northern plant.

121 **Early Purple Orchid*** *Orchis mascula*
Short/medium perennial. Leaves narrow oblong, pointed, usually *blotched* purplish-black. Flowers purple, less often pink-purple or white, smelling of tom-cats; petals with one sepal forming a hood, the two other sepals *erect*, lip shallowly 3-lobed, spur long; Apr-June. Woods, scrub, grassland. T.

121 **Green-winged Orchid*** *Orchis morio*
Short perennial. Leaves narrow oblong, pointed, unspotted. Flowers purple, pink or white, fragrant, hood formed by all sepals (which are *green-veined*) and petals, lip shallowly 3-lobed, spur long; fewer and in more open spike than Early Purple Orchid; May-June. Grassland, open scrub. T.

121 **Lady Orchid*** *Orchis purpurea*
Medium/tall perennial. Leaves broad oblong, shiny, unspotted, mostly in a basal rosette. Flowers shaped like a *manikin*, all sepals and petals forming

72

the hood or 'head', and the long lip being lobed narrowly to make the 'arms' and *broadly* to make the 'legs'; hood *dark* purple, and lip *pale* pink, fragrant, spur short; May-June. Woods, scrub; on lime. B (rare), F, G.

121 **Military Orchid*** *Orchis militaris*
Short/medium perennial. Leaves broad oblong, unspotted. Flowers manikin-shaped, like Lady Orchid, but with a small central lobe between the 'legs', pinkish-grey with darker pink markings, especially inside the hood; spur short; May-June. Wood edges, scrub, grassland; on lime. B (rare), F, G.

121 **Burnt Orchid*** *Orchis ustulata*
Low/short perennial. Leaves oblong, pointed, unspotted. Flowers like miniatures of Lady Orchid, the hood *dark maroon* at first, becoming paler, the lip less markedly 4-lobed, white with pink dots, short-spurred, fragrant; May-June. Grassland; on lime. T, southern.

121 **Monkey Orchid*** *Orchis simia*
Short/medium perennial. Leaves broad oblong, shiny, unspotted. Flowers like Military Orchid but more delicate, and 'arms' and 'legs' of manikin *much thinner* with the central tooth accentuated to form the monkey's 'tail'; May-June. Grassland, open scrub; mainly on lime. B (rare), F, G.

121 **Bug Orchid** *Orchis coriophora*
Short perennial. Leaves narrow lanceolate. Flowers red-brown, all sepals (which are *green-veined*) and petals joined in a hood, the lip 3-lobed and dark wine-purple tipped red and green, spur short, *smelling of bed-bugs* (but a more southern darker red form with white bracts and a large central lobe to the lip is vanilla-scented); Apr-June. Damp grassland. F, G.

121 **Loose-flowered Orchid** *Orchis laxiflora*
Medium perennial. Leaves lanceolate, *unspotted*. Flowers purple, in a rather loose spike, hood formed from petals and one sepal, the two other sepals *spreading*, lip often only *2-lobed*, spur short; bracts and stem often purplish; May-June. Damp meadows. F, G.

122 **Pyramidal Orchid*** *Anacamptis pyramidalis*
Medium perennial. Leaves narrow lanceolate, unspotted. Flowers *bright pink* or rose-purple, sepals spreading, petals hooded, lip 3-lobed, spur very *long*, slender and curved, often foxy-smelling in a densely flattened *pyramidal* spike; June-Aug. Dry grassland, dunes, mainly on lime. T, southern.

MARSH and SPOTTED ORCHIDS
Dactylorhiza

Flowers with sepals spreading outwards and forwards like a bird's wing, and a broad lip. Frequently hybridise with each other.

122 **Early Marsh Orchid*** *Dactylorhiza incarnata*
Short/medium perennial. Leaves oblong, keeled, *hooded at tip, yellowish-green*, unspotted. Flowers very variable in colour, pink, purple, brick-red or yellow, lip with a small central tooth and looking very narrow because the sides soon fold *backwards*, spur straight; May-July. Damp grassland, marshes, fens, dune slacks. T.

122 **Southern Marsh Orchid*** *Dactylorhiza praetermissa*
Short/medium perennial. Leaves dark green, not hooded at tip, unspotted. Flowers rose-purple, lip broad, streaked and spotted darker, with a small central tooth, the sides *not* folding backwards, spur short, stout; bracts and upper stem often purplish; June-July. Damp grassland, marshes, fens, dune slacks. T, but rare in S.

122 **Broad-leaved Marsh Orchid*** *Dactylorhiza majalis*
Medium/tall perennial. Leaves broad oblong, *bluish-green*, sometimes dark-spotted. Flowers lilac-purple (bright purple or reddish in mountains), the shallowly 3-lobed lip with darker lines and spots, spur short; May-July. Damp meadows, marshes, on lime. T.

122 **Common Spotted Orchid*** *Dactylorhiza fuchsii*.
Short/medium perennial. Leaves narrow lanceolate, keeled, usually *dark-spotted*. Flowers pale pink, pale purple or white, dotted and lined with crimson or purple, lip markedly 3-lobed, spur long; June-Aug. Grassy places, open scrub, on lime. T.

122 **Heath Spotted Orchid*** *Dactylorhiza maculata*
Similar to Common Spotted Orchid but the lip has a wavy edge and a single small tooth. Heathy places on acid soils, including bogs.

122 **Elder-flowered Orchid** *Dactylorhiza sambucina*
Short perennial. Leaves pale green, shiny unspotted. Flowers either *yellow* with a purple-spotted lip and pale *green* bracts or *red-purple* with a purple lip and *reddish* bracts, often mixed in same colony, lip very shallowly 3-lobed, not fragrant; Apr-June. Mountain grassland. F, G, S.

122 **Fragrant Orchid*** *Gymnadenia conopsea*
Medium perennial. Leaves narrow lanceolate, unspotted. Flowers in an elongated spike, *pale* purplish-pink, *fragrant* (sometimes clove-scented), with spreading sepals, hooded petals, 3-lobed lip and *long* slender spur; June-July. Grassland, especially on lime, fens. T.

123 **Man Orchid*** *Aceras anthropophorum*
Short perennial. Leaves oblong lanceolate, keeled, shiny. Flowers *greenish-yellow*, in long dense spikes, petals and sepals forming a hood and lip shaped as a manikin (compare Lady Orchid, p. 73), often tinged red-brown, unspurred; May-June. Grassland, scrub, on lime. B, F, G.

ORCHID FAMILY

plate

123 Lizard Orchid* *Himantoglossum hircinum*
Short/medium greyish perennial. Leaves oblong lanceolate, soon withering. Flowers purplish grey-green, petals and sepals forming a hood, the *long straplike lip* 3-lobed, spur short; smelling strongly of billy goat; in a tangled, often elongated spike; June-July. Grassy banks, scrub, wood edges, dunes. B (rare), F, G.

123 Dense-flowered Orchid* *Neotinea intacta*
Short perennial. Leaves oblong elliptical, blunt, either unspotted or with *lines* of brownish spots. Flowers either greenish-white or pink, sepals and petals hooded, lip shortly 3-lobed, spur short, vanilla-scented, in a short *tight* spike; Apr-June. May be more conspicuous in fruit. Sandy grassland, dunes, limestone rocks. B (W Ireland, Isle of Man).

123 False Musk Orchid *Chamorchis alpina*
Low perennial, hard to detect among other vegetation. Leaves linear, *grasslike*. Flowers green tinged with violet or purple, sepals and petals hooded, lip yellowish, obscurely 3-lobed, unspurred, few in the spike; July-Aug. Damp grassland in *mountains*; on lime. S.

123 Musk Orchid* *Herminium monorchis*
Low perennial. Leaves oval, yellow-green, 2-3 near *base* of stem. Flowers greenish-yellow, petals and sepals spreading, lip 3-lobed, the middle lobe much the longest, spur very short or none; *honey-scented* (not musky); June-July. Grassland; on lime; in Britain prefers dry turf, on Continent damp places. T.

123 Frog Orchid* *Coeloglossum viride*
Low/short perennial. Leaves lanceolate, narrower up the stem. Flowers yellow-green tinged red-brown, sepals and petals hooded, lip strap-shaped, *forked* near tip with a *tooth* in the middle, spur very short; June-July. Grassland, often on mountains. T.

123 Lesser Twayblade *Listera cordata*
Low slender perennial, sometimes only 5 cm. Leaves *heart-shaped*, shiny, *a single pair* at base of stem. Flowers reddish-green, petals and sepals half-hooded, lip obscurely 3-lobed, the middle lobe conspicuously forked, unspurred; June-Aug. Moors, bogs, coniferous woods, often half-hidden among heather and moss or under braken. T.

123 Common Twayblade* *Listera ovata*
Medium perennial. Leaves *broad oval*, not shiny, *a single pair* at base of stem. Flowers yellow-green, petals and sepals half-hooded, lip forked, unspurred, in a long spike; May-July. Woods, scrub, grassland. T.

124 Greater Butterfly Orchid* *Platanthera chlorantha*
Medium perennial. Leaves broad elliptical, shiny, *a single pair* at base, much smaller and lanceolate up stem. Flowers greenish-white, *vanilla-scented*, sepals and petals spreading, lip long, narrow and undivided, spur very long, in a rather loose spike; pollen masses diverging; June-July. Woods, open scrub, grassland. T.

124 Lesser Butterfly Orchid* *Platanthera bifolia*
Similar to Greater Butterfly Orchid, but shorter and smaller, with less broad basal leaves and pollen masses parallel. Also on moors and in marshes.

124 Red Helleborine* *Cephalanthera rubra*
Short/medium perennial, slightly tinged purple. Leaves a narrow lanceolate, sometimes almost grasslike in deep shade. Flowers bright *purple-pink*, not opening widely, with an unspurred whitish lip; June-July. Woods, especially of beech, and scrub; on lime. T, but rare in B.

124 White Helleborine* *Cephalanthera damasonium*
Short/medium perennial. Leaves *broad lanceolate*, slightly bluish-green, narrower up stem. Flowers creamy white, the yellow base of the unspurred lip usually hidden because flower scarcely opens, bracts conspicuous and *leaflike*; May-July. Woods, especially of beech, shady banks; on lime. T.

124 Narrow-leaved Helleborine*
Cephalanthera longifolia
Slenderer than White Helleborine. Leaves longer, *narrower*, parallel-sided and darker green. Flowers pure white, opening more widely to reveal a much smaller orange spot at base of lip, with bracts too *small* to appear leaflike; May-June. Woods. T.

124 White Frog Orchid* *Pseudorchis albida*
Short perennial. Leaves narrow oblong, keeled, shiny, unspotted. Flowers *creamy white, fragrant*, sepals and petals hooded, lip 3-lobed, short-spurred; May-June. *Upland grassland*. T.

124 Autumn Lady's Tresses* *Spiranthes spiralis*
Low perennial. Leaves pointed oval, bluish-green, in a basal rosette which withers before flowering, leaving only a few scale-like leaves up stem. Flowers white, fragrant, the lip greenish, unspurred, with a frilled recurved margin, *spirally* in a *single* row up the spike; Aug-Sept. *Dry* grassland. B, F, G.

124 Irish Lady's Tresses* *Spiranthes romanzoffiana*
Low/short perennial. Leaves linear-lanceolate up the stem, no basal rosette. Flowers white or creamy white, greenish at the base, fragrant, unspurred, in *three spiral* rows on a spike consequently much broader than Autumn Lady's Tresses; bracts conspicuous; Aug-Sept. *Wet* grassy places, peat marshes, bogs. B, western.

124 Creeping Lady's Tresses* *Goodyera repens*
Low/short creeping perennial, with *runners*. Leaves pointed oval conspicuously net-veined, in basal *rosettes*, smaller and scale-like up the stems. Flowers white, fragrant (to some people unpleasantly so), in a *spiral* spike, the unspurred lip neither frilled nor recurved; July-Aug. *Woods*, especially coniferous, mainly in hills and mountains. T.

HELLEBORINES
Epipactis
Leaves usually broad elliptical, pointed. Flowers in one-sided stalked spikes; lip unspurred, in two parts

74

joined by a narrow waist, the base cupped, the tip more or less triangular.

125 Marsh Helleborine* *Epipactis palustris*
Medium perennial. Leaves narrow elliptical, keeled, folded. Flowers with sepals purple or purple-brown, petals *crimson and white*, and lip white with cup crimson-streaked and tip with a yellow spot and a *notched frilly margin*; also sometimes flowers yellowish-white with lip white; July-Aug. Fruit downy. *Fens*, marshes, dune slacks. T.

125 Dark Red Helleborine* *Epipactis atrorubens*
Medium perennial, *tinged red-purple*; stem downy. Leaves in two rows up stem. Flowers *dark wine-red*, fragrant, opening fully; June-July. Fruit downy.

125 Broad-leaved Helleborine* *Epipactis helleborine*
Medium/tall perennial, often tinged purplish. Leaves sometimes short and almost rounded, alternating *spirally* up stem. Flowers very variable, greenish-yellow to purple-red, unscented, opening fully, lip appearing rounded because point of tip recurved *underneath*; July-Sept. Woods, shady banks, less often open hillsides, dune slacks. T.

125 Narrow-lipped Helleborine* *Epipactis leptochila*
Short/medium perennial, slightly downy, tinged *yellow*. Leaves in *two rows* up stem. Flowers green, usually tinged white or yellow, *drooping*, sometimes not opening fully, the lip with cup mottled red and tip extended to a *point*; July-Aug. Woods, especially of beech, dunes; on lime. B, F, G.

125 Violet Helleborine* *Epipactis purpurata*
Medium perennial, purple-tinged, stems usually in a *clump*. Leaves narrow elliptical, spirally up stem. Flowers pale greenish-white (purplish-green outside), lip with cup usually mottled violet and tip recurved; bracts often longer than flowers; Aug-Sept. Woods, often of beech. B, F, G.

125 Dune Helleborine* *Epipactis dunensis*
Medium perennial; stem downy above, purplish below. Leaves in *two rows* up stem. Flowers pale yellow-green, *not fully opening*, lip with cup mottled red inside and tip recurved as in Broad-leaved Helleborine; lowest bracts *longer than flowers*; June-July. Dune slacks, pine plantations. B (Lancashire, Anglesey).

125 Green-flowered Helleborine* *Epipactis phyllanthes*
Medium perennial; stems hairless. Leaves variable, in *two rows* up stem. Flowers green, often tinged yellow or purple, drooping, *scarcely opening*, lip cup usually whitish; lowest bracts longer than flowers; July-Sept. Woods, dunes. B, F, G.

126 Birdsnest Orchid* *Neottia nidus-avis*
Short/medium perennial; stem *honey-coloured*. *No leaves* but scale-like bracts on stem. Flowers honey-brown like stem, with a somewhat sickly fragrance, petals and sepals small, lip large, unspurred, *2-lobed* (Broomrapes (pp. 56-7) have a 3-lobed lip); May-July. Woods, especially of beech, in deep shade. T.

126 Coralroot Orchid* *Corallorhiza trifida*
Low/short perennial; stem yellow-green. *No leaves* but a few scale-like bracts on stem. Flowers yellow-green or yellowish-white, sepals and petals spreading, lip obscurely 3-lobed, unspurred and marked with *red*; June-July. Woods, especially coniferous, in mountains, dune slacks. T.

126 Ghost Orchid* *Epipogium aphyllum*
Low perennial; stem *mauvish-yellow*. *No leaves* but a few tiny pale brown bracts. Flowers pale mauve and pale yellow, petals and sepals spreading, lip recurved, undivided, spur whitish, solitary or 2-3 in a spike; June-Sept, flowering most freely after a wet spring. Broad-leaved woods especially of beech, in deep shade, often in damp places. T, but rare in B.

126 Bog Orchid* *Malaxis paludosa*
Low perennial, sometimes only 5 cm high. Leaves oval, *2-4* up the stems, usually with tiny bulbils on their margins. Flowers yellow-green, sepals and petals spreading, the narrow lanceolate lip twisted round to appear at the top; July-Sept. Bogs and other wet *acid* places, almost always among *sphagnum* moss. T.

126 One-leaved Bog Orchid *Malaxis monophyllos*
Low/short perennial. Leaf *solitary*, more or less oval. Flowers greenish-yellow, sepals and petals spreading, the narrowly triangular unspurred lip twisted round to appear at the top; July. Damp places, usually among *sphagnum* moss. G, S, rare.

126 Fen Orchid* *Liparis loeselii*
Low/short perennial. Leaves broad lanceolate, shiny, yellow-green, a *single pair* at base of stem. Flowers yellow-green, petals and sepals spreading, the broad unspurred lip twisted round to appear at the top; June-July. *Fens*, marshes, dune slacks, *on lime*. T.

126 Violet Birdsnest Orchid *Limodorum abortivum*
Medium perennial; stem violet. No leaves but scales on stem. Flowers violet with a yellow tinge, *40 mm* across, petals and sepals spreading, lip undivided, spurred; May-July, flowering most freely after a wet spring. Woods, especially coniferous, shady banks. F, G.

Ghost Orchid, Coralroot Orchid and the two Birdsnest Orchids, together with Yellow Birdsnest (p. 41) are all *saprophytes*, plants without chlorophyll (green colouring matter) which feed on rotting vegetation with the aid of a fungus partner. They are not to be confused with the other groups of plants with no chlorophyll, the Broomrapes and Toothworts (pp. 56-7), which are parasites on the roots of other plants.

Index of English Names

Index of Scientific Names